It's Our Military, Too!

Women and the
U.S. Military

In *the series* Women in the Political Economy,
edited by Ronnie J. Steinberg

It's Our Military, Too!

Women and the U.S. Military

Edited by

Judith Hicks Stiehm

Temple University Press \ Philadelphia

Temple University Press, Philadelphia 19122

Copyright © 1996 by Temple University. All rights reserved

Published 1996

Printed in the United States of America

Text designed by Will Boehm

Library of Congress Cataloging-in-Publication Data

It's our military, too! : women and the U.S. military / edited by Judith Hicks Stiehm.
    p.   cm. — (Women in the political economy)
  Includes bibliographical references and index.
  ISBN 1-56639-455-4 (cloth : alk. paper).—ISBN 1-56639-456-2
(pbk. : alk. paper)
   1. United States—Armed Forces—Women. 2. Women in combat—United
States. I. Stiehm, Judith. II. Series.
UB418.W65I88 1996
355'.0082—dc20   95-49038

Contents

Preface   ix

PART I   VOICES AND FACTS

1   Soldiering: The Enemy Doesn't Care
If You're Female
Rhonda Cornum
3

2   Duty, Honor, Country: If You're Straight
Virginia Solms
24

3   The Creation of Army Officers and the Gender Lie:
Betty Grable or Frankenstein?
Billie Mitchell
35

4   Just the Facts, Ma'am
Judith Hicks Stiehm
60

PART II HISTORY AND ISSUES

5 The Military Woman's Vanguard: Nurses
Connie L. Reeves
73

6 From Underrepresentation to Overrepresentation:
African American Women
Brenda L. Moore
115

7 Gender and Weapons Design
Nina Richman-Loo and Rachel Weber
136

8 Gender Ideology in the Ethics of Women in Combat
Lucinda Joy Peach
156

9 To Fight, to Defend, and to Preserve the Peace:
The Evolution of the U.S. Military and the Role
of Women Within It
M. C. Devilbiss
195

PART III   REFLECTION AND SPECULATION

10   Pernicious Cohesion
Carol Burke
205

11   Telling the War Story
Susan Jeffords
220

12   Subverting the Gender and Military Paradigms
Miriam Cooke
235

13   The Civilian Mind
Judith Hicks Stiehm
270

About the Contributors   297

Index   299

Preface

Militaries are traditional institutions. When outsiders ask them to change, for example, by permitting openly gay men and lesbian women to serve in uniform, they are capable of energetic resistance. A phrase frequently used by opponents of change is "Not in my military/Army/Navy/Air Force/Marine Corps!" as though because they are in the military they own it.

In fact, civilians, including the Supreme Court, often do defer to the military. But the military's commander in chief is an elected official, and a majority of voters are women. Thus, it would not be incorrect for women collectively to respond to a traditionalist: "Well, you realize it's actually my military"—or at least, "It's my military, too!" Women have never constituted more than 13 percent of the U.S. armed forces, and even the most nontraditional and the most patriotic seem more wary of than enthusiastic about joining the military. But it is our military, and we have responsibility for what it is and what it does.

The purpose of this book is to encourage civilians, especially women civilians, to accept and exercise that responsibility. The first section provides basic information about the military, such as the rank structure. It also offers narratives by three active-duty women officers, each very successful but each with a different story and set of beliefs. Two of the three have chosen to use pseudonyms. The second section provides perspectives on specific groups of women who have chosen to serve—in particular, nurses and African Americans. This section also discusses issues related to physical differences between women and men, the combat exclusion, and the changing nature of the military's mission. The essays in the last section are written by civilian feminist intellectuals. None has had military experience, but all have worked for an extended period on the subject of war or the military. Their essays are intended as catalysts. So is the book.

Four conferences, acknowledged below, provided a forum for the development of many of these essays. The importance of such gatherings cannot be overestimated. Indeed, some of their organizers too are contributors to this volume: "Women and the Military" was held as a Quail Roost Conference and hosted by Richard Kohn of the Triangle Universities Security Seminar in April 1993. "Gender and War" was held at the Rockefeller Foundation's Bellagio Study and Conference Center and hosted by Miriam Cooke and Alex Roland in August 1993. "Institutional Change and the U.S. Military: The Changing Role of Women" was held at Cornell University and hosted by Mary Katzenstein and Judith Reppy in November 1993. "Peacekeeping: A New Role for Women and Men" was held in Washington, D.C., and hosted by Georgia Sadler for the Women's Education and Research Institute in December 1994.

In addition, Chapter 8, by Lucinda Peach, was developed with the assistance of the Indiana Center on Global Change and World Peace at Indiana University; an earlier version of the essay was published in the *Hamline Journal of Law and Public Policy*.

PART I   VOICES AND FACTS

Rhonda Cornum

Soldiering: The Enemy Doesn't Care

If You're Female

Should women be in the military? Should they be in combat? I must have been asked about these issues a thousand times since I was shot down in Iraq during the Gulf War. I don't think people think it's so remarkable that I've been in the Army, but do people really believe that being shot down in a helicopter and spending a week in prison makes you an expert on social/military issues? That seems pretty unreasonable to me. I think I do have an important point of view about such issues, but I believe my view is valuable because it is based on my experience of (at the time I was shot down) thirteen years in the military and six and a half months of being deployed. Being captured does, though, give one a certain amount of credibility. Still, when I'm asked what I think about women in the military, my opinion is based on my extended experience, not on stereotypes, not on philosophy, not on prejudice, and not on a one-week experience as a prisoner of war.

I was an unlikely person to join the military. I was a product of the late 1960s and 1970s—as my teenage daughter says, of "the hippie days." I was a graduate student in nutritional biochemistry at Cornell University and within a year or so of getting my Ph.D. when I gave a talk at a national meeting and a lieutenant colonel in the Army came up to me afterward and asked if I had a job when I graduated. He turned out to be the director of a research division at the Letterman Research Institute in San Francisco and was interested in hiring someone to do research on amino acid metabolism. There was one hitch. He said, "You have to be in the Army." Well, that was interesting. I'd never met anybody in the Army before. During high school I had never even met someone who was planning to join the Army. In college I was at least aware that there were people in the Army—Cornell had an ROTC contingent, but I had never met anyone who belonged to it. I didn't say "No thanks," because I've always been willing to think about new activities, but I had had no experience at all with people in the Army and certainly none with Army people who did biochemical research.

One thing I learned about being commissioned in the Medical Service Corps was that I would make a lot more money than I would as an assistant professor or postdoctoral fellow. I also learned I would have a beautifully equipped research lab and an equally beautiful view of San Francisco Bay from the third floor of the Letterman Institute. You add to that package having no teaching responsibilities—an opportunity to do only research—and I was sold. I was commissioned in the Army Medical Service Corps and went off to officer basic training in San Antonio, Texas, in the summer of 1978. Officer basic was not exactly what the lieutenant colonel had told me it would be. Most of the other students were second lieutenants who had just graduated from college or from Officer Candidate School and who were going to be leaders of medical platoons. They were going to be in the real Army, not the medical research institute version of the Army. While I was attending this summer indoctrination course, I discovered that I really liked it. I liked running in formation. I liked doing things as a group. The Army sort of took on the feeling of family.

Going to the field and accomplishing things as part of a squad was a new experience for me. I had been very competitive my entire life, but I had always done things as an individual. I showed dogs—you do that by yourself. I showed horses—you do that by yourself. I didn't participate in any organized team sports when I was in high school or college. And doing biochemical research involved pitting your brain against a problem. First you had to find the problem; then you had to find a way to solve it; finally you had to find the solution. This was not really a group experience either. For whatever reason, when I joined the Army I found I was ready to be a team member, and I had a great time in officer basic.

Then I went to San Francisco and to work. It was, as advertised, a great research environment. I discovered, however, that most people at Letterman were not particularly military. The majority of the physicians who worked there were participants in the Berry Plan. This plan had let them defer their required military service until after they had completed medical school. Though some of them had a real interest in doing research, most of them had no interest in the military or in the Army's mission. I did find a few people at Letterman who liked the Army, and I gravitated toward them.

I went to the Expert Field Medical Badge Course in Monterey, California, with another officer. We had a great time and worked very hard. In fact, that course, which involved doing medicine in the field, was harder than anything I had done to date. We both graduated. When asked by a surgeon in the office next to mine why I would do such a thing—go down there and get dirty and sleep in the woods and set up field sanitation sites—I answered, "Because I'm in the Army."

The experience of being a Ph.D. scientist in a medical research institute convinced me of several things. First, I really liked medical research. Second, it was frustrating not to have a clinical background. Third, it was discouraging to watch people make twice as much money as I did and produce no better quality research than I was producing. I decided that I should either go back to the university and do research with rats and chickens or go to medical school. There seemed to be more future in medicine, and so I applied to and was accepted at the Uniformed Services University of the Health Sciences (USUHS), in Bethesda, Maryland, also known as "the military medical school," or FEDMED U.

I suppose a note about my personal situation is important. I had gotten married as a senior at Cornell and had a daughter, Regan, by the end of my first year of graduate school. At that time my husband and I were somewhat caught up in "hippie ways." We lived in a log cabin, heated our place with wood, milked goats, grew our own vegetables, and so on. We had a great time, and it was a wonderful experience. But things were quite different in San Francisco. After two years there, we were divorced and agreed to joint custody of our daughter. At the same time that I made the decision to go to medical school, Regan's father decided to go back to school, and he was barely surviving on a graduate student stipend. Thus, I was responsible, at least financially, for Regan. That was a significant consideration in my choice of where to go to medical school. As a student at USUHS, I was paid a regular second lieutenant's salary. Admittedly, that was not as good as the senior captain's salary I had already been receiving, but it was a lot better than nothing. And it was overwhelmingly better than going into debt, not just to pay for medical school, but also to pay for child care and living expenses. I knew I liked the Army and I knew I wanted to stay in, so the fact that a USUHS education carried a significant commitment in terms of the amount of time I was obliged to stay in service was easily outweighed.

USUHS was for the most part a great experience. First, I met my husband, Kory, there. Second, I was exposed to senior medical officers who liked the Army, who thought the military mission was important, and who thought going to the field and participating in wartime training was important. And it was an opportunity to see that there was a variety of interesting career paths after medicine if one wanted to stay in the Army. Many of the USUHS students had been in the service previously or in ROTC. Some had been enlisted, some had been in other career fields, but we were a group of people who knew we would work together for the rest of our careers, and there was very little of the unpleasant competition you sometimes get in civilian schools. We all knew we would have a job when we got out. I didn't need to remind myself "I'm in the Army" anymore. The military was my life, not just a phase.

After I was accepted to the military medical school, I requested a TDY, or temporary duty assignment, to attend jump (parachute) school at Fort Benning, Georgia, before starting school. Once again, my friends in San Francisco shook their heads. They asked, "Rhonda, why are you doing this to yourself?" I had to admit it was just to prove I could—and to be surrounded by people who were "really" in the Army.

Following medical school graduation in 1986, Kory and I stayed in Washington. I began a general surgery internship at Walter Reed Army Hospital. During my internship I applied for and was accepted into a (military) urology residency. While we were medical students, though, Kory had convinced me that we should take the Army flight surgeon course. Why? Because in 1986, when we attended, part of the curriculum included teaching the physician students how to fly helicopters. In order for Kory (who was in the Air Force, not the Army) to participate in the course, we had to go while we were students. Once he graduated and was assigned to an Air Force base, he could only have attended the Air Force flight surgeon course, in which you don't get to learn to fly. Although I had once considered being a pilot, I had decided against it. This was partly because at that time women were allowed to fly only transport helicopters and medevac. No gunships for them! My personality definitely ran more toward the gunship aircraft.

Even then, I did not consider it reasonable to try to compete in an arena where I was not going to be treated equally. Medicine was not that way, I thought. I believed that as a medical officer I would be judged on ability and performance and not on gender.

Kory and I had a great time at the Army flight surgeon course. We took two of our thoroughbred horses (that we were in the process of steeplechasing) with us and maintained them at the Fort Rucker riding stable. Every day after class we'd go to the stable, pack the horses in their trailer, and go out to the tank trail, where there were miles and miles of sandy roads, and ride for an hour. That kept "the girls" in shape for the races we went to during the six weeks we were at flight school. Best of all, though, we learned to fly helicopters! It was more fun than I had imagined. I graduated number one in the class, although I hadn't actually realized until the end of the course that there was any sort of grading going on other than pass/fail. On the last day the most remarkable thing happened. The guy who was second in the class said, "Rhonda, I didn't realize you were in the running." (I guess I hadn't looked very nerdy over the past six weeks.) I looked him in the eye and said, "Well, I didn't even know we were competing."

Kory had always wanted to be an Air Force flight surgeon. Denver, where I had been accepted for the urology residency, had no Air Force bases nearby—at least none that had fighters. I believed that if I was competitive now for a residency, then I'd be competitive later as well, and that being a flight surgeon was an opportunity to do a "military relevant" job. I, too, decided to become a flight surgeon.

It was at this point that I had my first clear experience with gender discrimination in the medical corps. We wanted to go to two bases in North Carolina. I could go to Fort Bragg with the 82nd Airborne. Kory could go to Seymour Johnson, where they were just starting to receive two-seat F-15s. We drove down for a weekend, met the people who were then in those jobs, looked at homes and farms. When we got back to Washington, though, I was told that I couldn't go because a flight surgeon in the 82nd would be considered a combat slot and women were not eligible. Yes, I was irritated. But as an intern I didn't have time to be irritated very long. We had just enough time to look for another opportunity for both of us to do what we wanted to do. Eventually, we settled, and the Army and Air Force personnel assignment officers also settled. Kory would go to Eglin Air Force Base in Florida, and I would be assigned to Fort Rucker, Alabama.

When I got to Fort Rucker in July 1987, I was met with a surprise. Because I was senior (having been in service prior to medical school), I was made chief of primary care. I was pretty surprised to be taking care of dependent family members and retirees, but I looked at it as a new opportunity. I had never run a clinic, I had never even worked in a clinic, and I had certainly never had other doctors working for me. In addition, I was responsible for the emergency room, staffing, credentialing, training, and more. I had a pretty steep learning curve, but it was fun finally to have a decision-making position again. I was actually sad when I had to leave the primary care clinic, but that didn't last long because I was next assigned to the Aviation Medicine Clinic, where I took care of flight students and instructor pilots.

In order to apply what I'd learned in my seven weeks of aviation medicine, I thought it was important to build rapport with the aviators. One way to do this was to make medical care convenient and to make myself available for discussion and consultation, so I started driving out to one of the airfields every morning at six o'clock, before my duties at the hospital began. I learned a great deal from this. I learned about the training mission and about student pilots, and, I confess, I noted some great research opportunities.

Because of my experience and interest in medical research, I was next transferred to the U.S. Army Air Aeromedical Research Laboratory, located at Fort Rucker. In this assignment the rapport I had established with the permanent instructor pilots proved really helpful. If I ever needed subjects for any study, I always had more than enough volunteers. If I needed class participation, I always got 100 percent. This rapport also proved to be valuable when I was deployed to the Gulf, because I had personally met every instructor pilot in the Apache helicopter group during the years I had been at Fort Rucker and had also spoken to every student who went through Apache training between 1988 and 1990.

I also knew a lot of people in other aviation units when we deployed. No matter how big an organization is, and the Army certainly is big, it is the personal relationships that both make it fun and make it work.

The first year at the research lab was great. We did studies looking at simulator sickness, sickness in an enclosed cockpit where the pilot's only visual interaction with the outside world is through an externally mounted camera. We examined sleep/wake, rest/work cycles in units that were deployed and how those cycles affected performance. We evaluated some of the experimental systems being designed for the new LHX helicopter. In August 1990, I was returning from Fort Hood, where a study on work/rest cycles was going on, and was at the Dallas airport waiting for my next flight when news of Iraq's invasion of Kuwait was announced. In fact, I was watching television in the airport with my friend Moshe Cohen, an Israeli lieutenant colonel who was the commander of the first Israeli Apache helicopter unit.

When we heard the news, we looked at each other and back at the screen. I asked him, "What do you think you are going to do?" He said, "I think

I'm going back to Israel early. How about you?" I wasn't sure. Fort Rucker has very few units that are normally deployed, but I had a feeling.

I got home late that night and was at the store the next morning when the commander of the 229th Attack Helicopter Battalion called looking for me. When I got home, my husband told me, "Colonel Bryan's looking for you." "What for?" "He couldn't say over the phone." At that point I knew. His unit was going to be deployed, and he wanted me to go. The next two days were a whirlwind. I had to get reassigned from the research lab to the 229th. I knew all the pilots and the commander quite well, but I had to meet the medics. I had to see what kinds of equipment and supplies and facilities were available. I had to plan for the medical aspects of the deployment. And none of us knew what the conditions would really be like when we got there. Through all this and like everyone else, I had to deal with the fact that I was leaving my husband and daughter and wasn't really sure if I'd ever be coming home.

That's a very interesting concept. Although I had always known it could happen, it's quite different when it really does. It never occurred to me not to go. If LTC Bryan thought his unit would do better if I went with it, then it probably would. And I had a lot of friends in that unit. I could never have even considered letting them down.

As the first two days turned into the first ten days, we frantically packed trucks, found equipment, and then waited for airlift to take us to Saudi Arabia. The fact that I was female never entered a conversation. Finally, we got in our trucks and our helicopters, bused and convoyed up to Fort Benning, and over several days deployed the battalion to the 101st Division in Saudi Arabia. We were offloaded in Dhahran for the first week. We and thousands of other soldiers lived in big open hangars. The only latrine facilities were the ones that were there for the British aerospace and Saudi employees. Showers were taken (such as they were) under fire hoses that were hung up over rafters in the hangars. Sometimes we used the emergency showers that were to be used if you spilled paint or gasoline on yourself. Sleeping facilities were wherever you laid down your sleeping bag. There was no privacy, and it didn't seem to bother anyone. Eventually, everyone arrived. The helicopters were all reassembled, and we went to the base that was to be our home for the next several months until we finally deployed into the desert.

Our base was the King Fahd Airport. Half-built, it consisted of several miles of runway, an unfinished hangar and terminal, and a huge parking garage. There were some buildings on the other side of the runway and a large trailer park. The brigade lived in the parking garage. My home was a parking space, complete with white lines on the floor to separate me from the person next to me. I was fortunate. Because I was a major, I had my own parking space. Captains and below had two people per parking space. Interestingly, my being female seemed to make no difference to most people.

But it did to one person. She was a headquarters company commander, and she was very concerned about being female. As soon as I got there, she stopped me and said she thought we should take all the women ("all the women" was about five in our battalion and five in the rest of the battalions combined) and have them live together in the parking garage, separate from their units, the people they worked with. She asked if I would take this idea to the commander of the brigade, because she knew that I knew him. I said I would certainly talk to him about the issue. Later that day I talked both to him and to the deputy commander and told them I thought it was the most ridiculous thing I'd ever heard of—that the one thing we could do to depress esprit de corps and to promote jealousy and harassment was to segregate the women from their units and treat them differently. The women stayed with their units.

The buildup phase of Desert Shield involved a lot of hurry up and wait. When we arrived, there had been talk of having to fight our way off the airplane, but no one really knew what would happen when we got there. As the days turned into weeks and then to months, it became clear that we were not about to be invaded. Nor were we about to invade. More and more stuff and more and more people poured into Saudi Arabia. Those of us who were there relentlessly sought out things to do. We planned, we did training missions, we played volleyball, we wrote letters, we built gym equipment with sandbags and pieces of iron. From various kinds of packing material we built furniture to supplement the meager furnishings we had been able to carry in our duffle bags. My birthday came and went. Thanksgiving came and went. Finally, Christmas came and went.

And then we deployed. There were rumors about where we were going and what we were going to do there, but on a miserably cold, rainy, icy day in January we deployed to the middle of the desert. We set up camp, dug foxholes, strung concertina (barbed) wire, set up tents. I think the reality of going to war finally began to hit everyone. By this time, after five months in the country, I felt very confident about the skill of the medics in our battalion, as well as about my being able to provide sufficient medical aid. We had taken care of some training accident victims (luckily, none from our unit) as well as motor vehicle accident victims and those with accidental gunshot wounds, things that medics rarely see when assigned to a garrison in the states. Still, we were nervous, the weather was terrible, and had we been faced with invading tanks from the north, we would have been unable to fly our aircraft against them or even to convoy our trucks out of the way. It was, in fact, a great relief to everyone when the air war finally started. Then we knew they would be unable to launch a preemptive ground attack—because we had already launched an air attack.

I remember the beginning of the air war very well. Everyone was up listening to their radios and watching the sky as the streams of fighters, bombers, and tankers were overhead. The excitement and anticipation was electric. No, you shouldn't get the impression that everyone was anxious to go kill Iraqis. I don't think that was it at all. But the months of waiting were finally over, and it had become clear that we would not go home except through Iraq.

I think some of it was the feeling of being part of something bigger than oneself—of being a part of a military that is strong and mighty and efficient. There's pride and there's excitement in being a part of that. I think everybody felt that. And again, I don't think I felt it any differently because I was female.

Following the successful beginning of the air war, we were repositioned several hundred kilometers farther to the west, in the middle of the desert. Once again, after the flurry of setting up tents and establishing latrines, it was hurry up and wait. There were more training missions, however, and planning took on a much more serious tone. It was obvious we had not been writing war plans for exercise. Before the ground war began, and before we actually moved our entire camp into Iraq, we did some armed recognizance missions across the border. I participated as a member of the search-and-rescue team. Because of the long distances the Apaches could fly without having to refuel, it was important to be available if one of our aircraft was shot down or had an engine problem or other accident. So a Blackhawk with one of the medics would follow the attack company's battle formation several kilometers behind. That way, if there was a problem, we would be available for immediate rescue or first aid. On one of our missions we came on an encampment of Iraqi soldiers. Using sign language, that is, pointing the Apache gun at them, we persuaded them to lay down their weapons and surrender. The lead aircraft of the mission directed our Blackhawk to retrieve the surrendering prisoners. We flew up, got off, and began to gather the prisoners. They brought the first few back to the plane. I searched them as they got onto the aircraft and then guarded them while the others went back to retrieve the rest of the prisoners. It didn't seem strange to me that I should be doing this. I was there, there wasn't any medical care to be given, and it was something that needed to be done. I felt no ethical dilemma. Not only was I not doing any harm to anyone—the Hippocratic oath states, "I will do no harm to my patients"—but healthy Iraqi soldiers were clearly not patients. Besides, they were probably being saved, not harmed, by becoming our prisoners.

This was perhaps the most exciting day of the deployment. We had gone on a mission and had actually successfully accomplished something and we have done so with no loss of equipment or personnel. I played only a minuscule role, but it was important to feel included, and I certainly understood why people wanted to participate in this and other missions. It was really a great feeling to be a part of this. Once again, I am convinced that I did not feel differently nor did anyone think I should feel differently because I was female. Being a girl just didn't matter. I tried to explain this in a letter to my mother:

> Dear Mother:
>
> I have gotten several letters from you lately (thank you, by the way!), and I have been debating about what to write. I could lie, and say I am safe in a nice quiet medical job somewhere, but (A) I don't lie, and haven't for twenty years; and (B) I'd rather you know what I'm really thinking and feeling about being here.
>
> Five days ago I was (I think) the first American female service member to fly into Iraq, get out of my aircraft, be a part of taking the first prisoners of war that the 101st took, and fly back out with these guys in my helicopter. No, I wasn't scared. It was in fact the most exciting thing since sex I've done. No, this is not a particularly romantic war, but going into combat is the real reason people stay in the army. It isn't the money, because I could not possibly make as little as I do if I was a civilian. It isn't the lifestyle, because I haven't lived like this since Freeville, New York. But it is in some ways—it is a personal test to see if you have the "right stuff." And let's admit it—that's me. I seem to gravitate to doing things that are difficult just because I crave challenge. And the army likes me for it! And I like, no, I love what I

do. It was like being a surgery intern at Walter Reed. That is the most difficult internship offered by the army—and I liked it!

I feel what I'm doing here is important, and I am very proud to be doing it. My family (husband and daughter) are happy with me. . . . So go to the library or something—but it doesn't help me focus on what I need to do here to worry about you worrying about me!

I love you; I'm glad you are doing well. Please, just laugh at some of my stories, be proud of me doing my patriotic thing, fly your flag. Sure, we've got body bags—I'm even considering using one as an outside liner for my sleeping bag, warm and dry!

> Love always,
> Rambo Rhonda (it's a joke)

Finally, the word came. We had begun the big air assault on Iraq. It went quickly, more quickly than anyone thought it would, and with nowhere near the casualties we had been warned to expect. I felt I was ready. I felt that I had prepared the medics as much as could be done for the possibility of 25 percent casualties, the number we had been told could result from ground combat.

After several days we were flat-out jubilant. It was obvious that the objective of driving the Iraqis out of Kuwait had been successful. During this part of the war, I confess, taking prisoners was not nearly so exciting; we had, in fact, stopped taking them. When we saw small bands of Iraqis, we would stop and pick up their weapons but let them keep marching south as we moved north.

On the morning of 27 February, we broke camp yet again and began moving farther north and east, toward Basra. The helicopters, as always, left first, with the trucks convoying twenty-four to forty-eight hours later. As we landed the Blackhawks, we dropped off loads of people and supplies and equipment. The helicopters stood in a long line and hovered to get gas at a large forward refueling area. After filling our Blackhawk, we continued shuttling people and equipment to the new but very temporary battalion headquarters. Then a radio transmission came through. It was our operations officer on a handheld radio asking, "Number one, do you have gas? Do you have the 'doc'? Do you have all her stuff?" Our pilot answered yes to all the above. Then we heard our new mission. An F-16 pilot had ejected approximately thirty-five minutes from our location. He was on the ground; he had at least a broken leg and was going to be captured if somebody didn't go and get him. We were the closest unit with helicopters, and our mission was to go and pick him up. We were pretty excited. This was the only *real* rescue mission we had a chance to do, since, fortunately, not one of our aircraft had been hit.

Two Apaches that had paralleled us in the large refuel line took off with us. We sped across the desert toward the coordinates we had been given. As we flew, the crew and I planned how we would do it. They'd hover down, we'd jump out, one would carry the stretcher, one would carry the weapons, one would carry a splint to mobilize his leg, and then we would bring him in. These were the very things we'd practiced many times.

As we flew close to the ground, we saw the truck convoys. Some of the men waved; we waved back. We felt very confident, but within a minute of our last wave we came under heavy Iraqi gunfire. In less than another minute, with the tailboom blown off our Blackhawk, we crashed.

The first thing I clearly remember following the crash was looking up and seeing five Iraqi soldiers with rifles pointed at me. When one of them grabbed me and pulled me up, I realized I was injured. My right arm, which was already fractured, separated. Later I found that both arms were broken between the elbow and the shoulder and that I had a bullet in my back.

I was dragged from bunker to bunker getting interrogated and being passed up the chain of command until finally someone made a decision to send me to prison. Along the way, another survivor, Sergeant Troy Dunlap, was also captured. When we were brought together under the most miserable conditions, I realized just how important being with another American, another Army guy, was to me. And it didn't matter that he was in the infantry and I was in the medical corps. It didn't matter that he was enlisted and I was an officer. And it surely didn't matter that he was male and I was female. We were taken to separate prison cells the first day we were captured. On the second day we were taken to another facility and left alone together for a few hours. During that time we compared notes, discussed what had happened, and made sure that our stories about where we were and what we were doing there corresponded.

But there were some funny events. As we were whispering, one time he looked at me and said, "Ma'am, you're really brave." I looked back at him and said, "What'd you think I was going to do, cry or something?" He said, "Yeah, I guess I thought you were." I said, "Well, that's okay. I thought you were, too." It is interesting what our expectations were. His were based on

Tail of the Blackhawk helicopter in which Cornum crashed.

Courtesy of Rhonda Cornum.

Rhonda Cornum in her parking-garage home in the Gulf.
Courtesy of Rhonda Cornum.

Rhonda Cornum, CW2 Bill Tompkins, and their aid station—ready for the land war. Courtesy of Rhonda Cornum.

Recovering POWs Bill Andrews (front row, center), Rhonda Cornum (behind Andrews), and Troy Dunlop (behind Cornum's left shoulder).
Courtesy of Rhonda Cornum.

Two Arabs (in cockpit) who offered help to Rhonda Cornum and crew when their chopper came down. Courtesy of Rhonda Cornum.

gender; mine were perhaps based on age, or, perhaps, just on experience, who knows.

On the third day of our captivity we were taken from our cell, blindfolded, and put on a bus to Baghdad. By this time, the third survivor of our eight-member crew had been located. He had a fractured pelvis and a badly broken leg and was taken on a stretcher onto the same bus. Additionally, we met up with Captain Bill Andrews, the F-16 pilot we'd gone to rescue. As we bounced our way to Baghdad, one of the few real difficulties of being female became apparent. It is much easier to urinate if you're a male with two broken arms than if you're a female. Other than that, there seemed to be very little difference between us as we jostled our way in the dark to Baghdad.

When we got there, the two severely injured people, Sergeant Daniel Stamaris from our wreck and me, were taken to the prison ward of the Rasheed Military Hospital. Sergeant Dunlap and Captain Andrews were taken to the prison where other Allied prisoners of war were being kept. At the military medical facility we were evaluated. Sergeant Stamaris underwent stabilization of his pelvis and external fixation of his leg. I underwent reduction of my fractures and the casting of both my arms, from my shoulders to my wrists. After that, as before, it was wait, wait, wait. I feel confident that the care we were given was at least as good as we would have received had we been wounded Iraqi soldiers, and I felt pretty good about that. That is certainly what we would have done and what we did do with wounded Iraqis.

On the sixth night of our captivity, soldiers came in the middle of the night, blindfolded us, and took us to the prison where the other Allied prisoners were being held. We were given yellow POW costumes that everyone wore home and ill-fitting Iraqi sneakers. Once again, we were blindfolded and marched onto a bus. Next we were marched off the bus into the lobby of a hotel. At that time, our blindfolds were removed, and we were welcomed with the words, "You're safe. You're with the Red Cross."

That day and night there was much celebration. We all heard the news that the war had been over for almost a week, what had happened, and the conditions of surrender. Mostly, we told one another stories of what had happened to us. It was pretty funny. In this hotel, which the Red Cross had commandeered, there was a separate room for each of us, but the last thing in the world that anybody wanted was to stay in a separate room. We'd been primarily in solitary confinement for anywhere from a week to a month. So we created a big slumber party. In my room there were two double beds.

We had three guys per bed, somebody on the couch, and several people on the floor, and we talked and told stories all night long. The next afternoon we were taken (this time not blindfolded) to another bus and then to the Baghdad International Airport, where Swiss Air came to pick us up. Three hundred Iraqi prisoners were returned, and then the twenty-one of us were taken back to Saudi Arabia. The ride home was also jubilant. As we passed into Saudi airspace, a British Tornado jet came up and flew wingtip to wingtip with us, and, as he peeled off, a U.S. F-15 came up and flew in close formation all the way to Riyadh. There we were greeted by General Schwarzkopf and numerous cheering dignitaries as we got off the airplane. We were then sent on an Air Force 141 to Bahrain, where we were taken to the USS Mercy (a Navy hospital ship) for some medical attention and psychiatric evaluation before we came back to the States.

Each unit that had a prisoner sent a member to meet that prisoner and to fill him or her in on what had happened after their disappearance. Some of them brought tapes. One guy even watched his own airplane being shot down through the camera of his sister ship. Dan Grant, a warrant officer in Charlie Company whom I had frequently flown with, played cards and Yahtzee with and talked with for hours, was sent to meet me.

I heard about how the mission was received at home and how they had been told by the pilot of the Apache that was following us that we'd all been killed, that there was no way anybody could have survived the wreck. I was told about the wide swings of emotion that occurred when they went to the site and found only five instead of the eight expected bodies. My husband, who was also in Saudi Arabia (my daughter was with her father in North Dakota), had had a premonition that it was my aircraft that was shot down when he heard the Schwarzkopf briefing on the evening of 27 February. He had not heard officially until 3 March, however, that I was missing in action—but he was on the Mercy waiting when I got there.

It was wonderful to come back. After several days on the Mercy, we were flown on the semiretired Air Force One to Washington, where we were greeted by Secretary of Defense Richard Cheney, General Colin Powell, numerous dignitaries, but most important, our families. Then we split up to our respective services. I went to Walter Reed Hospital for several days, then back to Florida, where I received definitive medical care. I got my left arm operated on twice, had a graft put in my right knee, and underwent fixation of my broken right finger. It was also during this time (after the return from Washington) that the impact of our captivity on America became obvious.

We had no clue what a huge media event our captivity was until we were released. In particular, it seems my being captured and being held as a prisoner of war was a big deal. Personally, I couldn't see why. I hadn't done anything different from what everybody else did. I wasn't any more or less brave than anybody else, but as I said, I was suddenly an immediate expert on women in the military and women in combat. The truth is, I think exactly what I have always thought. It's just that now my feelings and opinions are based on experience.

I think women are just like men; women who are motivated to be in the military have the same range of reasons as men. In terms of performance, there's also that same range. I think some women will be terrific, some will be brainless, and the vast majority will simply do their job and do it well. And I think the percentages of women in these categories will be approximately the same as for the men. The things that are really important are loyalty and integrity, moral courage, a sense of humor, dedication, and commitment. I don't think those things are any better represented in either sex. I think there should be no positive and no negative discrimination based on gender—or, for that matter, on race or anything else. I think a person's potential and his or her demonstrated performance should be the only criteria used in the assignment of people or in their selection for future training.

I can't say I recommend that anybody get captured. Personally, I'd have been much happier if we'd flown in, picked up Captain Andrews, and flown back. We'd have been delighted, but I do have to find some piece of good news in everything. The fact is that we failed in rescuing Captain Andrews, and that five guys were killed and the three of us were captured. I have to find some way to find something positive out of that experience. So for myself, I choose to look at it as an opportunity to demonstrate that, at least with an "n of one" experiment, we know that women behave the same when they are captured as men do. This is significant, since the potential for being captured is one of the key arguments used by those trying to keep women from holding important military positions. If it had to happen, I'm as glad it happened to me as anybody. And I'm glad to have had the opportunity to do interviews and appear in numerous publications. I'm glad I've had the chance to demonstrate what women can do.

I'm doing the same thing now as I would have been doing had I never gone to Saudi Arabia. I'm back in a medical center and in surgical training. Yes, I confess, I'm once again in a male-dominated specialty; I'm a fourth-year resident in urology, a specialty that has approximately 2 percent women. And what's important about that is that there is no magic percentage of any minority that is required to be successful. What's important is that one has to identify with the activity, whether it's being a pilot, being a urologist, being a fire fighter, being a schoolteacher. One must identify with the activity, not with race or the gender of the other participants. I pick mentors based on their teaching ability and their example. I don't pick them based on their gonads.

There seems to be a belief in some kind of critical mass theory—that you need 8 percent or 10 percent or 12 percent of any particular subgroup in order for any individual to be successful. I think that's wrong. All that happens, then, is that we select people primarily for their membership in a subgroup rather than for their ability to do whatever it is they're trying to accomplish. Then we have failures. Then the majority bases its opinions on the lowest performer in a minority, not on the highest.

One of the things I often say when I have to give a talk someplace is that if you're going to be first, you have to be best. In addition, when people are trying to integrate themselves into a field or an activity that was previously closed, the newcomer often tries to change the behavior of that group. That is a mistake. It happens in many circumstances, for example, when women started becoming doctors and men started becoming nurses. When you are a small minority, you can't expect to change the behavior of the group. You may or may not choose to participate in it. I've been a physician for a long time, I've been a urologist for some time, and I still don't play golf; I probably never will. But I surely don't try to say that I'm being discriminated against because I'm not included in my colleagues' golf games. I have learned to watch professional sports, but, I have to say, that was more the influence of my teenage daughter than it was of my mostly male colleagues.

Another interesting thing I hear is that somehow allowing women into traditionally male environments will make the women lose their femininity. I've always been in traditionally male-dominated environments, and I can't say that I think I've lost mine. In my life, masculinity and femininity are very personal. It has to do with how you interact with each other in a personal, social, intimate relationship, not how you act at work. It's true that at work I have occasionally been told I had some pretty big cohonas and it was meant as a compliment (I think). Also, I think that's one of the things we struggle with as a society—separating how we act and interact professionally from how we act and interact personally.

There are lots of funny stories about people's prejudices and expectations, and it starts when we're very young. One of my favorites comes from the time I was in San Francisco and my daughter was four. She was in kindergarten, and one of her classmates came home with her every day and was picked up by her mother at our house. When this little girl first came in, I heard my daughter ask her, "And what kind of doctor is your mother?" Obviously, Regan thought everyone must do what I do.

When one evaluates how our society views women, we have to remember that the majority of adults, including those who are in decision-making and powerful positions, look at their childhoods and at their own life experiences. Their expectations for women, then, are built on what their mothers and sisters and wives do. It's no wonder they can't imagine women flying jets, firing rifles, or being captured in a war. Again, their opinions, like everyone else's, are based on their experiences. And their opinions won't change until their experiences change. Take, for example, Sergeant Dunlap, the young man I was captured with. He'd been in the infantry for several years. There aren't any women, either enlisted or officers, in the infantry, so his primary interaction with women was with his mother, his sisters, the girls he went out with in high school, and his wife. He certainly hadn't seen any women who did what he did, so there's no reason to be surprised that he was surprised (favorably) when I behaved like a soldier when we were captured.

During an interview we did together, he was asked, "What do you think about women in combat?" And he said, "I don't think they should be there." Then he was asked about me specifically: "Would you go to war with Dr. Cornum again?" He said, "Of course. I'd go anywhere with Major Cornum." What does that mean? It means that his experiences did affect his thinking but not enough to generalize to all women. And I don't blame him. That's why I think it's so important to have women who are competitive and have the ability and will to be successful—and to take those women and allow them to compete for and in everything. Then the rest of the military can base their opinions on successful women instead of relying on memories of their mothers, their wives, their girlfriends, and their sisters. I have to admit that if I had to form my opinion of women based on my mother and my two sisters, I probably wouldn't be an advocate of women in combat either. But then, when I consider old boyfriends, my father, and my brother, I'm not sure I'd want men either!

One of the questions I am frequently asked is, "What did the Iraqis think when they found out that you were a woman?" Well, I have to admit that when they pulled off my helmet and a lot of dark brown hair came flowing out, they did seem pretty surprised, but they certainly weren't overwhelmed by it. I think they were mostly surprised that we were there at all. And it was much more surprising that we were there on an aircraft and that they had shot us down. I guess what I'm trying to say is that it made much more difference to the American media than it did either to the U.S. soldiers in the Gulf or to the Iraqis.

What did I, and what do I, hope others will learn from my experience? First, that attitude is everything, and that a sense of humor, optimism, and determination will get you through anything. Second, that prejudice is based on ignorance, and that the only effective way to fight prejudice is with experience. Given the opportunity and rational leadership, men and women work together and bond just fine, particularly during conflict and adversity. It's pretty simple: we must all judge others on what they do, not what they are.

NOTE

For a fuller account of Lt. Col. Cornum's experiences, see Rhonda Cornum, *She Went to War: The Rhonda Cornum Story* (Novato, Calif.: Presidio Press, 1992).

2

Duty, Honor, Country: If You're Straight

"You wanna *what?*"
"You have got to be kidding me, Virginia."
"Well, *that* certainly is interesting."
"Go get 'em, gal!"
"You'll have to cut your hair!"
"Yeah, right!"
"Where?"

These are some of the responses I encountered from family, friends, and professors when I announced my decision to apply for admission to the United States Military Academy in the fall of my sophomore year in college. I was a good student and a varsity athlete, seemingly well on my way to graduating with a degree in biology and a life of defending the earth's ecosystems. There was something missing, though. I felt some sort of void in my life, which defied identification. I felt a lack of fulfillment, but that seemed like an absurd emotion for a twenty-two-year-old. Still, I could sense this untapped store of potential lying dormant just beneath the surface, and I wanted to learn how to tap into it. I knew, somehow, I would have to change my life completely to do that. I knew I would need to seek an institution that would challenge me beyond what I could then imagine, that would unsettle my confident sense of empowerment, that would shake up my world.

I had grown up in a house full of West Point memorabilia, but I did not really have an understanding of what they meant. I knew my father had graduated from there, and that it was a college, but that was about all. My father hardly ever spoke about West Point, not for any particular reason, but more for lack of a reason to. The military was just the last topic of interest in my family's whirling life. In fact, we were lucky to speak to one another at all as we rushed in and out of the house on our separate ways. So I grew up without any sense of connection to my father's cadethood and brief military service.

It was my godmother who laid down the gauntlet for me. I was wandering around in my own private world when I unexpectedly received a letter from her. It read like a manifesto of my life's destiny. She had recently visited West Point as an ambassador of America's women who had never had an opportunity to attend the academy. She sat very still one night in front of the Plain (West Point's hallowed parade field) and came face to face with what it might be like to be a part of an institution that is about what is real, what matters, and what lasts. She wrote me the letter sitting right there, in the moonlight, amid all the rich history and tradition of service, a letter encompassing the promise of duty performed with unrelenting standards, and the spirit of uncompromising honor that tied it all together. You could have blown me over with a feather. I fancied hearing a few hushed bars of "God Bless America" in the background as I read the letter. I was hooked.

Thus began my illustrious career as the most unlikely candidate in the history of the institution ever to open an application file. I began by applying very late. Most of my soon-to-be classmates had started their candidate processes a year earlier. I was a bit behind, and it was only because of the creative problem solving of my region's West Point liaison officer (an individual trained by the West Point Public Affairs Office in the art of helping cadet candidates through the application and appointment procedures) that I was allowed to be in the running at all. I was refused interviews with two of my state's congressional representatives and one of my state's senators. I did have an interview with one of my state's representatives, after which I was offered a nomination to the Coast Guard Academy, to which I was not applying. I was put on a waiting list for an interview with the only remaining senator. Each cadet candidate must have a nomination from one of his or her state congressional representatives in order even to be considered for admission to West Point.

I was called one morning in early November by a harried congressional staffer who asked how quickly I could drive to their office (four hours away); they had just received a cancellation for the final interview of the entire season. I leaped into the car and drove to the interview with my hair on fire, and was soon told my odds. They had one nomination to offer, and there were 230 applicants interviewing. I was given that nomination. Again, you could have knocked me over with a feather. Nearly two months later, I was offered an appointment under the Early Admission Program, reserved for cadet candidates who have outstanding files. I figured they felt sorry for me, being such an old woman and agreeing to give up two years of college to begin all over again at the Academy. I graciously accepted and sealed my fate as a young army officer in training.

The United States Military Academy is not a place for the mildly curious or faint-hearted. I learned this very quickly. Once my bags were taken from me and I hugged my parents goodbye, I was on my way to an entirely new life, nothing like I had ever expected or imagined. By that first afternoon, I was marching in rank and file, devoid of any semblance of my former self, at least outwardly. I was "New Cadet Solms," no longer "Virginia," no longer distinguishable from any of my classmates by anything other than my call name. "New Cadet Solms" for the first eight weeks, "Cadet Solms," "Maggot," "Kraut," "Beanhead," "Smack," and a few unmentionables for that entire first academic year.

I got the hang of it, though, and excelled both at academics and at cadet life. By the end of my plebe year, I had been chosen as one of thirty-two cadets (roughly fourteen hundred began in my class that year) to take key leadership positions in the summer. For the next year and a half, I continued to develop as a person, an athlete, and a leader and was nominated to participate in the Second Class (i.e., junior class) Leadership Selection Boards. This was a fairly grueling process consisting of carefully scrutinized cadet career performance evaluations and inquisition-board-like interviews, all in an effort to choose the five best leaders in that class. These five cadets are then assigned to important leadership positions charged with running the Corps of Cadets during their First Class (senior) year. We started those boards, that year, with roughly one thousand cadets, and I was chosen as one of the remaining five. This was an unprecedented event, because of my gender, and it created somewhat of a stir in and around West Point, as well as in the press.

I highlight this particular aspect of my cadet career, because it illuminates the context within which I came of age as a woman and a lesbian. I think that until my senior year I was devoid of a sexual thought. I dated some, but I somehow deferred intimacy to everything else. I think this was a function of the sheer pace of the institution, as well as the awkward position women cadets found themselves in. In order to survive with some grace and aplomb, you really had to become a sexually neutral being. I'm sure this is no news to any woman who works in a male-dominated profession. Success was dependent on our not being sexually repulsive or attractive to our male superiors, peers, or subordinates. I'm not sure this fact was manifested consciously in our acts or our developing leadership styles; rather, it was somewhat of an invisible manifesto mandated by male cadet responses to our behavior. And you could see it in almost all of us. While we worked so hard to be not provocative in any way, our male classmates were escorting (exploring their own sexuality with) busloads of college coeds shipped in by the infamous West Point Hostess in conjunction with the social directors of the various women's schools surrounding the academy. Sexual maturation, however, was not part of the leadership agenda for female cadets at West Point, and I believe volumes can be written about that particular inadequacy and the impact it has on gender relations at all the academies and throughout all the services.

In light of this, it was no wonder that I didn't come to understand my sexual orientation until I was nearly twenty-six years old and well on my way to an outstanding career as an Army Aviator. My coming out was extremely slow and painstaking. It was full of struggle and shame and fear and loathing. It flew in the face of everything I understood as "normal" and "okay." It confronted my expectations for myself and my future. It was terrifying. In my hubris-ridden mind, I was "Wonder Woman," indefatigable, empowered, boundless. Lesbians were not any of those things. Lesbians were some subculture of angry feminists making political statements about a world in which they could not cull "success." Lesbians were ugly and dragged their knuckles and played a lot of softball. They belonged to a lower socioeconomic stratum. They were permanently disenfranchised, unreconcilable to "real" society. And I was one of them. Yipes!

I began to rearrange my entire universe to accommodate this discovery. I talked it over with my parents and family members at length, meeting with varying degrees of support and chagrin. I talked with friends, all of whom offered me more love and respect than I gave myself. And slowly, slowly I came to understand myself as a closeted lesbian thriving in both an institution that outlawed me and a society that defied me. And slowly, slowly I began my movement from the shadows of inertia into the brilliance of action. After much gnashing of teeth and wringing of hands, I decided to continue

Virginia Solms "moving mountains" with a little help from her helicopter. *Courtesy of Marlin and Juliette Ritzman.*

Virginia Solms performing one of the airlifts necessary to bring a
skilled technician to a critical task or evacuate a casualty to a hospital.
Courtesy of Marlin and Juliette Ritzman.

being who I was, a good leader of aviation troops. I decided that it was critical for me to live my life, with dignity, as I always had. Along with that, however, came an acute understanding of my obligation to fellow gays and lesbians who were fighting bravely and visibly in a world that punished them. I decided that if I was going to remain invisible in order to lead soldiers, which felt like nothing less than my soul's mandate, then I needed to find a way to contribute to positive social change. I began to get involved in gay and lesbian politics on campuses and in cities near my geographical assignments. I became an innovator of sorts by empowering the small gay and lesbian leadership through teaching principles of organizational change and development from behind the scenes. It was the best I could do, since I chose not to leave the military on the basis of my sexuality.

It was in the midst of this whirlwind of growth, personal empowerment, and efficacy that Judith Stiehm asked me to write something about my life and experiences in the military. This seemed an easy enough task, but it turned out to be more difficult than I ever expected.

I've never written about what it is like being a woman or a lesbian in the military, not formally, and not with an intended audience. Of course, I've written letters home and to my friends, but I've never been asked to represent my life in a way that is accessible to those who do not know me or do not know the military. When I was first confronted with the idea, I thought, "Ah, it'll be a cinch. I'll just write what I *feel.*" After two weeks of staring at a blank screen and then avoiding the screen altogether, I realized that writing about something so close to the heart would be just as challenging as living the life I was asked to convey. When I pondered the strangeness of being struck apoplectic each time I tried to write about my life as a lesbian Army aviator, I had the revelation that I never conjoined my sexuality and my profession in my conscious thoughts. Not *really.* Not in a way that would allow me to turn the two topics over in one hand for examination. I had always held them separately. Safely extricated from each other. But the Army doesn't work like that. It is not a nine-to-five job. It is not a career. It is not a trade. It is a life, and it happens twenty-four hours a day, seven days a week, fifty-two weeks a year. It is infinite and pervasive. It knows no boundaries. Except gender and sexuality, of course. But those two boundaries are cultural, administrative fabrications born of habit and convenience. The convenience of ignorance and sloth. Women and lesbians in uniform do not experience the Army's professional imperatives differently than men do. They perform no differently. They feel no different. They, like everyone else, are well within the normal variances of the humanity that is the American soldier. The gender and sexuality classifications are inane.

Having said all that, I wonder, then, what it is I should say about my life as a lesbian and a military pilot. What can I say about the fact that in order to serve I must recognize and honor the distinctions made about my sexuality and my gender? I must be an idiot, because I have dedicated my life to an institution that does not even recognize my existence as salient or worthy. But somehow my commitment rises far above what the military culture claims as fact or reality about the limitations of my gender or sexuality. The contract I have made with this country is that I will put everything I've got into honoring the lives of its children.

There are as many reasons for joining the service as there are kids signing up every day. Some join because they feel a sort of obligation or duty, some join because they are not yet mature enough for college, some join because they do not yet have the financial security to do what it is they really want to do, and some join because they are flat out of any better ideas. None of this matters. What *does* matter is that soldiers are members of an organization that is used as a tool for asserting political will. We are methods of achieving balances of power and global reckoning. We take orders from civilians in our nation's capital who define our enemy for us. And many times, their reasons are obscured in rhetoric and diplomacy. In light of this sobering reality, the element I concentrate on is that kid who, for whatever reason, finds himself or herself responsible for the lives of others.

That is a terrific responsibility for an eighteen-year-old, and the transition from carefree high school senior to helicopter gunner is critical. It is my moral imperative to guide these young souls toward taking responsibility for their own understanding of the grave duties they have chosen. And it is only when they fully understand, that they can make a conscious choice about whether or not this is really what they want to do with their lives. In addition to guiding soldiers toward consciousness, I ensure that they are trained and challenged to the utmost of their capacity and that they fully embrace the fact that the skill with which they perform their functions determines the survival of many others. It is non-negotiable that they understand and accept the critical interdependence of all soldiers involved in every mission. This is the only way I, or any leader, can bring everyone home alive.

I am an officer and a leader in the profession of arms. My life is about the management of violence. The instruments of that violence, on the surface, may seem to be the sophisticated war weapons I fly or fire, but in reality they have nothing to do with it. It is those people, those young, courageous, dedicated, crazy, wonderful kids, who offer me their trust and confidence for just a little part of their lives. And no matter how much I scrutinize this, I cannot find a place that belongs solely to my gender or sexuality. I cannot know why it is against a policy for me to lead soldiers into combat or against a regulation for me to be an officer at all. I cannot understand why the institution would adopt a regulation that asks me to lie about myself, at the same time that it asks of me exacting standards of integrity and moral courage. There is nothing courageous about the closet. There is nothing of integrity about remaining hidden. It flies in the face of everything I am about and everything the United States Military Academy taught me about duty, honor, and country.

A certain bitterness rooted in the ambivalence created by all this absurdity grows quietly in me, and every day I must watch it carefully. Every day of my life, I wake up and put on an emotional suit of armor. And I know I am better than most: more qualified, better trained, and adroit at problem solving. It shows in the everyday indicators that make up professionalism: dedication, vision, and commitment. Even the Army decorates me with inordinate accolades. Yet I must gracefully sidestep inquiries about my personal life, and I must bow out of conversations about loved ones, and I must consistently resist requests for visits to my home. I must, in fundamental ways, remain aloof from my fellow soldiers—the very people who deem me so valuable to the team. The very people for whom I will lay down my life.

So what is my life as a lesbian officer in Army aviation? Well, it is all I have mentioned and much more. It is about the joy of being challenged by the brightest and the dullest people on the planet. It is about the exhilaration of "slipping the surly bonds of earth and touching the face of God." It is about the overwhelming fulfillment when a tremendously complex mission is conducted flawlessly. It is about feeling very much like an outcast. It is about being despised in ways that are not readily apparent. It is about being fearful most of the time. It is about feeling awkward at most social functions. It is about trying to reconcile personal integrity with the will to continue serving this nation. It is about fighting the urge to become a public social campaign. It is about unmitigated elation and abysmal disillusion. It is about honesty and deception, courage and cowardice, commitment and treachery, jubilation and misery. At times, my being an officer feels like an unquestionable destiny, and at times, it is untenable.

And now it seems clear to me why it was so difficult to write about this life of mine. It highlights for me, on more than an intellectual level, the grave injustice our military politics and regulations generate. And it seems clear why I've never held my sexuality and my profession together in the same hand. They feel awkward there and heavy somehow, but right nonetheless. Oh so right. Just like my place as a leader in this institution.

POSTSCRIPT

February 1996 marked the second anniversary of the "don't ask, don't tell, don't pursue" policy related to homosexuals and military service. Billed as an easing of the difficulties for homosexuals in the military (no one doubts there *are* homosexuals in the military), the new policy, now based on federal law rather than executive policy, seems to have had little effect on a service member's risk of being investigated or discharged.

The Washington, D.C.–based Servicemembers Legal Defense Network (SLDN), which provides legal representation to individuals targeted under the policy, also monitors and reports on the policy's implementation. SLDN found that 722 people were discharged as gays or lesbians or bisexuals in 1995—more than in 1994, the first year of the new policy, and more than in the last two years of the old policy. The Marine Corps and the Army have had about the same percentage of total discharges for some time: 6 and 23 percent respectively. However, the Navy, which used to constitute more than half the discharges, now constitutes about a third of the discharges, while the Air Force has greatly increased both the percentage and the number of its discharges. It has also pressed criminal charges (as opposed to administrative charges) against some individuals for consensual adult relationships.

Women constitute 13 percent of the U.S. military but 21 percent of Department of Defense (DOD) discharges and 30 percent of the cases brought to SLDN. SLDN argues that women who report sexual harassment or rape are often, in retaliation, accused of lesbianism and that witch-hunts, particularly against women, continue to occur.

In the second year of implementation SLDN documented seventy-seven "don't ask" violations. It also described how normal social conversation can force gays to lie if private conversations are held as reportable and allowable as evidence. SLDN documented eighteen violations of "don't tell" in 1995. While it has been established that statements about sexual orientation may be made with impunity to lawyers, chaplains, and security personnel, statements to family, church members, friends, and health personnel have been used as evidence even though individuals believed their statements to be protected as "personal and private." SLDN argues that the "don't pursue" policy "has been roundly violated" by (1) asking service personnel to identify suspected homosexuals (i.e. fishing to see what can be turned up), (2) initiating investigations on the basis of information that is not "credible," and (3) selectively pressing criminal charges against suspected homosexuals but not pressing or threatening criminal charges against heterosexuals for illegal consensual behavior. (Internal Navy, Air Force, and DOD memoranda offer a different interpretation of what is and is not appropriate inquiry and evidence.)

SLDN now lists fourteen gay, lesbian, or bisexual service members who are serving openly in the military while challenging potential separation. It also notes that other openly gay service members have not received media attention or experienced adverse action. The percentage of service members discharged annually for homosexuality is low: less than one-half of 1 percent. Still, it should be noted that while officers serve continuously, enlisted personnel (the bulk of the military) serve for specified periods of time and may or may not be allowed to reenlist. It is likely that denial of reenlistment is used as a way to remove gays from the military, although no data are available to corroborate this.

Since the primary reason offered for excluding homosexuals is that having to incorporate them into work groups where they are not wanted creates inefficiencies, it is relevant to note that there are costs for discharging gays and lesbians too. SLDN estimates $20 million in training costs per year, quite apart from costs related to investigations and discharge procedures.

NOTE

To explore this issue from a variety of viewpoints see Wilbur J. Scott and Sandra Carson Stanley, eds., *Gays and Lesbians in the Military: Issues, Concerns and Contrasts* (New York: Aldine de Gruyter, 1994).

Billie Mitchell

3

The Creation of Army Officers and the Gender Lie:

Betty Grable or Frankenstein?

They say that in the Army the women are mighty fine,
They promise Betty Grable and give you Frankenstein.
Oh, I don't want no more of Army life,
Gee, but I wanna go,
But, they won't let me go,
Gee, but I wanna go home.[1]

"If I Were a Man, I'd Join the Navy"[2]

Army Regulation 360-5 requires that soldiers submitting articles for publication must first have their work reviewed by an official "who know(s) the subject matter and audience" (1986, 13). I complied in preparing this essay for publication. It was reviewed and heavily criticized by senior officials, and, although I was never ordered not to publish, neither was I given explicit clearance. They said the methodology was flawed and the argument weak. They doubted, in fact, that it was a scholarly paper at all. All this commentary was so authoritative that I became briefly convinced that the work was, indeed, deeply flawed. In the course of revising it, and in the hopes of trying to understand the specifics of their objections, I found myself engaged in a long conversation with one of the reviewers. Not only were most of my assertions unprovable by respectable quantitative means, he explained, but my perceptions about what women think and even my own experiences were utterly false. He argued that there was equality between men and women throughout the Army, because the Army adheres to the Judeo-Christian ethic of "Love thy neighbor."[3] At West Point, the primary focus of my study, there is no room for gendered discrimination, since men and women are held to the same leadership standards. Responding to my experience that military men regard military women as both objects of desire and threats to their identity as soldiers, he countered that he had never heard any complaint of gender discrimination by the female officers he had worked with, and none of his male colleagues had ever been guilty of harboring such thoughts. His experiences were true, mine were false, and therefore my essay lacked any foundation in reality. At this point, I knew I was on to something. The extreme, cathected fury with which he and his colleagues reacted—so out of proportion to the provocation offered by this unexceptionable piece of feminist writing—suggested to me just how deeply structures shape perceptions and what profound limits structures place on the imaginations of those who uphold them. I could not hope for a better illustration of what I call "the gender lie" at the heart of military thinking: the notion that because intentions are "good" and standards are "gender-blind," there cannot be any gendered tension in the military except in the pathological thinking of a female malcontent.

This chapter has dual foci: the American Army's gender lie of the woman officer's equality, and how women respond to it. Inherent in these issues is the larger question of women's relation to war. Susan Gubar has pointed out that although feminists have criticized warfare on the grounds of the "infinite sequentiality of world wars, technological advances in destructive capabilities, the obliteration of a safe homefront, the destruction of whole populations, and the ideological threat of fascism," they have also felt profoundly threatened by war *as women*:

> Why did literary women also fear that male vulnerability in wartime would result in violence against women? . . . They were grappling with male-authored images that reified gender arrangements as rigidly as they had been demarcated in the Victorian period, but in a newly eroticized way. Even women occupied at vocational jobs that had never before been available to them could hardly escape the conclusion that the female community had been no less occupied than all the other foreign territories that had been laid waste. (Higonnet et al. 1987, 230)

If women on the outside have felt the military as such a profound threat to their well-being, how can women on the inside cope? How do these two groups of women view each other? Military women, by and large, are not feminists, and feminists take a mixed view of military women. Odd. Military women are at the forward edge of the gendered battlefield but are generally not politicized and are concerned more with making a wage than with making a point (Katzenstein 1990). Furthermore, military women, by law, receive equal pay for equal work, since soldiers are paid by a (relatively) genderless calculation of time in service and rank. Statistically, women do well in promotion and, although they typically have a shorter military longevity, seem to be attaining rank and command with increased frequency. These realities may serve to dim feminist awareness among military women. After all, how many women in America have such mandated and governmentally monitored equal opportunity? Imbedded in such a system, military women often see women on the outside as crybabies, and feminists have been subject to such bad press that few military women would identify with the appellation anyway. After all, women soldiers have to work with men constantly. Good relations are essential.

Nonetheless, there are real barriers for women in the military, and women soldiers know it: no woman will be chief of staff without combat unit command experience. Outside aviation units, such duty is currently prohibited. Proportionally fewer women than men receive hazardous-duty pay; proportionally fewer are on "jump status," which offers extra pay to soldiers who take regular paratrooping missions. Astonishingly, military women voluntarily put up with a subculture that abhors their presence in it; this well-documented culture of misogyny routinely manifests itself in harassment, if not physical violence, toward women (see, for example, Faludi 1994).

Feminists are right to be bewildered and even ambivalent about military women. On one hand, military women are fighting the good fight for equality. On the other, they have been co-opted into accepting not only a male standard of success but one that professionalizes violence, has been responsible for the misery and death of women and children across all time and space, and glamorizes violent and demeaning sexual imagery as symbols of both victory and death. Feminists have every right to ask military women, "Are you for us or against us?"

In the hullabaloo over women in combat, and in the disagreements between women soldiers and feminists, precious little discussion of consequence has been devoted to the military women themselves, why they made the choices they made, and how they cope. The most provocative discussions in this regard have developed around Tailhook and Shannon Faulkner's quest to be a Citadel cadet;[4] unfortunately, provocation has not made for clarity. Most recently, Paula Coughlin—the "whistleblower" of the Tailhook scandal—has been recast as "slut," the role of "bitch" having been taken to its limit. At first, she was condemned in testimony for her abrasive manner (uncontrollable), foul mouth (too masculine), and unattractiveness as a woman and officer (dyke). Recent testimony has placed her on the scene at Tailhook, having her legs shaved by men in the main lounge (willing whore). On the day her multimillion-dollar victory in court was announced, a colleague of mine referred to her as "the babe." But even people who are not vested in any particular outcome to her case and are not easily duped by the Navy's typecasting of her are honestly perplexed by her and by women like her. While Citadel lawyers are busy turning Shannon Faulkner into a tool of the "feminists," or else some sort of psychological hermaphrodite (no *real* woman would want to go to the Citadel), others honestly ask what could possess a woman to bring on herself and her family all the wrath her challenge to "Southern male tradition" (i.e., the patriarchy) has brought (especially, they say, when she could have gone to West Point "carefree"). Americans don't understand why military women do the crazy things they do.

This is one explanation.

"You Can't Assume That Just Because I'm in a Dress I Left My Dick at Home"[5]

Recently, someone I didn't know at a party asked me why I'd joined the Army. I have been asked this question over a hundred times; I have given every imaginable answer, trotting out explanations from the most practical to the most esoteric, sometimes talking too much, sometimes not saying enough. This time I said simply, "Well, my mother was in the Army during World War II." That was immediately accepted as a full and complete explanation for my military service. Because women in the military are such an anomaly, people hardly know what questions to ask or what answers are sufficient.

I myself can't possibly explain why women join the Army. There are too many women and too many reasons. But I can say something about why the

Army is appealing to the women who are in it. Offering this explanation has a special political danger.

The "organized" opponents of women in the Army focus on a variety of biologically deterministic arguments; most notably, they point to women's comparatively lesser upper-body strength. Although advocates of women in the Army have sought to argue that upper-body strength in women can be developed and that today's heavy equipment could be redesigned, the cultural bottom line in America is that women are intrinsically different and that such difference should not be the subject of debate when it comes to national security. Given this, at least one thing women have been able to do is to demand a more refined application of the upper-body-strength argument. This demand has worked for women in the realm of air combat, since modern equipment has made upper-body strength in the cockpit inconsequential; women now fly combat aircraft. The demand has not worked in the Field Artillery, where soldiers must lift rounds and shove them into gun tubes. During the Cold War, when automated long-range weapons systems were the norm, women were in the artillery. There are fewer than fifteen female Field Artillery officers in the Army today. In 1994 no women from West Point's graduating class joined the branch. Nonetheless, in the cacophony over these issues, military women have identified main opposition voices. They are the known enemy.

It is the "unorganized" opponents of women in the Army—"the-men-we-have-to-work-with"—who complicate any discussion of women's motivations for joining the profession of arms. In opposing women's presence in the Army, "the-men-we-have-to-work-with" routinely focus on the supposed hypersexuality of women soldiers, who somehow manage the feat of being prostitutes and lesbians simultaneously. Consequently, like witches who cause the cattle to die or the beer to go sour, Army women are responsible for poor morale and unit unreadiness. Sometimes their presence emasculates units. Other times the opposite obtains: displaying prowess, men fight over sexual rights to women soldiers.

Here is where any discussion about the motivations of military women might be politically problematic. At first glance, most arguments that purport to isolate the motivations of women in the military on the grounds of gender and sexuality (e.g., tough gals like doing guy stuff for reasons of power) appear to "the-men-we-have-to-work-with" as penis-envy arguments. Much has been said about the rather obvious sexual fears and insecurities at the base of this perspective (what a flurry of discussion about showers surrounded the debate on homosexuals in the military!):

After trying to fit women into his masculine conception, seeing them as envying that which they missed, [Freud] came instead to acknowledge, in the strength and persistence of women's pre-Oedipal attachments to their mothers, a developmental difference. He considered this difference in women's development to be responsible for what he saw as women's developmental failure. (Gilligan 1982, 7)

As soon as the debate on women in the military broaches the subject of sex and gender, "the-men-we-have-to-work-with" say, "See, I told you; they are all a bunch of confused women who think they want to be men." I myself have been accused of wanting to be a man because I sought to achieve the highest possible score on the *women's* physical readiness test! "The-men-we-have-to-work-with" would love for military women to admit to a pathology as proof of their own ludicrous claims about the bisexual promiscuity of the women in their units and all the problems they bring (which usually translates into being turned down for sex or having to take orders from a woman).

The argument I make is that this is where the real battle lies for women, because the reasons women are in the Army *are* gendered and sexual and they *are* about challenging male structure (even if military women aren't fully aware of it), but this shouldn't be used as an argument to formulate policy that discriminates against women and protects the sentiments and feelings of "the-men-we-have-to-work-with." If you think I am overstating the possibility that this could happen, consider the current "don't ask, don't tell, don't pursue" homosexual policy, which can easily be construed as protecting the basest sexual instincts of heterosexual men at the expense of the civil rights of homosexuals, that is, as a policy designed to maintain the status quo of sexualized power relationships.

Women want to be leaders in the Army. The story of women in uniform is one about living on the edge of one's gender. Military women are not men. They're not women. This is a story about being a woman who's a man. This is about the narrowest sort of sartorial, behavioral, sexual space between man and woman. This is about phallic women. To be a successful Army officer is to be, by definition, a man. At best, Army women are "threshold people:"

These persons elude or slip through the network of classifications that normally locate states and positions in cultural space. Liminal entities are neither here nor there; they are betwixt and between the positions assigned and arrayed by law, custom, convention, and ceremonial. As such, their ambiguous and indeterminate attributes are expressed by a rich variety of symbols. . . . Liminality is frequently likened to death, to being in the womb, to invisibility, to darkness, to bisexuality, to the wilderness, and to an eclipse of the sun or moon. (Turner 1990, 147)

The future entering female class at the Citadel will have its own story to tell, but for now, I focus on women at West Point, eighteen years since the first woman arrived in 1976. This case is a model for understanding male fear of military women and female desire for sexualized military power.

Getting to the Point

The presence of women cadets at West Point is arguably the most overstudied sociological phenomenon in the world, and West Point, as an institution, may be one of the most self-reflective. I will not recount the now well known history of women at West Point and the controversies that accompanied them there. These ranged from the fundamental—whether their presence would require a redefinition of the academy's purpose and identity—to the mundane—the degree to which their presence would diminish the experience of men—to the farcical—whether women's Full Dress would or would not have coattails (or more honestly, whether female buttocks were to be revealed).

When will "women in the Army" and "women at West Point" disappear as issues? What will it take? We have tons of evidence that the performance of women in both institutions is fine, in some cases excellent. Even the chairman of the Joint Chiefs of Staff can't get it right; when General Shalikashvili was asked what he thought of women in the Army (isn't this old business?) he replied that he "felt great" about women in the Army. To me that is something less than if he felt nothing in particular about it. That's the problem: the particularity of women in the Army. For their part, the media's overindulgence in the issue, I can't help but think, is a result of the sexiness of it all: a diminutive woman in men's clothes running around with a rifle is not news, but it's great footage. I think there is something else going on besides the spectacular footage, and that is the issue of phallocracy: if you've got the phallus, you're in charge. When we are all in uniform—heterosexual women and men, and gay women and men—we can't ever be sure who's got the phallus and who wants it, and by this I mean both those who want "to have it" sexually and those who want to own it. That creates a great deal of anxiety. Marjorie Garber has already made a bold step toward deconstructing this:

> Women joined the Army . . . because they like to dress up in uniforms. Men who wore uniforms did so in part because they unconsciously understood them to be "fancy dress" [drag]. Whatever the specific semiotic relationship between military uniforms and erotic fantasies of sartorial gender, the history of cross-dressing within the armed services attests to a complicated interplay of forces, including male bonding, acknowledged and unacknowledged homosexual identity, carnivalized power relations, the erotics of same-sex communities, and the apparent safety afforded by theatrical representation. (Garber 1992, 55–56)

There is an undiscussed competition for the phallus at West Point, and women are in a peculiar predicament, obviously, with regard to this competition: "For someone like me, it had been a daily struggle to 'get with it' physically. I kept banging my head against the wall, trying to be a man. It was a relief to discover that it wasn't necessary" (Denise Gavin in Barkalow 1990, 232). Why did Gavin feel that while at West Point she was trying to do the impossible? Perhaps it is because every conversation with male cadets about the integration of women at West Point ends up at the same irreducible point: women cannot expect equality from the institution or equal treatment from men unless women's standards on the Army Physical Readiness Test are identical to men's. This could mean that more push-ups and sit-ups and faster two-mile run times must be demanded of women, or it could mean less should be demanded of men; it doesn't matter. In the male-cadet mind, only this would be true equality. Thus, every conversation on this topic ends up trapped in Professor Higgins's dilemma: "Why can't a woman be more like a man? Women at West Point are under pressure to prove themselves capable as cadets, as women, as athletes, and as scholars. When "capable" is measured by your peers against a male standard, then either you have to find a way to be a man or you have to find a way to fake it. What are the consequences if a woman cadet rejects this entire construct? First, peers have influence on cadets' military grades, influence that ultimately affects class standing, which in turn has numerous serious implications for longer-range career decisions such as military specialty and location of first assignment. The second, and more important factor, is the reality of close-quarters barracks life, of peer pressure, and of the shame and embarrassment that come with "failure." Indeed, that military men are often called "girls" if they aren't tough enough is a well-documented phenomenon. What could possibly be worse than being known as a girl?

Thus, women at West Point have to fake being men. Jacques Lacan offers a third term between "having" the phallus and "being" the phallus: "seeming." Garber argues that this is the space occupied by the transvestite (Garber 1992, 122). I believe that this is the political option chosen by women at West Point and by women Army officers in general: we are the model of the "codpiece daughter"—the figure of the phallic woman.

West Point accepts about twelve hundred candidates each year who are deemed to have the best potential for development as a "leader of character" in our armed forces. This potential is evaluated on three dimensions: intellectual ability, demonstrated leadership, and physical aptitude. Measures on each of these dimensions are combined to create a "whole candidate score" (WCS). The academy does not use a quota system per se; the number of women admitted for each class year is driven by class composition goals, that is, 10 percent is the lowest number of women that would allow each squad to have a woman in it. The upper end of the target area for women in the Corps is 15 percent. Currently, the Corps is 12 percent female, the 15 percent figure has never been achieved. The problem, according to the academy, is that there aren't enough women in America who excel in the three aspects of WCS, are interested in the military, want courses in math-science-engineering, and want to go to school in a physically demanding environment. The women who are admitted presumably want all these things. They score as well in their WCS as the men who apply; they have slightly higher academic and leadership predictors and a slightly lower physical aptitude predictor. Women have had slightly higher SAT verbal scores, proportionally greater incidence of having been valedictorians or salutatorians, and proportionally greater incidence of having been in the National Honor Society, and in general they match men's percentages of participation in student government and varsity letter winning. Women stress that their motivation for being a cadet is the quality of the academic program and a desire for their personal self-development. The profile of a woman cadet: intelligent, athletic, orderly, attentive to detail, and interested in self-improvement. "In recent years, higher percentages of women have applied, been qualified, and admitted, but these percentages have never met the upper end of the composition objective for women" (U.S. Military Academy 1992, 10). Every woman earns her place in the academy; they'd take more if there were more. The West Point woman is a rare creature.

Despite the fact that women compare very favorably with men in the admissions process and earn their way into West Point by every measure of potential, it is particularly interesting that West Point men are convinced that West Point women are replacing better-qualified men. West Point women—indeed, all military women leaders—are seen as inferior replacements for men. A West Point senior once said to me, oblivious to the homosexual implications, that it was objectively clear that men had "more perfect" bodies than women. To support his colleague, another cadet added the commodifying analogy that having women at West Point was like using Volkswagen replacement parts on a Mercedes Benz (that male cadets see cars as a metaphor for sex is an inescapable conclusion of most of the faculty).

Staying in "For the Duration"—Surviving and Excelling

For Americans, no other place matches West Point. It is history, tradition, and rare natural beauty rolled into one. It is a primary source of our national values. It is for young citizens the very embodiment of personal challenge. It is opportunity.
U.S. Military Academy, brochure

The official purpose of West Point is to provide the nation with leaders of character who serve the common defense. The official mission of the academy is to educate and train the Corps of Cadets so that each graduate will have the attributes essential to professional growth throughout a career as an officer of the Regular Army, and to inspire each to a lifetime of service to the nation. The program at West Point includes academic, physical, and military instruction. Although not a measured parameter, social success is of extreme importance. This means that proving oneself to "the-men-we-have-to-work-with" is essential.

Academically, the performance trends for men and women appear almost identical over time. In the first two years, men make the Dean's List with greater frequency; by the junior year, the percentages for both sexes are even; and by the senior year, a higher percentage of women receive Dean's List honors. Men and women receive the Superintendent's Award for Excellence in Academic, Military, and Physical Programs and the Distinguished Cadet Award for Excellence in Academics at essentially the same rate (U.S. Military Academy 1992, 22). Overall, women have been less likely than men to take elective courses in math, science, and engineering but are more inclined toward elective courses in the humanities and social sciences. Women have done exceptionally well in scholarship competitions. Since 1980, women have made up 33 percent of the Rhodes Scholars and 18 percent of the Marshall Scholars chosen from graduates of West Point. Women are only 11 percent of the Corps. (U.S. Military Academy 1992, 24).

At West Point, all seniors are required to take the Graduate Record Exam, and although in the civilian world the GRE is taken only by a select group of students aiming toward graduate study, academy cadets perform significantly better than national norms. Women perform better in the verbal and analytical areas whereas men perform better in the quantitative area (U.S. Military Academy 1992, 22).

The attrition rate for men and women is proportionally the same, although women are less likely than men to leave the academy for academic reasons and are more likely to leave for medical and personal reasons. Men are more likely to leave for conduct, military and academic deficiency, and honor violations. By far, most cadets, regardless of sex, leave the academy for reasons of "motivation" (U.S. Military Academy 1992, 25).

The physical program is designed to cultivate a healthy military lifestyle, promote fitness, encourage a lifetime of sports, and nurture qualities of courage, self-sacrifice, initiative, perseverance, aggressiveness, and the will to win. Cadets receive instruction in gymnastics ("kinesthetic awareness"), combatives ("striking and grappling"), and aquatics ("survival and conditioning"). All plebe physical education instruction is coeducational except for boxing (men) and self-defense (women). Note that women take "self-defense," not "martial arts." Upperclass men and women take all physical education electives together.

Personal physical fitness is assessed three times yearly. The Army Physical Fitness Test (push-ups, sit-ups, two-mile run) is administered twice yearly. The West Point Indoor Obstacle Course is also administered several times to assess general conditioning and agility. This is an extraordinarily grueling event; trashcans are set up at the end of the course for cadets who need to throw up after the test.

Physical program activities are conducted in accordance with Public Law 94-106 (directing that women be eligible for admission to West Point and stipulating that "commissioning [requirements] of female individuals shall be the same as those required for male individuals, except for those minimum essential adjustments in such performance standards required because of physiological differences") and the West Point Doctrine of Comparable Training. At the start of integration in the late 1970s, there was little consensus regarding what, if any, performance standard adjustments these differences justified or even whether differences existed or adjustments were necessary. After a great deal of testing, results indicated that there were physical performance differences between men and women that required standard adjustments. The Doctrine of Comparable Training sought to address this issue by establishing that physiological differences between men and women would be recognized through comparable, rather than identical activities and standards so that cadets of both sexes would be challenged to equivalent levels of performance that would be increased over time as their physical abilities improved. Separate grading scales are used for men and women on several tests. Although men normally must perform more repetitions of an event, lift more weight, or perform an event in a shorter time period, they achieve the same grade that a women doing fewer, lifting less, or taking longer would get. The only exception is on the Army Physical Fitness Test, where women must do more sit-ups than men to receive the same grade. Average plebe scores, which produce average grades by gender, look something like this: push-ups (men) 69, (women) 39; sit-ups (men) 80, (women) 81; two-mile run (men) 12:43, (women) 14:46. On average, men typically perform the Indoor Obstacle Course Test one and a half minutes faster than women (U.S. Military Academy 1992, 35–45).

The majority of intramural sports are coeducational without special rules based on gender. Women compete in all sports except football, wrestling, boxing, and rugby. In swimming, women compete with men. In three-on-three basketball, one woman per team must be playing at all times. Similar rules apply in club sports.

Several practices were stopped and others started when women joined the Corps. For example, because of the high incidence of stress fractures in women, the Corps switched from running in combat boots to running in sneakers. Because of women's smaller hands and lesser grip strength, women could not successfully run while carrying the M-14 rifle. Rifle exercises were eliminated, and partner-resistance exercises were added. Aerobics and jazz and ballroom dance were added to the curriculum. (Ballroom dancing is a particularly popular course for male cadets.)

Military training begins with Cadet Basic Training—Beast Barracks—where "New Cadets" (plebes) are trained in basic soldier skills, are prepared to join the Corps of Cadets, and are inspired to internalize the ideals of West Point and the U.S. Army. This training includes drill, athletic competition, road marches, bivouacs, first aid, mountaineering, combat movement techniques, nuclear-biological-chemical warfare, and rifle marksmanship. At the end of Beast, New Cadets are "accepted" into the Corps of Cadets (and drop the official appellation "New"); their roles as "followers" are reinforced and, it is hoped, a duty concept is developed. "Acceptance" is not the same as "recognition," which occurs late in the spring semester and allows upperclassmen and plebes to interact more informally. By the time they are sophomores ("yearlings"), cadets are beginning to exercise increased responsibility as team leaders and are receiving advanced military training. In their third ("cow") and fourth ("firstie") years, they serve as the trainers and senior leaders of the Corps. Requirements and standards in the military program are not gender-specific; men and women cadets must negotiate the same developmental challenges.

The most visible indications of military success at West Point are cadet rank and duty position. Cadet Captain is the highest rank awarded. The percentage of women cadet captains is directly proportional to their presence in the Corps (about 11 percent). According to official academy sources, this fact is a product of the performance of women and

> also reflects the philosophy underpinning selection of the cadet chain of command. . . . An effort is made to select a chain of command that appropriately recognizes the demographics of the Corps of Cadets so as to provide representative role models for all cadets. No cadet, however, is awarded cadet rank purely on the basis of demographic affiliation. Cadet rank is earned. (U.S. Military Academy 1992, 31)

"Pure Testosterone"[6]

What does all this mean? According to this official description of the program, it sounds as if, with the exception of a few details of physical training, women and men are fully equal at West Point. What is missing from this account is the success or failure of women *socially*. Again, it's "the-men-we-have-to-work-with" who *are* the social environment and are also the judges, jury, and executioners if they are not pleased with or if they are intimidated by the performance of women. Ostensibly, the administration at the academy has tried to mold cadet behavior to be accepting to women. But by drawing attention to the differences between men and women, these programs have often had the reverse effect. In fact, the whole construct of West Point—from uniforms to physical environment—is so heavily masculinist that it makes the social success of women permanently unattainable.[7] Life at West Point is life according to the male model. By constructing the academy in this way, it is actually the administration that controls the discourse. "The-men-we-have-to-work-with" are not free actors but the tools of a long-standing masculine perspective perpetuating the myth of male superiority and female pathology. This is a big gender lie: the academy encourages implicit acceptance of, as Carol Gilligan has put it, "male life as the norm," and "they have tried to fashion women out of a masculine cloth. . . . It all goes back, of course, to Adam and Eve—a story which shows, among other things, that if you make a woman out of a man, you are bound to get into trouble. In the life cycle, as in the Garden of Eden, the woman has been the deviant" (Gilligan 1982, 6).

Despite the fact that every cadet woman earned her entrance into the academy through outstanding performance in high school, athletics, and extracurricular endeavors—generally entering West Point with higher whole candidate scores than men—women graduate with slightly lower grades academically, militarily, and physically. Overall grade average (encompassing the three areas) at graduation is approximately 2.78 for women and 2.81 for men. The difference is slight but noticeable, since one would assume that women, being slightly more accomplished in high school, would end college slightly more accomplished. Isn't it possible that women who are more qualified do less well than lesser-qualified men because what cadets are being tested on at West Point are their abilities in the art of being male? If the male-centeredness of West Point is a factor in the performance of women cadets who graduate, what about women who don't? In fact, the most substantial difference between men and women at West Point is in graduation rates. Approximately 70 percent of the men who have entered West Point since 1976 have graduated. The same statistic for women is approximately 60 percent. Authorities at West Point have found an empirical understanding of gender-based attrition differences "elusive" (U.S. Military Academy 1992, 54).

The changes women brought to West Point—simultaneously insignificant and revolutionary—irk "the-men-we-have-to-work-with." Who are these men? A preliminary report on women at West Point concluded that "sex-role attitudes of male cadets are more traditional than those of male officers or male enlisted personnel in the Army as a whole. The differences are substantial: about two-thirds of USMA cadets would rank as more traditional than the most traditional one-third of the officers, for example" (Vitters, Kinzer, and Willis 1977, 27).[8] One might think that these more traditional men would treat women differently than men, would expect women at West Point to be treated differently by the institution, and would, in fact, advocate different treatment for women. As a rule, men with the more traditional sex-role attitudes tended, not surprisingly, to be against rapid integration of women into the Corps of Cadets (Vitters et al. 1977, 27). "Women took 'self-defense'—consisting of judo and karate—instead of boxing and wrestling. These adjustments were unpopular with many men who wanted absolute equality of treatment for the sexes, regardless of the exception guaranteed to women by the law which admitted them to the Academy" (Vitters et al. 1977, 26).[9] Did the most traditional men in the Army really want "absolute equality" qua equality? Could it be that they really wanted women to box and wrestle with men? Could it be that these men somehow didn't believe that female cadets were women, but rather some strange creature neither male nor female, à la Shannon Faulkner? Could it be that they perceived women cadets as having a "softening," and therefore threatening, effect on their formerly all-male environment? Could it be that the male cadets wanted to humiliate women, wanted to establish an atmosphere where women would fail, where women would be punished for trespassing on male terrain? Could it be that, to prove they did have "more perfect" bodies and the privilege that came with muscle power, male cadets just wanted to get into the academy-sanctioned ring and hit women?[10]

There is a tradition among West Point graduates: if you think the Corps of Cadets is as good as it was when you were a part of it, you say, "The Corps has not." If you think the Corps has degraded since your day, you say "The Corps has." For many "old grads" and current male cadets, one of the most conspicuous examples of the degradation of the Corps is the presence of women. Despite the fact that the mission, purpose, and core values at West Point haven't changed, this West Point has lost the romance and mystery of "the old Corps"—a time when "men were men," when "family values" prevailed, and when women and minorities knew their places. With every change meant to accommodate women, male cadets become more and more desperate to preserve the status quo while outwardly demanding a system of absolute equality over one of comparable equality.[11]

> Many upperclass cadets cite reasons for holding to traditional beliefs.
> Among these are: (1) a persisting belief that women do not belong in
> military academies; (2) a pervasive awareness that the Academy's top
> leadership originally opposed the admission of women; (3) a percep-
> tion that USMA officials may have "overreacted" to this change, as
> evidenced by the amount of time devoted to lectures, surveys, brief-
> ings, and the assignment of officers to "special positions" to work on
> this event; and (4) a widespread perception, among both men and
> women, that women have received "inequitable treatment" as plebes
> by other cadets and officers. Men cite instances of women being
> dated by upperclass cadets and of media coverage focusing exclu-
> sively on women. . . . On the other hand, women cite numerous in-
> stances of experiencing particularly harsh treatment. (Vitters et al.
> 1977, 27)

There were some instances of upperclass men "recognizing" women cadets
before they were officially allowed to. One interpretation of this was that
they were simply overcompensating for some unduly harsh treatment the
women were receiving. Another possibility is that these men didn't take the
women seriously as cadets but saw them as little sisters, potential dates, or
even mascots. If so, the behavior of upperclass males, at best, smacks of pa-
ternalism. At worst, since all cadets know that to recognize a cadet early is
to isolate that cadet and to make others feel that the recognized cadet is getting special treatment, it is also possible that women who were recognized
early were set up to be rejected by their peers.

"What's a Girl to Do?"

*Women learned that to survive they had to walk a tightrope—feminine, but
not too much so; assertive, but only in small doses. Management of self and
presentation of self became necessary and often tricky endeavors for women.
Most tried to walk a fine line trying to adjust themselves to a narrow definition
of appropriate female cadet behavior which involved not allowing oneself to be
either too military or too feminine, but also not too little of a soldier or too little of a woman.*

> Alan Vitters, Nora Kinzer, and Mary Willis
> "Women at West Point"

If women cadets stand out as women, they mark themselves as losers in the competition and are condemned. Note that it is a rare day that a woman cadet is seen in her cadet-issue skirt (granted, it is more common now than in the late 1970s but still very unusual), a profound marker in a culture where 90 percent of the population is trousered. Most women go the full four years without wearing it. One woman cadet told me a story about the skirt and about women as women as West Point. Her company declared one day "Old Corps Day," when cadets would imitate the Old Corps (the good old days) by wearing their high-waisted pants and tucking their long four-in-hand ties into their shirts. The women were distressed, since the whole implication of "Old Corps" meant a West Point without them. In a rare moment of unanimity all the women in her company agreed to protest this implication with a profound "in your face" act: showing up at morning formation in skirts and pumps. The next morning came, and indeed there were a good number of women (though not all) dressed as promised. The men were outraged and accused the women of bad faith, a lack of camaraderie, and gross insensitivity to the needs of the cadet community at large. The men dismissed the women's complaint that any "Old Corps" concept naturally excluded them as mere "political correctness." They isolated and ostracized the women who participated, and it was a long time before wounds were healed and old friendships resumed. This woman cadet never forgot the incident, and in the back of her mind there remained the image of the skirt as a weapon that could not defeat pants in a political battle. Woman as woman was no match for man as man.[12]

If the women cadets cast themselves as men, they will still be condemned by their threatened male colleagues.[13] The violence of men who discover that gender is not as it seems is well documented in art and life. Recall, for example, the reaction of Fergus (a character we come to like) when he is confronted with Dil's anatomical gender in The Crying Game or the real-life murder by defenestration of a cross-dresser in Paris Is Burning whose john presumably discovers something for which he was unprepared. When this film was viewed by students of mine at West Point, even the gentlest man among them agreed that he "could not be held accountable" for how he might react in such a situation. Thus, the most famous example of woman as man at West Point—Carol Barkalow's account of her cadet years in the first class of women—always elicits vitriolic commentary.

One caption in Barkalow's book reads, "Plebe math class. . . . I'm the only woman in the room. Can you tell? Another picture shows her "throwing a slightly startled National Guard [male] lieutenant over [her] shoulder during a self-defense demonstration"; soldiers are in the background looking on. In another picture she is demonstrating her ability to break boards with a swift chop in the Delaware governor's office. The governor looks impressed. In every photograph she is shown in men's clothes, doing men's things with men. A fact of military life for women? Perhaps. But that is certainly no explanation for the most provocative of all: the victory photo of Barkalow from the Roanoke Valley Women's Body Building Competition in May 1986 which ran in her post paper and thus also fell under the gaze of her male soldiers.

> I felt like the creature in Mary Shelley's *Frankenstein*. These men had inculcated their values in me, had created me, and now they were calling me a monster. If I were a man, I felt certain the battalion would have been proud that the 57th Trans was getting such a fit commander. . . . Because I was female, the automatic assumption about the effect of the photograph was that my soldiers would *not* respect me; they would regard me as a "sex symbol," instead of a leader. This was, ironically, the very circumstance I'd spent a good part of my professional life trying to avoid. (Barkalow 1990, 231)[14]

Barkalow presents a feminist account of her colonization, and the "economy of the male gaze" is described with striking clarity. The soldiers watching her martial arts performance, the governor, the soldiers viewing her posed/exposed picture in the paper—pelvis forward, open, penetrable—are imperial viewers, and she is subordinate, a performer. [15] There is an implicit sense throughout the book that Barkalow's body has been colonized and that her identity has been erased, replaced with "female cadet" or "woman officer," as in "daughter" or "wife." It is the masculine gaze and its inherent political domination that has turned her into an object of desire, either sexually, as with the photo in the paper, or through her skill—another form of sensuality and power. The male viewers are impressed by this (though not happy about it), and she is a reminder that they lack "perfect dominion"; they colonize her, take her as a model, repairing their own lack. She cannot help but excite the appetite; she is wealth and a sensual resource for which men have an unrestrained passion and appetite. Furthermore, and this makes her threatening, she excels at "manliness," that is, she is able to "win at games." This is too much of a challenge to gender roles. The male gaze on her—sight as an exercise of power—is also a form of surveillance. It must be, because her deliberate self-display could easily devolve into seduction.[16]

It is Gavin, not Barkalow, who recognizes that the entire enterprise of creating a convincing impersonation of a man while at West Point, of creating the perfect illusion, is problematic:

> Having been a company commander in the Signal Corps, I have witnessed other qualities—like courage, stamina, and teamwork—which have counted a lot toward my assessment of officers and enlisted soldiers. Far more than how many pull-ups they can do. . . . I've seen women who have somehow made it as soldiers on pride and adrenaline alone, and musclebound men who bungle things miserably. . . . All this finally led me to understand that what really matters in the military is competence, compassion, and the ability to make the Office-NCO relationship work. This realization cast a whole different light on my West Point experience, where I had gone through moments of dark despair.[17]

If you can't be a woman at West Point (the skirt-and-pumps model), or a man who's really a woman (the Barkalow model), maybe you can be a woman loosely disguised as a man. Indeed, this is the common avenue for most women cadets. This way, they can fake enough mannishness to get by in a masculine environment without sparking anyone's anxiety, because everyone thinks they know who's who and what's what. This is the equivalent of an old wartime style of GI drag, "the comic routines, chorus lines or 'pony ballets' of husky men in dresses playing for laughs" (Garber 1992, 56).

> "drag may become so incorporated into the fabric of a culture . . . may answer so precisely that culture's own desire that it ceases to provoke and becomes entertainment," as in the case of female impersonators. . . . Drag can also be an important destabilizing element that, in performance, "questions the limits of representation." "The imperfection of her imitation is what makes her appealing, what makes her eminently readable. Foolproof imitations of women by men, or men by women, are curious, but not interesting." (Oscar Montero in Garber 1922, 149)

To be successful as a woman at West Point you have to submit to a Hasty-Pudding-type fancy-dress code. Many of the faculty have pointed to the relatively new fact of women cadets who wear makeup and keep their hair long as an indication that women now feel more comfortable at West Point. Indeed they do. They have broken the code that Barkalow and her classmates could not; thus, the women who are most successful at West Point don't seem to compete openly for the phallus; instead, they wear men's clothes, take on the conservatism of the men as their own, distance themselves from the motives and aspirations of feminism, and give enough markers of themselves as women (a little eye shadow goes a long way) while they command cadet companies, letter in sports, and perform well in the classroom. In other words, they create an elaborate spoof and attain personal success and some degree of collective success for women, but well inside a discourse established by and for the convenience of the men-we-have-to-work-with.[18]

Conclusion

I shoot an M-16, I rappel out of a helicopter, I go on twelve-mile road marches.
. . . Sometimes that's intimidating to a guy.
                    Quoted in Joseph Berger
                    "Making Old Cadet Attitudes Die—Or
                    Just Fade Away"

It is axiomatic that, despite comprising more than 50 percent of the American population, in a democratic political culture, women experience life in a minority status. It is also true that such a life experience is not technically, theoretically, consonant with democratic values of inclusion. But there it is. You can imagine, then, what life would be like as a woman when women make up only 11 percent of the population in an authoritarian, rather than a democratic, culture that is organized around such values as, say, physical strength. What we have at the academy is the most difficult aspects of American political life, for women, without any of the tempering qualities of democratic society. Granted, democratic society leaves a great deal to be desired for women—but at least in democratic society women have value as women. To understand this, we feminists must put aside our more esoteric complaints about the patriarchy and our co-optation into the patriarchal discourse for a moment and admit that, for better or worse, we are integral to American society. Women are not integral to the military, however. Any job performed by a woman could be performed by a man. Women in the military have the constant sense that they are replaceable.

In my scholarly thinking and in my life as a feminist I have always been very suspect of the traditional ways in which women have been "offered" power—via motherhood, for example, or "power over the home," which is problematic for the obvious separation of public and private that it demands. Nonetheless, I was newly empowered and had an authenticated credibility with cadets when I became a mother. I became "certified" not only by my male peers but by my female cadets, who always asked for the particulars of career and family management techniques.

When I announced to my boss that I intended to have a baby while stationed at West Point, he was delighted but requested that I time the delivery for the summer months, since there was no other instructor to take my class in my absence. As a good follower, it never occurred to me, at the time, that there was anything wrong with his request. Fortunately, I delivered two days after the semester ended. But what if I hadn't? Would I have been a bad soldier if my baby had come early?

The overriding question for every woman soldier is, How do I survive in this man's Army? Women started deciphering this problem in earnest in 1976 when the first class of women came to West Point. Their problem wasn't about a lack of loving relationships; it wasn't about being only 11 percent of the population; it wasn't a matter of physiological difference.

It was about power. Women in uniform, like homosexuals, are hiding something. What homosexuals harbor, if you listen to the heterosexual rhetoric, is desire. They are posers, not real men. What women hide is their lack. If you are a man, it is very scary to find out that the soldier with the lack can perform the same task as well as you can, when your culture has put so much energy into linking the task and the phallus. You see, men have created this monster: the phallus and the work of a soldier owe something to each other. Their discourses of power are linked (see Cohn 1987). Thus, there is a problem if the job that requires a phallus can be done without one. What's the use of the phallus then? If women can do all the jobs of men in the Army, then men are facing a crisis of definition, a crisis of disempowerment. This is the threat women bring to the Army.

NOTES

The ideas expressed in this chapter are those of the author and do not purport to represent the official positions of the United States Military Academy, the Department of the Army, the Department of Defense, or the United States government.

1. This is a stanza from a famous "jody," or song that soldiers sing while marching. This jody is about all the lies the military tells its soldiers, for example, "They say that in the army the coffee is mighty fine" ("tastes like turpentine"), "the pay is mighty fine" ("they give you a hundred dollars and take back ninety-nine"), "the food is mighty fine" ("a chicken jumped off the table and killed a friend of mine").

2. This World War I Navy recruiting poster showed a young girl in a sailor's uniform.

3. I note in passing that his analogy places "woman," automatically, as the "neighbor" at the margin and not the self at the center, the object about whom a decision on proper treatment is made.

4. The Citadel is not a branch of the Army and, as an institution, should not be confused with service academy programs.

5. Anonymous in Garber 1992, 147.

6. This is the unofficial motto of the West Point Skydiving Team. Women have served on this team occasionally, but not for long periods of time.

7. "Masculinist" is a complicated word. Here I mean that it appeals to male aesthetics (see Stiehm 1981, 49). Stiehm tells a great story about a cadet woman who jokes that the reason women quit the academy was because the uniforms were the wrong color. Stiehm notes that "the palette is so masculine and sober that even a glimpse of a Baltimore oriole is experienced as a visual assault" (p. 120).

8. I am purposely using data from the early period of women at West Point to provide an understanding for the cultural setting that developed at that time. Comments by women cadets as reported by Joseph Berger in 1994 in the *New York Times* strongly indicate that this culture prevails and that women's strategies for coping are the same now as then (see note 18).

9. Indeed, as Stiehm has noted, "West Point, thinking infantry, tried to make its women cadets as similar to its men as possible" (1981, 145).

10. American sports creed is nothing less than an ideology and . . . athletics is not only associated with character development, discipline, competition, and fitness but it is also linked to religiosity and nationalism. Violence is central both to the military and to the most popular U.S. sport, football, but the crucial commonality may be that of ordeal. An ordeal involves victory, but it also tests limits" (Stiehm 1981, 147).

11. What was good for men was good for women, but not vice versa. "Prominent were fears of 'reverse discrimination,' a sense of loss of 'pride and discipline,' and literal interpretations of 'equality' that used males as the measure (e.g., the idea that women's heads should be almost shaved, as were men's, was acceptable, while the idea of men's wearing women's haircuts or clothing was so unimaginable as not to be queried)" (Stiehm 1981, 123). See also p. 155, for the assumption that men could teach women in physical education classes but women couldn't teach men.

12. These comments were made in a seminar on gender politics at USMA, Department of Social Sciences, spring 1993. A story is told by Stiehm (1981, 170) about Air Force Academy track-team women who won a race by running together with their slowest member and crossing the finish line hand-in-hand with much hoopla. "Their display of unity was unacceptable. Why it was unacceptable is still not crystal clear."

13. Women are issued both a men's long four-in-hand tie and a women's tab-collar tie. Most women eschew the four-in-hand because the men razz them about wearing it; however, some women do wear it. I have seen some women bend the gender lines provocatively by wearing the men's tie only when they are wearing the skirt. Although the total effect of this outfit is a kind of nineteenth-century conservatism, male cadets view it as an inappropriate co-optation of their sartorial rights—or, more psychologically, it shocks, as it is "the coexistence, in a single body, of masculine and feminine signifiers: the tension, the repulsion, the antagonism which is created between them. . . . Painted eyebrows and beard; that mask would enmask its being a mask" (Severo Sarduy in Garber 1992, 150). Part of the fear, on the men's part, is the possibility of discovering the "feminine" in themselves. Garber goes on to note that on stage, this method of mixing sex-role referents is called "working with pieces" and points to the artifactuality of the feminine, that is, what is feminine is overtly "tagged" (p. 152).

14. The reference to Frankenstein is remarkably apt not just for all the obvious feminist allusions Barkalow is making but because of the close relationship between creation and destruction it connotes. The faculty members who detest Barkalow's book (and perhaps Barkalow herself) are universally graduates of the academy. In some sense they are all Frankenstein monsters, too. But now as faculty they are responsible for creating more creatures in their own image. Yet, in the end, they destroy the monster not by fire but by vituperative commentary.

15. I recall hearing a senior officer at West Point glow that Kristin Baker, the first female selected to hold the academy's highest cadet rank ("First Captain"), had refused to succumb to the goading of a television talk-show host who tried to get her to bark orders on camera. The officer was delighted with her "professionalism." The implication is that it is at least "professionalism" that Barkalow lacks . . . and obviously more.

16. The "economy of the gaze" and the related ideas presented here are drawn from a presentation Anne Norton made at the Massachusetts Institute of Technology, 9 November 1990.

I have heard that the members of the first class of women agreed, before graduation, that none of them would write public accounts of their experiences and that many in Barkalow's class felt betrayed by the publication of her book. The existence of this pact, if real, marks a profound awareness on the part of these pioneering women to avoid the economy of the male gaze. I suspect, however, that the story is apocryphal. First, women at West Point avoid the appearance that they are caucusing around gender lines (they do not, for example, ever sit together in classes), and I doubt they would have even gotten together to talk about such a thing. Second, there were sixty-two graduating women in 1980, and I can't imagine sixty-two individuals agreeing not to publish in perpetuity. This story is probably another way to smear Barkalow's character, that is, she even went against her word (and a man's word is his bond). Even if such a pact was made, it is a bit absurd, and a bit immature, to hold everyone to it, given the possibility of intervening variables.

17. Gavin as quoted in Barkalow, 1990, 232. The analysis Barkalow makes of Gavin's quotation is bizarrely asymptotic: she gets close, but she just doesn't quite accept Gavin's full rejection of the "man-who's-really-a-woman" model. Her interpretation of

Gavin is that she "realized inherent in the work of any female soldier is the call to invent, or reinvent, herself." I doubt Gavin would agree. It is precisely the reinvention that they both submitted to which Gavin rejects for a "true-to-oneself" utopian model. Barkalow's idea of reinvention is that it is necessary, for "women who cling to traditional ideas and images of female identity may find very few places to gain a foothold." Her examples of traditionalism include pantyhose, high heels, skirts, long nails (called "bird's talons"), highly done-up hair (the "center of one's existence" for some women, according to Barkalow), makeup ("painted face"), and the behavioral roles of "coquette," "temptress," or "helpless damsel in distress" (note how extraordinarily condescending these descriptions are and how closely they mimic male criticisms at their worst). Barkalow misinterprets Gavin to support her own preference for the freedom of the "bob-haired, uncorseted, trouser-clad women of the 1920s who mimicked male attitudes and dress," and her preference for freedom from "the obligations of domestic drudgery"; she found it "a relief to assume a role among men" (pp. 232–33).

18. In a 1994 *New York Times* article, West Point women alluded strongly to the permanence of this third strategy and its success. Erin "forces" her body to comply with the demands of a grueling physical environment; she makes "her voice deep to command a platoon of men" (Berger 1994, B1). Kandice adds that emotionality equals "wimpy" and thus must be curbed. The prevailing sentiment among the women interviewed was that any "natural femininity" had to be carefully tempered with just the right dose of toughness. These quotations affirm the "tightrope" analogy made in 1976: "Female cadets have also come to appreciate many of their own qualities: how tough they can be when necessary, yet how much they cherish the chance to defy stereotypes and be feminine, to wear a dress or let their hair down. . . . In this physical world, women say they often have to tailor their personalities to earn the respect of male comrades. 'I've learned how to be more aggressive, because it's not really me. . . . You have to be a good actress.' 'If you don't assert yourself, you will be trampled' " (Berger 1994, B1).

REFERENCES

Barkalow, Carol. 1990. *In the Men's House*. New York: Poseidon Press.
Berger, Joseph. 1994. "Making Old Cadet Attitudes Die—Or Just Fade Away." *New York Times*, 7 November, p. B1.
Cohn, Carol. 1987. "Sex and Death in the Rational World of Defense Intellectuals." *Signs* 12: 687–718.
Enloe, Cynthia. 1983. *Does Khaki Become You?* Boston: South End Press.
Faludi, Susan. 1994. "The Naked Citadel." *New Yorker*, 5 September.
Garber, Marjorie. 1992. *Vested Interests: Cross-Dressing and Cultural Anxiety*. New York: Routledge.
Gilligan, Carol. 1982. *In a Different Voice: Psychological Theory and Women's Development*. Cambridge: Harvard University Press.
Higonnet, Margaret Randolph, Jane Jenson, Sonya Michel, and Margaret Collins Weitz. 1987. *Behind the Lines: Gender and the Two World Wars*. New Haven, Yale University Press.

Katzenstein, Mary. 1990. "Organizing on the Terrain of Mainstream Institutions: Feminism in the United States Military." In Mary Katzenstein and Hege Skjeie, eds., *Going Public: National Histories of Women's Enfranchisement and Women's Participation within State Institutions.* Oslo: Institute for Social Research.

Stiehm, Judith. 1981. *Bring Me Men and Women: Mandated change at the U.S. Air Force Academy.* Berkeley: University of California Press.

Turner, Victor. 1990. "Liminality and Community." In Jeffrey Alexander and Steven Seidman, eds., *Culture and Society: Contemporary Debates.* Cambridge, Mass.: Cambridge University Press.

U.S. Army Regulation 360-5. 1986. 24 December.

U.S. Military Academy. 1992. *Report on the Integration and Performance of Women at West Point for the DACOWITS.* West Point: USMA.

————. 1993. Brochure. West Point: USMA.

Vitters, Alan, Nora Kinzer, and Mary Willis. 1977. "Women at West Point." *Assembly* 35 (December): 26–27), 115, 136.

Judith Hicks Stiehm

Just the Facts, Ma'am

- There are four military services: the Army, which is the largest: the Marines, which is the smallest; the Navy, which has a special relationship with the Marines; and the Air Force, which is the youngest. The Coast Guard is a uniformed service and has an academy to train young officers, but it is under the Department of Transportation. In wartime it comes under the command of the Navy (Table 4-1).
- In the military, rank matters. Officers and enlisted are ranked separately, but all officers outrank all enlisted. Enlisted and officers correspond roughly to those military personnel with high school diplomas and those with college degrees, respectively. A small number of enlisted are given the opportunity to become officers, but most military people spend their careers as only one or the other. Thus, young and inexperienced officers can find themselves giving orders to much older, highly competent, and experienced enlisted personnel. This is similar to business and governmental organizations that have clerical and executive tracks. There, too, a new M.B.A. can be highly dependent on a skilled and experienced administrative assistant.
- Although wearing a uniform emphasizes what is shared by military people, uniforms also distinguish each individual from every other individual. Much of the time military people wear their (last) name on their uniform. Perhaps the next most important information one gets from "reading" a uniform is an individual's service and rank. In general, Air Force personnel wear blue, Army personnel wear dark green in cold weather and khaki in warm, the Navy wears midnight navy in cold weather and

Table 4-1: Active-Duty Personnel, September 1994

Service	Number	Percentage
ARMY		
Men	467,235	29.2
Women	69,284	4.3
Total	536,519	33.6
NAVY		
Men	411,148	25.8
Women	52,317	3.3
Total	463,465	29.1
AIR FORCE		
Men	356,566	22.3
Women	65,755	4.1
Total	422,321	26.4
MARINES		
Men	166,546	10.4
Women	7,671	0.5
Total	174,217	10.9

Note: There are 36,505 members of the Coast Guard, of which 33,449 are men and 3,056 are women.

khaki in warm weather and on board ship (unless dress whites are called for), and Marines wear dark green in the cold, khaki in the heat, and sometimes a magnificent dress uniform with blue pants with a red stripe.

Insignia are worn on hats, on shirt collars, on shoulder boards, and on sleeves. Special uniform patches and pins tell about an individual's special training (for instance, in missiles), special tours (for instance, in Vietnam), and special service or accomplishments (for instance, serving on the presidential honor guard).

Some special units wear special clothing (for instance, the Airborne's red beret), and work uniforms (for instance, the camouflage uniform, or "cami") may differ from the daily uniform.

- The draft ended in 1973. All U.S. military personnel are now volunteers.
- Officers typically enter service through a service academy (West Point, Annapolis, the Air Force Academy) or (more often) through university ROTC programs. Entrance to the academies is very competitive, and a high proportion of admirals and generals are academy graduates.

This page, clockwise from top left: Army maternity uniform; Dressed for work; A family in which both Mom and Dad are officers; At play—in fact, at a ball—in uniform. *Top left photo courtesy of Judith Hicks Stiehm; remaining photos on this page courtesy of Connie L. Reeves.*

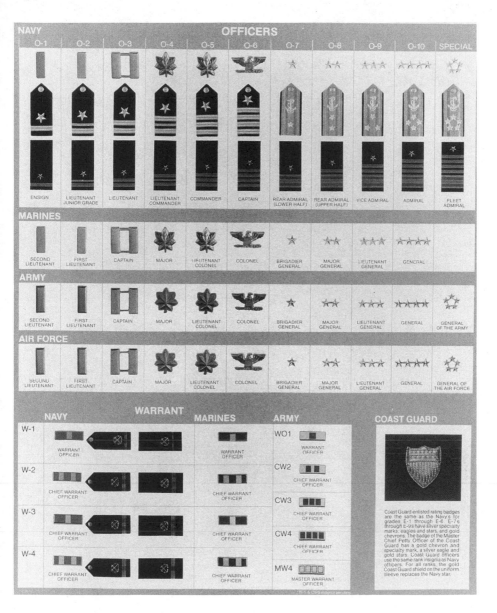

Rank and insignia of U.S. military officers.

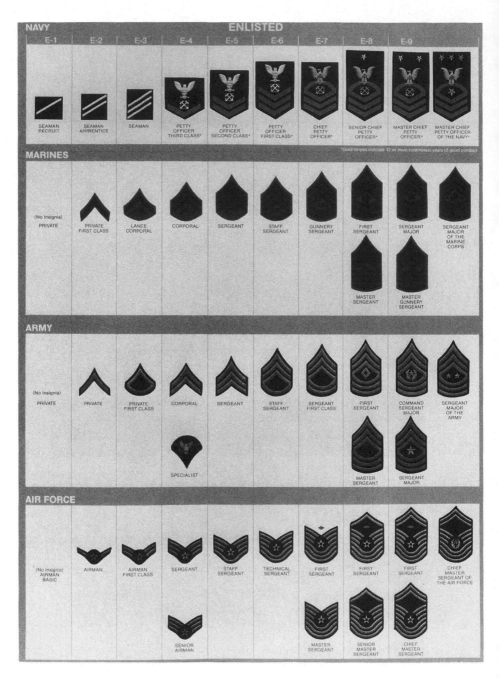

Rank and insignia of U.S. military enlisted personnel.

- Enlisted personnel sign a contract for a tour of specific length and may (or may not) be eligible for reenlistment. They are recruited for service, but many who wish to join are ineligible. In fact, 30 to 35 percent of eighteen-year-olds do not meet today's enlistment standards. In most cases this is because of a failure to meet educational standards or a failure to score high enough on the Armed Forces Qualifications Test, the AFQT. The good news is that uniformed personnel have chosen to serve and that they are "more qualified" than the citizenry as a whole. The bad news is that the military is both self-selected and selective. Such militaries can grow away from and come to think they know better than the civilians they are supposed both to protect and to obey.

  Officers are almost always college graduates. The majority enter through college Reserve Officer Training Programs (ROTC). A significant minority are graduates of one of the military academies: West Point, Annapolis, Air Force. In wartime or when the military is rapidly expanding, one way to become an officer is by attending Officer Candidate School (OCS). "Regular" officers (as contrasted to "Reserve" officers) may resign once they have fulfilled any legal commitments (e.g., military academy graduates owe five years). Officers must continue to be promoted to stay in service, however. Since the military is downsizing, at present, competition for promotion to senior ranks is great.

- The military was desegregated before schools were desegregated in the United States. Still, there is a continuing concern that minorities are underrepresented among officers and overrepresented among junior enlisted, who are likely to get hazardous assignments. Women are greatly underrepresented both in the officer corps and among enlisted. Historically, laws and policies prevented women from serving in the military's essential role—combatant. Therefore, only a limited number could be usefully employed by the military. The laws that prevented women from serving in combat planes or on combat ships have now been changed, and the Army has reassessed the policies that seek to shield women from combat. Thus far, however, there has been no noticeable increase in the proportion of women.

  Table 4-2 shows the distribution of active-duty forces by rank, sex, and ethnic group in the Department of Defense (DOD) as a whole and in the individual services at the end of 1994. Warrant officers make up a special personnel group that includes individuals who often have a special expertise but lack the qualifications necessary to hold regular of-

Table 4-2: DOD Personnel, 1994

		Percentage			
	Number	White	Black	Hispanic	Other
OFFICERS					
Army					
Women	10,889	71	20	3	6
Men	74,270	83	10	3	4
Navy					
Women	7,978	83	9	3	5
Men	53,821	88	5	3	4
Marines					
Women	642	84	9	5	2
Men	17,237	89	5	3	2
Air Force					
Women	12,322	83	10	2	5
Men	68,682	90	5	2	3
TOTAL					
Women	32,338	79	13	3	5
Men	220,935	87	6	3	4
ENLISTED					
Army					
Women	58,395	42	48	4	6
Men	392,965	61	28	6	6
Navy					
Women	44,339	61	28	8	4
Men	357,327	70	17	7	6
Marines					
Women	7,029	59	26	10	5
Men	149,289	72	14	11	4
Air Force					
Women	53,433	69	24	4	4
Men	287,884	77	15	4	3
TOTAL					
Women	165,745	57	33	5	5
Men	1,214,009	69	20	6	5

Note: Percentages may not total 100 because of rounding.

ficer rank. They constitute 7 percent of officers—a small group, but one that provides essential skills and experience. In the discussion that follows, warrant officer data are presented as part of officer data.

There are roughly six enlisted persons for each officer. Women are slightly more "officer-heavy," because many nurses are women and all nurses are officers. Black men are greatly underrepresented as officers except in the Army; they are greatly overrepresented as enlisted personnel; in fact, they serve at double their proportion in the population as Army enlisted. Hispanic men are greatly underrepresented as officers and are underrepresented as enlisted except in the Marines. (According to 1991 census figures, blacks constitute 12 percent of the U.S. population and Hispanics constitute 8.5 percent.)

Women constitute about 12 percent of the military. Note that black women are slightly overrepresented among women officers but almost triply overrepresented among women enlisted. Hispanic women are only slightly less well represented than Hispanic men as enlisted but equally represented as officers. (Black women are concentrated in the Army). Overall, about 30 percent of military personnel are minorities; over 40 percent of military women are minorities.

Officers in ranks 7 to 10 are generals and admirals, "flag" officers. There are about 950 of them. In 1994, 31 were black men, 10 were Hispanic men, and 11 were women, one of whom was black. (The heads of each of the Nursing Corps are now generals/admirals, so there are "automatically" three women who hold flag rank.)

Among enlisted personnel, minorities are distributed across the ranks vertically. Women, though, experience the "higher the fewer" phenomenon. The percentage of minority officers diminishes with rank in a pattern similar to that of enlisted women. Women officers, however, experience even more truncation. Indeed, the percentage of women falls sharply beginning with the rank of lieutenant colonel, and in 1994 only one woman had more than one star, although some 450 men did. Women's advancement has had no legal cap for more than twenty-five years, but the combat restriction has severely constrained it.

- The especially low number and percentage of women in the Marines stems from the fact that the Marines are predominantly combat troops; the Marines use Navy personnel for most of their support functions. For example, there is no Marine Nurse Corps, although the Navy, Army, and Air Force all have substantial nurse corps.

- Virtually all Air Force slots are open to women. Even when women were not allowed to fly combat aircraft, more than 90 percent of Air Force slots were open. Nevertheless, the Air Force has 16, not 45 or 50, percent women. Further, enlisted women have not advanced to the top ranks of the Air Force as minority men have, and Air Force officer women especially drop off with increase in rank. The paradox, then, is that although the Air Force has had only minor legal restrictions, its proportion of women has been only slightly higher than that of the other services, and its women have not done much better (for example, four generals to the Army's three) at the highest level.

- Military personnel enjoy many family support services, notably medical care and commissaries, but they move regularly, across the country and around the globe. Often they are required to serve unaccompanied tours, that is, without their families. In fact, military personnel are probably more international than any other subset of the U.S. population. The mobility of military life also means that one is likely to have a new boss/commander every year or two. Thus, flexibility is important to an individual's success within this hierarchical institution.

- Until the mid-1970s, women received no benefits for their dependents and were discharged when they became pregnant. Now more than a third of military women have children, and even if they seek discharge, some pregnant women are required to complete their service commitment.

- Military women serve in a wide range of military occupations, but in 1993 almost half of women officers (as opposed to 13 percent of men officers) served in the health professions. Seventeen percent of women officers held administrative positions. This means that about one-third of the women were doubly nontraditional, that is, served in the military and also in a field other than health or administration.

- Enlisted women were distributed differently. While about a third were in administrative slots, only 15 percent were in health services. This means that about half were in a variety of other, "nontraditional" fields.

- Although one general was not a college graduate in 1993, less than 2 percent of officers lacked college degrees. Four percent of enlisted women and 3 percent of enlisted men had college degrees; some even had Ph.D.s.

- Among NATO countries only Canada has as high a percentage of women in its military as the United States. There are two quite different circumstances that seem to increase the number of women who serve in the military. One is wartime. The second is in liberal democracies where the military is all-volunteer and where there is an emphasis on providing equal opportunity for all citizens. Thus, in the United States, women were consistently less than 2 percent of the military until after the draft ended. Within eight years that number had increased to 8.5 percent; today it stands at 12 percent.

- Military personnel think in terms of a twenty-year career. Many can or must retire by age forty to forty-five. The continuation rates for women and men are almost identical.

- Change at the top comes slowly, because the military "grows its own." That is, one (mostly) enters at the lowest enlisted or officer rank and progresses through the ranks until one leaves or retires. Lateral entry is unusual. Therefore, it takes a long time to get new kinds of people into policymaking positions. On the other hand, the military is a youthful institution. Most personnel do not stay in service twenty years. More than half the officers are lieutenants or captains, and more than half the enlisted are in ranks E-1 to E-4. Thus, the composition of the military overall can be changed rather rapidly.

- Forty-one thousand women, or 7 percent of the U.S. military total, participated in the Persian Gulf War. Five military women were killed there, and two became POWs.

  Eight hundred Army women participated in the 1989 invasion of Panama, and two women commanded companies in that invasion. Air Force women participated in the invasion of Panama and in the 1986 attack on Libya. One hundred seventy Army women took part in the invasion of Grenada in 1983.

- In the Department of Defense, women were serving in five of 28 positions requiring Senate confirmation in 1994. One was serving as Secretary of the Air Force.

- As well as military personnel on active duty, each service has a reserve system of trained individuals who can be called to duty. In addition, states have National Guard units.

- A military made up of volunteers has to pay well enough to compete with civilian employers. Basic pay rates per month are shown in Table 4-3. There are a variety of ways individuals can receive extra pay. These include serving in hardship posts or in combat and having special skills, for example in nuclear engineering.

Table 4-3: 1995 Regular Military Compensation

Navy		Army	Years of Service	Salary
COMMISSIONED OFFICERS				
0-10	Admiral	General	26	132,196.81
0-9	Vice Admiral	Lieutenant General	26	125,516.63
0-8	Rear Admiral (Upper Half)	Major General	26	115,478.48
0-7	Rear Admiral (Lower Half)	Brigadier General	26	104,403.57
0-6	Captain	Colonel	24	89,032.68
0-5	Commander	Lieutenant Colonel	20	76,127.24
0-4	Lieutenant Commander	Major	14	61,740.60
0-3	Lieutenant	Captain	8	50,269.12
0-2	Lieutenant Junior Grade	First Lieutenant	4	41,830.07
0-1	Ensign	Second Lieutenant	2	29,473.26
ENLISTED MEMBERS				
E-9	Master Chief Petty Officer	Command Sergeant Major	26	53,959.84
E-8	Senior Chief Petty Officer	First Master Sergeant	22	45,112.32
E-7	Chief Petty Officer	Sergeant First Class	16	37,918.07
E-6	Petty Officer First Class	Staff Sergeant	10	31,978.26
E-5	Petty Officer Second Class	Sergeant	6	27,634.87
E-4	Petty Officer Third Class	Corporal	3	23,109.05
E-3	Seaman	Private First Class	2	20,793.61
E-2	Seaman Apprentice	Private	2	18,697.63
E-1	Seaman Recruit	Private	2	16,963.01

Source: Adapted from data supplied by the *Army Times*.

Note: This table shows the average annual "salary" for each rank. The figures combine basic pay, the Basic Allowance for Quarters, the Basic Allowance for Subsistence, the average Variable Housing Allowance, and the tax advantage from untaxed allowances.

• Good sources of information about women military personnel are: Defense Manpower Data Center, 1600 Wilson Boulevard, Arlington, VA 22209; *Minerva: Quarterly Report on Women and the Military*, a journal published by Linda De Pauw; and *Women in the Military*, an annual report published by the Women's Research and Education Institute, Washington, D.C.

PART II HISTORY AND ISSUES

Connie L. Reeves

5

The Military Woman's Vanguard: Nurses

Women have served as nurses for and in the military of the United States since colonial days. Surprisingly, however, this special story has not been told adequately. During the nation's wars, American military nurses have endured the same conditions and privations as the soldiers with whom they served. Nurses, like soldiers, have been killed by enemy fire, have been captured and made prisoners of war, and have received decorations for their valor.

Unlike the soldiers, however, nurses had to fight to be accepted on the battlefield and in the military. In the early days, nurses were usually soldiers' wives, who were viewed as a drain on the Army. Later, women were perceived as intruding into the male realm of military nursing, and questions were raised as to whether it was seemly for women to be viewing and touching men's bodies (Weatherford 1990, x). Even after they became accepted as ministering angels on the battlefield, they struggled to attain military rank and to be an integral part of the military. And although military nurses were desperately needed in all the country's wars, lessons learned about their value were usually forgotten until the next war. Still, by winning the struggle for integration and acceptance, female military nurses were in many ways the forerunners of today's women in the military.

The military has always needed nurses, and this need increased when soldiers began to be seen as citizens deserving medical care rather than as cannon fodder for the state (Weatherford 1990, ix). As medical advances occurred during each war, often by leaps and bounds, mortality rates dropped and more nurses were required to care for the patients. Nursing as a profession was based on the efforts of courageous women who insisted on nursing the wounded during the Crimean War in the mid-nineteenth century. The skilled nursing care received by soldier-citizens led to demands for comparable care after they returned to civilian life, thus establishing the foundation for nursing outside the military. The public accorded enormous respect to military nurses for their wartime service, which led to increased public esteem for nursing as a profession.

Nursing provided a major opportunity for women to obtain an education and to work without being castigated for losing their femininity or stepping out of their "proper role" as nurturer. During the first half of this century, nurses were viewed as romantic and heroic figures, models of virtue and purity—ideal women. At the same time, they laid the groundwork for feminist thought by seeking equal pay for equal work, breaking barriers to become working wives and working mothers, and institutionalizing their profession. American women military nurses were also the vanguard of the modern woman with respect to working and obtaining new freedoms.

This chapter is a preliminary effort to synthesize the history of American women military nurses from the earliest days through the Vietnam War. To date, the history of military nurses has been portrayed as part of the whole history of nursing, as part of the history of medical care, or in separate nursing corps histories. Further research will result in a more complete record.

In following the thread of the evolution of women military nurses, I have made a distinction between untrained and trained nurses. No disparagement is intended to the thousands of women who learned nursing skills at home and cared for their families and communities, but, if they had no formal schooling, I have considered them untrained. Trained nurses I have taken to be those who graduated from a formal system of nursing instruction, instituted by a religious order, hospital, or nursing school.

Up through the Civil War, I have discussed all forms of nursing as they led to the evolution of the professional military nurse. From the Spanish-American War forward, however, I have limited my discussion to military nurses and have not included the thousands of Red Cross nurses or civilian volunteer nurses who served overseas and at home.

Colonial America: Nursing at Home

In the early days of America, few people had a formal medical education and few received hospital care. According to the Puritans, disease was God's punishment for sin and deserved no alleviation. In New England the minister often served as the local doctor, being the best-educated man in town. Women, who had learned nursing skills at home or through apprenticeships, provided bedside medical care for family and friends as part of their womanly duties. Sometimes they nursed in the community for pay, particularly as midwives or for the poor. The early settlers had access to hospitals, however, as early as 1658 in Manhattan and 1731 in Philadelphia. These first hospitals served as almshouses, orphanages, and insane asylums, as well as facilities for the sick. The attendants were people of the "roughest character," who were little more than housekeepers, often unable to read or write and prone to drunkenness. Not until 1771, shortly before the War of Independence, did nursing attendants receive formal instruction (Dock and Stewart 1925, 144–45; Spruill 1972, 267–75; Reverby 1987, 2, 12; Dolan 1978, 107,111).

From time immemorial, women have followed armies to battle and dressed their wounds, sometimes as assigned laundresses who often changed bandages in addition to washing them. Britain was the first nation to employ female nurses in its army regularly, and by 1750 almost all nurses were women. Military planning provided for one nurse for every ten patients and a chief matron to supervise the nurses. Early British hospital ships have been described as "stinking, disease-ridden, floating warehouses" that physicians were forbidden to board. In 1705, five British women naval nurses served on a hospital ship in the Mediterranean to care for the sick, bathe patients, disinfect clothing and bedding, and shave patients' heads and beards. A staff of fifteen women nurses with their matron served aboard the hospital ship Union, also in the eighteenth century, receiving combat-ship patients who, in earlier days, would have been thrown overboard when the shipboard surgeons, physicians, and surgeon's mates were unable to save them (Gabriel and Metz 1992, 114, 119–20, 131; Dolan 1978, 116–17).

Although no country had a medical service with sufficient trained staff, supplies, hospitals, or battlefield evacuation, all had made progress toward institutionalizing medical care by the middle of the eighteenth-century. The Massachusetts Bay Colony had decided as early as 1676 to provide a surgeon for every five hundred troops, thus preceding the eighteenth-century awareness among nations that states must supply medical care for their soldiers. In the years before the Revolution, each colonial militia company had its own surgeon and surgeon's mate. In July 1743, medical personnel were designated as noncombatants who were authorized safe passage to their units, were required to care for wounded enemy soldiers (which increased the patient load), and could not be made prisoners of war (Gabriel and Metz 1992, 101, 110).

The first military hospital in the colonies was built in 1762 in New York to house the wounded from the French and Indian Wars, but no medical school appeared until 1765. Each colony provided the medical staff and supplies for its own regiments, drawing from a total pool of four hundred trained physicians or surgeons. The only trained nurses at this time were women of religious orders, particularly the Sisters of Charity and the Beguines, who succeeded in alleviating the poor diet, uncleanliness, and unsanitary conditions found in most hospitals (Gabriel and Metz 1992, 131–32; Dolan 1978, 111).

Revolutionary War: The Continental Army Hires Female Nurses

When war began in 1775, the colonies were not prepared for the immensity of their undertaking. Each colony had its own small army, but a united federal force did not exist until the Continental Army was authorized on 14 June 1775. The need for a medical department was immediately recognized after the Battle of Bunker Hill on 17 June. Basic necessities for soldiers were unavailable, and medical supplies, instruments, and drugs were scarce. Up to this point, only five hospitals existed in the colonies. The Massachusetts Bay Colony had to appropriate private homes in Cambridge and Boston as military hospitals, despite the resistance of local citizens to hospitals in their midst. Because of the dearth of trained nurses, Catholic nuns offered their services to the military (Gabriel and Metz 1992, 131; Shields 1981, 7; Donahue 1985, 284–85; Dolan 1978, 108, 115).

On 27 July 1775, the Second Continental Congress authorized a Medical Department for the new army of twenty-thousand men and established three "hospitals," one each to support the northern, middle, and southern theaters of operation. These "hospitals" had no fixed facilities but were composed of a medical staff that followed the army and provided medical support as needed. Each staff included a director, a chief physician, four surgeons, an apothecary, twenty surgeon's mates, a clerk, two storekeepers, a nurse for every ten patients, and a nurse matron for every one hundred patients. General George Washington specifically requested female nurses so that men could be treated and freed for battle, and he wanted matrons to supervise the nurses and oversee the wards. A nurse was authorized 2 dollars a month plus a daily ration—equal to a sergeant's pay—and a matron received 15 dollars a month and a daily ration. By contrast, surgeon's mates received 50 dollars a month, and senior surgeons, who were officers, were paid 120 dollars a month plus six rations a day. By the end of the war, a nurse's pay had increased to 8 dollars a month (Gabriel and Metz 1992, 131; Kerber 1980, 58–60).

The Continental soldier found his greatest threat came not from the battlefield, where he had a 98 percent chance of living, but from disease (which caused 90 percent of all military deaths), including respiratory illness, dysentery, malaria, typhus, typhoid, venereal disease, pneumonia, pleurisy, scabies, and smallpox. In 1776, 5,000 men (25 percent of the army) died from illness. In December 1777 at Valley Forge, 2,898 men in a force of 11,000 (26 percent) were unfit for duty because of illness. The "flying hospitals" that accompanied armies on the move tended to be unsanitary huts near the front rather than aid stations that could improve a soldier's chance of recovery. The lack of transportation forced many soldiers to make their own way from the front to the rear, and a third of those who received transport died before reaching the rear. The field hospitals in the rear were little more than dirty and overcrowded log huts, halls, churches, or sheds in which fever and epidemics raged. Those who received medical treatment faced a 25 percent mortality rate, a high probability of amputation, and the likelihood of maggots in their putrefied wounds (Gabriel and Metz 1992, 106–7, 143; Meier 1991, 17–18; Dolan 1978, 116).

Male surgeon's mates performed most of the skilled tasks; female nurses carried out primarily custodial tasks—emptying chamberpots, washing patients, and sweeping wards—and sometimes cooked. The women dispensed medicine and monitored diets only when the surgeon's mates were unavailable. Nurses introduced innovations, however, to keep patients comfortable and help them recover, including stone jug hot-water bottles, combination lamps and food warmers, varying sizes of china feeding cups, and "go-chairs" (wheelchairs) and fan chairs (wheelchairs with fans). A popular part of the patient's diet provided by nurses was warm "pap" (milk in which oatmeal had been cooked and strained and to which beaten egg yolks, butter, and orange flavor were added) and beef tea, an extract of beef juices (Kerber 1980, 59; Dolan 1978, 110, 116; Willenz 1983, 10).

In 1778, the medical condition of the army began to improve. The office of Purveyor General was established to ensure that only the truly needy received medical services. Regimental commanders visited their sick soldiers, the flying camp hospitals prioritized patients, the Army published sanitation and cleanliness regulations, smallpox inoculation began for soldiers, lime juice eradicated scurvy, standardized medicine chests went to every regiment, and standard preparations for medicines appeared (Meier 1991, 19, 24, 28, 32–34, 36).

Records document the employment of women as nurses during the Revolutionary War. Mary Pricely was one of those who served on board colonial warships. In 1777, Maryland paid her for her service as a nurse on the *Defense*. In 1779, one matron and one nurse cared for 133 patients at a hospital in Philadelphia. Four nurses were responsible for 100 patients at a general hospital in Hillsborough, North Carolina. At the end of the war, an inventory found seven matrons and thirty nurses on duty serving the military at seven hospitals, nursing 4,000 men. A biography was written in 1791 of Mary Waters, an army nurse, although it was never published. In addition to the paid army nurses, hundreds of women followed their husbands to battle to care for them, nursing others as well (Donahue 1985, 285; Gabriel and Metz 1992, 134–35; Holm 1992, 3; Kerber 1980, 74; De Pauw 1982, 91).

Once the Revolution was won, the military medical department demobilized along with the army. Patient care reverted to regimental surgeons and surgeon's mates, assisted by military wives and laundresses. Not until the War of 1812 did an institutionalized military medical service reappear. Not until the Civil War did the nation desperately need women nurses again (Gabriel and Metz 1992, 136; Shields 1981, 7; Donahue 1985, 285).

The Early Nineteenth Century: Florence Nightingale Professionalizes Nursing

In civilian life, only the poorest people went to hospitals, which were occupied by the seriously ill. Death rates in hospitals reached 50 percent, and patients were shamefully neglected. Matrons tried to hire nurses of good character but often had to use hospital "inmates," whether retired prostitutes, former criminals, or the aged. Doctors often appointed the elderly as ward nurses so they could obtain better meals. Charles Dickens, in the 1850s, developed the character Sairy Gump, a caricature of the hospital nurse so frightening that it helped propel social reform. Epidemics of diseases such as cholera, yellow fever, smallpox, diphtheria, scarlet fever, dysentery, typhus, and typhoid occurred regularly, transmitted through contaminated water supplies and disease carriers. Most people were nursed at home by women, despite the problems in providing a proper diet and keeping the patient's room appropriately cool or warm and free from smoke. Religious orders provided the only high level of nursing care in hospitals and established the model for nurses in the future—gentle, disciplined, selfless, orderly, patient, skillful, tactful, charitable, dignified, and poised, qualities that were also attributes of the ideal woman and mother (Dolan 1978, 134–35, 137–38; Kalisch and Kalisch 1987, 10, 12–14).

By 1802, the United States had only 2 surgeons and 25 mates in its military medical corps, scattered among garrison and frontier posts. Military hospitals did not exist, as the army simply built huts for the sick and wounded as needed. The Army Reorganization Act of 1818 laid the foundation for the modern military medical department when Congress authorized a surgeon general for the medical corps. During the Mexican War, the 7,000-man army grew to 100,000 men; in contrast, its medical corps increased only from 71 to 250 officers. Tents housed the regimental hospitals, where primary medical care was given, and the Army created general hospitals as needed. The Army did not have the nurses, supplies, physicians, cooks, or stewards required to tend the wounded. The result was a deadly war for the U.S. Army, with respect to mortality rate, with 10,790 soldiers dying from disease and 1,458 from enemy fire (Gabriel and Metz 1992, 179–80).

By the 1840s, paid nursing became more prevalent with increasing numbers of child nurses, nursemaids, wet nurses, midwives, and monthly nurses (who assisted for one month after delivery of a child). Any woman could claim to be a nurse, but primarily widows in their thirties and forties without family obligations did so. Dickens, in a linguistic study of the word nurse, explained that since nursing was associated with maternity care (nourishing a child), women nurses were expected to treat patients with the same love they showed their children. Moreover, since nuns were some of the first hospital nurses, all nurses were still expected to work for altruistic rather than monetary reasons (Reverby 1987, 13, 15, 20; Kalisch and Kalisch 1987, 15).

Although the Crimean War did not involve the American military, the effects of that war, particularly as related to nursing, greatly influenced the United States. When British citizens learned in 1854 that thousands of soldiers in the Crimea were dying of cholera and battle wounds in the midst of disease, filth, and vermin, with no beds, blankets, soap, or towels, with few utensils and inedible food, they demanded action from their government. The British secretary of war, Sir Sidney Herbert, asked Florence Nightingale, a thirty-four-year-old superintendent of the Institution for the Care of Sick Gentlewomen, to become superintendent of the Female Nursing Establishment of the English General Hospitals in Turkey. She departed six days later with a personally selected corps of women nurses. Within six months of their arrival, Nightingale and her 125 nurses had reduced the death rate of the army from 42.7 percent to 2.2 percent by focusing on sanitation and nutrition. They provided clean linens and hospital gowns, washed the patients and the wards, and established diet kitchens, a laundry, recreation rooms, reading rooms, and education classes for the patients. Nightingale transformed the army medical system and conquered the prevailing opposition to the presence of women supporting an army in the field (Naythons 1993, 42; Dolan 1978, 159–60, 163; Kalisch and Kalisch 1987, 16; Donahue 1985, 242–44; Gabriel and Metz 1992, 170, 173).

A grateful nation presented Nightingale with fifty-thousand pounds, which she used in 1860 to establish the Nightingale Training School for Nurses in London, the first professional nursing school. Nightingale believed that nursing was a calling but also an art that had to be learned. She felt that a good character and respectability were critical in a nurse and established the new concept that nurses would be not under the control of doctors but under a hospital matron. Her book *Notes on Nursing* (1859) was widely distributed and praised. Her school became a model for nursing training around the world and was the first step in making nursing a respectable profession for women. Nightingale also became a worldwide authority on hospital planning and administration, and her book *Notes on Hospitals* (1859) greatly influenced medical care in the U.S. Civil War. Moreover, Nightingale's work served as an inspiration to J. Henri Dunant, who founded the international Red Cross to provide volunteer nursing on battlefields and who achieved the signing of the Treaty of Geneva, which recognized Red Cross nurses and their hospitals as noncombatants (Donahue 1985, 245, 247–48, 252, 253; Kalisch and Kalisch 1987, 18; Naythons 1993, 42; Dolan 1978, 161, 163–65, 167; Reverby 1987, 49, 51).

Civil War: Thousands of Women Serve as Army Nurses

When the Civil War began, the American military was once again not prepared for numerous casualties or ill soldiers. In 1860, the Army of twenty-six-thousand men, located on the frontier, included thirty surgeons, eighty-three assistant surgeons, and no nurses. Twenty-four of the medical officers left to join the Confederacy. There was no organized medical corps, no ambulance corps, no field hospital capability, and no nursing corps. Wounded men sometimes lay on the battlefield for days before receiving medical care. Soldiers had nursed patients with the assistance of laundresses and officers' wives up to the time the war began, but the Union and Confederacy both recognized very quickly that men would be needed in their regiments and not in hospitals. Moreover, soldiers who were given up by their commanders to perform nursing duty were usually misfits, and "poor soldiers make poor nurses." In addition, male patients preferred to be nursed by women. The need for female nurses became imperative (Gabriel and Metz 1992, 187; Stivers 1975, 328; Culpepper 1991, 320–22; Dolan 1978, 175; Naythons 1993, 48, 74; Donahue 1985, 285; Reverby 1987, 44).

Religious orders of women quickly volunteered. The Catholic Sisters of Charity, Sisters of St. Joseph, and Sisters of the Holy Cross were three of the twelve religious orders that supported both the Union and the Confederacy with six hundred sisters throughout the war. Many had received nursing instruction, particularly the Sisters of Charity, and had helped establish well-run and organized hospitals, the best in the United States. A monument memorializing their efforts now stands in Arlington National Cemetery, entitled "Nuns of the Battlefield." Protestant women and their religious nursing groups, most of whom had received their training at home, also nursed sick and wounded soldiers. These women neither asked for nor received compensation for their services, although, in the North, President Abraham Lincoln authorized them to purchase any supplies needed as they served in barns, warehouses, tents, the rotunda of the Capitol, the Senate and House buildings, and permanent hospitals. Despite their best efforts, the religious orders could not care for all the wounded, and lay nurses were desperately needed (Dolan 1978, 175–75, 186; Culpepper 1991, 317; Stivers 1975, 328; Donahue 1985, 280, 282–83, 285; Naythons 1993, 74; Gabriel and Metz 1992, 193).

In 1860, the New England Hospital for Women and Children opened a nursing school for women, and in 1861, a women's hospital in Philadelphia established another; nevertheless, few trained nurses were available for the war effort. Women in the North, led by Dr. Elizabeth Blackwell, the first female physician in the United States, organized the Women's Central Association of Relief, which successfully pressured President Lincoln to establish the U.S. Sanitary Commission in 1861 to ensure that soldiers received proper medical care. The commission, with close ties to Florence Nightingale and comprising mostly women, assumed a major role in the Army's medical service by coordinating the efforts of all relief organizations in the country; sending nurses where they were most needed; inspecting hospitals and enforcing sanitation standards; guaranteeing blankets, shoes, and medicine for soldiers; providing green vegetables to prevent scurvy; planning hospital construction; and collecting and distributing medical supplies and equipment. The largest relief organization in the war, the Sanitary Commission had seven-thousand local chapters that raised $5 million in cash and $15 million in supplies (Dock and Stewart 1925, 129, 146, 150; Holm 1992, 7; Donahue 1985, 290–92; Massey 1994, 32–33; Dolan 1978, 179; Oates 1994, 9).

When newspapers depicted the harsh reality of life in the military camps—no medicine, no drugs, no surgical dressings, no ambulances, and dirty and unsanitary conditions—Northern citizens became incensed and, like the British during the Crimean War, insisted that the government correct the situation. In a move analogous to the British request to Florence Nightingale to establish a nursing corps in the Crimea, the secretary of war appointed Dorothea Lynde Dix superintendent of the female nurses of the Union Army on 10 June 1861. Dix, a sixty-year-old crusader for the mentally ill and founder of thirty psychiatric hospitals in the United States, was not a nurse but had volunteered to recruit nurses for the Army. Her responsibilities included recruiting and equipping an Army nurse corp, organizing military hospitals, supplying nurses to hospitals, and receiving and disbursing supplies. After October 1863, no nurse would work in a military hospital without her certificate of approval (Dolan 1978, 177–78; Donahue 1985, 230–31, 292–93; Brocket and Vaughan 1993, 103–5; Masse 1994, 46; Naythons 1993, 42; Holm 1992, 8; Oates 1994, 9–10).

In accordance with the times, Dix required that her nurses be between the ages of thirty-five and fifty; matronly and plain-looking; highly educated; neat, orderly, sober, and industrious; dressed in brown, gray, or black dresses without ornamentation, hoop shirts, or jewelry; qualified and of good character; and willing to serve for six months or the duration. On 3 August 1861, Congress authorized the surgeon general to employ women nurses in military hospitals (at a ratio of one for every two male nurses) at $12 a month plus one daily ration (male counterparts received $20.50 a month), and in short order, Dix had two-thousand nurses ready to serve throughout the country. Neither Dix nor her nurses held military rank, but they were given administrative rank equal to a ward surgeon's. Unfortunately, some nurses were ignorant of their status and found themselves doing menial labor when male surgeons and military officers resisted their intrusion by limiting their work to scrubbing floors, washing windows, preparing food, and overseeing supplies. Eventually, nurses carried out more skilled tasks such as dressing wounds and feeding patients and were supported by a female corps of cooks, housekeepers, and attendants. By war's end, six-thousand Army nurses supplied by Dix had served the Union in general hospitals, in field hospitals, and on the battlefields (Dolan 1978, 178, 180; Donahue 1985, 293–94; Oates 1994, 23; Masse 1994, 44, 47; Naythons 1993, 42, 74; Culpepper 1991, 345; Smith 1988, 25–34; Brocket and Vaughan 1993, 35–36, 45–46; Holm 1992, 8; Shields 1981, 8, 74; Gabriel and Metz 1992, 193).

Some women who are well known today for other achievements served as Union Army nurses. Louisa May Alcott worked at Union Hospital in Georgetown, Washington, D.C., for six weeks from 1862 to 1863, supervising a forty-bed ward, dressing wounds, dispensing medicine, reading to patients, and writing letters for them before she succumbed to typhoid fever. The mercury in the calomel medicine with which she was treated made her an invalid and shortened her life; still, she wrote her famous book, Little Women, after the war. Harriet Tubman, a former slave who, after escaping to the North, returned to the South nineteen times to help three-hundred slaves find freedom, served as a Union Army nurse or matron at the Colored Hospital in Fort Monroe, Virginia. Sojourner Truth, a former slave who became an abolitionist, evangelist, speaker, author, suffragist, and Lincoln's counselor to the freedmen of Washington, also served as a nurse to the Union Army. Dr. Mary Edwards Walker closed her medical practice in 1861 and, when denied acceptance as a military physician, became a Union Army nurse. In 1864, she received a commission as a lieutenant in the Medical Corps, becoming the first female doctor in the Army and an assistant surgeon. Later in the year, she was captured by the Confederates and held prisoner for four months. For her war efforts, Walker was awarded the Congressional Medal of Honor, the first and only women to have ever received that honor (Dever and Dever 1995, 146; Donahue 1985, 301, 306–7; Naythons 1993, 75; Dolan 1978, 183–84; Holm 1992, 7; Spiegel and Spiegel 1994, 27–29; Gabriel and Metz 1992, 192).

Many women who had no special claim to fame also served as Army nurses. One was Sarah Edwards, who was a spy, courier, and soldier in the

Union Army as well as a nurse. Cornelia Hancock, assigned to a field hospital after the Battle of Gettysburg, remarked that the operating table in the woods "literally ran blood" and a nearby wagon was "rapidly filling with amputated legs and arms." Jane Swisshelm was reported to have worked from six in the morning until midnight in a hospital nursing fifteen hundred men, dressing wounds, and providing refreshment (Holm 1992, 6; Dolan 1978, 184; Naythons 1993, 74).

The most famous nurses of the Civil War were not Union Army nurses. Clara Barton, who had been a clerk in the U.S. Patent Office when the war began, rushed to nurse wounded soldiers who arrived in Washington on 19 April 1861. Not willing to take orders or share authority with Dix, religious orders, or the Sanitary Commission, Barton established an independent relief organization to provide supplies for the Army and its hospitals, often using her own money to purchase the needed medicine, clothes, and linen and distributing the goods directly to soldiers in the field. Known as the "little lone lady in black silk," Barton nursed soldiers in hospitals and on the battlefields, whether they were Union or Confederate, black or white. After the war, she personally marked twelve-thousand graves and was instrumental in founding the first National Cemetery at Arlington; in 1882 she organized the American Red Cross and for twenty years served as its first president (Oates 1994, 4–5, 10, 17; Dolan 1978, 175; Brocket and Vaughan 1993, 115–27; Naythons 1993, 42; Donahue 1985, 294; Holm 1992, 7).

Mother Bickerdyke (a.k.a. Mary Ann Ball), a Quaker widow clothed in a calico dress, Shaker bonnet, and shawl, was another renowned nurse. She began nursing as a volunteer at the beginning of the war and soon became an agent of the Sanitary Commission. Nursing soldiers from Tennessee to Georgia, serving under fire in nineteen battles, fighting for the rights and well-being of the ordinary soldier, she was loved by her patients, who called her "Mother." In 1863, she was the only female nurse caring for two-thousand patients in a field hospital near Chattanooga. In addition to organizing diet kitchens (one of the major contributions of Civil War nurses was providing nutritious food for soldiers), laundries, and an ambulance service; supervising nursing staff; and distributing supplies, she could be found roaming the battlefields at night to ensure that the living wounded were removed to hospitals and given medical care. In memory of her service, the United States launched the hospital ship *Mary A. Bickerdyke* in 1943 (Donahue 1985, 298, 300; Dolan 1978, 175–77; Culpepper 1991, 339; Brocket and Vaughan 1993, 172–86; Naythons 1993, 42).

The Confederate Army initially did not appoint a superintendent of nurses as the North had done, relying instead on individuals and state and local organizations to provide medical care. Women were more restricted in the South from serving as nurses because of the pervasive belief that it was improper for women to handle men's bodies or work with men. Even so, perhaps one-thousand women from religious orders and the laity volunteered as nurses while other women gave up their homes for hospitals and convalescent centers. The Army of the Confederacy accepted its first and only female officer when President Jefferson Davis awarded a captain's commission to Sally Louisa Tompkins, who had nursed patients at Bull Run and supervised a private hospital in Richmond, and who needed military rank to requisition supplies. In 1861, the Confederate government took over private hospitals, but President Davis allowed an exception for hers. Tompkins refused to accept payment for her services and built a reputation as capable of nursing the most critical patients. In September 1862, the Confederate Congress authorized monthly pay for Army nurses at the rate of thirty dollars for a ward matron, thirty-five dollars for an assistant, and forty dollars for a chief nurse. Unlike the North, however, the South did not set standards or qualifications for Army nurses. As the war progressed, Confederate Army nurses moved hospitals and patients several times as the Army continually retreated, complicating their already enormous job. As in the North, Southern men had their favorite nurses, among them Betsy Sullivan, known as "Mother of the First Tennessee Regiment" (Masse 1994, 44–48; Gabriel and Metz 1992, 193; Willenz 1983, 13; Donahue 1985, 304–6; Dolan 1978, 185).

Nightingale advocated housing patients with different illnesses in separate buildings placed in a semicircular fan arrangement, called a pavilion hospital. By the end of the war, the Union and Confederacy had built 204 large pavilion hospitals with a total of 137,000 beds. The largest hospital in the Western world was outside Richmond with 150 pavilions formed into five divisions, served by forty to fifty surgeons and assistant surgeons per division. The Sanitary Commission assisted in developing a mobile pavilion hospital. The pavilion-style hospital remained the model for the next seventy-five years for both military and civilian hospitals (Naythons 1993, 62; Dolan, 1978, 178; Gabriel and Metz 1992, 192, 194; Oates 1994, 31).

In 1861, the military established an ambulance corps with its own uniforms and insignia, providing ambulances, drivers, and litter bearers for each regiment. Regimental hospitals served as frontline aid stations, brigade hospitals were one-half mile removed from the front, division hospitals were a mile from the front, and general hospitals were well into the rear. Mobile surgical field hospitals were developed with operating tables and pharmacies near the front line. Litter bearers carried the wounded first to regimental and then to brigade hospitals, where horse-drawn ambulances then took them to division hospitals. Soldiers going on to general hospitals or convalescent centers were transported by hospital trains or hospital ships. This method of evacuating patients became a model for other countries for decades (Donahue 1985, 288; Gabriel and Metz 1992, 188–90, 194; Naythons 1993, 48–49, 54).

Steamboats converted to "floating hospitals" could carry eight-hundred wounded men, had operating and rehabilitation rooms, and were some-times used to isolate smallpox victims. The four Catholic Sisters of Mercy and five black women who volunteered and served on the first Navy hospital ship, Red Rover, nursed the wounded after the siege of Vicksburg and can be thought of as the first American Navy nurses. As nurses with the Sanitary Commission's transport service, they were paid fifty cents a day. One of the Sisters marveled at the modern 450-bed hospital with its three-hundred-ton icebox, two kitchens, elevator for immobile patients, a laundry, two water closets on every deck, and bathrooms. With a full complement of nurses and surgeons, Red Rover transported 23,738 patients on the Ohio, Missouri, and Illinois Rivers. Mother Bickerdyke was the nurse in charge of the City of Memphis, the Sanitary Commission's largest hospital ship, and nuns also served on Superior and Empress. By 1862, the Union Army had fifteen steamboats on the rivers, each with a qualified surgeon and assistant surgeon aboard, and seventeen oceangoing steamers. By the end of the war, they had carried 150,000 wounded men from the front to Army and Navy hospitals (Donahue 1985, 288; Naythons 1993, 42; Gabriel and Metz 1992, 189–90; De Pauw 1982, 101; Stivers 1975, 320, 323, 330–31).

Soldiers in the Civil War died five times more often from disease than battle injuries, and the mortality rate for all soldiers was 25 percent, with approximately 620,000 men dead at war's end (360,000 Union and 260,000 Confederate). The Springfield rifle minié ball caused 94 percent of all battle injuries, and as septicemia, gangrene, and tetanus were usual complications, amputations became the most common battlefield operation. Shortages of medical supplies led to substitutions for fighting infection; anesthesia began to be used on a wide scale, sanitation was improved with the use of antiseptics, and opium and opium-based drugs (laudanum and opium with ipecac) alleviated pain. Medical supply and equipment tables were established, a medical record system for tracking casualties was developed, and female nurses were used in a more far-reaching manner than ever before. In addition to treating wounds and diseases, nurses had to help their patients overcome their fear of hospitals (Gabriel and Metz 1992, 181–82, 185–87, 194–95; Culpepper 1991, 334).

Between the Union Army nurses, the religious orders, the relief organizations, and the volunteers, as many as ten-thousand women, called "Florence Nightingales" by the public, may have served as nurses during the war. When the war ended in 1865, the Army decided it no longer needed female nurses and sent them home, caring for its patients once again with male soldiers and the attached laundresses. The returning nurses, except for the Sisters of Charity, sometimes faced disparaging comments about their war work from men who thought women should stay out of nursing. At least twenty Union nurses died during the Civil War, and 10 percent of those who served fell ill from disease; nevertheless, Congress waited thirty years before providing Army nurses with a small pension for their services (Oates 1994, 376; Naythons 1993, 74–75; Masse 1994, 43, 63–64; Donahue 1985, 287; Culpepper 1991, 344).

Late Nineteenth Century: Nightingale Nursing Schools Appear in America

By 1870, ten-thousand civilian nurses existed in the United States, albeit without formal training or schooling. In 1873, Linda Richards was named "America's first trained nurse" when she graduated from the first hospital-based nursing program built on the Nightingale model in the United States. Students received nursing training in exchange for providing hospital labor, a tradition that continued for many decades. After 1873, women with formal training were called trained or graduate nurses and, in contrast to traditional nurses, were young and single. Women without formal training became known as professed nurses, practical nurses, nurse's aides, attendants, subsidiary nursing workers, or ward helpers. By 1880, there were 157 graduate nurses in the United States; by 1900, there were 3,546. The number of nursing schools increased from 3 in 1873 to 15 in 1880 and 432 in 1900 (Naythons 1993, 52; Shields 1981, 9; Kalisch and Kalisch 1987, 20–21; Dolan 1978, 194; Dock and Stewart 1925, 146; Reverby 1987, 3, 5, 21, 29, 41. 75).

By 1869, the military medical service had decreased by 161 medical officers from the high of 15,236 Union and Confederate medical officers who had
served during the Civil War, and women nurses were not needed in the Army,
as soldiers provided patient care. Nevertheless, the increasing lethality of wars
in the nineteenth-century added to the impetus of nations to develop national
military médical corps and to improve medical care so that army manpower
could be protected. Radical improvements in transportation and communication during the century led to opportunities among medical personnel to share
knowledge, spurring medical developments. Increased use of anesthesia permitted surgeons to spend more time operating on a patient and trying to re-
pair injuries rather than hurriedly amputating limbs. The hypodermic syringe,
stethoscope, X-ray, and quinine were remarkable inventions that improved
medical care available to soldiers. In addition, hospitals came to be seen as safe
and as places to get well. According to Susan Reverby, "the invention of the
modern hospital depended on the invention of the trained nurse" (1987, 39).
In 1873, there were 178 hospitals; by 1909, there were 3,300; and by 1919,
the number had grown to 7,000 (Gabriel and Metz 1992, 145–46, 148–49,
191, 194; Kalisch and Kalisch 1987, 21; Reverby 1987, 39, 62).

The Spanish-American War: Contract Nurses Serve and Die Overseas

Battling typhoid fever epidemics in military camps, along with yellow fever, malaria, and dysentery, became the immediate concern after the
Spanish-American War broke out in 1898. Diseases were causing ten times
the deaths as battle injuries and almost lost the war for the United States. The
Army Medical Department knew that its 983 members could not adequately
serve a 28,000-man Army and tried to recruit six-thousand male nurses. Sufficient trained female nurses existed and nursing schools had been turning
out graduates for twenty-five years, but no system was in place to procure
or recruit them for military service. The Nurses' Associated Alumnae of the
United States and Canada (later the American Nurses' Association), a new
organization, offered its services to Surgeon General George M. Sternberg
but was turned down since it was not recognized as the official voice for
nurses. The Daughters of the American Revolution (D.A.R.), under the leadership of Dr. Anita Newcomb McGee, physician and D.A.R. vice-president,
had formed the D.A.R. Hospital Corps and also volunteered to fill the breach

(Holm 1992, 8; Cosmas 1994, 251; Shields 1981, 8, 10; Dolan 1978, 220; Donahue 1985, 327). Sternberg had reservations about women serving in the field with male soldiers (despite their Civil War record) and believed their presence would necessitate the "expense of luxuries" such as bureaus, rocking chairs, and other items. Despite his concerns, on 28 April 1898, Sternberg requested and received congressional authority to appoint female nurses under contract, but without military status, for thirty dollars a month plus one daily ration. One day later, he established the Nurse Corps Division to manage the military nursing requirement and placed McGee in charge, appointing her acting assistant surgeon general in the U.S. Army (Shields 1981, 9–11; Holm 1992, 8–9; Donahue 1985, 327; Dolan 1978, 220).

McGee established admissions standards for the contract nurses, requiring character references and endorsements from their training schools. She developed a system of personnel records and evaluated credentials and, by July 1898, acquired twelve hundred volunteers from the Sisters of Charity, Sisters of Mercy, Sisters of the Holy Cross, the Red Cross, nursing school superintendents, and others as "contract nurses of the Army." The first nurses were appointed in May 1898, and from 1898 to 1909, fifteen hundred women signed contracts. The maximum number of contract nurses on duty at any one time was 1,158 on 15 September 1898. The nurses served in Army hospitals in Cuba, Puerto Rico, the Philippines, Hawaii, China, Japan and the United States and on the USS *Relief*, a newly purchased 750-bed hospital ship with six women nurses on board, equipped to operate for six months (Donahue 1985, 327; Shields 1981, 10–11; Dolan 1978, 220; Dock and Stewart 1925, 181; Willenz 1983, 14; Cosmas 1994, 249).

Initially, the nurses found themselves working in hospitals where male corpsmen, without training and experience, had allowed unsanitary and unhealthy conditions to develop. Moreover, they lacked appropriate supplies and proper shelter. One nurse, stationed in Puerto Rico, remarked that they drove to camp in ambulances pulled by mules; worked day and night; hauled water in barrels for more than a mile; tended patients in crowded tents filled with typhoid fever, dysentery, and diarrhea; and had no access to ice or diet kitchens. Twelve nurses died of typhoid fever and one of yellow fever. Clara Louise Maass, one of the first contract nurses, died while willingly undergoing a yellow fever experiment in Cuba in 1901. She had served during the Spanish-American War in Florida, Georgia, Cuba, and the Philippines and was buried with full military honors (Shields 1981, 10–11; Donahue 1985, 327, 329, 331, 333; Dolan 1978, 221).

In 1899, when the war was over and the typhoid fiver epidemic under control, the number of contract nurses was reduced to seven hundred. That same year, the first Army regulation on the Nurse Corps was published, increasing a nurse's monthly pay to $40 when in the United States and $50 when serving overseas. The regulation also defined a nurse's duties and privileges, such as quarters, rations, transportation expense, leave, sick care, uniform, and badge. By June 1900, though, only 210 nurses remained under contract (Shields 1981, 11).

The Early Twentieth Century: The Army and Navy Nurse Corps Are Established

The "indisputable contribution of the contract nurses" convinced Sternberg that nurses should be a permanent part of the Army medical system, despite the belief of many men that no women should be granted military status. Although most of the contract nurses had been under Army control, confusion resulted when others were paid by the Red Cross or the D.A.R. McGee wrote the legislation to establish the female Nurse Corps as a branch of the Army Medical Department. In the Army Reorganization Bill of 1901, Congress created the Nurse Corps (female) as an auxiliary of the Army; the name was changed to the Army Nurse Corps in 1918. The Corps would include only fully trained nurses (hospital school graduates), who would receive letters of appointment in the Regular Army for three years and could apply for reappointment. The nurses still had not received military status: they had no military rank, no pay equal to male officers, no retirement benefits, and no veterans' benefits. On 28 February 1901, the Nurse Corps consisted of 202 "charter" members, and on 15 March 1901, Dita H. Kinney, a former contract nurse, became the first superintendent, serving until 1909. In 1902, Congress fixed the authorized strength of the Nurse Corps at 100 nurses for the next ten years, increasing it to 125 in 1912 and 150 in 1914 (Holm 1992, 9; Shields 1981, 12–14, 16; Dolan 1978, 285–86; Donahue 1985, 331).

The Navy Nurse Corps was established by Congress on 12 May 1908 and was considered an integral part of the Navy. Esther Voorhees Hasson was appointed the first superintendent of the Corps in October 1908, and in that same month, twenty Navy nurses, named "the sacred twenty," reported to the U.S. Naval Hospital in Washington, D.C., for orientation and duty. By 1910, some Navy nurses were being assigned overseas. On Guam, in 1911,

Navy nurses established a nursing school for native women, and in Samoa, they established another. When World War I began, the nursing services of both the Army and the Navy were prepared to send nurses to the battlefields (Holm 1992, 9; Dolan 1978, 286; Willenz 1983, 14; Donahue 1985, 331).

The surgeon general established a pool of thirty-seven reserve nurses from women who had previously served four months in the Nurse Corps and were willing to come on active duty when ordered for emergencies. In 1909, the American Red Cross formed the Red Cross Nursing Service, a reserve corps of hospital graduate nurses to supplement the Army and Navy Nurse Corps and the Red Cross. Selected nurses were required to be members of the American Nurses' Association, the Army Nurse Corps, and the Red Cross Nursing Service. Under Jane A. Delano, second superintendent of the Army Nurse Corps, the Red Cross became the primary reserve of nurses for the military. By June 1913, four thousand reserve nurses were eligible and willing to serve on active duty (Shields 1981, 13–14; Donahue 1985, 297; Dolan 1978, 286).

World War I: Ten Thousand Military Nurses Serve Overseas

World War I created an enormous, worldwide, insatiable demand for nurses. When war began in 1914, the American Red Cross immediately sent nurses and doctors to France, England, Germany, Austria, Serbia, and Russia. By 6 April 1917, when the United States entered the war, 403 Regular Army nurses and 170 Reserve nurses were on active duty at general hospitals in Texas, Arizona, and New Mexico as a result of incidents on the Mexican border. Thanks to Delano, an adequate supply of nurses was available for military service, and the Red Cross Nursing Service went into action procuring, recruiting, and equipping nurses for overseas duty. The first 400 Army nurses sailed for Europe in May 1917 to serve with the British Expeditionary Force in France and were welcomed at Buckingham Palace by King George. One month later, 1,176 nurses were on active duty. On 2 October 1917, General John J. Pershing requested an Army Nurse Corps member to supervise nursing activities for the American Expeditionary Force (AEF), and Bessie S. Bell, chief nurse at Walter Reed, reported on 13 November (Shields 1981, 14; Donahue 1985, 397–98; Dolan 1978, 287; Holm 1992, 10; Mecca 1995).

Military nursing encountered new wounds in World War I. Mustard gas burned and blistered patients, caused tremendous agony, and burned the hands of nurses who touched the residue of gas on the patients' clothes. Shrapnel caused most wounds, and head and face injuries were especially common. Since battles lasted for days, "shell shock" became a frequent battle injury. The unmoving front lines with water-filled trenches resulted in 200,000 casualties from trench foot and trench fever and 115,361 from frostbite. Unsanitary conditions worsened by rats, maggots, and lice increased infections, resulting in thousands of amputations. Shock, severe hemorrhage, and communicable diseases such as dysentery and malaria were other challenges facing nurses. Except for the flu epidemic of 1918, the mortality rate from disease was less than in previous wars. Despite the Geneva Convention, nurses worked under threat of air attack and traveled the seas under at risk of torpedo attack. Medical care became the AEF's greatest concern (Mecca 1995, 5; Dolan, 1978, 287; Donahue 1985, 404; Gabriel and Metz 1992, 243).

Female military nurses did not serve at the frontline aid stations (advanced dressing stations)—although civilian nurses did—but did serve occasionally in field hospitals located outside artillery range above five miles from the front. The frontline aid stations treated emergencies, had mobile laboratories and X-ray machines, and prepared the wounded for transport to field hospitals. Field hospitals provided emergency surgery, pain relief, nourishment, treatment of shock, dressing of wounds, and splint application. Evacuation hospitals (casualty clearing stations), located twenty to twenty-five miles from the front, included full complements of female nurses and were the first locations where all medical services were provided. In some parts of France, the nurse-to-patient ratio was one to sixty. Within twenty to twenty-four hours, the wounded were removed by train, ambulance, or barge to base (general) hospitals far in the rear. The U.S. Army operated fifty medical barges on French waterways and sent 6,875 motorized ambulances to France. During the war, the United States built 333 hospitals in France and 91 in the United States. Castles, chateaux, and private homes in France harbored auxiliary hospitals (Donahue 1985, 404; Gabriel and Metz 1992, 240, 250; Dolan 1978, 287; Mecca 1995, 8).

In May 1918, the secretary of war established the Army School of Nursing at Walter Reed Hospital in Washington, D.C., and in San Francisco to create more nurses for the war. The three-year course, centered in Army hospitals, attracted thousands of applicants, as the Army paid for all tuition, board, lodging, laundry, and textbooks. Although the war had already ended, five-hundred nurses graduated from the program in 1921. The Vas-

Sanitary Commission nurse with patients in Fredericksburg during the
Civil War. Courtesy of U.S. Army Center of Military History, Washington, D.C.

Contract nurses serving aboard a hospital ship during the Spanish-American War. *Courtesy of U.S. Army Center of Military History, Washington, D.C.*

American Red Cross worker giving chocolate to the wounded in France, 1918. *Courtesy of U.S. Army Center of Military History, Washington, D.C.*

Nurse Maxine Lykins of Albany, Missouri, digging a slit trench
minutes after landing in Anzio, Italy, 1944.
Courtesy of U.S. Army Center of Military History, Washington, D.C.

Air evacuation team leaving for overseas duty, 1944.
Courtesy of Virginia E. Garnett.

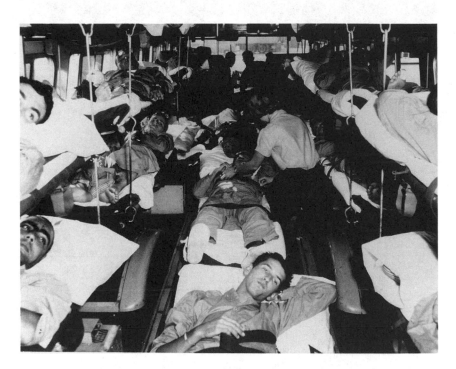

Tan Son Nhut, South Vietnam: Second Lieutenant Pat Hines checking safety belts aboard an ambulance bus taking patients to an aircraft for evacuation to Japan. *Courtesy of U.S. Air Force.*

sar Training Camp for Nurses, a three-month program of theoretical training to prepare women for entry into two-year-and-three-month programs
at selected nursing schools, was also developed in 1918 (Dolan 1978,
288–90; Donahue 1985, 399–402).

The peak strength of the Army and Navy Nurse Corps combined was more
than 23,000 nurses, with the Army Nurse Corps strength on Armistice Day,
11 November 1918, at 21,480 women and the Navy Nurse Corps at 1,551.
The Army Nurse Corps had expanded from 400 nurses and the Navy Nurse
Corps from 460 nurses since the beginning of the war eighteen months earlier. More than 10,000 nurses served overseas in Belgium, England, Italy,
Serbia, Hawaii, Puerto Rico, Siberia, and the Philippines. They worked in all
levels of hospitals, except for frontline aid stations, including mobile hospitals, hospital trains, hospital ships, and convalescent centers. In July 1918,
Congress authorized the nurses a monthly pay of $60. Many remained in Ger-
many with the occupation forces until the United States departed in 1923 or
aided with relief efforts in Asia after the war (Donahue 1985, 404–5, 407;
Shields 1981, 14, 16; Willenz 1983, 15; Holm 1992, 10; Dolan 1978, 287).

Although no military nurses died from enemy fire, 260 nurses died while
on active duty, many from pneumonia, meningitis, and flu. Decorations
awarded to Army nurses included the Distinguished Service Cross (a combat
medal second only to the Congressional Medal of Honor) to three nurses, the
Distinguished Service Medal (the highest noncombat award) to 23 nurses, the
French Croix de Guerre to 28 nurses, the British Royal Red Cross to 69 nurses,
and the British Military Medal to 2 nurses. Thirty-eight nurses remain buried
in U.S. cemeteries overseas (Holm 1992, 10; Donahue 1985, 407).

The Navy Nurse Corps was much smaller than the Army Nurse Corps, and
its nurses could be sent to overseas locations only where the Navy maintained facilities. The first Navy nurses assigned to transport duty sailed on
the USS *George Washington*, and the first Navy nurses to serve on a hospital ship
boarded the USS *Relief* in 1920. A total of 1,224 Navy nurses served in the
United States while 327 served overseas in Britain and France. The Navy
Cross, the highest decoration in the Navy, was awarded to four Navy nurses
during World War I. One of them, Lenah S. Higbee, second superintendent
of the Corps, was also the first woman for whom a combat ship, the de-
stroyer USS *Higbee*, was named (Holm 1992, 11; Donahue 1985, 407).

Nurses embodied for America an incredibly heroic and saintly role for
women throughout the war, increasing the respect accorded the nursing
profession and working women (Kalisch and Kalisch 1987, 49).

Between the World Wars: Military Nurses Receive Relative Rank

The military had learned during World War I that, although nurses supervised orderlies and corpsmen and were perceived to be on a level with officers, their lack of rank caused endless confusion and difficulty. On 4 June 1920, the National Defense Act rewarded military nurses for their heroic contributions during the war by providing them, at long last, with relative rank as officers from second lieutenant through major. Rank insignia on their uniforms was authorized, but nurses still did not receive the pay and allowances or other rights and privileges enjoyed by their male peers. On 30 June 1921, the Army Nurse Corps consisted of one major, four captains, 74 first lieutenants, and 772 second lieutenants. Further steps forward occurred on 13 May 1926, when nurses received retirement eligibility based on length of service and, on 20 June 1930, when they were authorized disability retirement. Social expectations for female nurses continued to be restrictive, however, as pregnant unmarried nurses or those who married while in the military received dishonorable discharges, a punishment usually reserved for serious criminal offenders (Holm 1992, 11; Donahue 1985, 331, 407–8; Shields 1981, 18–19).

The only military women's organization not demobilized after World War I were the Army and Navy Nurse Corps, although their numbers were considerably reduced. By 1935, the Navy Nurse Corps included only 332 women, smaller than at the beginning of World War I. Military nurses were more accepted than the women who had served in the women's military auxiliaries, because military nursing was finally viewed as "women's work" after long decades of opposition by men. A monument dedicated to Army and Navy nurses, entitled "Spirit of Nursing," was unveiled in 1938 in a plot reserved for military nurses at Arlington National Cemetery. The women's auxiliaries, with their typists, clerks, and ambulance drivers, though, were still perceived as a threat to male-dominated fields of the male-dominated military (Holm 1992, 16–17; Donahue 1985, 407, 432).

During the 1920s and 1930s, a military nurse earned a far better living than the average civilian woman. The government gave her room and board, medical care, and free laundry. She had access to graduate education and the opportunity to travel. On the eve of World War II, the average military nurse had been assigned to the Philippines, Alaska, Hawaii, Panama, or China. Her work was limited to an eight-hour day, giving her a lot of free time, and being outnumbered by men, she had more dates than she could handle. Military nurses were living it up and loving it. A shortage of nurses in the United States existed, however, as more civilians began using hospitals (Weatherford 1990, 3, 16).

World War II: Nurse Prisoners of War, Nurses on Beachheads, and Flight Nurses

On 8 September 1939, when a state of limited emergency was declared in the United States in response to the war in Europe, the Army Nurse Corps included 625 nurses and the Navy Nurse Corps 430. By April 1941, the Army Nurse Corps was recruiting seven-hundred women each month. On 27 May 1941, a state of national emergency was declared, and Reserve nurses were ordered to active duty. In the summer of 1941, Congress appropriated funds for graduate nurse refresher training and nurses' dormitories and classrooms. By December 1941, the Army Nurse Corps had expanded to 7,000 nurses and the Navy Nurse Corps to 787. By 30 June 1942, there were 12,475 Army nurses and nearly 1,800 Navy nurses on active duty. Almost a year after the United States entered the war, nurses remained the only women being mobilized (Weatherford 1990, 16; Tomblin 1993a, 33–34, 38; Dolan 1978, 306; Holm 1992, 45; Bellafaire n.d., 3, 6).

Since the Spanish-American War, the Philippines had been a quasi-colony of the United States. Almost a hundred Army and Navy nurses were assigned there. By 27 December 1941, the Japanese were advancing toward Manila from the north. Two Army nurses were taken prisoner. General Douglas MacArthur, commander of the U.S. Army Forces in the East, ordered 34 Army nurses to evacuate to Corregidor, a rock island about thirty miles to the southeast. Eleven Navy nurses were taken prisoner in January 1942 and removed on 8 March 1942 to Santo Tomas Internment Camp in Manila, where they provided nursing care for thirty-five hundred confined civilians until they were moved to Los Banos in May 1943 (Bellafaire n.d., 4–5; Weatherford 1990, 2; Frank 1988, 83–87; Tomblin 1993a, 38–39).

MacArthur ordered 50 Army nurses (and one Navy nurse) to depart for the Bataan Peninsula to establish two emergency hospitals to support the U.S. and Filipino forces. The Navy nurse stated that everyone worked from 7 A.M. until 10 P.M., with each nurse caring for two hundred or three hundred patients. Food, equipment, beds, medicine—all were in short supply.

By April, the full day's ration was a half cup of rice with a few pieces of mule meat. Patients shared beds, and nurses slept in triple-decker bamboo and rattan bunks under the trees. Malaria, dysentery, beriberi, and dengue fever ran rampant. On April 8, the Japanese were within several hundred yards of overrunning the hospitals when all 51 nurses were evacuated to Corregidor. Corregidor's hospital was built deep into the rock and provided safety from Japanese bombing. When surrender seemed imminent in late April, the 85 nurses were ordered to evacuate the island. Twenty-one reached Australia; the other 64 became Japanese prisoners and were sent to Santo Tomas (Weatherford 1990, 4–6; Bellafaire n.d., 5–6; Frank 1988, 84–87; Shields 1981, 20).

Five Navy nurses, training native nurses and corpsmen on Guam, became prisoners of war when the Japanese took over the island on 10 December 1941. On 10 January 1942, the nurses were sent to a prison camp in Zentsuji, Japan, and were released in June 1942 as exchange prisoners. The 1st Cavalry Division liberated the 66 Army nurses at Santo Tomas on 3 February 1945, after 32 to 37 months of internment, and the 11 Navy nurses at Los Banos on 23 February 1945, after 37 months of internment, and each was presented with the Bronze Star. In all, 82 Army and Navy nurses became prisoners of war in the Pacific in World War II (Tomblin 1993a, 39–40; Weatherford 1990, 6–7; Frank 1988, 83–87; Holm 1992, 45, 91, 97; Shields 1981, 21).

After the experience in Bataan, the Army realized that "nurses were not ethereal angels of mercy but human beings who had to have some of the same training given to male recruits to help them save their own lives" (Weatherford 1990, 7). In July 1943, nurses started attending a four-week training course after they were commissioned. They went on twenty-mile hikes with thirty-pound packs, chlorinated water, pitched tents, used camouflage, identified lethal chemicals, defended themselves from enemy attack, learned field sanitation, experienced the gas chamber, set up and dismantled hospitals, maintained a sterile hospital environment in sand and wind, and completed a seventy-five-yard live-fire, low-crawl course (Weatherford 1990, 7–8; Shields 1981, 24).

In the European theater, women nurses found themselves hitting the beachheads just hours or days after the landing force. Sixty Army nurses climbed off their ship and into assault boats, loaded with helmets, packs, gas masks, and canteens, and landed on the North African beach with assault troops on 8 November 1942, the day of invasion. They immediately started nursing in abandoned structures, struggling without electricity, running water, major medical supplies, beds, or adequate sleep. They donated blood, gave the patients their C-rations, and slept on the ground. Another 140 nurses waded ashore at Oran and followed the combat units as they moved. In February 1943, several units were trapped behind German lines, including nurses who insisted on staying until the patients could get out. One of the nurses, 1st Lt. Mary Ann Sullivan, received the Legion of Merit for valor when they finally escaped from Kasserine Pass under enemy fire (Bellafaire n.d., 9; Weatherford 1990, 9; Holm 1992, 80, 91; Shields 1981, 22).

The Allies invaded Sicily on 9 July 1943, and nurses arrived three days later with the 10th Field Hospital and 11th Evacuation Hospital in the midst of a German bombing raid, which confined them to trenches and foxholes for several days. Every twenty-four hours, nurses admitted three hundred patients and evacuated two hundred to North Africa. On 22 January 1944, the Allies landed on the Anzio beachhead, accompanied by two hundred nurses. By June 1944, 25,809 battle casualties, 4,245 accidental injuries, and 18,074 medically ill patients had been admitted into Anzio field and evacuation hospitals (Bellafaire n.d., 16, 18, 20; Holm 1992, 91).

On 6 June 1944, the Allies invaded Normandy. Four days later, nurses with the 42d and 45th Field Hospitals landed on the beachhead. They had to bury the dead in order to make room for beds. Nurses from the 12th Evacuation Hospital followed the Allies as they moved toward Germany, establishing operations near the Siegfried Line, setting up a new hospital in Rheims, starting an evacuation hospital in a field near the Argonne Forest, working out of a hospital in Nancy, and moving to Luxembourg by 1945. The 44th Evacuation Hospital, during the 3d Armored Division's final push into central Germany in April 1945, treated 1,348 casualties in fifty-six hours. The 77th Evacuation Hospital treated weak and malnourished American and British paratroopers who had been prisoners of war, as well as German prisoners of war. When Dachau was liberated, the nurses of the 116th and 127th Evacuation Hospitals had a ghastly job—treating the severely malnourished, ill, and diseased victims of the concentration camp who "clung to the nurses as their saviors" but who often died within weeks of being freed (Bellafaire n.d., 20–21, 23–24; Holm 1992, 91; Weatherford 1990, 11).

In the Pacific, Army nurses remained outside combat areas and moved forward only when Allied control was in place. In 1942, they were stationed in Hawaii, Australia, New Zealand, Fiji, New Caledonia, New Hebrides, and

New Guinea. Army nurses arrived on Guadalcanal in June 1944 and, in July 1944, one month after Americans seized control, landed on Saipan, where half the nurses became ill with dengue fever. On 20 October 1944, the United States invaded the Philippines; nine days later, nurses landed on Leyte Island and began providing nursing care within three hours. Nurses arrived on Guam in December 1944 and Tinian in January 1945. Army nurses staffed the hospital ship USS Comfort, which, while supporting the wounded from Okinawa, was hit by a kamikaze plane; six nurses were killed. Flight nurses stationed on Guam embarked on 273 missions, evacuating 5,529 patients. As the Okinawa campaign ended, 81 nurses landed with their hospital on Iwo Jima, taking refuge in caves and air raid shelters during air attacks. Because of the immense number of casualties, nurses in the Pacific often exercised responsibilities reserved for doctors in civilian hospitals (Bellafaire n.d., 24, 27–28; Tomblin 1993a, 41–43; and 1993b, 46).

Navy nurses were found in base hospitals and on hospital ships throughout the world, particularly in the Pacific. Although hospital ships encountered dangers from enemy torpedo attacks, nurses aboard reported that they enjoyed comfortable beds, good food, and interesting ports of call. They treated and evacuated thousands of casualties from Tarawa, Guadalcanal, Iwo Jima, Kwajelein, and Guam, often within hours or days of marine landings. Seven hospital ships evacuated the wounded from Okinawa in the midst of kamikaze raids; Relief and Solace were both hit. Navy flight nurses helped evacuate 11,771 patients by air from Okinawa. In contrast to Army nurses, the Navy nurses were required to teach and be managers as well as provide nursing care. Because of the presence of corpsmen, who did the most menial and routine tasks, Navy nurses were able to concentrate on skilled nursing (Tomblin 1993a, 41–48; and 1993b, 37–50; Weatherford 1990, 11–12).

Air evacuation was one of the most dramatic new developments during World War II, and both the Navy and the Army established flight nurse training programs. Students learned survival techniques in ocean, jungle, desert, and arctic environments; high-altitude effects; parachute drill; responses to air attack; and crash procedures. The first class of Army flight nurses graduated on 18 February 1943, and the Army began evacuating patients by air from North America that same month. An evacuation plane, with a flight nurse and corpsman as medical crew, needed only ten minutes to load twenty-five passengers. The flight nurse handled men with "shell shock," gaping stomach wounds, and half their faces shot off; gave hypodermics, oxygen, and plasma; checked vital signs; relieved pain; stopped bleeding; and dressed wounds. Five hundred Army flight nurses in thirty-one medical air evacuation squadrons evacuated 1,176,048 patients during the war, losing only 46 patients, but 17 flight nurses, a higher loss than experienced by nonflight nurses. Aircraft which carried supplies in and patients out were not allowed to display red crosses and were subject to air attack (Bellafaire n.d., 13–15; Shields 1981, 22; Donahue 1985, 416; Weatherford 1990, 12).

The Army Medical Department used a chain of evacuation in all theaters of operation. Mobile field and evacuation hospitals, housed in tents, could be set up and dismantled by nurses as they followed the combat units. A staff of eighteen nurses at each field hospital provided triage for up to 150 wounded carried in by litter bearers and ambulances and then sent them to evacuation hospitals, staffed by fifty-three nurses who stabilized and prepped for surgery up to 750 patients. Hospital ships, hospital trains, and aircraft transported patients from evacuation hospitals to station hospitals, where critically wounded patients received surgery and special treatments, or to general hospitals, where special laboratory tests, diagnoses, and therapy were carried out (Bellafaire n.d., 12–13).

In July 1943, Congress established the U.S. Cadet Nurse Corps, a thirty-month, government-funded training program to produce nurses. Tuition, fees, and uniforms were free, and students received monthly stipends in return for a pledge to serve where needed for the duration of the war on graduation. Although the war ended before any nurses graduated, the program was an enormous boost to the nursing profession, and 95 percent of all nursing students in the country enrolled. In addition, racial barriers were removed, providing opportunities for black women to attend nursing schools and join the Army or Navy Nurse Corps (Bellafaire n.d., 7; Dolan 1978, 306; Donahue 1985, 306, 414; Holm 1992, 108).

The War Department decided in December 1943 that the Army Nurse Corps had sufficient nurses and ordered the Red Cross to close its nationwide recruiting network. In spring 1994, the War Department reevaluated, in view of projected high casualties, and decided that the Army and Navy Nurse Corps each needed ten thousand more nurses. Newspaper editorials suggested that American nurses were "shirking their duty and avoiding military service," but when they tried to join up, no recruiting apparatus was available. On 6 January 1945, President Franklin Delano Roosevelt announced that eleven hospitals were deploying overseas without nurses, that the average nurse-to-patient ratio was 1 to 26 rather than 1 to 15, and that the nation had no recourse but to draft nurses. The Nurse Draft Bill, with an exemption for married women, quickly passed in the House of Representatives by a vote of 347 to 42. Thousands of nurses applied for military service in response to the draft threat, filling the requirements for the war in the Pacific. The war ended before the Senate took action on the bill, but, if it had lasted just one or two more months, women nurses would probably have been drafted (Bellafaire n.d., 8; Weatherford 1990, 19–20; Donahue 1985, 419–20; Holm 1992, 109).

Not until 1942 did Navy nurses receive relative rank. In the same year, Congress increased the Army nurse's highest relative rank to lieutenant colonel and granted pay and allowances equal to an officer without dependents. Married nurses were permitted to join the Army in 1942, and since 80 percent of all Navy nurse resignations resulted from unauthorized marriages, the Navy began accepting married women in 1944. On 22 June 1944, Roosevelt signed an executive order making the Army and Navy Nurse Corps integral parts of their services, granting the nurses then on active duty full pay and privileges and temporary commissions for the duration of the war plus six months (Shields 1981, 22, 24; Donahue 1985, 408; Weatherford 1990, 21; Dolan 1978, 307).

Medals, citations, and commendations were awarded to 1,619 military nurses (1 out of every 40 who served) for their meritorious service and bravery under fire. They received the Distinguished Service Medal, Silver Star, Distinguished Flying Cross, Soldier's Medal, Bronze Star, Air Medal, Legion of Merit, Army and Navy Commendation Medal, Purple Heart, and Gold Star. The first Army nurse killed in the war, 2d Lt. Ruth M. Gardiner, died in an air evacuation plane crash in July 1943; a hospital was named after her in Chicago. The first women to receive the Silver Star were 1st Lt. Mary Roberts, 2d Lt. Elaine Roe, 2d Lt. Virginia Rourke, and 2d Lt. Ellen Ainsworth (awarded posthumously) for evacuating forty-two patients during a German bombing raid at Anzio on 10 February 1944; six nurses perished during the German counteroffensive. The Army Nurse Corps lost the most nurses: 201 died during the war, mostly from disease, and 17 are buried overseas (Bellafaire n.d., 19, 31; Dolan 1978, 307; Donahue 1985, 416; Holm 1992, 92; Shields 1981, 25).

The valor of nurses was undeniable. About sixty Red Cross nurses (half of whom joined the Army after the United States entered the war) were en route to England when their ship was torpedoed; they spent twelve days drifting in lifeboats. Four nurses received the Purple Heart when the British ship carrying them to Italy on 13 September 1943 sank after a bombing attack. Flight nurse Reba Zitella Whittle was wounded and become a German prisoner of war at Stalag IXC for five months when her C-47 crashed behind enemy lines in September 1944. During the Battle of the Bulge, five Army nurses stayed with two hundred patients too weak to be evacuated until Germans were within hours of arriving (Weatherford 1990, 8–9; Bellafaire n.d., 14, 17–19, 22–23; Gruhzit-Hoyt 1995, 37–49).

The harrowing story of the "Balkan Nurses" is not well known. On 8 November 1943, an air evacuation plane carrying thirteen flight nurses and other medical crew crashed in Albania behind German lines. Partisan guerrillas escorted the survivors on a two-month, eight-hundred mile foot journey through mountains and severe snowstorms, where they suffered from frostbite, dysentery, jaundice, and pneumonia. Three nurses who had been separated at the crash spent five months behind enemy lines before they returned, with partisan help, via car, donkeys, and torpedo boat to Bari (Bellafaire n.d., 17).

The peak strength of the Army and Navy Nurse Corps combined reached almost 69,000. At the end of the war, 57,000 Army nurses and 12,000 Navy nurses were on active duty in more than 1,000 Army hospitals and 350 Naval installations. They served everywhere soldiers and sailors did, in more than fifty nations, including the Aleutians, Wales, Trinidad, Iran, China, Burma, India, Ireland, England, Solomon Islands, Newfoundland, Puerto Rico, Panama, Iceland, North Africa, Germany, France, Italy, Hawaii, New Zealand, Philippines, Guadalcanal, Tinian, Manus, Saipan, Efate, Espiritu Santo, Guam, Tulagi, New Caledonia, New Hebrides, and New Guinea. In addition, they served on twelve hospital ships, on hospital trains, and on air evacuation planes. Their presence improved morale, because soldiers knew they would receive skilled nursing care. The fighting men were so grateful that hundreds signed a letter to the *Stars and Stripes* newspaper in Europe on 21 October 1944, thanking the women for volunteering to be there. Out of the 274,405 registered nurses in the United States, 75,000 applied to join the military, a higher percentage than any other skill or profession except perhaps doctors (Tomblin 1993b, 50; Shields 1981, 25; Holm 1992, 91–92; Donahue 1985, 395, 415; Gruhzit-Hoyt 1995, 14; Bellafaire n.d., 16).

On return from the war, women found themselves eligible for all veterans' benefits, including the new G.I. Bill. On 16 April 1947, the Army-Navy Nurse Act established the Army and Navy Nurse Corps as permanent staff corps within their respective services and authorized permanent commissions for women up to lieutenant colonel (Army) and commander (Navy). The chief of each Corps would hold a temporary commission in the rank of colonel or captain, the highest rank for a military woman. On 1 July 1949, the Air Force Nurse Corps was established when the Army and Air Force agreed to separate their medical activities. To form the nucleus of the Air Force Nurse Corps, 1,199 nurses, primarily World War II veterans, transferred from the Army Nurse Corp (Donahue 1985, 331, 408, 418–19; Dolan 1978, 307; Shields 1981, 28, 31; Holm 1992, 108; Bellafaire n.d., 31).

Korea: Nurses in the MASH

When war broke out on 25 June 1950, Capt. Viola B. McConnell was the only Army nurse stationed in Korea, and she helped evacuate seven hundred Americans to Japan, receiving a Bronze Star for her efforts. The first combat units landed in Korea on 1 July 1950, and 57 Army nurses arrived in Pusan on 5 July. They immediately established their hospital and, on the following day, began receiving casualties. On 8 July, 12 of the nurses moved with a Mobile Army Surgical Hospital (MASH) to the perimeter at Taejon. The Army Nurse Corps had 3,460 nurses on active duty on 15 July 1950, and by August, 100 nurses were stationed in Korea. Within a year, the number of Army nurses expanded to 5,397, with 540 serving in twenty-five separate facilities in Korea, supporting troops during amphibious landings, the advance toward the Yalu River, the retreat from the Chinese, and the effort to push the Chinese north of the thirty-eighth parallel. Most nurses were World War II veterans and had joined the reserves at the end of the war, not imagining that they would be called up again so soon. No nurses died from enemy action, but Maj. Genevieve Smith died in a plane crash en route to be chief nurse in Korea (Donahue 1985, 421; Holm 1992, 149–50; Shields 1981, 33–35).

Of 77,788 wounded men during Korea, only 1,957 died, thanks in part to the MASH and air evacuation. A MASH, a sixty-bed hospital with ten doctors, twelve nurses, and ninety corpsmen, could move, set up in any location, and be ready to treat several hundred patients within hours. With its own helicopter detachment to transport the critically wounded, the MASH became the first hospital in the chain of evacuation for the soldiers and was instrumental in improving care and morale. The Air Force Nurse Corps received its first major challenge carrying out air evacuation in Korea. In one day, 5 December 1950, air evacuation lifted 3,925 patients, and by the end of the war, 350,000 had been evacuated. Air Force nurses served throughout Korea until 27 July 1953 (Gabriel and Metz 1992, 257; Donahue 1985, 422, 426).

After Korea: Military Nurses Aid in Humanitarian Missions

The government established another program to recruit nurses on 30 December 1953, called the Registered Nurse Student Program. Registered nurses in their final year to obtain a bachelor's or master's in nursing could receive financial assistance in the form of pay and allowances in the grade in which they were commissioned, thereby obligating them to serve two years on active duty as a Reserve officer. The Army Student Nurse Program, beginning 18 April 1956, was another recruiting attempt that provided pay and allowances of an entry-level enlisted person during training, a commission to second lieutenant, and the obligation to serve two or three years on active duty (Shields 1981, 37, 40).

In 1956, the first Army Nurse Corps officers other than the chief of the Corps were promoted to the temporary grade of colonel in the Army of the United States, and in March 1958, the first women were promoted to the permanent grade of colonel. Men were allowed to join the Army Nurse Corps in 1955 (Shields 1981, 41, 43; Donahue 1985, 408).

During the years following Korea, nurses continued to serve around the world, mostly on humanitarian missions. They nursed refugees in November 1956 during the Hungarian uprising; supported ten thousand American troops in Lebanon during the crisis in 1958; aided earthquake and tidal wave victims in Chile in 1960; were ordered to active duty on 1 October 1961 for the Berlin crisis; assisted hurricane victims in Texas in 1961 from hospital ships; helped earthquake victims in Iran in September 1962; nursed in Honduras in 1962 to combat a gastroenteritis epidemic; deployed worldwide during the Cuban missile crisis in 1962; assisted earthquake victims in Yugoslavia in 1963 and Alaska in 1964; and supported military troops in the Dominican Republic from 1965 to 1966 (Shields 1981, 41, 44–47, 51–52, 54; Holm 1992, 226).

Vietnam War: Military Nurses Serve from Beginning to End

The first nurses arrived in Vietnam on 29 April 1956. Maj. Frances K. Smith, her sister Maj. Helen D. Smith, and Maj. Jane Becker were assigned to temporary duty with the U.S. Military Assistance Advisory Group (MAAG) (Vietnam) to train South Vietnamese nurses and provide medical care to MAAG personnel. In March 1962, a contingent of 10 Army nurses with the 8th Field Hospital arrived in Nha Trang to support Army personnel. On 17 May 1962, 11 Army nurses arrived for duty in Korat, Thailand. By 1965, Army and Navy nurses were also stationed in Saigon and Soc Trang, Vietnam. When the U.S. military buildup began in earnest, the numbers of medical personnel increased. Army nurses arrived in Saigon in April 1965 as part of the 3d Field Hospital. Air Force flight nurses began arriving in 1965 with the 9th Aeromedical Evacuation Group in Saigon, evacuating patients to Japan, Okinawa, the Philippines, and the United States, and clinical nurses arrived in Cam Ranh Bay and other bases in Vietnam and Thailand. In October 1965, the hospital ship USS *Repose* with 29 Navy nurses aboard sailed in for duty. By 31 December 1965, 215 Army nurses were serving in Vietnam; by February 1966, 37 Air Force nurses had arrived. Another 29 Navy nurses arrived in 1966 on the hospital ship USS *Sanctuary* (Shields 1981, 41, 49, 55; Donahue 1985, 427; Holm 1992, 226).

The total strength of the Army Nurse Corps in August 1963 was 2,928 nurses, assigned to Alaska, Hawaii, Japan, Puerto Rico, Korea, Thailand, Okinawa, Turkey, Iran, Ethiopia, Germany, France, and Italy, in addition to Vietnam, but each military branch recruited nursing students for Vietnam. The Walter Reed Army Institute of Nursing (WRAIN) began offering financial assistance for a four-year nursing program on 1 May 1964 to women who would then come on active duty for three years. On 15 December 1964, married applicants could finally receive commissions in the Army. Army Reserve nurses were ordered to active duty on 11 April 1968, with assignment in Vietnam. Also by 1968, 280 Army nurses were assigned to the Medical Command in Japan. Most military nurses volunteered for Vietnam, for the challenge, out of patriotism, or from a sense of adventure (Shields 1981, 51–53, 57–58; Marshall 1987, 6).

Nurses soon learned that Vietnam was a totally different war than World War II. Booby traps, punji sticks, claymore mines, high-velocity bullets, napalm, and white phosphorus resulted in shredded bodies and patients who endured agonizing treatments. Chinook helicopters could evacuate one hundred soldiers within minutes of being wounded and fly them immediately to nearby hospitals, creating increased casualty loads of patients who often would not survive. Nurses hated "playing God" during triage—setting aside the men expected to die, the "expectants," and treating the more survivable cases. Nurses did emergency tracheotomies so men would not choke on their own blood; separated burned clothing from burned skin, which often appeared the same; had men's feet come off in their hands when they removed their boots; and found live grenades in stomachs. Rockets and mortars fell around them as they worked, sometimes up to seventy-two hours without rest. They had not been trained to treat the typhoid, tuberculosis, malaria, dengue fever, and bubonic plague of patients in their care, nor were they prepared for the multitude of drug addicts. Nurses in Vietnam were noncombatants in a combat situation and saw more death and destruction than the average soldier. A few years older than the men they served, nurses became their mother figures, "frontline therapists," and sometimes confessors—often they were the first to deal with a soldier and the last to be with him as he died. These responsibilities created enormous stress for nurses, who, although patriotic volunteers who had sought the challenge of war nursing, began to question the seemingly pointless waste of human life, particularly of nineteen-year-old boys (Freedman and Rhoads, 1987, 1–5; Marshall 1987, 6–7; Smith 1992, 53; Holm 1992, 106, 225, 232–33).

Some men arrived in hospitals amazed at finding American women so close to the front lines. *Repose* and *Sanctuary* cruised the Vietnamese coast between Da Nang and the Demilitarized Zone (DMZ). Army nurses could be found at Quang Tri, within thirty-five kilometers of the DMZ. Although women worked six or seven days a week, they were always willing to go to a firebase or to Vietnamese villages under the Medical Civil Action Program. On occasion, the Army wanted to evacuate nurses from areas under fire, and invariably, they refused. Eventually, hospitals in Vietnam became fixed facilities when the road network could not be secured. Army nurses worked in field hospitals, surgical hospitals, evacuation hospitals, MASH units, convalescent hospitals, and hospitals for prisoners of war. They also served in the new Medical Unit, Self-contained, Transportable (MUST) hospital, consisting of inflatable rubber shelters with electricity, air conditioning, heat, running water, and waste disposal. The Army established all-male nursing units in 1966 and tried to assign only men in combat areas. The concept failed, however, because the male patients wanted female nurses (Holm 1992, 227, 232; Marshall 1987, 5; Donahue 1985, 431).

Soldiers were moved so quickly and efficiently through the medical system, thanks to the dedicated nurses, the air evacuation system, and the hospital ships, that only 2.6 percent of the 133,447 wounded patients between 1965 and 1970 died. Air Force nurses worked out of casualty clearing stations and evacuation hospitals, as well as being stationed in Da Nang and Cam Ranh. By the end of the war, 54 Air Force flight nurses were working in Southeast Asia, picking up patients in Vietnam and Thailand and transporting them to the Philippines, Japan, and Okinawa. A flight nurse's day was extremely long, starting at 4:30 A.M. in the Philippines, readying the plane with medical supplies, flying four hours to Vietnam, loading casualties, enduring the return flight, and offloading patients to waiting ambulances. 1st Lt. Jane A. Lombardi received the Bronze Star for loading thirty-seven patients, twenty-six of whom were on litters, onto a C-141 at Da Nang under enemy fire. Another 67 Air Force flight nurses with the Military Airlift Command escorted patients to the United States in C-141 airplanes set up like hospital wards. Flight nurses often assumed the roles of doctors, giving blood transfusions and intravenous feedings and declaring medical emergencies. In the Air Force, nurses believed that flight duty was the ultimate achievement. The Army had 116 air ambulances, each with five to seven UH-1E helicopters that could carry six to nine patients each, and every division had its own medical detachment with "dust-off" medevac helicopters (Holm 1992, 233–34; Gabriel and Metz 1992, 259–60).

Approximately 6,250 military nurses served in Vietnam from March 1962 to March 1973, accounting for 80 percent of all military women present. Army, Navy, and Air Force nurses (the Marines had no nurses), in addition to caring for U.S. military personnel, provided medical care to Vietnamese civilians and, on occasion, to Viet Cong prisoners in special hospital wards. All the women received combat pay, and many were awarded combat medals. The Purple Heart was given to each of four Navy nurses who were injured in a Viet Cong bombing. The Vietnam Veterans Memorial lists the names of the eight women (seven Army and one Air Force) who died during the war: 1st Lt. Sharon Ann Lane, 2d Lt. Elizabeth Ann Jones, 2d Lt. Carol Ann Elizabeth Drazba, Lt. Col. Annie Ruth Graham, Capt. Eleanor Grace Alexander, 1st Lt. Hedwig Diane Orlowski, 2d Lt. Pamela Dorothy Donovan, and Capt. Mary Therese Klinker. Six died in helicopter crashes in 1966 and 1967 and one in a plane crash in 1975. Lane was killed by a Viet Cong rocket attack on her hospital in 1969 and was awarded the Purple Heart and Bronze Star posthumously (Marshall 1987, 4–5; Willenz 1983, 35; Saywell 1986, 226; Holm 1992, 7, 228, 242; Shields 1981, 59, 62; Freedman and Rhoads 1987, 1; Van Devanter 1983, 78).

Conclusion

Women have always seen a need to care for men in battle. At first, they followed their husbands to war and cared for them and their compatriots. Then a few were hired by the Army expressly to nurse soldiers. With each successive war, more nurses found themselves on or near the battlefield, although male military nursing continued to predominate in peacetime. In the Civil War, army nurses encountered prejudice and harassment from men who did not welcome their presence. The contributions of women nurses to the medical care in the Crimea and the Civil War led to the establishment of formal nursing schools and the rise of nursing as a profession. Formally trained nurses served as contract nurses in the Spanish-American War, laying the foundation for the Army and Navy Nurse Corps. The military could at last provide trained nurses on short notice when it entered World War I. Women began working more outside the home and developing careers along with independence. With women in the military as nurses, the way was open for women to join in other roles, and the women's auxiliaries were born. The military nurse during World War II was a role model to thousands of young girls, who entered nursing in droves. Nursing became a respectable profession, leaving the memory of Dickens's Sairy Gump far behind.

Eventually, military nurses became part of the military establishment. Their presence in Korea and Vietnam was, on the whole, accepted and desired. The long road they had traveled to reach this point, however, was virtually forgotten. Women in the auxiliaries and women's services had their own battles to fight for integration and inclusion and did not seem to remember the groundwork that had been laid by military nurses. The newest generation of women in the military do not even think of military nurses as soldiers, indicating a severe lack in the military of educating women about their own history. This loss of institutional knowledge has had ramifications during debates about the roles of women in combat, whether in the media, before Congress, or by the public, because the stories of military nurses who have been prisoners of war, killed by enemy fire, shipped home in body bags, denied privacy, and been on the front lines rarely surface. Women find themselves fighting the same misconceptions over and over again even though there is a wealth of history on which to draw.

For many years, "most of the nurses did not see their activities as significant in a historical sense; the selflessness of nurses' training was so inbred that they made little attempt during or since [World War II] to draw attention to their record. The result is that they have largely been forgotten, and debate today about the possibility of women in combat generally takes place in a vacuum that is ignorant of the precedents" (Weatherford 1990, 23). This statement is as true of nurses of the Civil War period and Vietnam era as it is of World War II. Despite women veterans' success in building the Vietnam Women's Memorial and the current drive for the Women in Military Service for America Memorial, the public does not remember their sacrifices or contributions. Men, in particular, find it incomprehensible that women served in wars, in combat conditions, and on battlefields. Since the history of women military nurses is not well known, opponents have been successful in presenting frightening arguments about keeping women out of combat. Yet when the past contributions of women military nurses, the conditions in which they served, and their attitudes at the front and under fire are reviewed, one realizes that women have already handled every situation and that the public can live with the circumstances in which its women are placed.

Nurses have bound the wounds of this nation from its inception and continue to do so today. Wherever our soldiers, sailors, airmen, and marines go, our nurses follow—usually without much fanfare. Military nurses have been in combat and can expect always to be in combat. They are the "invisible" soldiers.

REFERENCES

Bellafaire, Judith A. n.d. *The Army Nurse Corps: A Commemoration of World War II Service.* Washington, D.C.: Center of Military History.

Brocket, L. P. and Mary C. Vaughan. 1993. *Women at War: A Record of Their Patriotic Contributions, Heroism, Toils, and Sacrifice during the Civil War.* Philadelphia: Zeigler, McCurdy; Boston, R. H. Curran, 1867. Reprint, Stamford, Conn.: Longmeadow Press.

Bullough, Vern L., Olga Maranjian Church, and Alice P. Stein. 1988. *American Nursing: A Biographical Dictionary.* New York: Garland.

Cosmas, Graham A. 1994. *An Army for Empire: The United States Army in the Spanish-American War.* Columbia: University of Missouri Press, 1971. Reprint. Shippensburg, Pa.: White Mane.

Cosner, Shaaron. 1988. *War Nurses.* New York: Walker.

Crawley, Martha L. 1989. "The Science of Right Living: The Navy Medical Department in the Progressive Era." Ph.D. dissertation, George Washington University.

Culpepper, Marilyn Mayer. 1991. *Trials and Triumphs: Women of the American Civil War*. East Lansing: Michigan State University Press.

Denney, Robert E. 1994. *Civil War Medicine: Care and Comfort of the Wounded*. New York: Sterling.

Denver, John P., and Maria C. Dever. 1995. *Women and Military: Over One Hundred Notable Contributors, History to Contemporary*. Jefferson, N.C.: McFarland.

De Pauw, Linda Grant. 1982. *Seafaring Women*. Boston: Houghton Mifflin.

Dock, Lavinia L. and Isabel Maitland Stewart. 1925. *A Short History of Nursing: From the Earliest Times to the Present Day*. 2d ed. New York: G. P. Putnam's Sons.

Dolan, Josephine A. 1978. *Nursing in Society: A Historical Perspective*. 14th ed. Philadelphia: W. B. Saunders.

Donahue, M. Patricia. 1985. *Nursing, the Finest Art: An Illustrated History*. St. Louis: C. V. Mosby.

Frank, Mary E. V. 1988. "Army and Navy Nurses Held as Prisoners of War during World War II." *Minerva: Quarterly Report on Women and the Military* 6, 2:82–88.

Freedman, Dan, and Jacqueline Rhoads, eds. 1987. *Nurses in Vietnam: The Forgotten Veterans*. Austin: Texas Monthly Press.

Gabriel, Richard A. and Karen S. Metz. 1992. *A History of Modern Medicine*. Vol. 2: *From the Renaissance through Modern Times*. Contributions in Military Studies. no. 125. Westport, Conn.: Greenwood Press.

Gruhzit-Hoyt, Olga. 1995. *They Also Served: American Women in World War II*. New York: Carol Publishing Group.

Holm, Jeanne. 1992. *Women in the Military: An Unfinished Revolution*. Rev. ed. Novato, Calif.: Presidio Press.

Kalisch, Philip A., and Beatrice J. Kalisch. 1987. *The Changing Image of the Nurse*. Menlo Park, Calif.: Addison-Wesley.

Kerber, Linda K. 1980. *Women of the Republic: Intellect and Ideology in Revolutionary America* Chapel Hill: University of North Carolina Press.

LaForte, Robert S., and Ronald E. Marcello. 1991. *Remembering Pearl Harbor: Eyewitness Accounts by U.S. Military Men and Women*. Wilmington, Del.: Scholarly Resources.

Marshall, Kathryn. 1987. *In the Combat Zone: An Oral History of American Women in Vietnam, 1966–1975*. Boston: Little, Brown.

Massey, Mary Elizabeth. 1994. *Bonnet Brigades*. New York: Alfred A. Knopf, 1966. Reprint, Lincoln: University of Nebraska Press.

Mecca, Jo-Anne. 1995. "'Neither Fish, Flesh, nor Fowl': The World War I Army Nurse" *Minerva: Quarterly Report on Women and the Military* 13, 2:1–19.

Meier, Louisa. 1991. *The Healing of an Army, 1777–1778*. Norristown, Pa.: Historical Society of Montgomery County.

Naythons, Matthew. 1993. *The Face of Mercy: A Photographic History of Medicine at War*. New York: Random House.

Norman, Elizabeth M. 1990. *Women at War: The Story of Fifty Military Nurses Who Served in Vietnam*. Philadelphia: University of Pennsylvania Press.

Oates, Stephen B. 1994. *A Woman of Valor: Clara Barton and the Civil War*. New York: Free Press.

A Piece of My Heart: The Stories of Twenty-Six American Women Who Served in Vietnam. 1986. Told to Keith Walker. Novato, Calif.: Presidio Press.

Redmond, Juanita. 1984. *I Served on Bataan*. Philadelphia: Lippincott, 1943. Reprint, New York: Garland.

Reverby, Susan M. 1987. *Ordered to Care: The Dilemma of American Nursing, 1850–1945*. Cambridge: Cambridge University Press.

Samuelson, Nancy B. 1987. "Mother Bickerdyke: She Outranked Everybody but God." *Minerva: Quarterly Report on Women and the Military* 5, 2:111–25.

Saywell, Shelley. 1986. *Women in War: From World War II to El Salvador*. Markham, Canada: Penguin, Reprint, New York: Penguin.

Schneider, Carl J., and Dorothy Schneider. 1991. *Into the Breach: American Women Overseas in World War I*. New York: Viking Press.

Shields, Elizabeth A., ed. 1981. *Highlights in the History of the Army Nurse Corps*. Washington, D.C.: Center of Military History.

Smith, Nina B. 1988. "Men and Authority: The Union Army Nurse and the Problem of Power." *Minerva: Quarterly Report on Women and the Military* 6, 4:25–41.

Smith, Winnie. 1992. *American Daughter Gone to War: On the Front Lines with an Army Nurse in Vietnam*. New York: William Morrow.

Spiegel, Allen D., and Andrea M. Spiegel. 1994. "Civil War Doctress Mary: Only Woman to Win Congressional Medal of Honor." *Minerva: Quarterly Report on Women and the Military* 12, 3:24–35.

Spruill, Julia Cherry. 1972. *Women's Life and Work in the Southern Colonies*. Chapel Hill: University of North Carolina Press, 1938. Reprint, New York: W. W. Norton.

Stivers, Reuben Elmore. 1975. *Privateers and Volunteers: The Men and Women of Our Reserve Naval Forces, 1766 to 1866*. Annapolis: Naval Institute Press.

Straubing, Harold Elk, comp. 1993. *In Hospital and Camp: The Civil War through the Eyes of Its Doctors and Nurses*. Harrisburg, PA.: Stackpole.

Tomblin, Barbara B. 1993a. "Beyond Paradise: The U.S. Navy Corps in the Pacific in World War II (Part One)." *Minerva: Quarterly Report on Women and the Military* 11, 1:33–53.

———. 1993b. "Beyond Paradise: The U.S. Navy Corps in the Pacific in World War II (Part Two)." *Minerva: Quarterly Report on Women and the Military* 11, 3/4:37–55.

Van Devanter, Lynda, with Christopher Morgan. 1983. *Home before Morning: The Story of an Army Nurse in Vietnam*. New York: Beaufort.

Weatherford, Doris. 1990. *American Women and World War II*. New York: Facts on File.

Willenz, June A. 1983. *Women Veterans: America's Forgotten Heroines*. New York: Continuum.

Brenda L. Moore

From Underrepresentation to Overrepresentation:

African American Women

Whenever I mention research I am doing on African American women who served overseas during World War II, my listeners almost invariably reply, "I didn't know black women served in the military during World War II!"

The fact is that as early as the American Revolution, African American women supported military troops as cooks, laundresses, seamstresses, and nurses. Virtually every history book on African Americans documents slave and abolitionist Harriet Tubman's service as a spy for Union troops during the American Civil War. But Tubman was not the only African American woman to participate actively in the Civil War. In her book *Reminiscences*, Susie King Taylor tells of her experiences maintaining military equipment and nursing wounded men who were assigned to the First Carolina Volunteers, the first Negro regiment organized by the Union Army (Taylor 1968). Contributions made by countless other black women during the Civil War, many of whom were promised freedom from slavery as compensation for their services, remain undocumented (see U.S. DOD 1991, 137). In subsequent years, thirty-two African American women, serving as nurses during the Spanish-American War helped the United States rise to the status of imperialist power. Initially rejecting the services of African American women, the military later recruited them—primarily because of the misconception that blacks were immune to typhoid fever, a disease that killed many of the soldiers who fought in that war. During World War I, some African American women performed military duties to release men for combat, and others served in the Nurse Corps (U.S. DOD 1991, 140). African American women have served this country in every war.

Military organizations have consistently reflected the larger society, including its race and gender norms, which for more than a hundred and fifty years justified the exclusion of women and racial minorities from regular military service. Protecting the community through military service has historically been viewed as the responsibility of full citizens, individuals who possess such rights as owning property, participating in the exercise of political power, and sharing in the nation's economic wealth and security.[1] For decades, full citizenship in the United States, including the duty of national defense, was reserved for white men. This policy of exclusion was part of the code of local state militias that predated World War I, as well as the nation's first large, standing, federal army, authorized by the National Defense Act of 1916.[2] Thus, women and minorities have been excluded from active participation in the defense of the nation until a crisis erupted, and then they have been used as white men saw fit. Historically, African American women have willingly shared the burden of national defense out of a sense of moral obligation to the country but also in an attempt to demonstrate their worthiness for full citizenship. Their efforts were often in vain, however, because the services of women and minorities were forgotten as soon as the conflict was resolved.

World War II: A Turning Point

World War II created fundamental changes in military race and gender policies. Actually, racial policies were modified even before the United States entered the war, through the Selective Service Training Act of 1940. While prohibiting race discrimination against male volunteers and draftees, nevertheless this act upheld the norm of racial segregation by specifying that "there would be no intermingling between the races" (Lee 1966, 76). The policy further held that the number of "Negroes" would not exceed their percentage in the civilian population (Lee 1966).[3] Women, on the other hand, did not become members of the American armed forces until after Japan bombed Pearl Harbor. The Women's Army Auxiliary Corps (WAAC), established in May 1942, was converted to the Women's Army Corps (WAC) in 1943, giving women full Army status.[4] Both the Selective Service

Training Act and the act creating the WAAC were necessary before African American women could serve in the U.S. military.[5]

Following the War Department's lead, the Navy established its Women Accepted for Volunteer Emergency Service (WAVES) in July 1942; the Marine Corps opened its doors to Euro-American women in February 1943. African American women, however, were not accepted into the Marine Corps during the war at all (Johnson 1974, 33–41); they were authorized to enter the Navy only in December 1944, as a result of a direct order from President Franklin Delano Roosevelt. Fewer than one hundred African American women served in the Navy, the first three of whom began their training at the Naval Reserve Midshipmen's School at Northampton, Massachusetts, in November 1944 and graduated that December. Black members of the WAVES served in racially integrated units, and according to Mildred McAfee Horton, former director of the WAVES, racial integration was accomplished without incident (Horton 1971, 44–49).

In contrast to the WAVES, the Women's Army Auxiliary Corps admitted black women from the time of its inception. According to War Department policy, African American Waacs (members of the WAAC) were to serve in racially segregated facilities, and their numbers were not to exceed 10.6 percent of the WAAC/WAC (the proportion of African American women in the general population). Forty African Americans were among the first 440 to graduate from Officer Candidate Training at Fort Des Moines, Iowa, on 29 August 1942. These women were selected from a pool of college graduates. Approximately 850 African American Wacs served with the Six Triple Eighth Central Postal Directory Battalion (6888th) in England and France in 1945 (Moore 1996). That battalion was commanded by Major Charity E. Adams of Columbia, South Carolina, a twenty-seven-year-old who interrupted her graduate studies at Ohio State University to enter the first WAAC Officer Candidate Training class in 1942. The 6888th was the only African American WAC unit to serve overseas during World War II.[6]

African American Waacs/Wacs came from all walks of life, ranged in age from eighteen to fifty, and entered the military from every region of the nation. Some of them were reared in racially segregated communities of the South; others grew up in ethnically diverse neighborhoods in the North and Midwest (Moore 1996, 93). Some were the daughters of ministers, schoolteachers, and technicians; others were children of tobacco field hands, farmers, and domestic workers. Before entering the military, a few black Waacs/Wacs had completed college and had worked as schoolteachers (one of the few professional occupations open to educated African American women in the 1930s and 1940s); others had far fewer educational opportunities (Moore 1996, 89). War Department documents reveal that in May 1943, 66 percent of black women recruits scored in the lowest aptitude category on the military's aptitude test, compared to 15 percent of white women recruits in that category (Treadwell 1954, 593).

These statistics are not surprising in light of the racial discrepancies then characteristic of U.S. occupational and educational institutions. As late as the mid-nineteenth century, for example, it was illegal in some parts of the country for African Americans to be educated. Even during World War II, African Americans had limited access to educational and economic institutions and were vulnerable to social injustice and political exclusion (Myrdal 1944; Wilson 1980; Lieberson 1980). The African American population was still concentrated in the southern region of the country, where, in many areas, they had been disenfranchised since Reconstruction (Franklin and Moss 1988; Garraty 1975). African American women were virtually excluded from any prestigious occupation. According to the 1940 U.S. Census, approximately 4 percent of African American women in the labor force were professionals (teachers, medical doctors, lawyers, etc.), while the majority of African American women were domestic workers, farm laborers, and service workers such as beauticians, lodginghouse keepers, janitors, waitresses, and midwives. These are some of the characteristics of the civilian world that African American women left to join the Army (Moore 1996, 84–86).

A central factor in the decision of many African American women to join the military was the expectation of greater educational and occupational opportunities when the war was over. For others, participating in the struggle to "make the world safe for democracy" seemed like the right thing to do, a response to the slogan, "Uncle Sam Needs You." Before the war ended, there were 6,500 African American Waacs/Wacs, 120 of whom were officers (Johnson 1974, 6, 15).

A major source of tension for the African American woman serving in the Army was the War Department's policy of racial segregation, as well as problems associated with inappropriate assignments and inferior treatment. Regardless of their education, skills, and talents, black officers in senior grades were never given positions of authority over white officers junior to them. For the most part, black officers were narrowly assigned to work as company officers in all-black units and seldom attained even the rank of captain (Putney 1992, 134–35). In December 1943, 4 percent (103) of all African American Wacs were officers (in comparison, 10 percent [5,753] of all white Wacs were officers) (Treadwell 1954, Tables 1, 10, 11). The highest-ranking female black officers during the war years were Majors Charity Adams and Harriet West. Adams, battalion commander of the 6888th, was promoted to lieutenant colonel in December 1945, three months before she was discharged (Moore 1993). In comparison, the highest-ranking white female officers were Colonel Oveta Hobby, the WAC director, followed by approximately twenty-eight lieutenant colonels and fifty-seven majors (Treadwell 1954, Tables 1, 10, 11).

In addition to having limited promotional opportunities, the African American Wac officer was often socially isolated and deprived of access to many recreational facilities, including the officer's club. In her published memoirs, Charity Adams Earley reveals that when she was stationed at Fort Des Moines, she was severely reprimanded by a white male officer for going to the officer's club. Earley recalls that he addressed her as follows:

> So you are the Major Adams, the negra officer who went into the officers club last night. I don't think any colored person has ever been a guest there before. What were you doing there? Who had the nerve to invite you there? I don't believe in race mixing, and I don't intend to be a part of it. I understand that you are from South Carolina. Well, I am too, and that makes it worse. I'll never accept whites and coloreds mixing socially, but I think that I might be able to ignore it if you came from any other state. I can't stand having a negra from the same state that I come from socializing with the same people I do. Don't let being an officer go to your head; you are still colored and I want you to remember that. You people have to stay in your place. (Earley 1989, 107–8)

The problem was exacerbated by the limited number of black male officers, combined with the military's nonfraternization policy, which forbade Wac officers to date enlisted men. Some black Wac officers were prosecuted for violating this policy (Putney 1992, 129).

Because of the Army's policy of racial segregation, many qualified African American women refused to join the WAC, and some African American Wacs got angry and resigned, as indicated in the following statement by Private Ann Aikens:

I was sworn in the WAC on the 5th of February, 1943, and received basic training at Fort Des Moines. Conditions on the post were pretty fair. We only had segregated service clubs. After I completed my training I was sent to Fort Clark, Texas. . . . When I went to the movies I met Jim Crow. . . . San Antonio was the nearest town and there we were barred from all recreation centers. . . . From there I went to Camp Gruber, Okla., in June 1944. This camp was definitely not one for colored as provisions had been made for white Wacs only. . . . The morale of our group became very low. . . . We were finally sent to Fort Sam Houston, Texas. . . . Civilians employed at the depot made it very unpleasant for us. . . . We were not allowed to work at the hospital (Brooks General). . . . Until we are able to live together as a people, colored units should be sheltered from the inconveniences of the south. (Cited in Moore 1996, 77–78).

Other African American women remained in uniform and resisted unfair and unequal treatment. Sometimes African American Wacs protested inferior job assignments, claiming that they were not assigned to military jobs but given menial tasks instead. Although the War Department often asserted that because a large number of Negro women scored low on the military's standardized placement test they were unassignable, many African American Waacs/Wacs demonstrated that because of racial biases, they were not assigned to occupations for which they were qualified. One such case took place at Fort Deven's Lovell General Hospital, where four black Wac orderlies went on strike in March 1945, maintaining that although they had been trained as medics, a white male commanding officer ordered them to "mop walls, scrub floors, and do all the dirty work" (cited in Moore 1996, 78). The women were court-martialed and initially sentenced to dishonorable discharge and one year of hard labor. After a thorough investigation spurred by black activist groups and three congressmen, it was decided that the court was improperly convened and the women were reinstated (Moore 1996, 78; Putney 1992, 61–65).

Another act of resistance against racial discrimination was the case of WAC Band No. 2.[7] Because black Waacs/Wacs were prohibited from joining the (white) WAC band at Fort Des Moines, they formed their own band in August 1943. WAC Band No. 2, consisting of twenty-six Negro women, soon gained national acclaim for their performances. On 18 July 1944, the band was deactivated by military officials, who claimed that it was unauthorized. Members of the band, other African American Wacs, several black political organizations, and the black press appealed to the War Department and directly to President Roosevelt. The protesters successfully exposed the blatant racism in a policy that prohibited African American Wacs both from joining the white WAC band and from organizing a band of their own. Consequently, by August the War Department reversed its decision to eliminate the Negro WAC band.

African American Waacs/Wacs continued to raise racial issues and receive support from civilian organizations. Throughout the war religious and political organizations such as the National Association for the Advancement of Colored People, the National Council of Negro Women, and the Young Women's Christian Association supported black Waacs/Wacs in their struggles for racial equality in the military (Moore 1996). Racial segregation remained a reality in the Army until 1950, however, when racial quotas were eliminated and women of all races were assigned to integrated units.[8]

Interestingly, African American women who were able to endure the racial and gender inequities that existed in the WAAC/WAC during World War II often recalled their military service as a positive experience. In retrospect, some of the women believed they had reached a higher level of maturity and learned how to live and work with others. One African American woman veteran reflected on her military service:

> I'm sure it enhanced my life quite a bit. I just think that the training and the assignments I had and the maturity that I developed during this period of time certainly prepared me to handle the situation in the civilian world. I was young and had never worked or been away from home, or experienced any of the real life outside of home. And during that period of time I had an opportunity to have four more years of maturity with responsibilities and everything. So I mean I felt that when I came out of the military, I was really prepared. (Moore 1996, 157).

Other women said military service helped them develop self-confidence. Gladys Carter noted that military service had "a great impact on my life and the type of person I turned out to be. I always was assertive, and a person interested and concerned and would get involved. But I think the military gave me more direction. It gave me the willingness to take on a job, take on a challenge. I just think that I can do anything damn well if I put my mind to it. I think the military had a lot to do with that" (Moore 1996, 156).

There is little doubt that the military was a turning point in the lives of many African American women who decided to pursue a military career. Military careerists by necessity assumed new roles, entered relationships with people of different backgrounds, and developed new concepts of themselves. Completing military training and receiving recognition for accomplishments are two of the ways military service has boosted the self-esteem of many African American women. Margaret Barbour, for example, attended several military schools and was awarded nine medals while on active duty, including the World War II Victory Medal and the European-African-Middle Eastern Service Medal. After growing up on a farm in Virginia, Barbour entered the military for "a better way of life." Her twenty-seven years of military service afforded her both personal growth and economic stability (Moore 1996, 175–78).

Other women spoke of the educational opportunities they gained by taking advantage of the G.I. Bill. Willie Whiting, who joined the military shortly after she graduated from high school, stated that she knew she wanted to go to law school before she entered service. Military service, then, represented a means of achieving her ambition (Moore 1996, 169).

In a few instances the women I interviewed felt that their skills and talents were not used and therefore found their military service of little or no value to them in later years. Ruth Hammond stated that the military did not help her advance educationally or occupationally. She had completed college before entering the military and did not use the G.I. Bill afterward. Hammond is convinced that she was never able to find the job she felt she was qualified for because of racial discrimination. Hence, in this case, the military did not provide an avenue for upward mobility. Still, on a positive note, Hammond noted that she met and interacted with wonderful people while serving in the United States and overseas (Moore 1996, 155).

Military service overseas afforded African American Wacs an opportunity to travel to countries they had previously only read about. For many members of the 6888th, serving in England and France during World War II was an exciting and fulfilling experience. African American Wacs in Europe held all the occupational positions, from "kitchen police" to commander. This was a radical departure from the civilian environment in the United States, where virtually all powerful positions were occupied by men and women of European descent. What is more, while in Europe, members of the 6888th received a great deal of positive reinforcement from the British and French, who treated them with dignity and respect. This was also quite different from the social environment they experienced in the United States.

European service offered a new perspective, and many of the women indicated that they had greater expectations of themselves when they left the military than when they enlisted. (Moore 1993).

The number of African American women serving in the military sharply declined after World War II, as did the number of military women in general. Restricted to 2 percent of the total military strength, the number of women serving in the Women's Army Corps fell to 9,655 by December 1946. In 1948, the number of African American women dropped to 125 (Morden 1990, 85). Despite legislation such as the Women's Armed Services Integration Act of 1948, which gave all military women permanent status in both the active military and the reserves, and the 1967 act, which removed the 2 percent restriction, the number of women, black and white, serving on active duty remained low. Only a limited number of African American women served in the military during the Korean conflict and the Vietnam War (U.S. DOD 1985, 103). Indeed, the strength of the Women's Army Corps did not rise above 12,000 until the 1970s, when the number of women in the armed services began to soar.

1973: The All-Volunteer Force

The number of women on active duty increased threefold from 1973 to 1979, the number of African American women increased fivefold (Dorn 1989, 46–48; Moore 1991, 363–65). During the 1970s and 1980s, the increase in accession rates for black women was greater than that of women of other racial and ethnic backgrounds and greater than that of black men (Moore 1991). During this period, African American women served longer and did not separate from service before their terms had expired (Binkin et al., 1982, 52–53). African American women reenlisted more often than did women of different racial and ethnic origins; they also tended to be single heads of households more than any other segment of the military population (Moore 1991, 370–72). For the first time in American history, the percentage of African American women on active duty increased at a more rapid rate than that of white women. (The percentage of African American men was also growing rapidly.) This expansion is in stark contrast to African American women's underrepresentation during and after World War II. Why have such a disproportionate number of African American women been attracted to the military? A major factor in the increase was the end of the draft, which led to a decline in the participation rate of middle-class white males and to the active recruitment of minorities and women in an attempt to meet personnel goals. This was especially true in 1979, when despite its best efforts, the Army fell short of its recruitment goals (Gilroy, Phillips, and Blair 1990, 333).

The increased participation of women is also related to changed social norms. During the 1970s the United States began to be more receptive to the idea of women working outside the home and in nontraditional jobs. This attitude was reflected in the Equal Rights Amendment, which was passed by Congress in 1972 and ratified by 70 percent of the states (75 percent was required for ratification.) Moreover, women appeared to have become more favorably disposed toward military service and struggled for expanded roles in the military through such advocate groups as the National Organization for Women, National Women's Political Caucus, and the Women's Equity Action League. In March 1990, Congresswoman Patricia Schroeder addressed the Military Personnel and Compensation Subcommittee advocating that women be allowed to perform all military occupational roles (U.S. House of Representatives 1990). An organized effort to expand the career opportunities for women in the U.S. armed services, which is strongly supported by prominent middle-class white women, continues to this day. The Army's motto urging recruits to "be all that you can be" attracted many women who were struggling for careers in the civilian sector, but apparently it had a particular appeal for African American women.

The disproportionately high rate of African American women in the military today can also be explained by the fact that the military has more nearly achieved racial equality than most other American institutions. Therefore, the military has been seen as the only viable avenue for upward mobility by many bright and ambitious African Americans. The rate of African American women on active duty would probably be even higher if there were no restrictions placed on the number of women who can enter the military at a given time. Clearly, the military retains strongly masculine norms: each service has tolerated racial integration more than it has gender integration. African American males are overrepresented in the military, constituting approximately 16 percent of active-duty forces in 1993 while making up only 6 percent of the total population. Not only are there more African American men serving on active duty today than previously, but these men are assigned to positions of greater responsibility and exercise more authority over Euro-Americans than in any other institution in the United States (Moskos 1986).

Women, on the other hand, make up a mere 12 percent of the total military force although they constitute 50 percent of the total population. Un-

African American Waacs of the Thirty-second and Thirty-third WAAC
Companies in the dining hall at Fort Huachuca, Arizona, 1942.
Courtesy of the Women's Army Corps Museum, Fort McClellan, Alabama.

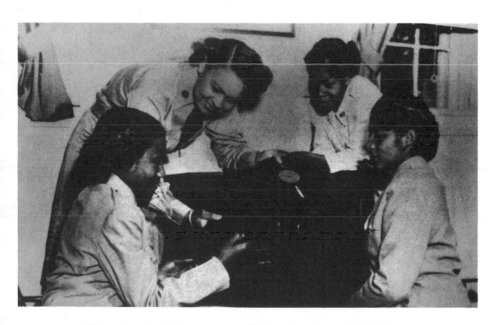

African American Waacs enjoying off-duty time during World War II.
Courtesy of the Women's Army Corps Museum, Fort McClellan, Alabama.

African American Waacs marching at Fort Huachuca, Arizona, 1942.
Courtesy of the *Women's Army Corps Museum, Fort McClellan, Alabama.*

African American Waacs at work at the Headquarters Annex, Fort Huachuca, Arizona, 1942.
Courtesy of the *Women's Army Corps Museum, Fort McClellan, Alabama.*

doubtedly, then, the U.S. military has not done as well in integrating women into the services as it has in employing African American men. Still, the military has been successful in employing African American women in comparison with civilian institutions.

For many African American women, military service represents job opportunity and security. Since the beginning of the All-Volunteer Force, the American military has come to resemble the civilian labor market in many ways. Today, military organizations rely heavily on monetary incentives in the recruitment of personnel; in turn, they are viewed as providing an employment opportunity. Because of the combined effect of racial and gender inequality, which excludes a disproportionately large number of black women from effectively participating in the civilian labor force, military service has provided an attractive alternative. Civilian African Americans experience higher unemployment rates than do men and women of European descent; further, their unemployment rates remain disproportionately high even when national unemployment decreases.

Since the All-Volunteer Force began in 1973, African Americans have been twice as likely as Euro-Americans to experience unemployment (Table 6-1). The black/white ratio remained higher than two even when the national unemployment rate dropped from 7.1 percent in 1977 to 5.8 percent in 1979, and from 9.6 percent in 1983 to 5.3 percent in 1989.

Table 6-1: Unemployment Rates for Americans Sixteen Years and Older, in Percent

Year	Total	Blacks	Whites	B/W Ratio
1973	4.9	9.4	4.3	2.2
1975	8.5	14.8	7.8	2.0
1977	7.1	14.0	6.2	2.2
1979	5.8	12.3	5.1	2.4
1980	7.1	14.3	6.3	2.3
1981	7.6	15.6	6.7	2.3
1983	9.6	19.5	8.4	2.3
1985	7.2	15.6	6.6	2.4
1987	6.2	13.0	5.3	2.4
1989	5.3	11.4	4.5	2.5
1990	5.5	11.3	4.7	2.4
1991	6.7	12.4	6.0	2.0
1992	7.4	14.1	6.5	2.2

Source: For 1973–87, U.S. Bureau of Labor Statistics, *Handbook of Labor Statistics*, Bulletin 2340, August 1989; for 1989–92, U.S. Bureau of the Census, *Statistical Abstract*, 1993, Table 625.

In addition, unemployment rates have been two to three times higher for African American women than for Euro-American women over the same period. On average, black civilian women from eighteen to twenty-four years of age were three times as likely to be unemployed from 1973 through 1988 as white civilian women in the same age cohort (Table 6-2). Although the black/white ratio is not as high for women in the twenty-five-to-forty-three age cohort, it averages over two. African American women, with fewer employment options than white women in the civilian sector, are thus more likely to enter the military for economic reasons.

Additionally, the exceptional economic problems faced by black men in the United States have exacerbated socioeconomic problems for black women. The high rates of joblessness, imprisonment, and homicide among black men are well documented (Larson 1988; Wilson 1987; 93–106; Jaynes and Williams 1989, 308–12). These facts add to the financial and emotional burdens of black women. One of the consequences of the economic plight of black men, then, is that African American women are more often single heads of households than any other segment of the American population. Findings of a recent study reveal that

> among separated and divorced women in 1984, two-thirds of blacks were household heads, compared with one-half of whites. . . . The proportion of separated or divorced black women who headed families increased from 40 to 66 percent between 1960 and 1984. Never-married

Table 6-2: Unemployment Rate of Black and White American Women, in Percent

Year	18–19 Years Old			20–24 Years Old			25–34 Years Old		
	Black	White	B/W	Black	White	B/W	Black	White	B/W
1973	34.2	10.9	3.1	18.4	7.1	2.6	10.3	5.1	2.0
1975	40.6	16.1	2.5	24.3	11.2	2.2	13.4	8.4	2.0
1977	40.4	14.2	2.8	25.5	9.3	2.7	13.6	6.7	2.0
1979	36.9	12.5	3.0	22.6	7.8	2.9	12.1	5.6	2.2
1981	39.8	15.3	2.6	26.4	9.1	2.9	14.9	6.6	2.2
1983	48.0	16.4	2.9	31.8	10.3	3.1	18.6	7.6	2.4
1985	36.4	13.1	2.8	25.6	8.5	3.0	15.1	6.2	2.4
1987	31.7	11.7	2.7	23.3	7.4	3.1	13.5	5.0	2.7
1988	29.6	10.8	2.7	19.8	6.7	3.0	12.7	4.5	2.8

Source: U.S. Bureau of Labor Statistics, *Handbook of Labor Statistics*, August 1989, Table 28.

white women rarely head families. . . . This was true also of black never-married women in 1960, when 6 percent did so; but by 1984, almost 25 percent of such black women headed families. (Jaynes and Williams 1989, 519)

It is understandable why many black women have entered the military: to make an honest living. They have used this opportunity well; African American women have been and continue to be a reliable and valuable asset to the armed services.

Recent Trends for African American Women: Service, Pay Grades, Occupations

While constituting 12 percent of the total female population in the United States, African Americans make up approximately 30 percent of all the women serving on active duty in the American armed forces. This figure increased from 25 percent in 1980 and has held steady at 30 percent since 1988. It is also noteworthy that the distribution of black women varies with regard to branch of service and status (enlisted/officer). In 1980, African American enlisted women were concentrated in the Army, and officers were almost equally distributed in the Army and the Air Force (Table 6-3). As of December 1993, 50 percent of all African American women officers and 52 percent of African American enlisted women were in the Army. The Air Force had the second largest proportion of African American women, followed by the Navy and last the Marine Corps. At the same time, 30 percent of white women officers and 26 percent of white enlisted women were in the Army,

Table 6-3: Percentage of Officer and Enlisted Women for 1980 and 1993

Race & Status	Army		Air Force		Navy		Marines	
	1980	1993	1980	1993	1980	1993	1980	1993
Black officers	44	50	45	32	10	18	0.01	0.01
Black enlisted	62	52	24	23	11	21	3.5	3.5
White officers	33	30	40	41	25	27	0.02	0.02
White enlisted	33	26	39	41	24	29	0.04	0.04

Source: Defense Manpower Data Center.
Note: Warrant officers excluded.

followed by 27 percent and 29 percent of enlisted in the Navy (see Table 6-3). the largest proportion of white women officers and enlisted women were in the Air Force. Only 2 percent of the white women officers and 4 percent of white enlisted women were in the Marine Corps.

Thus, over the last decade the proportion of African American enlisted women in the Army has decreased as their proportion has increased in the Navy, and it has been relatively stable in the Air Force and Marines. The percentage of African American women officers both in the Army and the Navy increased between 1980 and 1993. In the Air Force, their percentage decreased between 1980 and 1993. African American enlisted women, then, are less concentrated in the Army and more represented in the Navy; African American women officers are even more concentrated in the Army, less concentrated in the Air Force, and, like the enlisted women, more represented in the Navy. Although the percentage of African American women who are officers in the pay grades of O1–O3 (2d lieutenant, 1st lieutenant, and captain) has remained between 5 and 6 percent from 1983 to 1993, the percentage of O4s (majors) and, to a lesser degree, O5s (lieutenant colonels) has been increasing. The percentage of African American women who serve as enlisted women in pay grades E1–E4 (private through corporal) has been declining over the last decade, while E5s and E6s (sergeants and staff sergeants) and, to a lesser degree, E7s (sergeants first class) have been increasing. In fact, there has been a more than 100 percent increase in the proportion of African American women in the E5–E6 category (from 17 percent in 1980 to 36 percent in 1993); there has also been an increase in the percentage of E7s (from 0.4 percent in 1980 to 6 percent in 1993); and, for the same years, a slight increase in the percentage of African American women who are E8s (master sergeants).

The two occupational categories in which all active-duty military women are concentrated are administrative/support and medical services. The proportion of African American enlisted women in the administrative/support occupations peaked in 1982 at 48 percent and then began to decline. Still, in 1993, 42 percent of all African American enlisted women were in administrative/support occupations; their numbers soared from 1980 to 1982 in both the E1–E4 and E5–E6 categories. From 1982 to 1989, however, the number of African American women in the lower enlisted ranks (E1–E4) in administrative/support occupations fell, while their representation in the higher ranks (E5s, E6s, and E7s) continued to expand. Similarly, the percentages of African American women officers in administrative/support occupations dropped between 1985 (30 percent) and 1993 (20 percent). This decrease was mainly in the O1–O3 pay grade category. The trend, then, is that fewer African American women are entering administrative/support occupations and that those already in these fields are being promoted.

In 1980, 36 percent of African American women officers were assigned to medical occupations. Four years later, the percentage of African American women in medical occupations dropped to 28 percent and then continued to increase over the next nine years, reaching 44 percent in 1993. The biggest increase in African American women medical officers was in pay grades O4 (majors) and O5 (lieutenant colonels). Likewise, the proportion of African American enlisted women in medical occupations continually increased between 1980 and 1993, from 9 percent in 1980, to 14 percent in 1993. It is evident that since 1990 the increase in African American enlisted women in the medical occupations has been among those in the rank of E7 (sergeant first class). From 1980 to 1983, the number of E1s through E4s increased in the medical occupations before declining from 1983 to 1985 and then increasing again until 1988, when E1s through E4s once again began to decline. The E5s continued to increase until 1990, when their numbers fell slightly until 1992 and leveled between 1992 and 1993. In sum, African American women have been moving into medical specialties and have been successful in earning promotions there.

Women have made gains in recent years in two nontraditional occupations: as tactical officers and in the field of weapons for enlisted. The percentage of African American female tactical officers, though, dropped from a high of 6 percent in 1987 and 1988 to 4 percent in 1993. The decrease occurred primarily in the O1–O3 pay grade category. This reduction suggests that fewer African American women are entering tactical occupations but that those who are already there have been promoted. In weapons occupations, the percentages of African American women, like those of white women, have been increasing, from 1 percent in 1980 to 5 percent in 1993. The biggest increase occurred between 1987 and 1988 among E1s–E4s and E5s–E6s. Since 1991, E1s–E4s have dropped while E5–E6s, E7s, and E8s have steadily climbed. Again, the pattern shows a recent reduction in nontraditional occupations but success for those already in such fields.

In sum, the fact that women are concentrated in medical occupations does not appear to put them at risk for a large number of cuts during the military drawdown. On the contrary, the percentages of all enlisted women and women officers who are in medical occupations have been increasing.

Women are, however, losing ground in administrative/support occupations in the Air Force, Army and Navy. Still, they seem to be gaining presence in the weapons and tactical occupations, which appear to be offsetting their losses in the administrative/support fields. Although African American women have not been experiencing more cuts than white women, they are experiencing lower representation in the area of tactical occupations, which may have negative consequences for African American women officers in the future. There is also a significant decline in African American enlisted women in the E1–E4 pay grades, which indicates that they are not accessing the military today as they were in 1980. If this trend continues, it may significantly decrease the representation of African American women on active duty in the future. The cause of this decline is not yet known.

Conclusion

What is the meaning of the overrepresentation of African American and especially of African American women in today's military? In the past, some claimed that the disproportionately high rate of black participation in the military would discourage white participation. It was argued that as the number of black military personnel increased, the number of white Americans interested in enlistment would decrease (Schexnider 1980). Given the country's ambivalent attitudes toward African Americans, some social groups, such as clubs, neighborhoods, and schools, were erroneously devalued when the proportion of African Americans increased. This has apparently not been the case with the U.S. military, however. The successful, heavy recruitment of African Americans was an effect of their poor opportunities in the civilian sector. Their recruitment has not much affected the interest of white middle-class men in military service.

Some have argued that the overrepresentation of blacks in the American armed forces is nothing to be alarmed about but rather should be applauded because it is much better than being unemployed or even homeless. Several arguments in support of black male overrepresentation followed this line of reasoning in the 1970s and 1980s (Dellums 1975; Schexnider and Butler 1976; Schexnider 1982). These views, however, neglect the fundamental issue of choice for all Americans (Moore, 1996). Is the military the only alternative African American men and women should have to unemployment? The Army may have provided well, but what career options are available to African

American women in the civilian sector? Are African American women being forced disproportionately to bear the burden of national defense? The lack of career alternatives for the American black woman can no longer be overlooked. Indeed, a crisis may develop if the military drawdown curtails what has been one field in which African Americans have found success and security.

NOTES

1. The United States's definition of citizenship came from England. In addition to rights, citizenship is defined in terms of such responsibilities as national defense. See Marshall 1963, 78, 123–24.

2. For a good discussion of the evolution of the American armed services, see Segal 1989, 17–44.

3. Seventy-five percent of the African American men serving in the military during World War II were in the Army. The Navy employed approximately 150,000 black men, mainly as messmen, and the 17,000 African American men serving in the Marine Corps were primarily in service units. See Lee 1966.

4. In the Women's Army Corps, women had the same military pay, benefits, and discipline as men. See Treadwell 1954, 220–21.

5. A fuller discussion about how the Selective Training Act of 1940 and H.R. 4906 (the bill that established the Women's Army Auxiliary Corps) influenced the recruitment, assignments, and deployment of African American women is in Moore 1996.

6. In comparison, more than twenty thousand white Waacs/Wacs were stationed overseas during the war. One hundred eight black nurses also served overseas during World War II: thirty in Liberia, fifteen in the South Pacific, and sixty-three in England. See U.S. DOD 1991, 141–43.

7. The Army's designation for "Negro" was "No. 2."

8. Although President Truman signed Executive Order 9981 in 1948, mandating that the armed services be desegregated, the WAC was not desegregated until January 1950, when the 10 percent racial quota was also abolished. See Morden 1990, 85–87.

REFERENCES

Binkin, Martin, Mark Eitelberg, Alvin Schexnider, and Marvin Smith. 1982. *Blacks and the Military.* Washington, D.C.: Brookings Institution.

Dellums, Ronald V. 1975. "Don't Slam Door to Military." *Focus* 3,8 (June). Washington, D.C.: Joint Center for Political Studies.

Dorn, Edwin. 1989. *Who Defends America? Race, Sex, and Class in the Armed Forces.* Washington, D.C.: Joint Center for Political Studies Press.

Earley, Charity Adams. 1989. *One Woman's Army: A Black Officer Remembers the WAC.* College Station: Texas A & M University Press.

Farley, Reynolds, and Walter Allen. 1987. *The Color Line and the Quality of Life in America.* New York: Sage Foundation.

Franklin, John Hope, and Alfred A. Moss. 1988. From Slavery to Freedom: A History of Negro Americans. New York: Alfred A. Knopf.

Garraty, John A. 1975. The American Nation: A History of the United States since 1965. 2 vols. 3d ed. New York: Harper and Row.

Gilroy, Curtis, Robert Phillips, and John Blair. 1990. "The All-Volunteer Army: Fifteen Years Later. Armed Forces and Society. 16, 3 329–50.

Horton, Mildred McAfee. 1971. "Recollections of Capt. Mildred McAfee, USNR (Ret.)." In WAVE Officers of World War II, vol. 1. Annapolis: U.S. Naval Institute.

Janowitz, Morris, and Charles C. Moskos, Jr. 1974. "Racial Composition in the All-Volunteer Force." Armed Forces and Society, 1, 1:109–23.

———. 1979. "Five Years of the All-Volunteer Force, 1973–1978. Armed Forces and Society 8, 2:171–218.

Jaynes, Gerald D., and Robin M. Williams, Jr. 1989. A Common Destiny: Blacks and American Society. Washington, D.C.: National Academy Press.

Johnson, Jesse. 1974. Black Women in the Armed Forces. 1942–1974. Hampton, Va.: published by author.

Larson, Tom E. 1988. "Employment and Unemployment of Young Black Males." In Jewelle Taylor Gibbs, ed., Young, Black, and Male in America: An Endangered Species. Dover, Mass.: Auburn House, pp. 97–128.

Lee, Ulysses. 1966. United States Army in World War II Special Studies: The Employment of Negro Troops. Washington, D.C.: U.S. Government Printing Office.

Lieberson, Stanley. 1980. A Piece of the Pie: Blacks and White Immigrants since 1880. Berkeley: University of California Press.

Marshall, T. H. 1963. Class, Citizenship, and Social Development. Chicago: University of Chicago Press.

Moore, Brenda L. 1991. "African American Women in the U.S. Military." Armed Forces and Society. 17, 3:363–84.

———. 1993. "Serving with a Dual Mission: African American Women in World War II. National Journal of Sociology. 7, 1:3–43.

———. 1996. To Serve My Country, to Serve My Race: The Story of the Only African-American WACs Stationed Overseas during World War II. New York: New York University Press.

Morden, Bettie J. 1990. The Women's Army Corps, 1945–1978. Washington, D.C.: Center of Military History.

Moskos, Charles C. 1980. "Racial and Educational Composition of the All-Volunteer Army." Paper presented at colloquium, Ethnicity and Public Policy, University of Wisconsin, Green Bay, 30–31 May.

———. 1986. "Success Story: Blacks in the Military." The Atlantic 257 (May): 64–72.

Myrdal, Gunnar. 1944. An American Dilemma: The Negro Problem and Modern Democracy. New York: Harper.

Pitts, Lucia M. 1968. One Negro WAC's Story. Los Angeles: privately published.

Putney, Martha. 1992. When the Nation Was in Need: Blacks in the Women's Army Corps during World War II. Metuchen, N.J.: Scarecrow Press.

Randolph, Laura B. 1991. "The Untold Story of Black Women in the Gulf War." Ebony (September):100–107.

Sabrosky, Alan Ned. 1980. "Symposium: Race and the United States Military." *Armed Forces and Society* 6, 4:601–6.

Schexnider, Alvin J. 1976. "Expectations from the Ranks: Representativeness and Value Systems." *American Behavioral Scientist* 19, 5:523–42.

———. 1980. "Symposium: Race and the United States Military." *Armed Forces and Society* 6, 4:606–13.

———. 1982. "Black Americans in the Military: Too Many?" Paper presented at the Third Annual Conference on Ethnicity and Public Policy, University of Wisconsin, Green Bay, 14–15 May.

Schexnider, Alvin J., and John S. Butler. 1976. "Race and the All-Volunteer System." *Armed Forces and Society* 2, 3:421–32.

Segal, David R. 1989. *Recruiting for Uncle Sam: Citizenship and Military Manpower Policy.* Lawrence: University Press of Kansas.

Taylor, Susie King. 1968. *Reminiscences of My Life in Camp.* New York: Arno Press.

Treadwell, Mattie E. 1954. *U.S. Army in World War II Special Studies: The Women's Army's Corps.* Washington, D.C.: Department of the Army.

U.S. Department of Defense. 1985. *Blacks in Defense of Our Nation.* Washington, D.C.: U.S. Government Printing Office.

———. 1991. *Black Americans in Defense of Our Nation.* Washington, D.C.: U.S. Government Printing Office.

U.S. House of Representatives. 1990. *Women in the Military: Hearing before the Military Personnel and Compensation Subcommittee.* Washington, D.C.: U.S. Government Printing Office.

Wilson, William J. 1980. *The Declining Significance of Race.* Chicago: University of Chicago Press.

———. 1987. *The Truly Disadvantaged: The Inner City, the Underclass, and Public Policy.* Chicago: University of Chicago Press.

Nina Richman-Loo and Rachel Weber

7

Gender and Weapons Design

When Secretary of Defense Les Aspin announced the Clinton administration's new policy on women in combat in April 1993, he sought to implement a congressional mandate that would permit women to compete for all assignments in aircraft, including those aircraft engaged in combat missions (Aspin 1993). The Aspin policy was far-reaching and reflected the sentiments of advocates who had been urging an expanded role for military women for years.

Although the 1993 policy gives women a greater potential for receiving combat assignments, the technologies associated with these assignments, for example combat aircraft, constrain, if not actually preclude, the directive from being implemented. This chapter examines the role technology plays in facilitating or limiting women's military service. Logic tells us that technology should reduce dependence on human strength. To do so, however, the technology must take into account the characteristics of the humans who will use it. At the present time many military technologies have been designed for men. This affects women's use of those technologies and effectiveness in certain roles. The specific case of the development of the Joint Primary Aircraft Training Systems (JPATS) provides an illustration.

In 1993, Defense Acquisition Board (DAB) deliberations on the procurement of a proposed JPATS noted the need for changes in cockpit sizing to accommodate greater numbers of women in the new plane. Specifically, senior-level discussions in the Office of the Secretary of Defense (OSD) concluded that existing military aircraft were designed for a male population; an assessment of the physical accommodation of women in the planned JPATS revealed that the specifications then current would exclude a high percentage of women.

JPATS specifications are significant, because this plane will be the primary aircraft trainer used by the Navy and the Air Force. After successful completion of mandatory JPATS training, student pilots advance to intermediate trainers and, finally, to aircraft-specific training (Figure 7-1). Because all pilots will be trained in the JPATS, if women could not "fit" in the JPATS cockpit or if the cockpit could not "fit" women pilots, many women would be unable to pursue aviation careers in either the Navy or the Air Force.

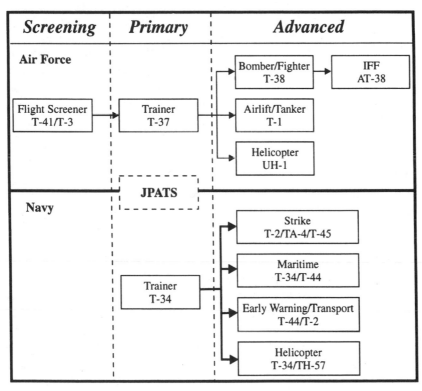

Figure 7-1: Defense Aircraft Training Pipelines

Inherent Bias in Existing Military Technologies

Department of Defense acquisition policy mandates that human considerations —that is, what is known about the capabilities and limitations of the human operator—be integrated into design efforts to improve system performance. After all, the best defense technology is useless if it does not take such capabilities and limitations into account. Indeed, human factors (i.e. human error) are the cause of more than two-thirds of operating mishaps (Richman-Loo and Weber 1993).

Despite the appearance of a "gender-neutral" policy, defense systems have traditionally been built to male specifications. Since women tend to be shorter and have smaller limbs, many of them may not be accommodated in current aircraft and ship design. In particular, they may have difficulty reaching controls and operating certain equipment. To understand how this occurs, we describe how weapon systems are designed with regard to the characteristics of potential operators.

The military relies on the concepts of ergonomics and anthropometrics to fit the soldier, sailor, and airman to the system. Ergonomics, also called "human factors," addresses human characteristics, expectations, and behaviors in the design of items. Ergonomic theories were developed during World War II when it became obvious that new and complicated military equipment could not be operated safely or effectively, or even maintained adequately, by many well-trained personnel. Effort was then directed to design equipment that would be more suitable for human use, and the term "human engineering" entered our vocabulary. Nonmilitary applications of ergonomic concepts include the design of transportation, communications equipment, and computer equipment.

Anthropometrics, on the other hand, refers to the measurement of dimensions and physical characteristics of the body as it occupies space and as it moves and applies energy to physical objects. These measurements can include variables such as age, sex, occupation, and ethnic origin. The military relies on data provided by the U.S. Army Nadick Research Development and Engineering Center in the "1988 Anthropometric Survey of Army Personnel." This survey contains data on more than 180 body and head dimension measurements of a population of more than nine thousand soldiers. Age and race distributions match those of the June 1988 active-duty Army, and minority groups were intentionally oversampled to accommodate anticipated demographic shifts in Army population (Gordon et al. 1988). Figure 7-2

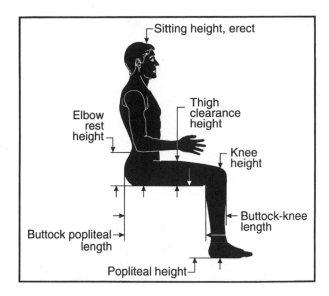

Figure 7-2: Some Body Dimensions Evaluated for Cockpit Design.
Source: McCormick and Sanders 1982.

depicts some of the body dimensions evaluated for cockpit design (Mc-Cormick and Sanders 1982, 314).

In the application of anthropometric data, system designers commonly rely on *Military Standard* 1472, "Human Engineering Design Criteria for Military Systems, Equipment, and Facilities." These military specifications, or "milspecs," as they are commonly known, are critical, for at each stage decisions are made that reflect the military's needs and goals. These decisions are ultimately embodied in the technology. Milspecs suggest the use of 95th and 5th percentile male dimensions in designing weapons systems if the accommodation of 100 percent of men would incur trade-off costs out of proportion to the benefits to be derived. Deciding what is a "trade-off cost" and when such costs are too high is a negotiated and often arbitrary process.

Because women are often smaller in all physical dimensions than men, the gap between a 5th percentile woman and a 95th percentile male can be very large (Richman-Loo and Weber 1993, 5). For example, the height of the 5th percentile woman in the Nadick study was measured at 60.15 inches, while the 95th percentile male in the same study was 73.48 inches (Gordon et al. 1989, 270). Because women who do not meet physical requirements for the equipment designed for men are deemed ineligible, milspecs are of crucial importance.

Accommodation is even further complicated when more than one physical dimension is involved or several dimensions need to be considered in combination. Further difficulties arise from the interrelationships between and among dimensions that may have low correlations with each other (i.e., sitting height and arm length). Thus, in certain military applications, as many as half of all Naval aviators would not be accommodated by a particular cockpit design if both the 5th and 95th percentiles were used for each of the thirteen dimensions evaluated.

There are many case studies that demonstrate how design limits the access of women because of specified anthropometric requirements. For example, accommodating women on ships has required the Navy to redesign hull fittings and equipment, to modify damage-control systems, and to provide protective clothing for smaller individuals. Abroad ships, living and working conditions are closely tied to mission accomplishment; thus, habitability, or what is called "human support space," also becomes an issue. Destroyers are currently being retrofitted to include separate berth and shower spaces for women (Key, Fleischer, and Gauthier 1993).

The JPATS

The difficulty and importance of the accommodation of women first received prominent attention during JPATS Defense Acquisition Board meetings. One specific JPATS requirement—the sitting height threshold—was examined for consistency with the newly published policy on women in combat. Although the JPATS sitting height specifications were based on the existing accommodation made in military aircraft, the 34-inch threshold of this single dimension excluded approximately 65 percent of otherwise eligible women (Figure 7-3).

Consequently, the undersecretary of defense (acquisition) directed that JPATS specifications be changed to accommodate at least 80 percent of eligible females, and he delayed release of the JPATS draft Request for Proposal (RFP) until a new threshold could be documented. (An RFP identifies systems requirements and provides solicitation instructions to potential bidders). The accommodation of men was not questioned.

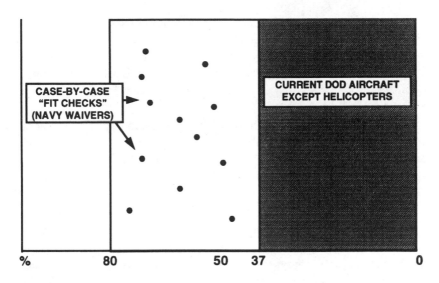

%   80   50   37   0

BASED ON DOD COCKPIT WORKING GROUP ESTIMATES

Figure 7-3: Current Accommodation of Female Sitting Heights in Defense Aircraft

The OSD convened a working group to develop a new sitting height threshold in May 1993 with representatives from Air Force and Navy JPATS Program Offices and from service acquisition, personnel, human factors, and flight surgeon organizations. A comprehensive triservice effort was necessary because this issue cuts across all services. It also reflected a trend toward acquisitions that would be used by more than one service.

The working group soon discovered it would be unable to develop new JPATS specifications until it would (1) assess cockpit accommodation techniques actually used by the Navy and the Air Force, (2) define a "JPATS-eligible" population, and (3) select data sets for the most accurate evaluation of cockpit accommodation. Furthermore, the JPATS "off-the-shelf" acquisition strategy, which requires the application of already developed technology, hindered many innovative solutions. If one is to design a wholly new aircraft, there are no limits to using technology to overcome accommodation problems. In the JPATS, however, the designers and the working group were prohibited from using newly designed ejection seats, escape systems, and flight controls. New or different technology such as adjustable sticks, seat-tilt mechanisms, and powered canopy closures could have solved or at least mitigated difficulties created by smaller-stature crew members, but the nondevelopment (i.e., "low risk") acquisition policies already in place precluded their use.

The Navy uses an anthropometric coding system to evaluate cockpit accommodation based on four measurements: sitting height, functional reach, buttock-to-knee length, and buttock-to-leg length. Since the Navy codes represent a range of sizes and do not use multivariate relationships, it is difficult to predict whether a borderline individual can or cannot successfully operate a particular aircraft. The Navy resolves this problem by performing subjective, visual, cockpit "fit checks" on individuals who fall into the indeterminate ranges; that is, the person is put in the cockpit to see whether or not she or he can reach everything that needs to be reached. This means, for example, that people with longer arms but shorter sitting heights, but who can reach controls, switches, and rudder pedals/brakes and who can see outside the cockpit, are accommodated. Thus, candidates who would have been excluded from pilot training by the original 34-inch sitting height threshold are allowed to receive that training.

The Air Force, on the other hand, requires only two measurements: minimum sitting height and stature, which are 34 and 64 inches, respectively. Unlike the Navy, the Air Force maintains a "fly one, fly all" policy, which requires that all Air Force pilots "fit" all Air Force aircraft. As a result, all potential aircraft to be used by the Air Force must be evaluated to verify that Air Force pilots will be accommodated. The Air Force does not perform "fit checks" but does occasionally grant waivers under special circumstances. The JPATS 34-inch sitting height threshold would have accommodated all current Air Force pilots but would have excluded many otherwise eligible women.

Since the working group was instructed to "accommodate 80 percent of eligible females," the group first had to agree on the meaning of this phrase. To some participants, "eligible females" implied those women who already qualified for pilot training. To the political appointees designated by President Clinton's administration, the terminology had a much broader meaning. Ultimately, the working group adopted the broadest possible definition—one that offered the greatest accommodation. Thus, it concluded that the "eligible female" population was defined by the following criteria: (1)

aged twenty-two to twenty-seven years, (2) met height and weight requirements for entry into the Air Force and Navy, and (3) exhibited a racial mix that matches the most recent Bureau of the Census data pertaining to U.S. college graduates. As a result, the constructed "eligible" population for JPATS would be quite different from current Navy and Air Force training system candidates, who had to meet minimum aviation entrance requirements that were based on the expectation that most aircrew would be male.

An aircrew member must be able to reach and operate leg and hand controls, see cockpit gauges and displays, and have the external vision required for safe operation. Other physical factors related to effective operation include the strength required to operate controls and the ability to tolerate forces produced by the aircraft's emergency escape system. Critical anthropometry design measurements, then, include sitting height, functional arm reach, leg length, buttock-knee length, and weight.

The working group quickly discovered that no large-scale anthropometric data base existed that contained the required data for the "constructed" population. An Army female officer data base derived from the "1988 Anthropometric Survey of U.S. Army Personnel" was therefore selected to serve as the source for defining the JPATS target female population (U.S. Department of Defense 1993). The working group adopted this source of data because it was representative of U.S. military populations and correlated well to previous anthropometric data collected by the National Institutes of Health.

Anthropometric data on 332 women officers, twenty-two years or older, were extracted from the 1988 survey as the target female population. A double check by Navy and Air Force representatives confirmed that the anthropometric characteristics would also represent women in the Navy and Air Force. The group chose the three most critical variables that it believed would help it best evaluate cockpit accommodation: total leg length, arm reach, and sitting height. A multivariate analysis of the target population's possession of total leg length and arm reaches at various sitting heights yielded the results shown in Table 7-1.

The working group selected the 32.8-inch sitting height threshold, since it complied with the direction to accommodate at least 80 percent of eligible females and could be accomplished using current technology, thus minimizing potential safety and technological risks. Examination of the data base also revealed that at 32.8 inches virtually all men in the United States would be accommodated (Table 7-2).

Table 7-1: Cockpit Accommodation of Target Population

Minimum Sitting Height	Percentage Target Population (Women) Included
34.0''	39
33.8''	51
33.6''	63
33.4''	72
33.2''	76
33.0''	79
32.8''	82
32.6''	84
32.4''	86
32.2''	87
32.0''	91

Table 7-2: U.S. Population Sitting Height Ranges

Percentile	Females	Males
1st	30.5''	32.59''
5th	31.31''	33.64''
10th	31.77''	34.17''
25th	32.58''	34.80''
50th	33.52''	35.99''
75th	34.48''	36.95''
95th	35.84''	38.29''
99th	36.74''	39.03''

The working group noted that standardization of data, both on airframes and on humans, was problematic. Further, accommodation of human beings in most other Air Force and Navy aircraft has never been measured. Consequently, after completion of primary training in JPATS, there may or may not be relatively few follow-on aircraft to which to assign smaller pilots. Another practical problem involves the fact that the three services use different standards in evaluating candidates for pilot training (Table 7-3). The Air Force considers only stature and sitting height. The Navy evaluates sitting height, buttock-knee length, buttock-leg length, and thumbtip reach but then "eyeballs" borderline candidates. The Army (which will not use the JPATS) adds arm span and crotch height. In joint programs such as JPATS, the use of different standards and measurement techniques by the different services makes accommodation difficult and will continue to cause problems

Table 7-3: Flight Training Physical Standards

Characteristic	Army	Navy	Air Force
Minimum weight	100 lb., men 90 lb. women	100 lb., men 100 lb., women	N/A
Stature (flight training)	64–76″ men & women	60″, men 58″, women	64–77″ men & women
Sitting height	Less than or equal to 40.2″	32–41″	34–40″, pilots 33–40″ navigators
Buttock-leg length	N/A	35–50″	N/A
Buttock-knee length	N/A	21.9–28″	N/A
Functional reach	N/A	28″ or greater	N/A
Total arm reach (span)	Less than or equal to 64.6″	N/A	N/A
Crotch height	Less than or equal to 29.5″	N/A	N/A

in joint service efforts. Consequently, the working group made the following recommendations:

Standardize anthropometric requirements among the services.

Standardize and implement cockpit measurement ("mapping") of all military aircraft to determine the range of current as well as future accommodation.

Develop a joint service aviation anthropometry data base and anthropometric measurement techniques to support design and evaluation of cockpits and pilot equipment.

Establish a joint service research effort to study whether physiological factors such as strength and tolerance to ejection acceleration forces differ between women and men.

Develop and fund advanced technology demonstrators and test articles, such as mannequins, to represent smaller-sized aviators.

After the working group's deliberations, the Air Force issued a revised JPATS draft Request for Proposal that included the 32.8-inch sitting height threshold. The RFP identified crew accommodation as a key source selection criterion. During the source selection process, prospective candidates were required to submit cockpit "mockups" which would be measured for their adherence to JPATS anthropometric requirements. Contractors exceeding the JPATS 32.8-inch sitting height requirement stand a greater chance of being selected.

John Deutch, then undersecretary of defense for acquisition and technology, concurred with the findings of the working group and legitimized solutions to the accommodation of women in defense aircraft by stating:

> I believe OSD should continue to take the lead in addressing this problem. Other platforms in addition to aircraft should be considered as well. We must determine what changes are practical and cost-effective in support of Secretary of Defense policy to expand combat roles for females. I request that you take the lead in determining specification needs. Further, you should determine the impact of defense platforms already in production and inventory. (1992)

Negotiating Accommodation

The decision to alter any technology is always affected by competing political, economic, and social factors. To examine how technological decisions are shaped by such factors, it is important to identify the groups that have a stake in changing a technology. In this section, we interpret the narrative we have just laid out in order to shed light on some of the factors affecting the decisions that were reached.

One could argue that negotiations regarding technological gender bias arose primarily as a result of changes made in policies concerning women in combat. Les Aspin publicly recognized that women would play a greater role in the military when he issued the directive in April 1993. That directive stated:

> The services shall permit women to compete for assignments in aircraft, including aircraft engaged in combat missions.
> The Army and Marine Corps shall study opportunities for women to serve in additional assignments, including, but not limited to, field artillery and air defense artillery.

Although the new policy gave women a greater combat aviation role and was intended to allow for their entry into many new assignments, the tech-

The smallest and the largest pilots JPATS was designed to accommodate.
Courtesy of Martin-Baker.

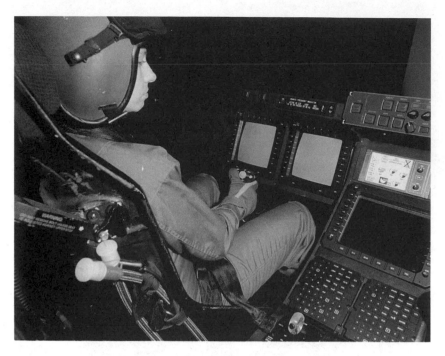

Above: Cockpit interior: Pilot's legs must reach rudder pedals for steering; arms must reach various other controls.

Below: Pilot being evaluated for cockpit "fit."

nologies associated with the new assignments, such as aircraft, prohibited the immediate implementation of the directive. The fact that existing systems could contain a technological bias against women's bodies despite the congressional mandate for accessibility brought policy specialists at the Pentagon into the debate.

Instead of "fitting the man to the machine" (already designed for men), it was seen as suddenly necessary to "fit the machine to the woman." Improving the accommodation of women could not be accomplished just by revising the JPATS specifications and changing its operational requirements, however. Altered requirements would also entail changing important and expensive technology, primarily for safety reasons. For example, reducing the sitting height to 32.8 inches would require significant cockpit modifications, largely because of the requirement for an ejection seat. Since the seat must be stationary to ensure precision during ejection, the ability to adjust the seat (as is done on an automobile, for instance) is significantly restricted. In addition, there was the possibility that the aircraft nose, rudder, and other flight controls would have to be modified to accommodate a smaller person. Because ejections of individuals with smaller statures and presumably lower body weights have yet to be certified for safety, test articles and demonstrations also would have to be developed to ensure safe ejection.

Performance characteristics of ejection seats are influenced by the weight of the occupant. Seat stability and control, harness fit, parachute opening shock, and spinal injury potentials are all affected when weight deviates from the design envelope. Additionally, parachute harnesses and other seat-related equipment may not fit properly when crew size deviates from design limits. Consequently, the working group reported that the "expansion of ejection seat capabilities to accommodate a lighter weight JPATS-eligible female population involves risks that cannot be fully quantified at this point in time. Preliminary assessment suggests that the risk will be higher in some aircraft. Therefore, ejection tests, physiological research, and performance data must be more fully analyzed before reasonable estimates of ejection seat upgrade approaches, costs, and schedules can be developed" (U.S. Department of Defense 1994).

Although the physical strength to operate controls and the ability to tolerate ejection force are required for cockpit accommodation and safe ejection, specific research has not been performed to determine whether strength, endurance, and ability to withstand high acceleration differ in women, particularly those with the smaller statures and lower weights that will be accommodated in JPATS. As most of the research has been conducted on men, knowledge of the risk to women aircrew in terms of female physiological responses to ejection forces and impact accelerations is incomplete.

Because of the need for these modifications, many believed that accommodating a "JPATS-eligible" population would be cost-prohibitive. Some senior defense officials opposed the change, maintaining that such alterations would delay the development of the JPATS and thus raise costs. Estimated costs associated with modifying the JPATS included changes to cockpit layout, aircraft structure, flight control systems, and ejection seats as well as the development of new anthropometric mannequins and the building of a new JPATS prototype. The Air Force estimated that original cost projections would increase the overall cost by approximately $600 million (U.S. Department of Defense 1994). A preliminary analysis on expanding accommodation in *all* aircraft concluded that a minimum multimillion-dollar, two-year effort would be required to measure cockpits for actual accommodation ranges, determine needed redesigns, and quantify costs.

Design changes that would accommodate and benefit women would benefit smaller men as well. Smaller men also have difficulty operating hatches, damage control equipment, and scuttles on ships (Key, Fleischer, and Gauthier 1993, 13). Nonetheless, the issue of cockpit accommodation was framed by its opponents as a women's issue. As the controversy continued about women in combat, the debate about altering military technologies was cast in terms of accommodating the differences in women's bodies.

There were pragmatists within the Department of Defense who believed that it was both practical and economical to integrate new human factors in acquisition specifications. Technologies built for the military as opposed to civilian markets tend to favor capability over maintenance and operability, and hardware over personnel. With decreasing budgets, however, pragmatists felt that these standards could no longer be the norm. Maintenance and operability matter.

To continue to study the issue, a working group effort was spearheaded by advocates of the OSD Human Systems Integration (HSI) program. HSI addresses how well "human factors" such as manpower, personnel, human engineering, training, and safety and health hazards have been included during weapon system design and acquisition. (Although each service has its own HSI program—Army MANPRINT, Air Force IMPACTS, and Navy HSI—their program implementation is quite similar.) During each acquisition stage, managers must document what human system risks exist in predecessor or comparable systems, what studies and analyses are planned to identify or mitigate human risks, and the status of these efforts before each milestone decision by the Defense Acquisition Board. It is through this process that design flaws, such as those involved in the JPATS, are raised for senior-level deliberation and resolution before the system proceeds to production.

Shrinking male personnel resources and the changing demographic pool of men from which the military recruits also mandate that human capabilities be more closely matched to defense technologies. As the ethnic and racial makeup of the nation changes, inclusion and accommodation of smaller men will be necessary. Judith Hicks Stiehm has noted that the services want their male citizens for any assignment and that "in the past and even now—the military seems to have accommodated men of many sizes" (1985, 221–22).

Enhanced accommodation has another important economic consideration. Pragmatists have pointed to the prospect of foreign military sales to countries with smaller-statured populations. Edwin Dorn, as the assistant secretary of defense for personnel and readiness, in a memorandum to the undersecretary of defense, stressed: "A reduced JPATS sitting height threshold will also expand accommodation of shorter males who may have previously been excluded from pilot training. For potential foreign military sales, this enhances its marketability in countries where pilot populations are of smaller average stature" (1993).

The pragmatists emphasized that cockpit accommodation would benefit all military members, because it required the acquisition process to consider differences concerning capabilities and limitations. By refusing to engage in a gendered discourse, they hoped to appeal to a broader segment of the population and to a Department of Defense with a historically male orientation.

Women's groups, both inside and outside the military, also supported the decision to alter the JPATS sitting requirement, but for different reasons. The fact that it was *women* who were being excluded by the operational requirements and by the technology was central to their decision to support the changes. In general, feminism in the contemporary military environment is organized around ideals of parity and equal opportunity regarding career opportunities (Katzenstein 1993). Insisting that career advancement be based on qualifications, not biology, many felt that physical restrictions that disqualified women limited women's mobility in the services. Through informed networks and more formal associations such as the Defense Advisory

Committee on Women in the Service, new activists set about to influence policy decisions about career opportunities for women.

Although the Tailhook scandal provided momentum for feminist groups in the military and brought gender issues to the forefront of national attention, the decision to accommodate more women in the JPATS cockpit was not without dissension. Some women officers who considered themselves feminists believed that cries for accommodation could be used against women politically. They insisted that demanding "special" treatment would single women out in an institution that, at least on the surface, seeks to eradicate differences between the sexes.

Conversely, a more radical position questioned the very assumptions behind the operational requirements. Is it really necessary, they asked, to possess a sitting height of 34 inches to fly defense aircraft? The lack of any test validation caused an outcry from women who had themselves flown the aircraft (during wartime) and had not experienced any accommodation problems. Thus, distinguishing legitimate requirements for efficiency and safety from the residue of years of assumptions and male bias should become the project of those who develop specifications and are responsible for system acquisition. Underlying this assertion is the belief that the technology itself can be neutral but that the context in which it is embedded is profoundly sexist (Winner 1985, 26–27).

Congress, too, weighed in with views on expanded accommodation for women. The Conference Report of the 1994 Authorization Act blocked release of the JPATS Request for Proposal until a deliberate Department of Defense effort to accommodate women was justified. The Conference Report pointedly directed the secretary of defense to perform two studies concerning accommodation of women and ejection safety in defense aircraft. Conference Report language documented conferee views that JPATS must balance cost savings with the largest user population possible and that it would be imprudent to expand the candidate population for a primary jet trainer when follow-on training and fleet aircraft could not safely accommodate the new population. Senior defense officials testifying before various subcommittees were often asked about department plans to modify cockpits and equipment to expand accommodation of women. Although leadership of the Senate Armed Services Committee passed from the moderate Sam Nunn to the conservative Strom Thurmond after the 1994 midterm elections, there is still significant congressional interest in this subject.

Conclusion

The JPATS case study sheds light on the gendered construction of technology in the military. The design of the cockpit as well as the debates surrounding JPATS accommodation of women delineate men and women as essentially different physical beings. As military technologies are discovered to exclude segments of an otherwise eligible population, they must be replaced with those technologies that are "gender neutral." The JPATS focused enormous attention on this previously unexplored and unexposed issue in defense systems acquisition.

As we have shown, some groups wished to emphasize biological differences between the sexes as a justification for women's ineligibility to fly combat aircraft. For various economic, political, and psychological reasons, the opponents of "fitting the machine to the woman" wanted to continue to use men as the design standard. Despite twenty years of increase in women's involvement in the armed forces, technology seems to have protected what has traditionally been a male occupation—pilots—from any threat. Stressing the physical differences between men and women and assuming the inalterability of aircraft is a way of keeping women out of combat aircraft. Judith Reppy notes that "it is not that women are not physically capable of flying these particular aircraft or that they are not equally exposed to danger in other aircraft; rather, denying women access to combat aircraft is a way of protecting a distinctly male arena" (1993, 7).

On the other hand, simply denying the differences between men and women serves to conceal the gendered dimension of military technologies. As Reppy notes, "closure in the design of these weapons [had] been reached in a time and context in which the idea of women as potential users was not considered; in effect, the current technologies were born gendered" (1993, 6). As we have seen, how such technologies become gendered may have little to do with operating requirements and much to do with social expectations about women's roles.

The economics of defense downsizing mandates that human capabilities play a more prominent part during technology acquisition. For instance, the development of "gender-neutral" technologies may enhance the marketability of U.S. technologies to foreign countries where human engineering has not been a priority despite smaller-statured populations. Finally, as we look to the future, we may find that high-technology systems will even further diminish strength and size requirements. Technologies such as "glass" or computer-automated cockpits and voice-activated systems may require less physical strength and may be more accommodating of women.

Since it is likely that the remaining combat exclusions such as submarines and ground combat will be removed in the coming years, we should begin now to build women into technologies for the future. The next generation of submarines is on the drawing board in preparation for the twenty-first century, and the design specifications being used will accommodate female anthropometric dimensions. Similarly, plans for combat vehicles and weapons should assume that "infantrywomen" will be among the intended users.

Imagine a society in which General Motors, Ford, and Chrysler built cars that could be operated only by men and a few women—or one in which automobiles were designed only for women and a few small men. Technology is not genderless!

NOTE

Acknowledgments: We wish to thank Judith Reppy, Mary Fainsod Katzenstein, Claire Gordon, Greg Zehner, David Rose, and Scott Price for their assistance and support.

REFERENCES

Aspin, Les. 1993. "Policy on the Assignment of Women in the Armed Forces." Memorandum. 28 April.

Deutch, John. 1992. "JPATS Cockpit Accommodation Working Group Report." Memorandum. 2 December.

Dorn, Edwin. 1993. "JPATS Cockpit Accommodation Working Group Report." Memorandum. 19 October.

Gordon, Claire C., et al. 1989. "1988 Anthropometric Survey of U.S. Army Personnel." U.S. Army Natick Research, Development, and Engineering Center, Natick, Mass. September.

Katzenstein, Mary Fainsod. 1993. "The Formation of Feminism in the Military Environment." Paper presented at conference, Institutional Change and the U.S. Military: The Changing Role of Women, Cornell University, November.

Key, Evelyn, Edward Fleischer, and Elizabeth Gauthier. 1993. "Women at Sea: Design Considerations." Paper presented at Association of Scientists and Engineers, 30th Annual Technical Symposium, 8 April.

Maze, Rick. 1993. "Fitting Seats for Women." *Navy Times,* 25 October.

McCormick, Ernest J., and Mark S. Sanders. 1982. *Human Factors in Engineering and Design.* New York: McGraw-Hill.

Reppy, Judith. 1993. "New Technologies in the Gendered Workplace." Paper presented at conference, Institutional Change and the U.S. Military: The Changing Role of Women, Cornell University, November.

Richman-Loo, Nina, and Rachel Weber. 1993. "Gender and Weapons Design: Are Military Technologies Biased against Women?" Paper presented at conference, Institutional Change and the U.S. Military: The Changing Role of Women, Cornell University, November.

Stiehm, Judith Hicks. 1985. "Women's Biology and the U.S. Military." Virginia Sapiro, ed., *Women, Biology, and Public Policy.* Beverly Hills: Sage. pp. 205–34.

U.S. Department of Defense. 1993. "JPATS Cockpit Accommodation Working Group Report." May.

———. 1994. "Studies of Joint Primary Aircraft Training System Accommodation of Women and Expansion of Universal Ejection Seat Capability." March.

Winner, Langdon. 1985. "Do Artifacts Have Politics?" In Donald Mackenzie and Judith Wajcman, eds., *The Social Shaping of Technology.* New York: Taylor and Francis, pp. 26–27.

Lucinda Joy Peach

Gender Ideology in the Ethics
of Women in Combat

Nearly forty-one thousand women served in the U.S. military in
Desert Storm, approximately 7 percent of the total forces (see Holm 1992,
xiii). Even though women were officially excluded from combat duty, they
were assigned to posts that positioned them in or near the line of fire (see
U.S. Senate 1991, 803; Association 1991, 18). (And, of course, the "line of
fire is an artificial construct, given modern military technology.) Throughout Desert Storm, women performed flight operations within the combat
zone; a number of women also participated in support and rescue assignments that were as physically demanding as combat and involved significant
risk.

In prior conflicts, too, many women in the armed services have served in
combat support and combat service support positions that have put them
within range of enemy fire.[1] For example, it has been estimated that approximately three-quarters of the women who served in the military in
Vietnam were subjected to combat conditions (see D'Amico 1990, 5; Dienstfrey 1988, 551). Yet none of these women was formally in a combat position (see Association 1991, 31–33; U.S. Senate 1991, 998).

The issue of whether women should participate in military combat challenges deeply held assumptions and beliefs about the nature of war, women,

men, and the military. It raises several competing concerns: the integrity of national security and defense capability, gender equality and justice, and family and citizenship responsibilities. Differences of opinion about these issues cut across the usual political and religious divisions, as well as differences of gender, military versus civilian status, and types of feminist and nonfeminist orientations.

Despite the renewed attention to the combat issue that has resulted from the media spotlight on women's participation in the Gulf War, little consideration has been given to the specifically moral and ethical dimensions of the issue. Embedded in the debates over whether—and if so, what—combat roles are appropriate for women are three distinct ethical positions or perspectives, which I have designated the *ethic of accountability*, the *ethic of justice*, and the *ethic of care*.

There are problems with each of these ethical approaches to the combat issue. First, proponents of one ethical position seldom recognize the considerations that are central to the other two. Thus, little effort is made to accommodate the concerns important to proponents of other approaches. Second, and more problematic, underlying and interwoven with each of these orientations are assumptions, prejudices, stereotypes, and myths about male and female "natures" and "proper" sex roles and behaviors (see Code 1991, 196). It is such ideas—what I call *gender ideology*—rather than established facts about women's or men's capabilities, that too frequently dominate the discussion of the three ethical perspectives to be considered. Although these perspectives each make assumptions about gender difference, the specific assumptions differ radically.

Background and Current Status of Women in Combat

The military is known as a male-dominated bastion of masculine tradition and practice. Yet as far back as the Revolutionary War, and throughout U.S. history, some women have always managed to serve in the military, including in combat roles (see Holm 1992; Larson 1990; De Pauw 1981). Nonetheless, before 1948, when the Women's Armed Services Integration Act was enacted, no women were permanently enlisted in the military. Rather, women were assigned to special "women's corps," auxiliary forces that were temporarily established to meet manpower shortages (see Holm 1992, 113–22).

Legislation permitted the secretaries of the services to discriminate between men and women, resulting in unequal enlistment and discharge procedures, dependency benefits, and promotion and combat restrictions. Statutory restrictions also limited women to 2 percent of the armed forces, even during the peak of U.S. involvement in World War II. Although no enlisted women were given combat assignments (nor were they trained for survival in a war zone), many of them worked in combat situations (see Reeves, Chapter 5 in this volume; Campbell 1990, 109; see generally Morden 1990; Treadwell 1954; Holm 1992, Chaps. 10, 11; Rogan 1981).

Most women were discharged from the armed forces at the end of World War II. After much debate, however, Congress passed the 1948 Integration Act, which established a permanent place for women in the regular military.[2] Although the 2 percent ceiling on women was lifted in 1967 in order to ease personnel shortages in connection with the Vietnam War, all branches of the armed services continue to restrict the percentage of women allowed to enlist (see Holm 1992, 192–203; Schumm et al. 1994, 500).[3] The services vary considerably regarding the opportunities made available to women, but they are similar in having excluded women from all combat positions until 1993.[4]

"Combat" is the ideological core of the military (see Enloe 1983, 138). What constitutes "combat," though, has often been vaguely defined, and definitions have been frequently altered (see Holm 1992, 337–38, 396–99; Association 1991, 11; Kornblum 1984, 359–60). From 1988 to 1993, the Department of Defense determined what was a combat position on the basis of a "risk rule," specifying that "risks of direct combat, exposure to hostile fire, or capture are proper criteria for closing positions or units to women" (U.S. DOD, Task Force Report 1988, 9; Schmitt 1994b).[5] This definition stated that direct combat "takes place while closing with the enemy by fire, maneuver, or shock effect to destroy or capture or while repelling assault by fire, close combat, or counterattack" (U.S. DOD 1991, 10-1, 2; U.S. DOD, Task Force Report 1988, 10–11).[6]

In 1993, Defense Secretary Les Aspin replaced the risk rule with a new definition of ground combat that bars women from units that engage the enemy with weapons on the ground while exposed to hostile fire and that involve substantial probability of direct physical contact with hostile forces (see Schmitt 1994b; Schmitt 1994c, A18; Lancaster 1994, A1; Pine 1994, A5). Under the new policy, then, exposure to risk, *alone*, became an insufficient ground for excluding women from a particular assignment. Nevertheless, women are barred from almost all assignments that involve operating offensive, line-of-sight weapons and from all positions entailing ground fighting. This includes armor, infantry, and field artillery, the three specialties that are considered the core of combat (see Schmitt 1994b; Schmitt 1994a, A7).

After Desert Storm was concluded, Defense Secretary Dick Cheney announced that "women have made a major contribution to this effort. We could not have won without them." General Norman Schwarzkopf stated that American military women had performed "magnificently" (quoted in Holm 1992, 470). Women's visible (especially the capture and release of Army officer Rhonda Cornum; see Chapter 1 in this volume) and noticeably exemplary participation in the Persian Gulf War sparked a reevaluation of the issue of combat roles for women. The performance of women soldiers had assuaged many fears about their capabilities, but as Congresswoman Pat Schroeder pointed out, the Gulf War showed that while women were as exposed to the danger of attack as many men in combat positions, the women were not given the status, recognition, or benefits that accompany positions carrying the "combat" designation (see Association 1991, 16–17).

In 1991, Congress lifted the ban on women flying combat aircraft. Despite the finding of a presidential commission appointed by President George Bush in 1991 that women not be given air combat assignments (the commission did hold that women should be allowed on combat ships, with the exception of submarines), Aspin ordered the military to drop most of its restrictions on women in combat aircraft. He also asked Congress to lift the ban on women's service on combat ships, which it subsequently did (see Rohter 1993). The USS Eisenhower, which completed a six-month tour of duty in April 1995, was the first Navy warship to sail with women (more than four-hundred of a five-thousand-member crew) (see Schmitt 1994d).[7]

These recent developments have not eliminated the debate over women in combat roles. Many inside and outside the military continue to be opposed to combat for women, and military leadership has engaged in a number of foot-dragging strategies to obstruct the integration of women into newly opened combat assignments (see Korb 1992; Palmer 1991).[8] For example, after Army Secretary Togo West's order to make more positions available to women, the Army first suggested that it could open another seven-thousand positions to women, but then the Army's vice-chief of staff, General J. H. Binford Peay, recommended a "pause" to let the situation "sort out for a while" (quoted in Schmitt 1994c, A18). Army Chief of Staff Gordon Sullivan objected on the ground that women lack the necessary physical rigor for such assignments and that they would cause morale and privacy problems (see Schmitt 1994c, A7, A18). Because of opposition from senior Army generals, West later abandoned plans to open thousands of positions, including the battalion headquarters of combat engineer, air defense, and field artillery units, and slots as crew members of a barrage artillery system.

Despite this initial reluctance, a month later the Army announced plans to open thirty-two-thousand positions that previously had been closed to women (Schmitt 1994b).[9] (Closed positions still include nearly 25 percent of Army job classifications, or about 67 percent of the actual jobs, including operating advanced field artillery weapons, service on Multiple Launch Rocket System [MLRS] crews, and flying aircraft carrying special operations troops.)[10]

The Navy opened aircraft carriers to women in 1994 but still excludes them from positions in SEAL Commando units, on nuclear submarines, and on mine sweepers (the latter ostensibly because of their cramped quarters). When the plane of the Navy's first female combat pilot, Lieutenant Kara Hultgreen, went down in October 1994, some male aviators and military leaders grumbled publicly that her accident proved that women were unfit for combat duty, even before evidence was retrieved indicating that the problem was engine failure (Schmitt 1994e).

As of 1995, some 67 percent of Army jobs and 62 percent of Marine Corps jobs remain closed to women (Schmitt 1994b). In addition, severe combat restrictions apply to virtually all ground combat positions such as field artillery, short-range air defense, and combat engineering, as well as military intelligence and "special operations" aircraft transporting crews (Pine 1994). These include most of the positions that are traditionally paths to advancement into the military's top ranks. This drastically constrains women's opportunities for top leadership (see Schmitt 1994b, A5).

Thus, despite recent policy changes, the situation of most military women in relation to combat has not been significantly altered. Gender ideology continues to operate at the core of the "combat" ethos, despite the appearance of gender equality on paper. (see Mitchell, Chapter 3 of this volume).

The Influence of Gender Ideology on the Debate

Before we turn to a discussion of each of the ethical perspectives on women in combat, it is helpful to introduce the notion of gender ideology and describe how it has functioned in relation to the combat issue. Gender ideology perpetuates traditional understandings of male and female roles. Such understandings are frequently the products of sexist attitudes and of values maintained by a still-patriarchal culture. Gender ideology presents stereotypes of males and females, which (1) preclude recognition of individual characteristics (2) often do not conform to reality (see Code 1991, 189, 197).

In the context of the combat issue, ideological notions about gender perpetuate myths not only about women but also about men, the military, and the nature of war and combat. In particular, the rationales forwarded to exclude women from combat frequently reflect the influence of one of two ideologically biased myths about the nature of men, women, and war: the myth that war is "manly" (and thus no place for women) and the myth that men are protectors and women protected (see Stiehm 1989).

The "Masculinity" of War

Traditional notions of gender identity link men with war and women with peace (see Jeffords 1989, 3; Enloe 1988).[11] This linkage carries over into the specific realm of gender and combat. Marine Corps Commandant General Robert Barrows (Ret.) testified at a congressional hearing that "combat is uncivilized and women cannot do it. Nor should they be even thought of as doing it. . . . I think the very nature of women disqualifies them from doing it. Women give life, sustain life, nurture life; they do not take it" (U.S. Senate 1991, 895). Expressing the same sentiments despite more enlightened rhetoric is the recent statement of Air Force Chief of Staff General Merrill McPeak: "Combat is about killing people. . . . Even though logic tells us that women can do that as well as men, I have a traditional attitude about wives and mothers and daughters being ordered to kill people" (quoted in Towell 1992).[12] Jean Elshtain concludes that the prevailing gender ideology associated with war characterizes men as "just warriors" and women as "beautiful souls" (Elshtain 1987, 144).

Throughout history, war has been a theater in which men could prove their masculinity and in which masculinity was deemed as a necessary prerequisite to success. "Femininity" has long been disparaged in the military, and much effort has been made to suppress and exclude any traits in male soldiers that could be considered feminine.[13] In basic training, new recruits are often characterized as feminine and effeminate and are called "ladies" or "girls" until they are able to prove their masculinity by exhibiting aggression and other "macho" characteristics (see MacDonald 1988, 16; Ruddick

1983a, 253; Michalowski 1982, 332). The male standard operates, sometimes explicitly but more often implicitly, in shaping the attitude that women
are out of place, if not in the military generally, then at least in combat.

The presence of women in the military has been viewed as depriving
"young men of their manhood" and as antithetical to the misogynistic attitudes bred by such basic training (Michalowski 1982, 332; Rogan 1981,
27). Similar sentiments have perpetuated the combat exclusion. For example, Senator Emanuel Cellar testified during congressional debates that
"women represent motherhood and creation. Wars are for destruction.
Women integrated with men in the carnage and slaughter of battle . . . is un-
thinkable. Can you imagine women trained by a drill sergeant to charge the
enemy with fixed bayonets and bombs? War is Death's feast. It is enough
that men attend" (*Congressional Record* 1971, 35–785).[14] The perception that
the virtues of "manliness" are necessary for effective combat soldiering,
virtues that women are considered intrinsically to lack, has contributed to
the maintenance of women's exclusion from most combat assignments.[15]
Given these stereotypic images, it is not difficult to understand how opponents can "equate women's participation in combat with the destruction of
womanhood, manhood, and American society" (Kornblum 1984, 385).[16]

The Myth of Protection

Accompanying and interrelated with the notion of war as masculine
is the myth that the purpose for which men fight is to protect women (see
Stiehm 1989, 6–7; Kornblum 1984). This myth is frequently evident in rationales that the combat exclusion is necessary to protect women from the
risks of battle and to protect their roles as childbearers and mothers. According to this myth, members of the military extend "a special regard for
women who must be protected as the symbolic vessel of femininity and
motherhood" (Karst 1991, 536). The myth that women are the weaker sex
who need to be protected by strong men portrays women as victims dependent on men rather than as autonomous agents capable of defending
themselves. The myth persists despite the incongruity of such imagery with
respect to women soldiers—or even women civilians, who are regularly
slain in war.

The little evidence that sheds light on Congress's original intent for the
combat exclusion suggests that it was based, at least in part, on notions of
proper gender roles that required men to protect women from the horrors of
the battlefront (see *Owens v. Brown*, 455 F. Supp. 291, 305 [D.D.C. 1978]).[17]

Modern weapons technology has blurred the lines between support and combat positions as well as between the "front line" and the "rear" (see Holm 1992, 403; U.S. Senate 1991, 803). Thus, although women were not permitted to fly fighter aircraft until 1993, they had been permitted to fly the tankers that refuel the fighters, making them a prime target for enemy fire. Similarly, although women were banned from Navy destroyers until 1994, they were allowed to serve on supply ships that are located in battle zones.

Again, modern combat doctrine can dictate that the first targets to be hit are command headquarters and supply houses located far from an elusive and increasingly illusory front line. These can be the very areas where women are concentrated. Yet although women have been allowed to serve in command headquarters, they are still excluded from MLRS crews, which can launch rockets at a distance of twenty miles from their targets (see Lancaster 1994, 17; Schmitt 1994a, A18). This suggests that part of the reason for excluding women from combat has to do with not wanting them in control of powerful weaponry; it is not merely a concern about protecting them from danger.

The ideological understandings of gender operating in these two myths underlie each of the perspectives on women in combat, although they take quite different forms. They are particularly evident in the rationales that would exclude women from combat roles. Only by attempting to disassociate ideological myths and stereotypes about gender from considerations relevant to these three ethics can we make a well-grounded assessment of the issue of women in combat.

Ethical Perspectives on Women in Combat

The Ethic of Accountability

The arguments most frequently raised in opposition to combat roles for women concern the need for military efficiency, effectiveness, and troop safety. These principles are part of an "ethic of accountability" according to which military leaders are deemed to have a special responsibility for the safety and protection of their troops as well as the efficient and effective accomplishment of the military mission. This includes a responsibility to ensure that the lives of the soldiers for whom one is responsible are not needlessly sacrificed (see, e.g., Hartle 1989, 52–53, 145; Huntington 1986, 23–24; Wakin

1986, 196; Gabriel 1982, 140). The accountability ethic assumes that high military standards cannot be maintained if women are allowed to occupy combat roles.

In particular, the efficiency rationale posits that the military's mission can be accomplished more economically by excluding women from combat positions than by including them. The assumption that the inclusion of women in combat roles leads to inefficiency is commonplace. Even Army Secretary West, who has fought to open more combat roles for women, characterizes the issue of women in combat in terms of a conflict between equal opportunity to serve and the Army's obligation to fight and win wars. As he puts it, "the question is how to best utilize the available resources to do the latter with the least compromise of the former" (quoted in Schmitt 1994c, A18).[18] The purported inefficiency of using women in combat positions has been based on several factors, including the lesser effectiveness of women soldiers and mixed-gender units, the cost of adequate physical and psychological screening of enlisted women for combat capability and preparedness, and the inefficiency of pregnancy, factors that are considered in greater detail below.

The efficiency rationale has been considerably weakened in the past two decades. Since the advent of the All-Volunteer Force in the mid-1970s, the military has become more dependent on its women soldiers, who overall have more education and fewer performance problems than men soldiers. Just as it became less efficient to keep African Americans segregated in the military in an earlier era, and as it is becoming inefficient to keep gays and lesbians either banned or closeted, it has now become less efficient for the military to keep women out of combat roles than it would be to integrate them fully, for, as we will see, the combat restrictions present obstacles to the most efficient and effective use of military personnel. Given women's indispensable and integral importance to the present-day military, it could be argued that it is more efficient to integrate them fully into all roles for which they are qualified rather than to continue to segregate them from combat positions.

The effectiveness rationale is also frequently advanced against including women in combat roles. In 1981, William D. Clark, acting secretary for the Army's Office of Manpower and Reserve Affairs, testified at a Senate Armed Services Manpower Subcommittee hearing that the Army was planning to cut back on the recruitment of enlisted women, not because of their inability as soldiers or because of the issue of their exposure to combat, but because of "feelings" of field commanders about problems with "combat effectiveness of the organizations as you have large numbers of women in them" (quoted in Holm 1992, 388). As late as 1994, senior generals criticized civilian leaders who wanted to open up more combat roles for women, arguing that they "let their idealistic goals interfere with military effectiveness" (quoted in Schmitt 1994c, A1).[19]

The military has used the accountability ethic to reply to arguments that restrictions on combat assignments for women deny them equal opportunity. It maintains that equal rights and opportunity can be met only to the extent they do not conflict with the military's fundamental purpose of national defense, a basic aspect of which includes combat effectiveness. From this perspective, the military "must not be used for social experimentation to the degradation of its war-fighting capability" (Nabors 1982, 51; see Association 1991, 48–49, 55; Tuten 1982). Essentially, the argument is that national defense takes priority over rights and justice (DiLucente 1992, 46; Golightly 1987, 48). As discussed below, however, the various rationales for the combat exclusion do not demonstrate that women's participation in combat roles would hinder national defense objectives.

Although the assumption that integrating women into combat would be deleterious to combat effectiveness and to the military's ability to mobilize in time of war is widespread (see, e.g., Mitchell 1989, 159; Kelly 1984, 103; Marlowe 1983, 194),[20] it is a slippery aspect of the accountability ethic to assess. Effectiveness is used to refer to a variety of situations, including mobilizing and deploying troops, success in battle as measured by outcomes (e.g., "mission accomplishment" or "the ratio of United States versus enemy killed and wounded in combat"), and the perceptions of hostile forces (e.g., Mitchell 1989, 159; U.S. Senate 1991, 798 [testimony of Sen. John Glenn]).

Several different arguments have been raised to support the position that women's participation in combat would be detrimental to the accountability obligations of military leaders. These include the contention that women's participation would interfere with the male bonding and lack of sexual distractions necessary for combat readiness, that women are physically and psychologically unfit for combat, and that their capacity for pregnancy and motherhood makes them unfit for combat roles. These arguments have been heavily influenced by one of the two myths about gender and combat discussed above, so much so that most of the arguments in opposition to combat roles for women can be subsumed under one myth or the other.

The masculinity myth is often evident in arguments that the male bonding necessary for unit cohesion and the lack of sexual distraction required for combat readiness, along with women's lesser physical and psychological strength, justify women's exclusion from combat roles. Conventional military wisdom is that "male bonding"—characterized as camaraderie and team spirit—is necessary to unit cohesion, itself a prerequisite to military effectiveness and efficiency. (For a counterargument, see Burke, Chapter 10 in this volume.) Male bonding is related to the accountability ethic in that unit cohesion is understood to be a function of interpersonal relations between military leaders and their troops and the leader's ability to create and sustain "those interpersonal skills that allow him to build strong ties with his men" (Gabriel 1982, 172–73). Opponents of women in combat roles often assume, but have not demonstrated, that bonding will not occur if male soldiers are required to share their duties with women (Mitchell 1989; Golightly 1987; see U.S. Senate 1991, 85–96).

The myth of the masculinity of war helps sustain the view that women and anything identified as feminine "must be effectively and finally eliminated from the masculine realm" in order to maintain the value of bonds between males (see Jeffords 1989, xiii, 168). Ideological understandings of gender are patent in the unsubstantiated, outdated, and anecdotal character of the evidence on which the male bonding argument relies. The military has not studied the impact of the integration of the forces on "male bonding" in actual combat recently, nor has it undertaken systematic efforts to instill male-female or female-female bonding in its soldiers (see Stiehm 1989, 236; Stiehm 1985a, 172).

More important, recent evidence indicates that bonding is not harmed by gender integration in combat units. The return of the USS *Eisenhower* in April 1995 after six months at sea "sorely disappointed" the naysayers, as a *Time* magazine journalist put it, since the mission "was a resounding success" (Waller 1995, 36). The ship suffered no decline in combat readiness and, according to the executive officer, Captain Doug Roulstone, performed "as well as if not better than before women were aboard" (quoted in Waller 1995, 36). Of the few sex-related problems that occurred, only one necessitated disciplinary action. The total number of disciplinary cases was less than on previous cruises, and the carrier's overall performance indicators showed improvement (see Waller 1995, 37).

A 1994 study of the effect of gender integration on unit readiness in the Army found that "when unit readiness was predicted from all the independent variables, no significant direct or indirect effects of gender were observed" (Schumm et al. 1994, 506). After reviewing other research on this area, the study's authors concluded that "it appears unlikely that having females within combat service-support units presents a substantial problem for military readiness" (Schumm et al. 1994, 307). In addition, military experience with female soldiers in the Persian Gulf War, supplemented by the limited studies that have been done under simulated combat and field conditions, indicates that the presence of women in combat units does not adversely effect combat effectiveness (see Johnson et al. 1978; U.S. Army Research Institute 1977; discussed in Holm 1992, 256–58; Devilbiss 1990, 18; Coyle 1989, 37–40; Moskos 1985; Devilbiss 1985).[21] It is likely that unit bonding depends more on shared experiences, including risks and hardships, than on gender distinctions (see Karst 1991, 537, 543; Opinion 1988, 138; Devilbiss 1985, 519; U.S. Senate 1991, 851–52).

In addition to the supposedly detrimental effect on male bonding, including women in combat roles is sometimes alleged to diminish troop effectiveness because of the inevitable sexual attraction and behavior that would follow from having mixed-gender units. Some express a fear that men will be preoccupied with winning the sexual favors of women rather than with concentrating on their mission (see, e.g., Mitchell 1989, 176–78; Golightly 1987, 46; Rogan 1981, 27).[22]

The fraternization argument ignores the capability of the sexes to interact with each other in nonsexual ways, particularly under the exigent circumstances of combat. The limited studies that have been conducted under simulated combat conditions show that gender-integrated combat units are as effective as all-male units and that members of such units develop brother-sister bonds rather than sexual ones (see Schumm et al. 1994; Johnson 1978; U.S. Army Research Institute 1977; Devilbiss 1990, 18; Coyle 1989; Moskos 1985). Fraternization is most likely to be a problem where there is ineffective leadership. Experience with African Americans in the military has shown that actual integration diminishes prejudice and fosters group cohesiveness more effectively than any other factor (see Holm 1992, 257; Moskos 1990, 74; Kornblum 1984, 412, 422).

Many proponents of the combat exclusion argue that military effectiveness and efficiency are compromised by women's lack of physical strength and stamina relative to men's (see, e.g., Mitchell 1989, 156–62; Golightly 1987). Military personnel have testified before Congress that few women would meet the physical standards for combat duty (see U.S. Senate 1991;

Cramsie 1983, 562).[23] The steadfastness with which the belief that women are physically ill-equipped for combat duty, in the face of evidence to the contrary, indicates the influence of gender ideology with respect to this rationale as well.

Military studies document that men have some advantages in upper-body and leg strength, cardiovascular capacity, and lean muscle (see U.S. Dept. of Army 1976; Kelly 1984, 100–101). Nevertheless, these tests do not show that women are incapable of meeting the standards required for combat duty. Nor do they factor into consideration the disparities in prior physical training and physical conditioning that contribute to men's better test results. Army reports, for example, indicate that some women *do* have the requisite upper-body strength. In addition, some women are stronger than some men, and women have performed well in the limited number of combat-type situations in which they have been tested.[24]

Physical strength is only one of many factors that determine the capability of persons for military combat. Bravery, intelligence, and technical skills are also important attributes. In addition, the nature of modern combat, with its emphasis on high-technology equipment, makes the issue of physical strength far less important than it was when war involved primarily hand-to-hand combat. Physical size and strength has minimal, if any, consideration when weapons are being fired at the touch of a button from a location far removed from the combat theater.[25] Equipment redesign and technological innovations can eliminate most needs for intense physical strength in many combat assignments (see Richman-Loo and Weber, Chapter 7 in this volume).[26]

The ideological dimension of the physical strength question is evident in the military's tendency to treat women's generally lesser physical strength as an insurmountable obstacle to women's combat participation rather than attempt to find strategies that would minimize its significance. Since the early 1980s, military personnel and others have suggested that combat roles be assigned on the basis of the physical strength required to perform them rather than exclusively on the basis of gender (see, e.g., U.S. Senate 1991, 865; Roush 1990, 11–12; Coyle 1989, 31; Proxmire 1986, 110; Segal 1984, 110; Nabors 1982, 61; Rogan 1981, 306). Such proposals would result in a fairer and more accurate measure of "fit" between persons and assignments than the current reliance on gender difference. Military leaders have failed to implement such a scheme, arguing that a performance-based standard may not be "cost effective" (see Association 1991, 54; Rogan

1981, 20), but their failure to demonstrate that this is the case suggests that the physical strength rationale for the combat exclusion is actually the consequence of gender ideology rather than cost-effectiveness.

Finally, another loosely related set of arguments under the ethic of accountability in support of the combat exclusion is based on psychological considerations. Some of these arguments are related to the masculinity myth, and others to the myth of protection. One argument reflecting the influence of the masculinity-of-war myth is based on the assumption that men are naturally more aggressive than women and that this "natural aggressiveness" would be "softened" by women's participation in battle (e.g., Mitchell 1989; Marlowe 1983, 191; Tuten 1982, 255).

There is no factual basis for the often-aired argument that female combatants would be psychologically weaker or less well equipped to handle the extreme psychological stresses of combat than men.[27] Such arguments have been refuted by the experience of military women such as Army (then) Major Rhonda Cornum, a flight surgeon whose aircraft was shot down during the Gulf War. Cornum and other military women's matter-of-fact attitude about survival in the face of physical injury and/or sexual abuse at the hands of their captors testifies to the ability of military women to cope as POWs (see Cornum, Chapter 1 in this volume; Reeves, Chapter 5 in this volume; Cornum 1992; Holm 1992, 455–59). Several U.S. Army studies, including the reactions of military women during World War II (as well as female POWs), also challenge the view that women are psychologically unfit for combat (see Gordon and Ludvigson 1991, 25; Dillingham 1990, 227–28).[28]

Another psychological argument is framed from the hypothetical perspective of the enemy. According to this rationale, women's participation in combat would be interpreted by hostile forces as indicating that U.S. forces were weak and ineffectual, thus diminishing the symbolic effectiveness of U.S. troops as icons of power and strength (e.g., Van Creveld 1993; Golightly 1987, 49). Such arguments are easily rebutted by counter indications that one side in a battle generally ignores the presence of women on the other side. Where military women have dealt with members of hostile forces, as female members of Operation Desert Storm did with Iraqi POWs, their gender generally did not result in different behavior (see Holm 1992, 463–64).[29]

Three key arguments for maintaining the combat exclusion have been particularly influenced by the other myth of gender ideology, the protection myth. These are that women's biological and psychological characteristics make them ill-suited to be POWs, that pregnancy interferes with combat effectiveness, and that women's roles as childbearers and childrearers make their assignment to combat inappropriate.

Under the protection myth, some have argued that if women were in combat, male soldiers would be more concerned about protecting them than fighting the enemy, thus compromising combat effectiveness (see Barkalow 1190, 260; Beecraft 1989, 43).[30] Related to this rationale is the view that women soldiers would be physically and psychologically unable to handle capture by hostile forces, because of the possibility of rape and other sexual abuse (see Mitchell 1989, 7, 182–92; Marlowe 1983, 195; Nabors 1982, 59; Rogan 1981, 26). This argument was featured in press coverage of the Gulf War in connection with the few female soldiers who become POWs.

The rationale that women need to be protected from the horrors of capture and imprisonment ignores the reality that men as well as women are raped in war and that women are subject to such sexual violence at home and by their fellow troops, as well as in the field of combat.

The protection myth, which calls into question the propriety of risking the safety of the nation's childbearers by exposing them to the risks of combat, is evident in the military's traditional approach to pregnancy. The military has historically argued that assigning women to combat would hamper combat effectiveness and efficiency because of their conflicting roles as mothers and potential mothers (see, e.g., Barkalow 1990, 238–41; Stiehm 1985b, 226; Nabors 1982, 56–58).[31] The Army in particular has expressed concern with the effects of pregnancy on "readiness," "mission accomplishment" and "deployability" (see Mitchell 1989, 6, 166–71; Stiehm 1985a, 266; Tuten 1982, 251).[32]

Pregnancy was one of the primary concerns of the Navy in sending women to sea on the USS *Eisenhower's* six-month mission (see Waller 1995; Pine 1995; Graham 1995). Out of more than four-hundred women on the crew, only fifteen left the ship early because they were pregnant, a far lower number than the overall pregnancy rates for Navy women serving on land (see Waller 1995, 37). Research has shown that the belief that female military personnel lose more duty time than men because of pregnancy-related reasons is unfounded, since males lose even more time for being AWOL and for desertion, drug and alcohol abuse, and confinement (see Holm 1992, 303).[33]

Given the procedures in place under the combat exclusion, however, pregnancy can interfere with the ability of the armed forces to mobilize troops rapidly for combat, since it cannot be predicted in advance which women will be pregnant and thus unavailable for deployment. Since military policy, at least in the Army, does not provide temporary replacements for pregnant personnel, having pregnant women in a unit also increases everyone else's work load. Pregnancy consequently has the potential to breed resentment among co-workers, even though the argument that enlisted women use pregnancy as a means of avoiding unpleasant tasks (which would theoretically include combat) (see, e.g., Tuten 1982, 251) is not supported by the evidence (see Graham 1995).

Thus, because of the way military units are currently structured, pregnancy can present a problem to the full integration of all women into combat forces. Pregnancy is a legitimate reason to exclude women from actually engaging in some forms of combat. It is *one* consideration that needs to be factored into the analysis of how and whether to integrate women into certain combat roles. But it does not justify the stringency of the current restrictions.[34] Only about 10 percent of servicewomen are pregnant at any given time (see Gordon and Ludvigson 1991, 22–23; Hackworth 1991, 27). Further, the experience of pregnancy varies widely as to how it affects a woman's job performance. Some women are able to carry on their normal activities into the latter stages of pregnancy. Most logistical problems relating to pregnancy, such as deployment plans, can be surmounted by careful planning.

Like pregnancy, motherhood and women's responsibilities to their families are viewed as antithetical to effective combat soldiering.[35] The protection myth reinforces the view that women need special protection because they are responsible, in turn, for protecting their children.[36] According to this argument, women not only bear children but also are primarily responsible for their care and nurture as the center of family life (see Mitchell 1989, 6, 171–76; Segal 1982, 274–75, 281–82).[37] Questioning military women's involvement but not men's whenever families are concerned also perpetuates the stereotype that mothers are more responsible for family life than are fathers.

Nonetheless, ideological assumptions about women's primary obligations to their families are widespread in American society. Although the public has been reluctant to send husbands and fathers off to war, surveys reveal that Americans continue to be more willing to send young fathers into combat than young mothers. Even supporters of combat roles for women have assumed that mothers would be more reluctant to risk their lives in combat than would men (see Campbell 1993; Lieberman 1990, 219).[38]

Since exempting all single parents and dual-service career couples from deployment would weaken military capability, and since women make up the larger percentage of single parents in the military, the problems of how the military should deal with single parenthood in times of troop mobilization and deployment implicate women more than men. The family obligations of mothers in the military, especially single parents, may consequently present practical difficulties for their ability to carry out combat assignments involving instantaneous readiness for mobilization and deployment.

Nonetheless, the problems surrounding mothers in combat roles are exacerbated by the ideological assumption that women *are* essentially mothers. In actuality, many military women are not mothers and have no immediate plans to become mothers. Most women entering the military are not (yet) mothers (see Stiehm 1985b, 229).[39] Treating all women as potential or actual mothers leads to the irrational result that men who are fathers can be required to participate in combat whereas women who are *not* mothers cannot (see Association 1991, 25; Segal 1982, 283).[40] Further, although most women traditionally have taken primary responsibility for protecting and providing for their children, not all mothers are primary caretakers. Many families have alternative arrangements for child care that make someone other than the mother chiefly responsible.

Finally, tradition should not be dispositive of who *should* be responsible for national defense in time of war. Fathers have equal responsibility for protecting and providing for their children, yet they have not been exempted from combat duty since the Korean War. In addition, the legislation mandating women's exclusion from combat does not exempt them from military *service* in time of war. Children of military parents are just as much in need of care and protection whether their mothers are assigned to combat duty or some other role. Allowing families to make their own decisions about child care in the event that the mother is called to serve in combat duty is more appropriate than maintaining the combat exclusion.

In addition to the rationales for the combat exclusion that are products of the gender myths we have just explored, a third reason offered under the accountability ethic is based on public and military opinions. These arguments are based on the premise that military leaders are accountable not only to their own troops but also to the general public. The Department of Defense, for example, has suggested that the real basis for the exclusion is "the will of the American people" (see Mitchell 1989, 153; Kelly 1984, 105–6). Representatives of the military have also argued that the public is "not ready" for women to come home in body bags. In the past, such arguments were supported by public opinion polls of both military and civilian populations. This rationale for excluding women from combat is fast becoming obsolete, however.[41] As the public's response to the Gulf War showed, by and large Americans have come to accept women in dangerous military roles (see Holm 1992, 464, 470).

Military personnel are divided over the exclusion issue, with the greatest opposition from male officers. The most support for combat roles for women come from female officers, with enlisted personnel of mixed opinion (see Stiehm 1989, 91–104). Here, as well, attitudes have changed from what they were in the 1970s, when a study found that a majority of military personnel believed that women should not be assigned to any combat positions (see Stiehm 1989, 91, 103). For example, a large majority of male and female Air Force pilots surveyed in 1987 indicated that women were physically and psychologically equipped to handle combat (see Stiehm 1989, 103).[42] A survey of military women in 1989 reflected a two-thirds majority in favor of repealing the combat exclusion. Survey responses indicate, however, that military women favor allowing women to *choose* combat roles but are reluctant to *require* combat duty (see Lieberman 1990, 219).

These opinion polls suggest that some of the unwillingness to support combat roles for women reflects concerns about disrupting traditional gender roles and the sexual division of labor they represent. The myths of war as the province of masculinity and the need for female protection are again evident. Such concerns are not significant enough to warrant the conclusion that gender-integrated combat units would not function effectively. Further, the trend of these polls clearly indicates that opinions about women's participation in combat are becoming more favorable. Congress and the Pentagon need to consider these changing attitudes.

A final aspect of the accountability ethic relates to pragmatic military needs for personnel. Military leaders have cited the lack of current necessity for more enlisted personnel, male or female, in combat or other positions, to justify maintaining the combat exclusion (see, e.g., U.S. Senate 1991, 896; Mitchell 1989,15). The recent "downsizing" of the military is thus undoubtedly one of the most significant factors determining what combat positions are made available to women in the foreseeable future. The experience of women in militaries in the United States and abroad indicates that women are allowed in combat roles only when it is perceived to be "necessary" (see Devilbiss 1990, 6, 35, 37; Campbell 1993).

Regardless of changes in the size and configuration of the modern military, however, the downsizing argument is flawed. In addition to its inegalitarian spirit, the combat exclusion functions in opposition to certain aspects of the accountability ethic itself. Banning women from all direct combat assignments prevents maximum use of the talents and capabilities of all members of the military, thereby reducing effectiveness and decreasing national security (see Proxmire, quoted in Gordon and Ludvigson 1991, 17; Lieberman 1990, 218). The exclusion also produces inefficiency. By requiring commanders to reconfigure their units in time of war so as to exclude all women whose current positions would run afoul of the combat exclusions, current restrictions on women's combat participation decrease combat readiness.

These inefficiencies are magnified in an era of shrinking availability of highly qualified, well-educated male recruits, despite recent reductions in troop strength. Relying on the necessity argument precludes consideration of how women might actually be an asset to combat effectiveness, especially with respect to assignments in which, for example, smaller physical size would be an advantage.

As we have seen, the major rationales forwarded under the ethic of accountability fail to justify maintaining the current restrictions on women's participation in combat roles. Such rationales are primarily based on gender ideology rather than demonstrated evidence of women's inability to perform combat duties effectively or men's inability to perform in the presence of women. As the following section reveals, a different form of gender ideology, one that presumes women's essential similarity rather than difference in relation to men, is predominant in the ethic of justice.

The Ethic of Justice

Proponents of increasing women's participation in combat generally base their arguments on an ethic of justice, especially principles of equal rights and responsibilities, equal protection of the laws, and basic fairness (see, e.g., DeCew 1995; Kohn 1993; Gordon and Ludvigson 1991; Association 1991; Lieberman 1990; Roush 1990). Military sociologist Charles Moskos notes that although the Army has a stated principal of equal opportunity for women, the actual "role of women continues to be a roiling source of contention" (Moskos 1991, 16).

There are several respects in which the prohibition on women in combat may be considered unjust. First, the combat exclusion treats women in the military differently than men. By excluding *all* women from the majority of combat positions, the exclusion treats women as an undifferentiated class. Yet women are not all similarly situated for purposes of the combat exclusion, since, as noted above, some women are qualified to perform combat roles.

Second, by excluding women from most combat roles, the exclusion limits the number of jobs available to military women, including some of the most elite positions.[43] Even though a majority of job classifications may be available to women, the number of actual jobs is far less, because many jobs are in the classifications designated "combat" (see U.S. Senate 1991, 806, 824). In addition, the combat restrictions limit women's access to certain noncombat jobs that are reserved for men who rotate through combat and noncombat positions (see, e.g., Gordon and Ludvigson 1991, 14; Kornblum 1984, 368). This in turn limits the number of women who are able to join the military. The combat restrictions thus severely restrict women's opportunities to participate in the job-training, educational, and other benefits that the military makes available to its employees.[44] The low proportion of women in the services also creates tokenism, which has an inhibitory influence on women's advancement and promotion (see Association 1991, 21; Karst 1991, 524; Dunivin 1988).

Third, the combat restrictions deny women access to certain leadership positions for which combat assignments have historically been prerequisites (see, e.g., Holm 1992, 412; Gordon and Ludvigson 1991; Karst 1991, 525). As Senator John Glenn stated, "One of the ways you advance in a military career is either performance in combat or prospective performance in combat" (U.S. Senate 1991, 797). Military leaders have acknowledged that the combat exclusion limits women's opportunities for career advancement (see Towell 1992, 2292; U.S. Senate 1991).[45] Even the Supreme Court has recognized that combat restrictions disadvantage military women by limiting their opportunities for promotion (*Schlesinger v. Ballard*, 419 U.S. 498, at 508–9 [1973]).[46]

The effects of the combat restrictions extend beyond the military, operating to deny women equal opportunities for advancement and promotion in the civilian world after discharge (see, e.g., Hackworth 1991, 25; Devilbiss 1990, 49; Lieberman 1990, 219). They also operate to deny women the full rights and responsibilities of citizenship, since citizenship is symbolically linked to one's defense of nation (see Karst 1991, 524–29; Segal and Segal 1983, 243).[47] If women are denied the obligations of citizenship, justice-ethic proponents argue, they cannot expect equal treatment in other spheres of public life. Thus, in order to become fully equal *citizens* with men, entitled to equal rights and responsibilities in the larger society as well as in the ranks of the military, women need to be permitted to exercise their equal responsibility to defend the nation, which includes the right to participate in combat (see Devilbiss 1990, 52; Rogan 1981, 286–87 [quoting Army captain Kathy Whitcraft]).

Excluding women from combat duty also creates an inequality that disadvantages men by putting full responsibility on their shoulders (see Gooch 1988, 133; Ferber 1987, 12). This situation can easily breed resentment among enlisted men about the unequal risks military women are required to take. Although the military environment of machismo may make it difficult for such feelings of resentment to be openly admitted by men, they may be manifested as general antipathy toward women, particularly when women's abilities are perceived to be judged by more lenient standards than men's. In particular, high-ranking military officials have linked the combat exclusion to sexual harassment, which remains a significant problem in the military, as the Tailhook scandal attests (see, e.g., Towell 1992, 2292; U.S. DOD, Task Force Report 1988, 1; Devilbiss 1985, 532–33).

Because the exclusion limits women's rights to equal opportunity inside and outside the military, as well as perpetuates stereotypes of women's inferior abilities and social status, the justice ethic prescribes that, as a matter of public policy, military women should be allowed access to combat assignments for which they are qualified. Although this argument is sound as a general principle, it is distorted by particular ideological notions of gender, albeit ones that are diametrically opposed to those drawn on by accountability proponents.

The justice ethic emphasizes similarities rather than differences between males and females, treating women as though they were essentially the same as men. It assumed that women *should* participate in all military activities men do, because military women are the same as men in the respects relevant to the combat issue. But as we have seen, this is not always the case, particularly with respect to physical strength, pregnancy, and roles as mothers and heads of families, all of which present certain difficulties. Proponents of a justice ethic tend to gloss these problems.

In addition, those supporting an ethic of justice often avoid the vexing question whether women should be *required* to participate in combat on the same terms as men, by framing the issue only in terms of whether women should be permitted to *volunteer* for such assignments. The majority of women in the military oppose *mandatory* combat roles. Yet the Supreme Court's pronouncements in *Rostker v. Goldberg* indicate that the constitutionality of female exemption from draft registration rests, at least in part, on women's exclusion from combat.

Moreover, granting equal opportunity requires that *both* men and women have responsibilities as well as rights in relation to combat.[48] In the context of the present all-volunteer military, this problem is not as acute as it would be in the context of conscription, since all enlistees can be considered to have agreed, implicitly or explicitly, to all the risks entailed in military service, including combat duty. Mandatory combat policy, however, would expose more enlisted women in the lower ranks to risk of harm than the women officers who have more strongly supported ending combat restrictions. In addition, proponents of the justice ethic have failed to consider the disproportionate impact of mandatory combat service on women of color and working-class women, for whom military employment is more of a necessity than an option.

Efforts to gain equal opportunities for women in the military through expanding combat assignments are criticized as reinforcing the notion that the military is so primary to the social order that women require access to its central function in order to find fulfillment. Some criticize the justice ethic for encouraging what they consider a male-gendered concept of citizenship, one linked to national defense and through it to combat. In this view, such a concept of citizenship obscures the larger issue of the legitimacy of the military as an institution whose central business can involve the large-scale killing of human beings (see, e.g., Brock-Utne 1985; Reardon 1993 and 1985). It also fails to challenge—and thereby serves to reinforce—the fundamental operating assumptions of the military, which have frequently had deleterious consequences for women (see Enloe 1983, 16; Tiffany 1981, 36). Making women subject to a draft would also make their opposition to certain military involvements as unjust wars more costly.

Such criticisms serve to highlight the failure of the justice ethic fully to consider differences *among* women and the implications of the combat issue for women inside and outside the military.[49] Such failures frequently result from ideological assumptions that women are essentially the same as men. The ethic of care provides a corrective, albeit a problematic one, to these oversights.

The Ethic of Care

Although generally absent from the legal and public policy debates surrounding women in combat, the ethic of care provides an important critical perspective on both the justice and accountability ethics. Recognition of a distinctive ethic of care has emerged within the last decade from the work of feminist theorists such as Carol Gilligan (1982), Sarah Ruddick (1989; 1983a), and Nel Noddings (1984). According to these theorists, females have a distinctive approach to ethics, one that is based on caring, responsibility, and relationality, as opposed to a "male" ethic focused on justice, rights, and autonomy.

The qualities of an ethics of care are considered to orient women more toward peace than war. Women's special empathy for nonviolence is sometimes viewed as stemming from their experiences of giving birth and nurturing human life. According to Ruddick, for example, "mothering begins in birth and promises life; military thinking is characterized by its justification of organized, deliberate death" (1987, 247; see Ruddick 1989; Pierson 1988b, 223).

The ethic of care is concerned with the protection of innocent life, especially the lives of women and children who are victimized by war and the militarization of society. From this perspective, the struggle to obtain equal opportunity for women within the military diverts attention from a critical analysis of the purposes and functions of military institutions, particularly as they affect the lives of women and children (see Jones 1990, 132; Tiffany 1981, 39). Proponents of the care ethic emphasize that the military as a whole is a patriarchal and sexist male-dominated institution that is oppressive to women. For example, they point out that the military not only discriminates against women who have volunteered to serve but also allows enlisted men to be sexually used, harassed, and raped (see Roche 1993, 2). They also emphasize that militarism is connected to other forms of patriarchal social violence, including the physical and sexual abuse of civilian women and children (see Enloe 1988, 411; Reardon 1985, 1–7; Stephenson 1986, 74, 86).

Women's military involvement, according to this view, merely strengthens the power of a fundamentally immoral institution. Rather than seeking to increase their participation in the military, such peace advocates conclude, women should devote their distinctive moral resources to developing nonviolent alternatives to war. In addition, advocates of a care ethic suggest that combat roles are antithetical to women's roles as peace workers rather than warriors. Many committed to the care ethic believe that it provides women with distinctive resources for opposing war and promoting nonviolence and peacemaking. The affirmation of human connectedness, cooperation, and dialogue promoted by an ethic of care is thus opposed to combat as a legitimate form of dispute resolution, because it condones the use of violence and killing.[50]

Just as those concerned with principles of justice neglect consideration of the morality of the military enterprise and the validity of war in general, those concerned with principles of care tend to be guilty of the opposite oversight. By refusing to acknowledge any legitimate role for the military in national defense and the defense of other nations from unjust aggressors, advocates of the care ethic generally fail to consider the morality of leaving men responsible for national defense while claiming a privileged position as "peacemakers." This stance encourages women not to contaminate their moral purity by participating in the military, at the same time taking advantage of the protection provided by men, who take sole responsibility for national defense. As Stiehm asks, "If women are not prepared to make a commitment to nonviolence as a way of life, and to advocate it for others (especially their 'protectors') as well, shouldn't they assume their share of responsibility for exercising legitimate violence?" (1989, 233; see Segal 1983, 203; Elshtain 1987, 243–44). Proponents of the care ethnic fail to acknowledge that women should accept proportionate risks and obligations for legitimate exercises of national defense.

In addition, since principles of care also involve taking responsibility for protecting others, particularly those with whom one is connected in relationship, the care ethic need not be aligned with pacifism. Maternal practices, for example, demonstrate the violence that many mothers are willing to use to protect their children from harm (see Stiehm 1988, 101; Ruddick 1989). If this responsibility to care for others is interpreted to extend beyond "one's own" to the protection of the innocent generally, it may seem morally necessary to engage in the use of armed force in certain circumstances. These oversights lead to a failure to recognize women's civic duty to participate in national defense, thus permitting the perpetuation of a largely male military and the accompanying ideology that women's role is to be "the protected."

Several aspects of the care ethic represent a simple reversal of the gender ideology dominating the accountability ethic. Whereas gender stereotypes of men animating the accountability ethic point to their "natural" affiliation with war, here it is argued that women's "natural" affiliation is with peace.[51] Whereas principles of justice assume the essential sameness of men and women, principles of care often assume that men and women are essentially different and have distinctive approaches to war and peace. Pacifist feminists who ally women exclusively with nonviolence cannot adequately account for the reality that many women take a pro-war stance in times of international conflict and that many women choose to join the military. In addition, those subscribing to this ethic commonly focus on the military as a whole as a fundamentally male institution, founded on distinctively male traits of aggression. Despite its critical insights into the deficiencies of the justice and accountability ethics, then, the ethic of care also reflects unsubstantiated assumptions that are attributable, at least in part, to the influence of gender ideology.

Conclusion: Combat Ethics Beyond Gender Ideology?

As we have seen, the dominant strand in each of the three ethical positions discussed here is linked to gender-biased assumptions about the nature of men and women in relation to war and combat. When assumptions about gender are unmasked and their influence is assessed, the implications of each ethic for the issue of women in combat can be significantly recast.

Each of the ethical perspectives provides an important perspective, one that should be considered in any complete analysis of the ethics of women in combat. Once outdated stereotypes and myths about women's capabilities and deficiencies are exposed in the ethic of accountability, the current restrictions on combat roles for women are revealed to lack persuasive foundation. Yet the protection of troop safety and the efficient and effective use of military resources remain paramount concerns.

The ethic of care is founded on many of the same assumptions about gender as the accountability ethic, leading to similar conclusions about the propriety of combat roles for women, although for radically different reasons. Looking beyond the ideological notions of gender underlying the care ethic leads to an awareness that care may also require that women engage in armed conflict in defense of innocent others.

The care ethic also provides an important corrective to certain deficiencies in the ethics of justice and of accountability. Its focus on concern for others points up the inadequacies of the accountability ethic, with its tendency to focus only on a military leader's responsibility to his own troops, ignoring the lives of innocent civilians who will be affected by his decisions (Walzer 1989, 67–72). In addition, the care ethic demonstrates the short-sightedness of the justice ethic's primary focus on attaining benefits for U.S. military women (and men) rather than encompassing a concern for *all* women, as well as children and other innocents of war. Principles of care suggest the importance of at least questioning, if not actively opposing, certain practices of the military. This requires a distanced perspective that is less likely to be held by those within the military, especially those engaged in combat roles.

Finally, the ethic of justice is weakened by its assumption of women's sameness to men and its consequent failure to assess the overall moral legitimacy of the military and of combat roles for either men or women. Nonetheless, it demonstrates the importance of making equal opportunity, equal protection of the laws, and fairness to both men and women primary considerations in the determination of how combat roles are to be allocated. Although complete gender-neutrality may be an unachievable ideal, it is possible to formulate an ethical approach to the issue of women in combat that is not as embedded in ideologically damaging assumptions about gender as the three approaches we have considered.

Nonetheless, these approaches each contribute a valuable aspect to an ethics committed to the ideal of gender-neutrality. The accountability ethic's concern for combat effectiveness and for the protection and safety of troops highlights the importance of requiring both men and women to demonstrate their combat capabilities in accordance with rigorous physical and psychological tests. The justice ethic's concern with equal opportunity and fairness stresses the importance in a democratic society of affording women as well as men the opportunity to prove themselves capable of satisfactorily performing combat assignments. The care ethic's consideration of the negative implications of militarism in general, especially with respect to the protection of and respect for human life, counsels careful evaluation of whether it is necessary to make combat duty mandatory or whether some gender-neutral type of conscientious objector status could be feasible even for enlisted personnel with respect to involvement in particular conflicts.

Where relevant, factors such as physical strength, psychological fortitude, bonding, troop cohesiveness, and the effect of pregnancy and maternity on military effectiveness and efficiency must be assessed on the basis of gender-neutral standards. It is likely that the implementation of such standards would greatly increase the numbers of women in the military, as well as their status, rank, opportunities for advancement, and the respect accorded them as members of the armed forces.

NOTES

1. Combat support positions provide direct assistance to combat arms; they include engineering, police, communications, and intelligence. Combat service support positions provide technical and administrative support to those in combat (see U.S. DOD, Task Force Report, 1988, 10). Former Army captain Carol Barkalow's experience as a military officer included her discovery that some women were used to fill combat support roles from which they were technically barred, depending on the attitude of the leadership within the particular unit (Barkalow 1990, 173).

2. Public Law 80-625, 62 Stat. 356. The act restricted women officers to positions of colonel and lower and permitted the services to discharge pregnant women as well as those who had small children in the home.

3. Women currently make up approximately 11 percent of the services overall, with the Navy at approximately 15 percent, the Air Force at 14 percent, and the Marine Corps at about 5 percent. The total of women in the reserves is about 13 percent (see Association 1991, 5). African American women disproportionately constitute about 48.7 percent of the Army's enlisted women, 26.8 percent of the Navy's, and 23.7 percent of Air Force's, although they make up only about 12 percent of the total female U.S. population (see Enloe 1993, 86; Moore 1991a, 363; Moore 1991b). Lesbians as well as gays are still not openly accepted in the military, despite recent political wrangling over the issue, and, outside the "Don't ask, don't tell, don't pursue" rule, remain subject to discharge if their sexual orientation is discovered (see Kohn 1993; Karst 1991; Berube 1990, 275–79).

4. Although the Integration Act excluded women from combat positions only on Navy ships and Navy and Air Force aircraft engaged in combat missions, all four branches of the armed services interpreted these provisions broadly to limit the participation of women (see Holm 1992, 399). In 1971, as a result of a court case challenging statutory prohibitions, Navy women were for the first time allowed on ships, although not warships (see Owens v. Brown, 455 F. Supp. 291 [D.D.C. 1978]).

5. In accordance with this rule, positions could be closed to women if they presented risks that were "equal to, or greater than, risks for direct combat units or positions with which they are normally in close proximity." If such risks were less than those for direct combat, they were to be open to women under the rule.

6. The services also have distinguished among "combat mission," "close combat," "direct combat," "combat support," and "combat service support" (see Association 1991, 12–14).

7. The Navy has stated its plans to open thirty combat ships to women in the three-year period beginning in 1995.

8. During Senate hearings on the bill to open combat pilot positions to women, held in June 1991, representatives from the Army and Marine Corps said they would not

alter their exclusionary policies if the law were changed. In contrast, representatives from the Navy and Air Force said they would "feel compelled" to make such positions available to women (see Korb 1992; Palmer 1991).

9. This move would open air defense artillery battalions, helicopters that fly cover for tanks, and battalion headquarters of combat engineers and special operations forces.

10. General John Shalikashvili, chairman of the Joint Chiefs of Staff, argued that carrying special operations forces justified excluding female pilots because such assignments would bring women too close to the front and consequently to participation in combat (Schmitt 1994b; Pine 1994; Harris 1994). Since the general explicitly did not include special operations missions delivering fuel and supplies, the clear implication of his directive was that he considered female soldiers competent to deliver goods but not human lives!

11. Men are identified as having such masculine traits associated with violence as hardness, toughness, and aggressiveness, whereas women are associated with the "peaceful" feminine attributes of softness, gentleness, passiveness, and fragileness (see Pierson 1988a, 211–12). Women are also traditionally identified with nature, the corporeal, childbearing and childrearing, and the private sphere of domesticity, attributes that are symbolically associated with peacefulness rather than violence and aggression. In contrast, men are viewed as cultural beings possessed of rationality and concerned with the public sphere of government, which in turn is identified with soldiering and citizenship, symbols of selfless devotion to a higher cause.

12. Even religious doctrines have been put forward in support of this ideology. For example, during hearings on the repeal of the combat exclusion provisions in 1979, the director of the Moral Majority testified that "women in combat roles violates the order of creation, will of God" (quoted in Holm 1992, 342). As Army captain Carol Barkalow notes, "The concept of a powerful woman who could actually kill somebody . . . is still too frightening for most people to grasp, much less accept" (1990, 258).

13. For example, a Navy report on integrating women into the Naval Academy states that "the waging of war . . . requires professional attributes and characteristics which are the antithesis of what we in this society consider essentially feminine qualities" (quoted in Jeffords 1989, 60; MacDonald 1988, 6).

14. A similar sentiment was expressed by the federal district court in *United States v. St. Clair* (129 F. Supp. 122, 125 [S.D.N.Y. 1968]), a case involving a challenge to the constitutionality of regulations exempting women from draft registration: "In providing for involuntary service for men and voluntary service for women, Congress followed the teachings of history that if a nation is to survive, men must provide the first line of defense while women keep the home fires burning."

15. Related to this view may be a reciprocal attitude that continuing combat as an exclusively male province is a way of preserving traditional forms of masculinity in society (e.g., D'Amico 1990, 7; Devilbiss 1990, 47; Hartsock 1989, 134).

16. For example, former Marine Corps Commandant Barrows testified at congressional hearings in 1991 that women in combat positions "would destroy the Marine Corps, something no enemy has been able to do in over two hundred years" (U.S. Senate 1991, 897).

17. Original Senate bills introducing the Integration Act contain some discussion of women as the weaker sex and of ships being inappropriate places for women to serve. In 1978, the federal court in *Owens v. Brown*, a case involving a successful challenge to the legislative ban on women on Navy ships, found that the prohibition "was premised on the notion that duty at sea is part of an essentially masculine tradition" and that it contained "a statutory purpose more related to the traditional way of thinking about women than to the demands of military preparedness" (455 F. Supp. 291 at 305; see Stiehm 1989, 109; U.S. DOD, Task Force Report 1988, 9).

18. A similar rationale was forwarded more than twenty years earlier in the report of a 1976 study of women in the Army, concluding that women should not serve in combat because of the dangers of "degrading mission capability" (U.S. Dept. of Army 1976, Chap. 11).

19. The perception that using women in combat roles is antithetical to accountability extends outside the military. In response to the military's testimony at the subcommittee hearings, for example, Senator Roger Jepsen stated that "our armed services are in being to provide national security . . . and not to provide the foundation for any social experimentation" (quoted in Holm 1992, 389). Lawrence Korb notes that the military fights all proposed changes in its social structure on the grounds that they are experiments that will impair combat effectiveness (1992, 31).

20. For example, a commentator writing in *Parameters: U.S. Army War College Quarterly* concludes that "combat readiness and full gender integration may not be fully compatible goals" (Hooker 1989, 36).

21. The results of a "secret" experiment integrating women into male anti-aircraft artillery combat units in 1942 indicated that mixed units of men and women performed even better than all-male units (see Campbell 1984, 38–39; Campbell 1993)! In addition, the experience of women in combat in other nations, as well as the successful integration of women into police and other traditionally male-only professions, provides useful analogies indicating that the participation of American military women in combat would not hamper unit or troop cohesion.

22. Reciprocally, rumors periodically circulate within the military that women in uniform are promiscuous and frequently engage in prostitution (see, e.g., Gooch 1988, 127; Campbell 1993).

23. For example, Commandant Barrows declares, "I do know from eight years of ground combat that few women could endure its savagery for long," because women lack the necessary "brawn" (quoted in Hackworth 1991, 25). Women's inferior physical capability is voiced especially loudly by enlisted men, who deny that women have the strength necessary for fighting on the front lines (see Kantrowitz 1991, 23; Mitchell 1989, 157–58, Stiehm 1989, 102). Some military women also have expressed skepticism about women's physical ability to handle combat assignments (see, e.g., U.S. Senate 1991, 847).

24. Because the combat exclusion has precluded the possibility of obtaining data about women's physical performance under actual combat conditions, gender-based assumptions and prejudices have continued to dominate policy discussions. Positive experience with women in traditionally all-male fields, such as police forces, that require skills similar to those used in combat supports the conclusion that many women

are capable of effectively carrying out numerous types of combat assignments (see Mc-Dowell 1992; Kornblum 1984, 392–93).

25. As Judith Stiehm argues, the question should not be "how strong women are, but how strong they need to be" for particular assignments (1989, 219).

26. Physical strength does matter occasionally, as when technology fails to function properly. For example, when forklifts broke down in the Persian Gulf, female as well as male soldiers had to haul heavy loads by hand (see Campbell 1992a). Such circumstances are the exception rather than the norm, however, and are not a legitimate ground for a blanket prohibition on using women in combat roles, including direct or ground combat.

27. But even assuming that women are less aggressive than men, there is still no evidence that this trait stems from biological causes rather than culture and socialization, which are malleable. The military has not offered empirical evidence to demonstrate that women cannot be trained to exhibit an appropriate degree of aggressiveness.

28. Like the physical strength argument, the psychological arguments against women in combat are undermined by the successful integration of women into comparable civilian institutions such as police forces (e.g., McDowell 1992). The disparity between allowing women to participate in police forces but not combat positions in the military leads to the absurd situation that women are allowed to kill other Americans but not foreigners.

29. In addition, it is just as plausible to suppose that the presence of women in U.S. combat forces would be viewed as evidence of strong U.S. resolve to succeed in a particular conflict, much as the presence of women guerrilla fighters was during the Vietnam War (see Holm 1992, 360; D'Amico 1990, 9; Kornblum 1984, 425–27).

30. Those opposed to the integration of women into the U.S. military's combat units often point to the Israeli experience with gender-integrated units, in which male soldiers were apparently so traumatized by the sight of female soldiers being wounded and killed that they were less effective, and enemy soldiers so macho that they would rather fight to the death than surrender to a woman (see Van Creveld 1993; Hackworth 1991, 26–27). After a few weeks of allowing women to fight, the Israeli military changed its mind and has not allowed women in combat positions since. The Israeli women who now serve with male combat units are to be removed in the event of war.

31. Alexander Webster, a chaplain for the Army National Guard, speculates about the "identity confusion that must confront any would-be women warrior who pauses for a moment to consider her potential for motherhood" (Webster 1991, 29).

32. As with the lack of data on gender-integrated units, however, there have been no studies of the impact of pregnancy on military effectiveness, because the combat exclusion has precluded the possibility of gathering data. In recognition of the lack of evidence, Navy Secretary Dalton called for the study of pregnancy's effect on combat readiness in February 1995 (see Pine 1995; Graham 1995).

Until 1975, women were automatically discharged from the military as soon as their pregnancy was discovered. This contributed to high attrition rates for women in the services. In 1975, the Department of Defense made such discharge for pregnancy voluntary (see Holm 1992, 125, 291–92, 297–303; Segal 1983, 207; Treadwell 1954, 200).

33. In addition, although pregnancy accounts for a significant percentage of military women's lost time, they lose *less* service time overall than do men. Men lose time especially for illness, drug and alcohol abuse, and disability (see D'Amico 1990, 8; Coyle 1989, 39).

34. The Navy adopted a new policy toward pregnancy in February 1995. The policy acknowledges that most pregnant women are able to perform their ordinary duties well but may have special needs (*New York Times* Editorial Staff 1995; Pine 1995; Graham 1995). Pregnancy cannot be used as a basis for lowering marks on performance reports or for demoting women to dissimilar billets after their return from pregnancy leave. Also, pregnant women are allowed to remain assigned to ships through the first twenty weeks of pregnancy, unlike in the Marine Corps, which attempted to ban the recruitment even of married people in 1993 and which requires that pregnant women be transferred off ships as soon as they learn they are pregnant (see Pine 1995).

35. As Air Force Major General (retired) Jeanne Holm explains, according to the family policy that had been maintained from the post–World War II era until the 1970s, it was assumed that "women's natural responsibilities as wife/mother were inherently incompatible with her military duties, and that wherever these two came into conflict, the former must take precedence, irrespective of her professional value to the service" (1992, 289).

36. This view was a basis for the opposition to President Carter's plan to make women subject to the draft in the early 1980s. Arguments of opponents gave congressional testimony that the administration had given inadequate consideration to "the induction of young mothers, and to the strains on family life that would result" (*Congressional Record*, 96th Cong., 2d sess., 1980, 126, pt. 25:S6532 [testimony of Senator Warner]).

37. This sentiment is evident in Chaplain Webster's claim that the paradigm of the citizen soldier may have been destroyed by the "social disruption and havoc among families wreaked by the mobilization and deployment of mothers of young children to the theater of operations in the Persian Gulf," including media images of "mothers wrenched from their offspring" (Webster 1991, 29, 24–25). Notably missing from Webster's assessment is consideration of the consequences of *fathers* being "wrenched from their offspring," thus perpetuating a gender-biased assumption that women, as mothers, are the more significant parents.

38. Pregnancy continues to be an issue for the public as well as within the military. A 1991 *Newsweek* poll found that 76 percent of the public is concerned about military women becoming pregnant and putting the fetus at risk (see Hackworth 1991, 2).

39. Attrition and reenlistment data for women indicate, however, that motherhood is a primary reason why women leave the military. And surveys show that a large majority of servicewomen want to have children (see Shields 1988, 109).

40. Such beliefs underlie the original Army prohibition on the enlistment of women who had children in certain age groups or the retention of women who become mothers (see Treadwell 1954, 496). This policy was reversed in *Crawford v. Cushman* (531 F. 2d 1114 [2d Cir. 1976]; see Holm 1992, 301–3).

41. Before 1977, surveys showed that one-half to three-quarters of the public rejected the propriety of women in combat roles (with men more likely to be opposed

than women), but those taken since the mid-1970s reflect a majority approval of at least some combat roles for women (see U.S. Congress 1977, 78; Segal 1982, 284–85; Davis, Lauber, and Sheatsley 1983, 32–34; D'Amico 1990, 12; Gordon and Ludvigson 1991, 24; Mitchell, 1989, 153; Beecraft 1989, 43; Stiehm 1989, 191; U.S. Senate 1991, 798, 985–86).

42. About 75 percent of the women officers questioned indicated that women should join combat arms. Slightly over 20 percent indicated that they would have entered a combat specialty when they enlisted had that option been available to them.

43. In addition, studies indicate that negative attitudes and perceptions about military women, particularly within the service academies, are linked to the combat exclusion (see U.S. Senate 1991, 866, 1211). In the early 1970s, the military service academies attempted to rely on the combat exclusion as a reason for not accepting women at all (see Holm 1992, 307–9, 311–12; Devilbiss 1990, 20). Congress and the president had to direct them to integrate in 1976.

44. These benefits include retirement benefits, medical care, low-cost insurance, veteran's bonuses, loans, and preferences in federal and state government employment and with home assistance loans, on-the-job training, and higher educational opportunities, both during and following service.

45. A General Accounting Office study completed in 1989 concluded that "people serving in combat specialty career fields are generally promoted more rapidly than people in non-combat specialties, and are generally promoted to higher levels" (U.S. Senate 1991, 806 [testimony of Hon. Christopher Jehn]).

46. In *Schlesinger*, the Court upheld Naval legislation affording women longer periods to achieve promotions than men, noting that the combat exclusion made it more difficult for women to qualify for promotions.

47. The Supreme Court has recognized that "the duty of citizens . . . to defend our government against all enemies whenever necessity arises is a fundamental principle of the Constitution" and that the duty of military service is inherent in citizenship (*United States v. Schwimmer*, 279 U.S. 644, 650 [1929]). The dissenting opinion of Justice Marshall in *Rostker v. Goldberg* (453 U.S. 57, 86 [1981]) argued that the combat exclusion denies women "a fundamental civic obligation."

48. As military sociologist Charles Moskos points out: "To allow both sexes to choose whether or not to go into combat would be the end of an effective military force. Honesty requires that supporters of lifting the ban on women in combat state openly that they want to put all female soldiers at the same combat risk as all male soldiers—or that they don't" (1990, 78).

49. This criticism itself fails to consider the race and class dimensions of the issue, however. Although women may not require access to combat to find fulfillment, for the many African American and working-class women for whom military service is more of a necessity than an option, access to combat roles takes on more urgency as a necessary means of enhancing career opportunities and goals.

50. Some who subscribe to an ethic of care reject the appropriateness of any military roles for women because of their "defeminizing" influence, which strips from soldiers of both sexes the "feminine" qualities of care, compassion, and tenderness and trains them to kill other human being (see Brock-Utne 1985, 32). In this view, women's

military roles can only perpetuate the very destructive and aggressive practices that feminists insist are immoral.

51. For a variety of views about the linkages between women and pacifism which challenge biological notions of women's inherent peacefulness, see Hunter 1991. The association of women with peace and peace movements is a long-standing one, extending back as far as the classical Greeks and Romans (see, e.g., Elshtain 1990, 256–57; Elshtain 1987, 139; Berkman 1990; Costin 1983). Nonetheless, most peace prizes are awarded to men, and most peace organizations are run by men.

The identification of women as "naturally" more peaceful than men has gained women's social protest movements significant political leverage (see Ruddick 1989; Pierson 1988b; Swerdlow 1993). Even today, public opinion polls support the arguments that women are more oriented to peaceful resolution of disputes than are men. Polls reflect that women consistently show less support for using force to achieve foreign policy goals than men do, with an average 15 to 20 percent "gender gap" on the issue of military involvement (Branscombe and Owen 1993; Gallagher 1993; Brock-Utne 1985, 33). These statistics indicate that women have a different voice on issues of war and peace, regardless of whether it is "natural" or the result of their socialization in a patriarchal society.

REFERENCES

Alonso, Harriet. 1993. *Peace as a Women's Issue: A History of the United States Movement for World Peace and Women's Rights.* Syracuse, N.Y.: Syracuse University Press.
Association of the Bar of the City of New York. 1991. "The Combat Exclusion Laws: An Idea Whose Time Has Gone." *Minerva: Quarterly Report on Women and the Military* 9, 4:1–55.
Barkalow, Carol. 1990. *In the Men's House.* New York: Poseidon Press.
Beecraft, Carolyn. 1989. "Personnel Puzzle." *Proceedings (of the U.S. Naval Institute)* 115, 4:41–44.
Berkman, Joyce. 1990. "Feminism, War, and Peace Politics: The Case of World War I." In Jean Bethke Elshtain and Sheila Tobias, eds., *Essays in History, Politics, and Social Theory. Women, Militarism, and War:* Savage, Md.: Roman and Littlefield.
Berube, Alan. 1990. *Coming Out under Fire: Gay Men and Women in World War II.* New York: Free Press.
Branscombe, Nyla, and Susan Owen. 1993. "Gun Ownership among American Women and Its Consequences for Social Judgment." In Ruth Howes and Michael Stevenson, eds., *Women and the Use of Military Force.* Boulder, Colo.: Lynne Reinner.
Brock-Utne, Birgit. 1985. *Educating for Peace: A Feminist Perspective.* New York: Pergamon Press.
Campbell, D'Ann. 1984. *Women at War with America: Private Lives in a Patriotic Era.* Cambridge: Harvard University Press.
———. 1989. "Coming of Age in the Women's Army Corps," foreword to *One Woman's War: Letters Home from the Women's Army Corps, 1944–46,* by Ann Boesanko Green. St. Paul: Minnesota Historical Society Press.
———. 1990. "The Regimented Women of World War II." In Elshtain and Tobias, *Women, Militarism, and War,* 107–22.

―――. 1992a. "Combatting the Gender Gulf." Minerva: Quarterly Report on Women and the Military 10, 3–4:13–41.

―――. 1992b. "WACs in Combat: The World War II Experience." Paper presented to the U.S. Military Academy, March.

―――. 1993. "Women in Combat: The World War II Experience in the United States, Great Britain, Germany, and the Soviet Union." Journal of Military History 57, 2:301–23.

Chapkis, Wendy. 1988. "Sexuality and Militarism." In Eva Isaksson, ed., Women and the Military System. New York: St. Martin's Press, pp. 107–13.

Code, Lorraine. 1991. What Can She Know? Feminist Theory and the Construction of Knowledge. Ithaca, N.Y.: Cornell University Press.

Congressional Record. 1971. 92d Cong., 1st sess. Vol. 117 (daily ed. 12 Oct.), pt. 27:35785 (testimony of Senator Cellar).

―――. 1980. 96th Cong., 2d sess. Vol. 126 (daily ed., 10 June) pt. 25:S6532.

Cornum, Rhonda. 1992. She Went to War: The Rhonda Cornum Story. Novato, Calif.: Presidio Press.

Costin, Lela. 1983. "Feminism, Pacifism, Nationalism, and the United Nations Decade for Women." In Judith Stiehm, ed., Women and Men's Wars. Oxford: Pergamon Press, pp. 301–16.

Coyle, Barry. 1989. "Women on the Front Lines." Proceedings (of the U.S. Military Institute) 115, 4:37–40.

Cramsie, Jodie. 1983. "Gender Discrimination in the Military: The Unconstitutional Exclusion of Women from Combat." Valparaiso Law Review 17:547–88.

D'Amico, Francine. 1990. "Women at Arms: The Combat Controversy." Minerva: Quarterly Report on Women and the Military 8, 2:1–19.

Davis, James, Jennifer Lauber, and Paul Sheatsley. 1983. Americans View the Military: Public Opinion in 1982. Technical Report no. 131. Chicago: NORC, University of Chicago.

DeCew, Judith Wagner. 1995. "The Combat Exclusion and the Role of Women in the Military." Hypatia 10, 1:56–73.

De Pauw, Linda Grant. 1981. "Women in Combat: The Revolutionary War Experience." Armed Forces and Society 7, 2:209–26.

Devilbiss, M.C. 1985. "Gender Integration and Unit Deployment: A Study of G.I. Jo." Armed Forces and Society 11, 4:523–32.

―――. 1990. Women and Military Service: A History, Analysis, and Overview of Key Issues. Maxwell Air Force Base, Ala.: Air University Press.

Dienstfrey, Stephen. 1988. "Women Veterans' Exposure to Combat." Armed Forces and Society 14, 549–58.

Dillingham, Wayne. 1990. "The Possibility of American Military Women Becoming Prisoners of War: Justification for Combat Exclusion Rules?" Federal Bar News and Journal 37, 223–30.

DiLucente, Lieutenant A., U.S.N.R. 1992. "Equality: A Step Backward." Proceedings (of the U.S. Naval Institute) 118, 2:46–48.

Dunivin, Karen. 1988. "Gender and Perceptions of the Job Environment in the U.S. Air Force." Armed Forces and Society 15, 1:71–91.

Elshtain, Jean Bethke. 1987. *Women and War.* New York: Basic Books.

————. 1990. "The Problem with Peace." In Elshtain and Tobias, *Women, Militarism, and War,* pp. 256–66.

Elshtain, Jean Bethke, and Sheila Tobias, eds. 1990. *Women, Militarism, and War: Essays in History, Politics, and Social Theory.* Savage, Md.: Rowman and Littlefield.

Enloe, Cynthia. 1983. *Does Khaki Become You?* Boston: South End Press.

————. 1988. "United States." In Isaksson, *Women and the Military System,* pp. 395–415.

————. 1993. "The Right to Fight: A Feminist Catch-22." *Ms.* 4 (July–August): 84–87.

Ferber, Martin. 1987. *Combat Exclusion Laws for Women in the Military.* GAO/T-NSAID-88-8. Washington, D.C.: General Accounting Office.

Fullinwider, Robert, ed. 1983. *Conscripts and Volunteers: Military Requirements, Social Justice, and the All-Volunteer Force.* Totowa, N.J.: Rowman and Allanheld.

Gabriel, Richard. 1982. *To Serve with Honor: A Treatise on Military Ethics and the Way of the Soldier.* Westport, Conn.: Greenwood Press.

Gallagher, Nancy. 1993. "The Gender Gap in Popular Attitudes toward the Use of Force." In Howes and Stevenson, *Women and the Use of Military Force,* pp. 29–44.

Gilligan, Carol. 1982. *In a Different Voice: Psychological Theory and Women's Development.* Cambridge: Harvard University Press.

Golightly, Lieutenant Neil (U.S. Navy). "No Right to Fight." *Proceedings (of the U.S. Naval Institute)* 113, 12:46–49.

Gooch, Robert, Master Chief Sonar Technician, U.S. Navy. 1988. "The Coast Guard Example." *Proceedings (of the U.S. Naval Institute)* 114, 5:124–33.

Gordon, Marilyn, and Mary Jo Ludvigson. 1991. "A Constitutional Analysis of the Combat Exclusion for Air Force Women." *Minerva: Quarterly Report on Women and the Military* 9, 1–34.

Graham, Bradley. 1995. "Navy Adopts a Gentle Response to Service Programs." *Washington Post,* 7 February, p. A4.

Hackworth, Colonel David. 1991. "War and the Second Sex." *Newsweek,* 5 August, pp. 24–28.

Harris, Adrienne, and Ynestra King, eds. 1989. *Rocking the Ship of State: Toward a Feminist Peace Politics.* Boulder, Colo.: Westview Press.

Harris, John. 1994. "Shalikashvili Tries to Exclude Female Pilots from Certain Missions." *Washington Post,* 7 May, p. A3.

Hartle, Anthony. 1989. *Moral Issues in Military Decision Making.* (Lawrence: University of Press of Kansas.

Hartsock, Nancy. 1989. Masculinity, Heroism, and the Making of War." In Adrienne Harris and Ynestia King, eds., *Rocking the Ship of State: Toward a Feminist Peace Politics.* Boulder, Colo.: Westview Press, pp. 135–52.

Holm, Major General Jeanne, U.S.A.F. (retired). 1992. *Women in the Military: An Unfinished Revolution.* Rev. ed. Novato, Calif.: Presidio Press.

Hooker, Richard. 1989. "Affirmative Action and Combat Exclusion: Gender Roles in the U.S. Army." *Parameters: U.S. War College Quarterly* 19, 4:36–50.

Howes, Ruth, and Michael Stevenson, eds. 1993. *Women and the Use of Military Force.* Boulder, Colo.: Lynne Reinner.

Hunter, Anne E., ed. 1991. *Genes and Gender VI: On Peace, War, and Gender: A Challenge to Genetic Explanations.* New York: Feminist Press.

Huntington, Samuel. 1986. "Officership as a Profession." In Malkham Wakin, ed., *War, Morality, and the Military Profession,* 2d ed. Boulder, Colo.: Westview Press, pp. 23–34.

Isaksson, Eva, ed. 1988. *Women and the Military System.* New York: St. Martin's Press.

Jeffords, Susan. 1989. *The Remasculinization of America: Gender in the Vietnam War.* Bloomington: Indiana University Press.

Johnson, Cecil. 1978. *Women Content in the Army: REFORGER (REFWAC 77).* Alexandria, Va.: U.S. Army Research Institute.

Jones, Kathleen. 1990. "Dividing the Ranks: Women and the Draft." In Elshtain and Tobias, *Women, Militarism, and War,* pp. 125–36.

Kantrowitz, Barbara. 1991. "The Right to Fight." *Newsweek,* 5 August, pp. 22–23.

Karst, Kenneth. 1991. "The Pursuit of Manhood and the Desegregation of the Armed Forces." *University of California Los Angeles Law Review* 38, 3:499–581.

Kelly, Karla. 1984. "The Exclusion of Women from Combat: Withstanding the Challenge." *Judge Advocate General Journal* 33, 1:77–108.

Kohn, Richard. 1993. "Women in Combat, Homosexuals in Uniform: The Challenge of Military Leadership." *Parameters: U.S. War College Quarterly* 23, 1:2–4.

Korb, Lawrence. 1992. "Cheney Remains Silent on Thorny Issues." *Army Times,* 17 February, p. 31.

Kornblum, Lori. 1984. "Women Warriors in a Men's World: The Combat Exclusion." *Law and Inequality* 2:351–445.

Lancaster, John. 1994. "Aspin Eases Combat Policy." *Washington Post,* 13 January, pp. A1, A7.

Larson, C. K. 1990. "Bonny Yank and Ginny Reb." *Minerva: Quarterly Report on Women and the Military.* 8, 1:33–48.

Lieberman, Jeanne. 1990. "Women in Combat." *Federal Bar News and Journal* 37, 4:215–22.

MacDonald, Sharon. 1988. "Drawing the Lines—Gender, Peace, and War: An Introduction." In Sharon MacDonald, Pat Holden, and Shirley Ardener, eds., *Images of Women in Peace and War: Cross-Cultural and Historical Perspectives.* Madison: University of Wisconsin Press.

Marlowe, David. 1983. "The Manning of the Force and the Structure of Battle: Part 2— Men and Women." In Robert Fullinwider, ed., *Conscripts and Volunteers: Military Requirements, Social Justice, and the All-Volunteer Force.* Totowa, N.J.: Rowan and Allanheld, pp. 189–99.

McAllister, Pam, ed. 1982. *Reweaving the Web of Life: Feminism and Nonviolence.* Philadelphia: New Society.

McDowell, Jeanne. 1992. "Are Women Better Cops?" *Time,* 17 February, pp. 70–72.

Michalowski, Helen. 1982. "The Army Will Make a 'Man' out of You." In Pam McAllister, ed., *Reweaving the Web of Life: Feminism and Nonviolence.* Philadelphia: New Society, pp. 330–33.

Mitchell, Brian. 1989. *The Weak Link: The Feminization of the American Military.* Washington, D.C.: Regnery Gateway.

Moore, Brenda. 1991a. "African-American Women in the U.S. Military." *Armed Forces and Society* 17, 3:363–84.

——— 1991b "The Participation of African American Women in the U.S. Military: Past and Present Issues." Paper presented to the Inter-University Seminar on Armed Forces and Society Biennial Conference, 11–13 October.

Morden, Bettie J. 1990. *The Women's Army Corps, 1945–1978*. Washington, D.C.: Center of Military History.

Moskos, Charles. 1985. "Female GI's in the Field. *Society* 22, 6:28–33.

———. 1990. "Army Women." *Atlantic Monthly* 266, 2:70–78.

———. 1991. "How Do They Do It?" *New Republic*, 5 August, pp. 16–20.

Nabors, Robert. 1982. "Women in the Army: Do They Measure Up?" *Military Review* (October): 50–61.

New York Times Editorial Staff. 1995. "Sailing into Motherhood." *New York Times*, 11 February, p. 18.

Noddings, Nel. 1984. *Caring: A Feminine Approach to Ethics and Moral Education*. Berkeley: University of California Press.

Opinion. 1988. "No Right to Fight?" *Procedures (of the U.S. Naval Institute)* 114, 5:134–39.

Palmer, Elizabeth. 1991. "Senate Debates Rights, Role of Women Warriors." *Congressional Quarterly Weekly Report*. 49 22 June: 1687.

Pierson, Ruth Roach. 1988a. "Did Your Mother Wear Army Boots? Feminist Theory and Women's Relation to War, Peace, and Revolution." In Sharon MacDonald, Pat Holden, and Shirley Ardener, eds., *Images of Women in Peace and War: Cross-Cultural and Historical Perspectives*. Madison: University of Wisconsin Press, pp. 205–27.

———. 1988b. "'They're Still Women After All': Wartime Jitters over Femininity." In Isaksson, *Women and the Military System*.

Pine, Art. 1994. "Women Will Get Limited Combat Roles." *Los Angeles Times*, 14 January, p. A5.

———. 1995. "Marine Corps, Navy Assure Women Jobs Won't Suffer over Pregnancy." *Los Angeles Times*, 8 February, p. A7.

Proxmire, Senator William. 1986. "Three Myths about Women and Combat." *Minerva: Quarterly Report on Women in the Military*. 4, 4:105–19.

Reardon, Betty. 1985. *Women and the War System*. New York: Teachers College Press.

———. 1993. *Women and Peace: Feminist Visions of Global Security*. Albany: State University of New York Press.

Roche, Leigh. 1993. "Military in Crisis: Sexual Harassment and Rape in the Armed Forces." *National Coalition against Sexual Assault Newsletter* 1, 2:1–2.

Rogan, Helen. 1981. *Mixed Company: Women in the Modern Army*. New York: G. P. Putnam's Sons.

Rohter, Larry. 1993. "Era of Female Combat Pilots Opens with Shrugs and Glee." *New York Times*, 29 April, p. A1.

Roush, Paul. 1990. "Combat Exclusion: Military Necessity or Another Name for Bigotry?" *Minerva: Quarterly Report on Women in the Military* 13, 3:1–15.

Ruddick, Sarah. 1983a. "Preservative Love and Military Destruction." In Joyce Trebilcot, ed. *Mothering*. Totowa, N.J.: Rowman and Allanheld, pp. 231–61.

———. 1983b. "Pacifying the Forces: Drafting Women in the Interests of Peace." *Signs: Journal of Women in Culture and Society*. 8, 3:471–89.

———. 1987. "Remarks on the Sexual Politics of Reason." In Eva Kittay and Diana Meyers, ed., *Women and Moral Theory*. Totawa, N.J.: Rowman and Littlefield, pp. 237–60.

———. 1989. *Maternal Thinking: Toward a Politics of Peace*. Boston: Beacon Press.

Rupp, Leila. 1989. "Women's Place Is in the War: Propaganda and Public Opinion in the U.S. and Germany, 1939–1945." In Laurel Richardson and Verta Taylor, eds., *Feminist Frontiers II: Rethinking Sex, Gender, and Society.* New York: Random House, pp. 344–53.

Schmitt, Eric. 1994a. "Army and Marine Corps Offer Women More yet Less." *New York Times*, 31 July, pp. A7, A18.

———. 1994b. "Army Will Allow Women in 32,000 Combat Posts." *New York Times*, 28 July, p. A5.

———. 1994c. "Generals Oppose Combat by Women." *New York Times*, 17 June, pp. A1, A18.

———. 1994d. "New Top Admiral to Push Wider Combat Role for Women." *New York Times*, 4 May, p. A20.

———. 1994e. "Pilot's Death Renews Debate over Women in Combat Role." *New York Times*, 30 October, p. A7.

Schumm, Walter, Bruce Bell, C. Elizabeth Palmer-Johnson, and Giao Tran. 1994. "Gender Trends in the U.S. Army and a Discussion of Implications for Readiness and Retention." *Psychological Reports* 74: 499–511.

Segal, Mady Wechsler. 1982. "The Argument for Female Combatants." In Nancy Loring Goldman, ed., *Female Soldiers—Combatants or Noncombatants? Historical and Contemporary Perspectives.* Westport, Conn.: Greenwood Press, pp. 267–90.

———. 1983. "Women's Roles in the U.S. Armed Forces: An Evaluation of Evidence and Arguments for Policy Decisions." In Fullinwider, *Conscripts and Volunteers,* pp. 200–213.

———. 1984. "Testimony before the Subcommittee on Civil and Constitutional Rights of the Judiciary Committee of the U.S. House of Representatives, October 26, 1983." Reprinted in *Minerva: Quarterly Report on Women in the Military* 2, 1:108–14.

Segal, Mady Wechsler, and David R. Segal. 1983. "Social Change and the Participation of Women in the American Military." *Research in Social Movements, Conflicts, and Change* 5: 235–58.

Shields, Patricia. 1988. "Sex Roles in the Military." In Charles Moskos and Frank Wood, eds., *The Military—More Than Just a Job?* Washington, D.C.: Pergamon-Brassey, pp. 99–111.

Shields, Patricia, Landon Curry, and Janet Nichols. 1990. "Women Pilots in Combat: Attitudes of Male and Female Pilots." *Minerva: Quarterly Report on Women in the Military.* 8, 1:21–34.

Sorley, Lewis. 1981. "Competence as Ethical Imperative: Issues of Professionalism." In James Brown and Michael Collins, eds., *Military Ethics and Professionalism.* Washington, D.C.: National Defense University Press, pp. 39–54.

Stephenson, Carolyn. 1986. "Pacifism and the Roots of Feminism in the United States, 1830–1930: Individual Linkages." In Birgit Brock-Utne, Julianne Traylor, and Solveig, Aas, eds., *Women and Peace: A Report from a Conference.* Oslo: International Peace Research Institute, pp. 18–36.

Stiehm, Judith Hicks. 1985a. "Generations of U.S. Enlisted Women." *Signs: Journal of Women in Culture and Society,* 11, 1:155–75.

————. 1985b. "Women's Biology and the U.S. Military." In Virginia Sapiro, ed., *Women, Biology, and Public Policy*. Beverly Hills, Calif.: Sage, pp. 205–32.

————. 1988. "The Effect of Myths about Military Women on the Waging of War." In Isaksson, *Women and the Military System*, pp. 94–105.

————. 1989. *Arms and the Enlisted Women*. Philadelphia: Temple University Press.

Summers, Anne. 1991. "Pat Schroeder: Fighting for Military Moms." *Ms.* 1 (May/June): 90–91.

Swerdlow, Amy. 1993. *Women Strike for Peace: Traditional Motherhood and Radical Politics in the 1960s* Chicago: University of Chicago Press.

Tiffany, Jennifer. 1981. "The Equal Opportunity Trap." In Wendy Chapkis, ed., *Loaded Questions: Women in the Military*. Amsterdam: Transnational Press, pp. 36–39.

Towell, Pat. 1992. "Women's Combat Role Debated as Chiefs Denounce Sex Scandal." *Congressional Quarterly*, 1 August, p. 2292.

Treadwell, Mattie E. 1954. *U.S. Army in World War II Special Studies: The Women's Army Corps*. Washington, D.C.: Department of the Army.

Tuten, Jeff. 1982. "The Argument against Female Combatants." In Goldman, *Female Soldiers*.

U.S. Army Research Institute. 1977. *Women Content in Units Force Deployment Test (MAXWAC)*. Alexandria, Va.

U.S. Congress. 1977. Joint Economic Commission. *Priorities and Economy in Government: The Role of Women in the Military*. Hearings. 95th Cong., 1st Sess. (22 July and 1 Sept.), p. 78.

U.S. Department of the Army, Office of the Deputy Chief of Staff for Personnel. 1976. *Women in the Army Study*. Washington, D.C., Chap. 11.

U.S. Department of Defense. 1991. *Conduct of the Persian Gulf Conflict: An Interim Report to Congress Pursuant to Title V*. (Public Law 102-25). Washington, D.C.: U.S. Government Printing Office.

————. Office of the Secretary of Defense. 1988. *Report on the Task Force on Women in the Military*. January. Washington, D.C.

————. Task Force Report. 1988. *Risk Rule*. Washington, D.C.: USOSD.

U.S. Senate. 1991. Committee on Appropriations. *Utilization of Women in the Military Services*. Hearings on Department of Defense appropriations, H.R. 2521, pts. 4 and 6. 102d Cong., 1st sess.

Van Creveld, Martin. 1993. "Why Israel Doesn't Send Women into Combat." *Parameters: U.S. War College Quarterly* 23, 1:5–9.

Wakin, Malham. 1986. "The Ethics of Leadership I." In *War, Morality, and the Military Profession*, pp. 181–99.

————. ed. 1986. *War, Morality, and the Military Profession*. 2d ed. Boulder, Colo.: Westview Press.

Waller, Douglas. 1995. "Life on the Coed Carrier." *Time*, 17 April, pp. 36–37.

Walzer, Michael. 1989. "Two Kinds of Military Responsibility." In L. Mathews and D. Brown, eds., *The Parameters of Military Ethics*. Exeter, Great Britain: Pergamon-Brassey.

Webster, Alexander. 1991. "Paradigms of the Contemporary American Soldier and Women in the Military." *Strategic Review* (Summer): 22–30.

M. C. Devilbiss

To Fight, to Defend, and to Preserve the Peace:

The Evolution of the U.S. Military and the Role

of Women Within It

"To Fight, To Defend, and To Preserve the Peace": These have been watchwords of generations of Americans who have served their country in the armed forces. Throughout our history, some of these Americans have been women, and their persistent presence in the military appears likely to continue (Devilbiss 1991, 136). But what will be the watchwords of the U.S. military of the future? And what will be the role(s) of women in the military? This essay attempts to answer these questions by discussing the evolution of the role(s) of women within the context of the changing mission of the armed forces themselves.

The style of the chapter will be familiar to anyone who has served in the military. It is that of a military brief, a lecture (usually supported by slides or overheads) that provides trainees with official doctrine. Civilian readers may judge this form repetitive and overstructured, but the military finds it very effective in training its people. It is essential to the military that its forces know what to do and why to do it, and also that they remember what and why. Thus, training is continuous for all service members. Indeed, both enlisted and officers go to "schools" at regular intervals. Even officers may spend a full year at a "war college" after as much as two decades in service.

The mission is where most training begins and ends. As you read, imagine yourself in a darkened room, being addressed by a young officer in a clear, precise voice. She or he has almost certainly rehearsed or given the presentation a dozen times, and you will almost certainly hear it an equal number of times. . . .

The Military's Changing Mission and Structure: The Three Paradigms

This discussion is based on two premises: (1) The mission and organizational structure of the armed forces constantly evolves. Over the course of U.S. history, three major paradigms have characterized the military. They are the Offensive Model, the Defensive Model, and a third (emerging) model I call the Pro-fensive Model. (2) The role of women in the armed forces has also evolved, and the potential for their participation in the armed forces is greater in the Pro-fensive Model than in either of the other two.

The three major paradigms (assumptions) concerning the mission and role of the U.S. military are different; still, the three also share characteristics. Each has come to the forefront at a particular time, each has emerged in response to factors largely external to the military, each has dominated military tactical and strategic thought during its era.

The paradigms shape the armed forces' "sense of self," or organizational "self-concept"—its notion of what the military is "all about." This can be seen when we consider the "mindset" that characterizes each model. For the Offensive Model, it is the Conquest Mentality; for the Defensive Model, the Siege Mentality; for the Pro-fensive Model, the Flexible Power Mentality. A mindset not only expresses what the military stands for; it also specifies what individual members of the military should strive to be. Thus, an archetype of the "ideal warrior" is subsumed within each model. The ideal warrior in the Offensive Model is the Conqueror/Vanquisher; in the Defensive Model, it is the Defender/Protector; and in the Pro-fensive Model, the Peacemaker/Warrior.

The importance of both the mindset undergirding a paradigm and of the warrior archetype associated with it will become more apparent when we examine the Pro-fensive Model in detail. Now, however, we note when and how each of the paradigms arose and how they have guided U.S. military thought.

"To Fight . . .": The War Department and the Conquest Mentality

The first paradigm to appear was the Offensive Model, which, based on the Conquest Mentality, had as its individual ideal the Conqueror/Vanquisher. This paradigm dominated U.S. political-military thought from the late eighteenth century until well into the twentieth century. This was the time of the nation's birth and its geographical expansion. It was the foundation for a war of revolution, a civil war, and a series of wars and incursions across the North American continent.

Crucial to our understanding of the Offensive Model is the fact that the United States was born out of revolution, and more specifically, out of a revolution against European powers that possessed a larger and more powerful military. The prevailing perspective of the North Americans was similar to that of their European opponents—both had a Conquest Mentality. To both, the choice was simple: win or lose. According to this paradigm, then, war was about the imposition of the will of the conqueror on the conquered. Only one side won. Combat was the sole way to determine whose will was stronger and whose side would prevail. In theory and in reality, there were only two sides to a struggle; the conquerors and the vanquished.

The Conquest Mentality guided the newly organized Continental Army (and Navy and many local militia forces). Following the assumptions of this model, U.S. armies and navies in the eighteenth and nineteenth centuries first fought against European powers that sought to dominate them and then against the indigenous populations of North and Central America whose land and other resources they—who had won their struggle against their former colonizers—now sought. The Conquest Mentality is clearly seen in the nineteenth-century doctrine of Manifest Destiny, which justified seizure of the North American continent. It also dominated the bloody mid century civil war. An important legacy of the Offensive Model was both a way of naming the military and a way of thinking about it. This paradigm described the military's business as "fighting wars." The military was understood to be a combat organization designed to achieve complete and final victory. The U.S. Congress institutionalized this paradigm when, in 1789, it formally established a new federal department: the "War Department."

"... To Defend ... ": The Department of Defense and the Siege Mentality

The Offensive Model and its Conquest Mentality guided U.S. national security thinking throughout the nineteenth century and into the twentieth. Gradually, however, the United States began to see itself (and to be seen by others) as an emergent world power. By the beginning of the twentieth century, massive standing armies and navies (and the beginnings of air forces) were in place in many countries, and they were supported in the field on a scale previously unknown in human history. As large-scale and sustained warfare became possible, the United States began to think about defending itself, and others, from unimaginable horrors. Thus, the Conquest Mentality began to give way to a Siege Mentality. Indeed, by the mid-twentieth century, this new set of assumptions had almost completely replaced the Offensive Model as the military's paradigm.

In the Defensive Model, the military was seen as a protector against malevolent and ignoble "outside" or "foreign" powers. Indeed, the military was viewed as the only thing that stood between the people it protected and the obliteration of their values and way of life by forces representing something foreign, strange, even evil. The whole concept of the U.S. military changed. Far from being the Conqueror/Vanquisher, the ideal warrior became a Protector/Defender. The military became a defens(iv)e organization. What the U.S. military protected was the United States. What it was protecting the United States (and sometimes other nations) from were threats from fascism, nazism, and communism. In the era of the Cold War, the United States and much of the world were figuratively held hostage by these foreign threats. Thus, a Siege Mentality undergirded the new Defensive Model. In 1949, this paradigm shift was made concrete by a renaming: the War Department became the U.S. Department of Defense.

". . . And To Preserve the Peace": The Pro-fensive Model and the Flexible Power Mentality

It is not as easy to characterize the third, and just emerging, paradigm shift. Some of its major features, however, can be identified.

The name I have chosen for this model is "Pro-fensive." The prefix "pro" here refers to both "professional" and "proactive," two keys to the character of the new model. The Pro-fensive Model focuses on neither "hot" nor "cold" wars. In this paradigm, the military is neither strictly an offens(iv)e combat organization nor solely a defens(iv)e one. Rather, its mission and organization emphasize a "flexible response" to various kinds of political-military threats. It seems it is almost becoming a conflict-management institution rather than a war-waging institution (Devilbiss 1988, 6; Devilbiss 1992, 11). In this paradigm, the military's role is not just to respond to conflict but also to prevent conflict, and to manage both it and its consequences if fighting cannot be prevented. In this model, the military is oriented toward global alliances and it assumes interdependence. It does not vaunt either national prominence (the concern of the Offensive Model) or regional coalitions (the standpoint of the Defensive Model). Thus, at the dawn of the twenty-first century, the U.S. military's mission has again shifted in response to changing needs and conditions. Its "primary" mission of the past was combat (either offensive or defensive). Today, what were historically "secondary missions" (i.e., medical, evacuation, search and rescue, disaster relief, port safety and security, drug traffic interdiction, policing, peacekeeping, and nation building) have become, if not the core mission of the military, at least missions that occupy most of its time, personnel, and resources.

Part of the problem, if there is a problem, is that of naming this new paradigm. The military is still called the U.S. Department of Defense, reflecting an old paradigm. Moreover, the military's perception of itself remains that of a combat organization rather than that of an organization with a broader mission (cf. Devilbiss 1988, 6). Thus, there is sometimes a problem when the military is called to accomplish new kinds of missions, and this is happening more and more frequently. The old structure, the old training, and the old name are impediments to establishing a new mission, because the military still sees its ideal warrior as being either the Defender/Protector or the Conqueror/Vanquisher. The archetype of the Peacemaker/Warrior— the one who knows when to sheathe the sword and when to draw it, with emphasis on the former—has not yet won its place in a military that is, nevertheless, rapidly moving toward a paradigm that features it. Table 9-1 summarizes the three paradigms and their important elements.

Table 9-1: Three Paradigms of the U.S. Armed Forces

Model/Era	Mission	Ideal Warrior	Department Name	Operation	Use of Women (Ration to men)
Offensive 18th and 19th centuries	To Fight	Conqueror	War	Hot war Single-nation domination	Low (2:98)
Defensive Early to mid-20th century	To Defend	Protector	Defense	Cold war Regional coalitions	Medium (15:85)
Pro-fensive Late 20th century	To Preserve the Peace	Peacemaker/ Warrior	Pro-fense	Conflict management Interdependence	High (40:60)

The Evolving Role of Women in the Military

Our discussion of the evolving mission of the U.S. military provides the context of our discussion of the changing role(s) of women in the military. First, it must be remembered that women have always served in and with the United States armed forces. Second, the change in women's participation in the U.S. military can generally be described as a movement from peripheral roles to more central roles (Devilbiss 1994). Third, the roles women have historically played in the military and in war have been generally consistent with civilian concepts of femininity or ideas about "women's natures" (Devilbiss 1992, 9).

These points hold true even as the military's mission has evolved. Recall that the basis of the Offensive Model was the Conquest Mentality and that the warrior was seen as a Conqueror/Vanquisher. The idea of a woman as Conqueror/Vanquisher had little social approval. Therefore, under this paradigm, most military roles were closed to women.

It is easier to see women in a defensive or protective role, and therefore it is not surprising that the second paradigm (the Defensive Model) allowed for greater participation by women, especially as nurses (see Stiehm 1982 and Reeves, Chapter 5 in this volume).

But what about the role of women in the emerging paradigm, the Pro-fensive Model? It appears that under this paradigm there is the greatest potential for participation by women. In fact, this is already happening—and will continue to happen—for two reasons. First, combat roles that were previously closed to women (under both the Offensive Model and the Defensive Model) have become increasingly open to them. This is due to the increased acceptance of and participation by women in civilian occupations that have military counterparts, such as, police patrol officers, drug enforcement agency officers, and jet aircraft pilots. One can expect that as societal norms change about what jobs are "appropriate" for women, the military as a reflection of that society will also change, in particular by opening its doors to more "combat" specialties for women.

At the same time, the Pro-fensive Military, which makes less frequent use of those in the combat arms, can be expected to increase the number of soldiers, sailors, and airmen with "secondary" missions and specialties, such as military intelligence and communications. Here both traditional views about women's roles and women's previous participation in these secondary missions and specialties will support their increased participation. Put another way, in an organization that requires flexibility of response, negotiating abilities, and performance of constabulary functions, and whose assignments often include "humanitarian" and other "complex" missions, it is not only easy but "natural" to see women participating. This is because their participation is in keeping with general societal beliefs about "women's nature."

A problem arises, however, when the military sees these peacekeeping tasks as not its "real" mission (worse, it sometimes sees such tasks as antithetical to its mission) and insists on clinging to its old paradigms, in which it envisions its members not as peacemakers first and warmakers as a last resort but rather as warmakers, period.

Conclusion

At present, the conflict over the evolving nature of the U.S. military appears to be one between the "Hot" and "Cold" Warfare (Offensive and Defensive) Models and the Statecraft (Pro-fensive) Model. Traditionally, the military has seen itself as "strong" only when it fights or is prepared to fight. To engage in peacemaking is seen, at best, as an ineffectual model and, at worst, as a weak model for the military. The way out of this dilemma is, of course, to see war and peace activities not as either/or but as complementary and essential to each other. The Pro-fensive Model of the military is a strong model. It is a model of "both and." The choice that is to be made is how and when to exhibit what strength. In the future, "strength" or "might" or "power" will have to include the idea that a "warrior" organization not only can but must be both strong and restrained. The definition of military "strength" or "might" or "power" must, therefore, include the concept that in "gentler" missions, such as peacekeeping, there is a power that can exceed the strength of any army that has ever conquered. The Pro-fensive Model of a soldier in the new military, in the emerging paradigm of the twenty-first century, is thus that of the Peacemaker/Warrior. In fact, we already have such a model. It is the U.S. Coast Guard, whose variety of "peace" and "war" missions represents the direction in which the whole of our military organization is now evolving.

The implications of the Pro-fensive Model of the military are many, but two should be noted here. Such a model not only opens the door for an organization with equal numbers of women and men in its ranks and in its positions of authority but also creates the possibility of a new model for international geopolitical relations. Indeed, it may be that the twenty-first century will see the institutionalization of that change when a new organization evolves and is named the U.S. Department of Pro-fense. Reflecting the priority of its missions, its motto will then read, "To Preserve the Peace, To Defend, and To Fight."

REFERENCES

Devilbiss, M. C. 1988. "Defense in the Global Village: The Impact and Consequences of Global 'Megatrends' on the U.S. Military." Paper presented at the annual conference of the International Security Studies Section of the International Studies Association, Washington, D.C., 5 November.
————. 1992. "Women and War: A Conceptual Framework." *Daughters of Sarah* (Spring): 9–12.
————. 1994. "Best Kept Secrets: A Comparison of Gays and Women in the United States Armed Forces (The Hidden Life of Uncle Sam)." In Wilbur J. Scott and Sandra Carson Stanley, eds., *Gays and Lesbians in the Military: Issues, Concerns, and Contrasts.* New York: Aldine de Gruyter, pp. 135–48.
Stiehm, Judith Hicks. 1982. "The Protected, the Protector, and the Defender." *Women's Studies International Quarterly* 5, 3.

PART III   REFLECTION AND SPECULATION

Carol Burke

10

Pernicious Cohesion

Every day at the United States Naval Academy, midshipmen walk back and forth across "the yard" past memorials to their profession: a shiny black anchor big enough to dwarf the largest midshipman; an early-model fighter jet poised on the carefully mowed grass like an exaggerated lawn ornament; a bronze statue of Billy the Goat, whose testicles glisten from the polishing by plebes assigned the task; and Herndon Monument, a twenty-one-foot obelisk that, at the end of every year, the grounds' crew circles with a deep trench, greases with lard, and tops with a "dixie cup," the sailor's hat all freshmen must wear during their summer basic training.

To mark the end of each academic year and the end of plebedom, at a signal all members of the outgoing freshman class run from their dorm across the yard. The heftier linebackers are the first to hurl themselves into the trench, while the others scramble to construct a human pyramid secure enough to raise a midshipman to the top more quickly than any preceding first-year class. The classmate who topples the cap resting on top of the monument will be named admiral before any of his colleagues—or so the tradition goes, even though no midshipman who has removed the dixie cup has ever made admiral.

The noisy struggle typically takes over an hour, and every year female midshipmen join their male peers in the ritual that will measure their class against previous and succeeding classes. But a woman never gets far up the pyramid before her male counterparts toss her off, for no class wants to be the first to send a woman to the top of Herndon, a monument that in all its phallic splendor marks for many an exclusive, male rite of passage.

Between 1984 and 1991, I taught at the Naval Academy in the English Department. During my first couple of years, I was completing fieldwork for a book on the folklore of women in prison. While investigating the ways tradition functions within prison society to indoctrinate rookies, censure inappropriate behavior, explain the irrational, and inscribe a corporate identity, I discovered the relevance of the questions raised by my study of prison culture to another closed institution, the military academy. As a folklorist, I was fascinated by the wealth of folk tradition I found when I started looking at the academy of Annapolis—both the general military lore passed on from service to service and war to war, and the folklore and folk practices peculiar to the Naval Academy.

As students and faculty became aware of my interest in collecting academy lore, they brought me jokes scribbled on sheets of lined paper; lyrics to bawdy marching chants; latrinalia; legends; accounts of pranks, rituals, and rites of passage; stories of academy antiheroes; and personal narratives of life among the Brigade of Midshipmen. I jotted down the lyrics to cadence calls chanted by recruits as they "chopped" across the yard during summer basic training. I attended official and unofficial academy ceremonies. Midshipmen invited me to their highly frantic and outrageously campy skits, performed at night outside their dorm, in part to parody the administration and in part, I imagine, simply for the pleasure of dressing up in women's clothes.

The more I saw and heard, the more I wondered how female students managed to adjust to such a culture. Why do these women annually jump onto the mass of bodies scrambling to mount the greased Herndon Monument, when they know that they will be rebuffed if they come too close to the top? One female student once described her life at the Naval Academy as "living in a fraternity without being a full member." By surviving the first and most rigorous year at the academy, female midshipmen win membership in the Brigade of Midshipmen, yet they must continually negotiate their place in that fraternity. For women to boycott a ritual as significant as the climbing of Herndon would justify their critics' belief that they don't really belong.

Women who apply to the Naval Academy are distinguished by their independence and their inclination to take risks, yet they learn in their first year at the academy that to survive they must call no attention to themselves: "Although I had always been outspoken, I soon became more circumspect and developed a tendency to say only those things I was sure would not annoy anyone. This was especially true in classes. When I had questions, I usually left them unasked" (Schollaert 1988, 94).

Women students must simply accept traditions in which they cannot fully participate. And while the climbing of Herndon reminds them that certain roles are off-limits to them because they are women, other rituals prescribe feminine roles for women no midshipmen would choose. Each spring a delegation of Washington debutantes, the "cherry blossom princesses," descends on the Naval Academy; male midshipmen, excused from classes, escort them about the grounds. The presence of these women would not be so offensive to female midshipmen if they didn't have to hear the comments made by some male students that "it's nice to see a real girl for a change."

At the end of the year, the company with the highest military rating serves as the "color company," and one permitted to carry the colors in the ceremonial Color Parade held during graduation week before scores of invited guests and dignitaries. The midshipmen who commands the color company invites his girlfriend, whom the Naval Academy flies in, dresses in splendor, and enters in the parade as the "color girl." "A lovely tradition," claim its defenders; "An outdated ritual offensive to female midshipmen," say others. The offense to women resides not in a girl roughly their own age, dressed like a Southern belle, parading with them, but in the inevitable comparisons the spectacle elicits between the women in uniform and the costumed symbol of feminine beauty, the jewel of the parade. Some critics muse about the day when a female midshipman happens to be commander of the color company. Will there then be a "color boy"? Will an African American midshipman someday command the color company and invite his girlfriend to be the "color girl"? Were the ceremony eliminated, would the Color Girl Alumni Club, an organization of former color girls in their forties, fifties, sixties, and even seventies, who gather in Annapolis each spring to reminisce, come together instead to mourn the passing of a colorful tradition?

The social chairman who organizes the event explained to me that she orders the gown for each year's color girl months in advance, well before her selection. "We always order a size 12, so that it can be taken in to fit any girl chosen color girl." "But what if the woman is a size 16? Certainly no tailor can stretch a 12 into a 16," I said. "That would simply not be tolerated by the brigade; they wouldn't put up with someone of that size as their color girl," she responded.

Tradition not only makes explicit the standards for acceptable femininity; it also defines the inverse—the large, promiscuous woman. The acronym WUBA ("Working Uniform Blue Alpha") first appeared in 1976 to describe the freshly issued uniforms of the first female midshipmen, but within months male midshipmen employed it as a term for an unattractive female midshipmen. The expression appeared in misogynistic graffiti ("WUBA Go Home!"), in jokes, and in catcalls. Although officially censored, the expression enjoys wide currency today at the Naval Academy, sometimes jokingly said to stand for "Women Used By All."[1] Even today WUBA jokes circulate quickly among the brigade of midshipmen:

What's the difference between a WUBA and a warthog?
About two hundred pounds, but the WUBA has more hair.

How do you get a WUBA into her room?
Grease her hips and throw in a Twinkie.

What's the difference between zebras and WUBAs?
WUBAs fuck for their stripes.

The majority of the male student body stigmatizes women midshipmen as overweight and promiscuous. Ironically, with the intensive physical regimen required of all students, an overweight midshipman, male or female, is rare. When any students exceed their approved weight by a few pounds, they find their names and excess pounds posted on company bulletin boards. To many civilians, faculty and outsiders, female midshipmen seem underweight, a few each year anorectic.

Like WUBA jokes, marching chants (of which I collected more than two hundred during my years at the Naval Academy) cast women as mothers, unfaithful lovers, or monstrous whores. Take, for example, the Brobdingnagian Lulu:

Rich girl uses Vaseline, poor girl uses lard
But Lulu uses axle grease and bangs them twice as hard.

Chorus: Bang Bang Lulu. Bang away all day.
Bang Bang Lulu. Who ya gonna bang today?

Rich girl uses tampons, poor girl uses rags
But Lulu's cunt's so goddamn big she uses burlap bags.

Bawdy chants like this one have been officially banned at the Naval Academy for the past few years. Although midshipmen have largely ceased to sing such verse in public, some have continued to exchange misogynistic lore at small, all-male gatherings. As recently as 1991, members of the Male Glee Club entertained themselves on bus trips home with a lurid variation of the popular song "The Candy Man," called "The S&M Man":

Who can take a chainsaw
Cut the bitch in two
Fuck the bottom half
and give the upper half to you . . .

Chorus: The S&M Man, the S&M Man,
The S&M Man cause he mixes it with love
and makes the hurt feel good!

Who can take a bicycle
Then take off the seat
Set his girlfriend on it
ride her down a bumpy street . . .
(Chorus)

Who can take some jumper cables
Clamp them to her tits
Jump-start your car
and electrocute the bitch . . .
(Chorus)

Who can take an ice pick
Ram it through her ear
Ride her like a Harley
As you fuck her from the rear . . .

During my first couple years at the academy, informal groups opposed to female midshipmen proudly referred to themselves as "Webbites" after James Webb, Marine, novelist, former secretary of the navy, and outspoken critic of the admission of women. In a 1979 article in the *Washingtonian*,

Webb denounced the presence of women at the Naval Academy, charging them with "poisoning" and "sterilizing" the training of male officers and of achieving their rank unfairly: "This year, as women become seniors for the first time, the whole world will see women in high 'striper' positions, possibly even that of brigade commander. What the whole world may not know is that women did not attain these positions in the same way that men historically have" (1979, 275).

For the most misogynistic midshipmen, James Webb became a cult figure whose sexist "word" they proselytized to underclassmen. Although the administration officially banned Webbite organizations, a group calling itself the "WUBA Klux Klan" attempted to solicit new members from the freshman class as recently as 1991.

Although I discussed these practices and this folklore with my colleagues (both military and civilian), and although we shared our concern when we heard of humiliations endured by students, we also suffered a sense of our powerlessness to change long-standing traditions "in the Hall," an exclusively military sphere over which faculty had no influence. Civilians, who made up 50 percent of the faculty and who were ostensibly freer than their military colleagues to voice their criticisms, rarely objected. The freedom to act civilian in a military institution is a fragile one. To criticize military practices too fiercely might open a civilian to the discrediting charge of being "unmilitary." When we did express our concern about practices in the Hall (as I did in a meeting with the dean after students told me about the hate group, the WUBA Klux Klan), we rarely heard of any action taken.

In his opening address to the faculty in 1989, Admiral Virgil Hill, the recent superintendent of the Naval Academy, began with a breast joke. Not very bawdy as breast jokes go, it nevertheless manifested an insensitivity, which was signified again by the admiral's comment a year later about a female midshipman handcuffed to a urinal by a group of her peers, jeered at and photographed. (The incident took place after a snowball fight during which the woman had scored a particularly hard hit on another midshipman.) Hill described the episode as simply an example of "high jinks." The distraught victims of such pranks find it difficult to dismiss them so casually.

The Naval Academy, which uneasily incorporates a contemporary undergraduate education within the traditions of a nineteenth-century British boy's school with its pranks and intimidations, demands continual adjustments of all its members. Although we civilian faculty celebrated our autonomy in the classroom, we knew that at some level we, too, were caught

Commissioning Week: Academy superintendent presenting the colors
to the color company commander and the color girl.
Courtesy of the Baltimore Sun.

Human pyramid formed to facilitate the scaling of the well-greased
Herndon Monument. *Courtesy of the Baltimore Sun.*

up in the socialization process. Education in the classroom (modeled on the classrooms in which we were taught) constituted only one form of instruction. Every day upperclassmen grill plebes braced at attention along hallways, quizzing them on the details of ships and planes, items on the noon menu, current sports scores, and other arbitrary trivia. To every question these freshmen may respond with the fact solicited or with one of the sanctioned replies: "Yes, Sir"; "No, Sir"; "I will find out, Sir"; "No excuse, sir."

These interrogations teach the recruit not only that she or he must never guess at an answer but also that the cost of not knowing a piece of information, however insignificant, is certain public humiliation. Since 1991, a no-touching rule has forced the replacement of physical punishment with verbal insults uttered loudly enough for the entire company to hear. Endorsed by the majority of upperclassmen as essential to toughening those who can withstand the stress and to eliminating those who cannot, these practices (along with a host of other requirements, prohibitions, and punishments that apply only to freshmen) constitute the system known as "plebe indoctrination."

While we encouraged freshmen to think critically, the plebe indoctrination system punished criticism and independence. While we encouraged skepticism and analysis, the military system of training demanded nonreflective precision. While we did our best to inspire students to admire and examine literary tradition, the closed institution we joined and in which we labored used tradition as a tool to standardize its human product and to discipline both faculty and students into conformity with a government-issue world view.

And that world view prescribes certain gender imperatives, such as the assumption that defense of one's country and manliness are synonymous. In response to the recent embarrassment of the Tailhook scandal, those in the highest positions in the Navy have insisted on a simple and forceful restatement of what has been official policy for some time: "zero tolerance" in matters of sexual harassment. But official pronouncements alone will not ensure change. In order to change attitudes toward women in the Navy and in its premier institution, the Naval Academy, we must take a careful, albeit painful, look into the shadows at the traditions that constitute the institution, traditions that stubbornly resist change. Military academies of all branches of the military, as well as those of modern Westernized militaries, have failed to examine traditions both in light of their relevance to the practice of modern warfare and in light of their appropriateness to the training of an increasingly diverse labor force.

Unquestioned in today's military is the belief that training fundamentally transforms the individual. In the words of a former head of drill instructors at Parris Island:

> Military training exists to break [the recruit] down to his fundamental
> self, take away all that he possesses, and get him started out in a way
> that you want him to be. Issue him all new clothes, cut his hair, send
> his possessions home, and tell him he doesn't know a damn thing,
> that he's the sorriest thing you've ever seen, but with my help you're
> going to be worthwhile again.[2]

In practice, breaking the recruit down to his "fundamental self" often means stripping him of his clothes to expose not just his selfhood but also his manhood. In the 1970s, upperclassmen at the Royal Military College in Kingston, Canada, ordered first-year students to stand naked at attention outside their rooms while a stereo down the hall played love songs. The first cadet to achieve an erection was awarded a prize and the company permitted to return to bed.

At Australia's West Point, Duntroon, upperclassmen roused first-year students from their sleep and stripped and herded them into bathrooms, where they were taken out one by one to run a gauntlet. These second- and third-year students slapped freshmen with towels, belts, and suspenders and forced them to climb a ladder while fire hoses sprayed their genitals. They demanded that initiates perform songs and answer impossible questions. Each victim in turn was seated on a block of ice at the top of a slide. After repeating a loyalty oath, he was dubbed a member of the Corps with a sword that in later years was electrified to deliver a shock to the shivering rookie astride the block of ice. After the administration of the shock, the ice block and cadet were shoved down the slide into a vat of foul-smelling liquids. In some years, broken bottles were added to the vat, necessitating treatment for minor (in some years major) lacerations. With only small variations from year to year, this ritual continued from 1911 until 1976, when the Army's Duntroon merged into a tri-service academy incorporating Navy and Air Force cadets. Like the adolescent male rites of passage documented by Erich Neumann (1994), Emile Durkheim (1965); Mircea Eliade (1965), and Bruno Bettelheim (1955), this tradition ran the initiate through a series of ordeals, in which he often suffered some pain to the genitals, symbolically died, and was born again into the world of men. In a 1969 article in his alma mater's quarterly magazine, the R.M.C. *Journal*, a former graduate naturalized his experience by setting it in the context (both literally and figuratively) of another, more ancient rite:

> The end of the week came. The great event arrived, the initiation. We welcomed this as an aboriginal boy would welcome the "man" ritual. It was in the evening. . . . We were required to disrobe. We were led blindfolded to the sacred corroboree grounds. Females were forbidden to the area, although rumour had it that female eyes sparkled on the slopes of [Mt.] Pleasant.
>
> Questions were asked but answers were gagged. Songs had to be sung, but oiled waste plugged the notes. Finally, one had to slide down the symbolic slippery dip. A . . . bath at the bottom consummated our declining status. And all punctuated with wet and knotted towels on our naked torsos.
>
> Then it was over. How wonderful, we were now gentlemen cadets of the Royal Military College "de facto" and "de jure." Around us were the exalted ones, shaking hands, telling us that we were now of the order. (JHT 1969, 50)

The first year, or a portion of it, in every military academy, from Sandhurst to West Point, from Annapolis to Kingston in Canada, marks a period of transition from childhood to manhood, from civilian status to membership in the Corps. Upperclassmen debase their juniors in painful but customary ways. Rarely do upperclassmen invent new forms of humiliation; the most brutal merely increase the frequency of their aggression. In "plebe indoctrination," known in Australia as "fourth-class training" or, somewhat less flatteringly, "bastardization," three-fourths of the student body assumes the role of masters and one-fourth reluctantly plays the part of slave.

In 1992, an article in the Australian press on the abuse of first-year cadets prompted an inquiry into allegations that freshmen had been made to lick cream off a senior cadet's underpants, to simulate sex, and to suffer a "woofering," in which a cadet was handcuffed and had his head covered, his pants pulled down, and a vacuum cleaner applied to his genitals.[3] The freshmen who endured these abuses were typically accused by upperclassmen of some trumped-up charge and convicted in a kangaroo court (in a "morals trial" if one had been friendly with a female cadet or in an "atrocity trial" if one had associated with a girl others regarded as unattractive).

Before an excited audience of upperclassmen, the young male cadets received their punishment. In some instances they were ordered to perform "rvo's" (Reverse Vienna Oysters), in which one freshman would lie on his back while the other, atop him in missionary position, performed pushups to the cheers of an aroused crowd in sync with each wave of simulated sex. Ceremonies that mix the homoerotic and the humiliating enjoy a long history in male groups. Rituals like these, most of which have continued far past the integration of women into the military, are clearly part of the cultural legacy of the modern military. They facilitate the assertion of collective masculinity and both celebrate and restrain homoerotic enthusiasm. When much of the point is to cast out the female or to recast it in male terms, there is no part for women to play, except the role of victim.

Despite the fact that many military traditions have at their center acts of humiliation, they inculcate, according to their defenders, an esprit de corps essential to group cohesion. Military arguments against the integration of women (and of blacks and homosexuals) have often turned on the issue of cohesion. Without the rough-and-tumble enthusiasm of individuals who feel comfortable with one another, so the argument goes, the military unit would cease to be effective. Would a soldier trust and defend someone who was not his buddy?

Cohesion, as involved in these arguments, suggests a homogeneity that protects the group and makes it more efficient in the face of danger. In a recent review of the literature on cohesion, sponsored by the Office of the Secretary of Defense under RAND's National Defense Research Institute, Robert MacCoun (1993) distinguishes "social cohesion," the network of buddy relationships within a group whose members enjoy spending time with one another, from "task cohesion," a group's shared sense of a common goal. Task cohesion, according to MacCoun, may exist among group members who are not friends and who have little in common other than their shared task. Past military studies (Adams 1953; McGrath 1962; Tziner and Vardi 1982) found little evidence that group harmony plays any role in determining performance. In his recent examination of social cohesion, task cohesion, and group pride, I. L. Janis (1983) confirmed that only task cohesion showed any correlation to performance. Likewise, the abundant research on effectiveness in the nonmilitary workplace demonstrates the importance of task cohesion rather than of camaraderie (Locke and Latham 1990).

Few citizens would quarrel with a military regimen that seeks to instill loyalty, respect for authority, and a sense of the group before the importance of the individual. But in what ways do these service academy practices further such ends? Proponents defend ritual humiliation as the necessary ordeal designed to make strong leaders. Were the abuse of service academies essential to the forging of officers, would the Pentagon train most of its officers in ROTC and OCS programs, which lack the time-honored tradition of "plebe indoctrination"? And in what ways can a system designed to instill total compliance fashion true leaders? To justify such a system on the basis of its promotion of cohesion is problematic. To rationalize ritual humiliation as a necessary rehearsal for prison camp is even more bizarre.

Harsh treatment of the sort meted out to freshmen at military academies is defended to this day as essential to toughening those who can withstand the stress and to eliminating those who cannot. James Webb, one of the staunchest proponents of this treatment, defends this method of training:

> So how do you teach combat leadership? You don't do it with a textbook; you do it by creating a stress environment. My academic education at the Naval Academy always took a back seat to my military education. During our first year, I and my classmates were regularly tested and abused inside Bancroft Hall, our living spaces. We were pushed deep inside ourselves for that entire year, punished physically and mentally stressed to the point that virtually every one of us completely broke down at least once. And when we finished our first year we carried out the same form of abuse on other entering classes. That was the plebe system. It was harsh and cruel. It was designed to produce a man who would be able to be an effective leader in combat, to endure prisoner-of-war camps, to fight this country's wars with skill and tenacity. (1979, 148)

But remembering the abuse he suffered during his first year at the Royal Military Academy at Duntroon, an Australian former prisoner of war refutes Webb's hackneyed defense. (The possibility of becoming a POW is ironically also the most common of all excuses to exclude women from combat.) Recalling an upperclass bully, this Australian veteran writes:

> I was pleased when I heard after I came back from the war that he had been killed. I know my soul has been eaten into more by Fourth Class Training than by the three-and-a-half years I suffered as a prisoner of war under the Japanese. I bear no animosity against the Japanese for

their treatment of me, they were my enemies at the time, but I still bitterly resent what was done to me by fellow Australian cadets in my Fourth Class at the RMC. (Coulthard-Clark 1984, 125–26).

What we witness in the folklore and folk practices of service academies today is the passing along of officer culture from Britain to the United States, Canada, and Australia, a culture whose purpose is to construct class through the production of elites—the British boys' school culture of privileges and punishments. Such a fundamentally antidemocratic enterprise becomes harder to defend as threats to our national security lessen and as we begin to consider the cost of such traditional institutions.

As we reevaluate our military institutions in these post–Cold War years, we must consider the informal as well as the formal training they prescribe, and we must hold them accountable for misdeeds like those that took place at the 1991 Tailhook Convention. In an interview in which he was asked to comment on the Tailhook scandal, J. Daniel Howard, undersecretary of the Navy, declared, "Americans don't want a naval officer to behave like just any person in society. They expect a higher standard of behavior."[4] In fact, when we insist that assailants be prosecuted, we invoke no "higher standard of behavior." When we condemn those who witness a crime but fail even to notify police, we demand no superior moral standard than the decency and responsibility that come with citizenship. What happened at the Tailhook reunion was both traditional and criminal. The Navy's botched investigation of the affair is evidence both of the difficulty of uprooting the deep-seated misogynistic traditions that breed such behavior and of pernicious cohesion, the closing-of-ranks that thwarts change.

NOTE

Acknowledgments: The title of this essay was suggested to me by Judith Stiehm. The first half of it appeared as "Inside the Clubhouse," *Women's Review of Books*, 10, 5 (1993):20–21.

1. As recently as November 1994, midshipmen affirmed the persistent widespread familiarity of this expression and the body of lore that associates with it. For further discussion, see "Dames at Sea," *New Republic* (17 and 24 August), 1992, pp. 16–20.

2. The quotation is taken from a tape-recorded interview with Colonel Fred Fagan, U.S.M.C., Annapolis, Md., 1 February 1989.

3. Margaret Easterbrook. *The Age*, 4 May 1992, p. 17; Rod Campbell, "Three ADFA Cadets Admit to Woofering," *Canberra Times* 16 December 1992, p. 1.

4. Eric Schmitt, "Now at Navy's Bridge, Engaging Sexism," *New York Times*, July 4, 1992, p. 8.

REFERENCES

Adams, S. 1953. "Status Congruency as a Variable in Small Group Performance." *Social Forces*, 16–22.

Bettelheim, Bruno. 1955. *Symbolic Wounds: Puberty Rites and the Envious Male*. London: Thames and Hudson.

Burke, Carol. 1993. *Vision Narratives of Women in Prison*. New York: St. Martin's Press.

Coulthard-Clark, C. D. 1984. *Duntroon: The Royal Military College of Australia*. Sydney: Allen and Unwin.

Durkheim, Emile. 1965. *The Elementary Forms of the Religious Life*. New York: Free Press.

Eliade, Mircea. 1965. *Rites and Symbols of Initiation: The Mysteries of Birth and Rebirth*. New York: Harper and Row.

Janis, I. L. 1983. *Groupthink: Psychological Studies of Policy Decisions and Fiascoes*. Boston: Houghton Mifflin.

JHT. 1969. "The Duntroon Tradition." *Journal of the Royal Military College*, 50–51.

Locke, E. A., and G. P. Latham. 1990. "Work Motivation and Satisfaction: Light at the End of the Tunnel." *Psychological Science* 1:240–46.

MacCoun, Robert. 1993. "What Is Known about Unit Cohesion and Military Performance." In *Sexual Orientation and U.S. Military Personnel Policy: Options and Assessment*. Santa Monica, Calif.: Rand Corporation, pp. 283–329.

McGrath, J. E. 1962. "The Influence of Positive Interpersonal Relations on Adjustment and Effectiveness in Rifle Teams." *Journal of Abnormal Psychology and Social Psychology* 67:365–75.

Neumann, Erich. 1994. *The Fear of the Feminine and Other Essays on Feminine Psychology*. Princeton: Princeton University Press.

Schollaert, Stephanie. 1988. Letter to the Editor. *Proceeding*, August, p. 94.

Tziner, Aharon, and Yoav Vardi. 1982. "Effects of command Style Group Cohesiveness on the Performance Effectiveness of Self-Selected Tank Crews." *Journal of Applied Psychology* 67:769–75.

———. 1983. "Ability as a Moderator between Cohesiveness and Tank Crew Performance." *Journal of Occupational Behavior* 4:137–43.

Webb, James. 1979. "Women Can't Fight." *Washington* 44:145–48, 273–82.

Susan Jeffords

11

Telling the War Story

I listened once to Tim O'Brien, author of several prizewinning novels about the Vietnam War and himself a veteran of that war, as he sat and told stories to an audience of West Point cadets. After riveting their attention with tales of his first night "in country," of his base being mortared, of his sergeant, and of his friends being killed, he turned casually to his audience and said, "You know, of course, that none of what I've been telling you is true. These are all war stories."

War stories are some of the oldest recorded narratives in many cultures, from the Greek *Iliad* to the Vietnamese *Tale of Kieu*. War stories have been a fundamental part of American culture, too, whether in Mary Rowlandson's account of her captivity by Indians in the King Phillip Wars of 1676–77, Stephen Crane's classic tale of the Civil War in *The Red Badge of Courage*, Ernest Hemingway's *For Whom the Bell Tolls* about World War I, or the numerous Hollywood films about World War II for which John Wayne became the quintessential star.

But it is the Vietnam War that stands in most people's mind today as the war that showed, more than any other, that understandings of war are not rooted in indisputable historical facts but are instead a collage, a collection of experiences, emotions, understandings, misunderstandings, and memories. In other words, war stories are a collection of stories people tell about wars. What the Vietnam War showed as well was that many different people told war stories, and that who told them and who they told them to mattered. The publication of the Pentagon Papers in the *New York Times* in 1971, for example, showed how the government's public story about the war was far different from that revealed in internal discussions and documents. Conflict erupted between citizens who accepted the government's interpretation of "what the Vietnamese wanted" and citizens who had acquired a different understanding. And, of course, whatever American stories were told, they were sure to be different from the war stories being told by the Vietnamese (both North and South).

For several decades, the Vietnam War has continued to be the subject of diverse interpretations of what the war was about, of how it was fought, of who "won" the war, of what exactly the war accomplished, of what the American public thinks about those who fought in it (or, more recently, as shown in the 1992 presidential campaigns, what it thinks about those who did not fight), and of what long-term effects it had on the United States. Anyone who has ever visited the Vietnam War Memorial—itself the most controversial memorialization of a war in American history—and who has seen the numerous and various offerings made by observers at the wall knows just how diverse U.S. citizens' relationships to that war continue to be. From war medals to POW bracelets to cans of beer to burned American flags to wedding rings to running shoes: the things people leave at the wall give testimony to just how many and how very different kinds of stories there are to tell about the soldiers whose names are inscribed there.

In this essay I look at the way the Vietnam War was interpreted in popular culture and then draw some conclusions about the importance of understanding how and why war stories are told.

The Early Vietnam War Stories

A number of stories about Vietnam appeared in the 1950s and set the stage for many Americans' thinking about Vietnam. Graham Greene's The Quiet American (1956) is an allegorical tale about French, British, and American intervention in Vietnamese government affairs. The story is played out through three men's relationships to a Vietnamese woman. The book is devastatingly prophetic about the failure of American idealism about democracy in the face of different historical and cultural forces. When made into a Hollywood film a few years later, however, the story of "innocence failed" became one that celebrated American innocence and described it as a plausible way to understand Southeast Asia. At about the same time, theater and film audiences were being treated to one of the decade's biggest draws, South

Pacific, a story about a young American military woman who falls in love with a French planter on a South Pacific island during World War II.[1] Presented largely as a romance, the story reaches its happy ending when the American woman agrees to "adopt" the planter's two children by a Polynesian mother. This happy parentalism portrayed for American audiences a picture of Southeast Asians as childlike people who were in need of American protection, care, and guidance, an attitude that probably later helped reinforce the parentalism of many of the Cold War strategists who favored U.S. intervention in Vietnam.

One of the most famous popular narratives about the growing U.S. military involvement in Vietnam was John Wayne and Ray Kellog's *The Green Berets,* the 1968 film adaptation of a novel by Robin Moore. Wayne and Kellog collaborated closely with the Pentagon on the screenplay of the film, sending drafts for editorial approval and enjoying cheap "rental" of U.S. military equipment as props.[2] Stereotypical characters abound in the film. They include the cynical and uninformed journalist who criticizes the war though he's never been in Vietnam and who dramatically changes to wholehearted support for the war (even joining in the fighting) after seeing it for himself; the ruthless Viet Cong who massacre innocent villagers, rape girls, and torture prisoners; and the honest American soldiers, who give their lives to protect the Vietnamese's right to democracy. Replicating the ending of *South Pacific, Green Berets* has John Wayne telling a Vietnamese boy that he's "what this war is all about," again showing the Vietnamese as children who need American protection.[3] It is a film whose imagery carried great weight with large portions of the American population. The U.S. Army gave its sign of approval when it began showing the film to U.S. soldiers when they arrived in Vietnam, thereby shaping the attitudes of the young people most responsible for U.S. interactions with the Vietnamese.[4]

Most of the popular fictional representations of the Vietnam War at this time were "B" movies that showed Vietnam veterans as crazed misfits who brought home the violence of the war and practiced it in small American towns. Films such as *The Born Losers* (T. C. Frank, 1967), *Angels from Hell* (Bruce Kessler, 1968), and *Chrome and Hot Leather* (Lee Frost, 1971) competed with the nightly news programs of America's first "television war." While newscasters were generally supportive of the war during the early years, many came to believe that the war was unwinnable—or not worth winning. Walter Cronkite's declaration in his 1968 post-Tet offensive broadcast, titled "Who, What, When, Where, Why," that "it seems now more certain than ever that the bloody experience of Vietnam is to end in a stalemate"[5] was particularly influential.

These stories were being told at the time of vigorous and widespread antiwar actions, perhaps the largest in the history of the United States. In 1970, two years after the media's coverage of the Tet offensive began to change people's perceptions about the winnability of the war, and one year after the massacre of Vietnamese civilians at My Lai became widely known, one of the most important of Hollywood's antiwar statements was released, M*A*S*H* (Hal Ashby). Even though the film was about a medical unit serving in the Korean War, its comment on Vietnam was inescapable. It depicted a military system that cared more about regulations than soldiers, that was inherently racist,[6] and that fought the war with little regard for the people it was ostensibly fighting for. M*A*S*H*, then, provided an immediate and forceful story about the Vietnam War that spoke to many in the increasingly vocal antiwar movement.

What followed in the early 1970s was a spate of films that criticized both the Vietnam War and war in general, among them *Johnny Got His Gun* (1971), *Welcome Home, Johnny Bristol* (1971), and *Slaughterhouse Five* (1972). But in the mid-1970s, when the war reached its end with the final withdrawal of U.S. troops in 1973 and the fall of Saigon to North Vietnamese troops in 1975, and for a few years afterward, popular culture seemed to be trying to forget the war. Few films were made about the war, and fewer, if any, of significance.[7] Then, in 1978, some of the strongest Vietnam War films were released: *The Boys in Company C* (Sidney Furie), *Coming Home* (Hal Ashby), *Go Tell the Spartans* (Ted Post), *Who'll Stop the Rain?* (Karol Reisz), and the film that brought the war back to the box office, Michael Cimino's *The Deer Hunter*. This film's popularity stemmed not only from its stars—Robert de Niro, Christopher Walken, and Meryl Streep—but from the particular story it told about the war. In its most famous scene, three American POWs are shown being forced to play Russian roulette while Vietnamese soldiers gamble over their lives. In spite of its falsity, this scene provided a metaphor that crystallized the war for many viewers: American soldiers' lives had been gambled by their government and by the Vietnamese in a vicious game that led to unmerited deaths and random acts of violence and torture. The scene suggested that in the end the grand political and moral explanations for the war meant very little to the soldiers whose lives were governed by what seemed to be a perverse game of chance.

The Deer Hunter opened the door for a new kind of story to be told about the war, one in which (1) the war was acknowledged to have been a bad one (whether because it should not have been fought at all or because it was not fought well enough was a subject of disagreement and (2) the focus for incorporating the war into American history was the individual soldier/veteran rather than civilian or military leaders. This significant shift not only allowed the war to be discussed apart from its politics but also laid the groundwork for public interpretation of later wars, in which, as in the Persian Gulf War, both pro- and antiwar citizens spoke about war from the point of view of the participants, those who did the fighting.

Finally, Francis Ford Coppola released in 1979 what many people take to be the quintessential Vietnam War film, *Apocalypse Now*. The story is of an obedient captain sent on a mission to locate and kill a renegade colonel who had taken to fighting the war in his own way. *Apocalypse Now* offered viewers what can only be called a story about the weirdness of the war. From scenes of night fighting illuminated by Christmas lights and grenade launchers, to gung-ho majors determined to take a beach because it offered the best surfing in Vietnam, to soldiers who were indifferent toward a massacre of civilians and yet protected a lost puppy, Coppola's interpretation depicted a haunting underside to Americans' behavior in the war. In a plot that showed the only effective fighting being done outside the military, in Colonel Kurtz's army of Montagnard tribesmen, and revealed the decay of a military leadership that would send soldiers to kill one of their own, Coppola presented a vision not simply of military thinking but of America itself, as hypocritical, self-serving, corrupt, and violent. Whether through politicized self-interest or simple naivete, Coppola's story is of a military incapable of understanding, let alone of winning, the war.

Stories of the Next Decade

With many veterans stepping forward to confirm *Apocalypse Now*'s nightmarish vision of Vietnam, it seemed for some years that Coppola's war story might become the Vietnam War's lasting, defining public image. But in 1982, two years after Ronald Reagan had won a presidential election campaigning for a renewed and strong America, John Rambo hit the screens of U.S. movie theaters. Though drawn from David Morrell's pessimistic novel about a Vietnam veteran's failed readjustment to U.S. society, *First Blood* was turned by director John Milius from a vision of a dysfunctional vet into a commentary on American society itself. Unable to appreciate the service and commitments of heroic soldiers such as Rambo, the small town of Hope, Oregon, shuns him, tortures him, and finally hunts him like an animal— even using America's own home forces, the National Guard, to try to kill him. The unexpected box-office success of First Blood showed that a change had occurred in Americans' thinking about the war. Though First Blood offered much the same criticism as Apocalypse Now of bureaucracies, military hypocrisies, and self-serving patriotism, it ended not with a critique of the war and the military but with a strong attack on an American system that had apparently forsaken the ideals that had led it to fight the war in the first place. Moreover, the film implied that by abandoning its ideals, the society had abandoned the soldiers who fought for it. First Blood marked the return of the Vietnam veteran, not simply to the box office but to the heroic war story. At the same time, it signaled a change in the stories told about the war.

What followed was a series of movies about heroic Vietnam veterans: the Rambo sequels, Rambo, First Blood, Part 2 and Rambo 3; Chuck Norris's Missing in Action trilogy; and Uncommon Valor. The target of critique in these films was not the soldier, or even the military itself, but a government that came to be depicted as unwilling to do what was necessary to fight the war. This story was reinforced by messages coming from the Reagan White House. Reagan proclaimed the Soviet Union an "Evil Empire" and expressed his determination to fight the extension of communism around the globe; as he did so, the war stories about Vietnam began to shift away from the sentiment that the Vietnam War was a bad war to the conclusion that it was just not fought properly. The Rambo stories and others like them helped reestablish America's lost faith in its soldiers. The new war stories replaced stories about baby killers with stories celebrating soldiers' courage, commitment, and patriotism. It was a revision that was fundamental not only to Reagan's political successes but to public support for the wars fought by him and his successor, George Bush. Without the public and popular reassessment of the Vietnam War, and of soldiers and war in general, military action in Grenada, Nicaragua, Panama, and the Persian Gulf would not have been possible.

Since then, the Vietnam War has continued to serve as a topic for Hollywood in films such as Full Metal Jacket, Gardens of Stone, Bat 21, and Oliver Stone's trilogy, Platoon, Born on the Fourth of July, and Heaven and Earth; it also became the subject of two television series, Tour of Duty in 1987 and the much-acclaimed China Beach in 1988. Since the mid-1980s, however, there have been fewer popular references to the war itself than there have been to soldiers who fought in it. Without being about the war, numerous Hollywood films and television series have featured main characters who were veterans of the war—*The A Team; Magnum, P.I.; Miami Vice; Hill Street Blues*—and characters on soap operas have begun to "reveal" their Vietnam War experiences. Action-adventure heroes now claim Vietnam War experience as well, including Mel Gibson's character in *Lethal Weapon*, Jean-Claude Van Damme's character in *Universal Soldier*, and Steven Seagal's character in *Under Siege*. One of the country's most popular action comic books, *Predator*, is also about a Vietnam veteran.

Thus, after the commitment of U.S. troops to Vietnam, American popular representations of the war moved through several phases, from an initial support of the war in films such as *The Green Berets* to a sympathy for its veterans in films such as *Born on the Fourth of July*. This trend away from the war itself to the people who fought in it shifts the war from a national to a personal experience, making it possible for viewers to forget the specific historical and political forces that caused the war—colonialism, Cold War anticommunism, racism, military industrialization, and so on—and to recall only the personal traumas and training of specific individuals. Many people today feel that the Vietnam War was a "bad war" not because they understand and disagree with the policies and decisions that underlay it but because they sympathize with the veterans who have been made to seem victims of that war.

The Effects of Vietnam War Stories

Some of the films I've mentioned here were among the biggest box-office draws in their years of release, including *The Green Berets, Coming Home, Rambo,* and *Platoon*. Millions of people saw these films in movie theaters and on video, not only in the United States but also abroad, where films such as *Rambo* were among the top box-office successes, particularly in the Philippines and Japan. Much of popular understanding about the Vietnam War, then, comes precisely from movies like these, not from history textbooks or even conversations with the veterans these films are ostensibly about.

The power of films to shape public thinking about wars is shown most clearly in the statements of the soldiers who fought in the Vietnam War. Many of those soldiers recall that their desire to enlist in the military and to go and fight in Vietnam came from remembered Hollywood images of World War II, especially those from the films of John Wayne and Audie Murphy. In his autobiography, *Born on the Fourth of July*, which became the basis for Oliver Stone's film, Ron Kovic talks about the importance of Hollywood films: "I'll never forget Audie Murphy in *To Hell and Back*. . . . He was so brave I had chills running up and down my back, wishing it were me up there. . . . It was the greatest movie I ever saw in my life" (Kovic 1977, 54).

In his much-acclaimed autobiographical novel *A Rumor of War*, Philip Caputo, as he fights in combat, recalls, "I was John Wayne in *Sands of Iwo Jima*. I was Aldo Ray in *Battle Cry*" (Caputo 1977, 255). Or, as one of the soldiers in Mark Baker's collection, *Nam*, remembers, "I had flash images of John Wayne films with myself as the hero" (Baker 1981, 23). Thirty-six years after *The Sands of Iwo Jima*, the film *Top Gun*, which also involved a Vietnam War subplot (Peter "Maverick" Mitchell's father's plane was shot down in the war), served as another recruiting story, increasing the enlistments in both the Navy and Air Force pilot training programs.

Such examples indicate the force of mass media representations on individual decision making, but what I think is finally more significant is how war stories shape and are shaped by larger cultural attitudes. For although wars may be fought for immediately identifiable reasons of territorial dispute, treaty violation, or political change, much must be done to prepare a society to engage willingly in the fighting of a war, especially a long-term war. This is particularly important when success of military actions is seen to depend on the achievement of public support for large-scale, overt military engagements. Such support became a key criterion for military engagement in the Reagan administration. Caspar Weinberger, Reagan's secretary of defense, argued in 1980 that no wars should be fought without prior public support, a point he made explicitly in relation to the Vietnam War:

> Before the U.S. commits combat forces abroad, there must be some
> reasonable assurance we will have the support of the American people
> and their elected representatives in Congress. . . . We cannot fight a
> battle with the Congress at home while asking our troops to win a
> war overseas or, as in the case of Vietnam, in effect asking our troops
> not to win, but just to be there.[8] (Weinberger 1990, 442)

How, then, does the representation of warfare—in other words, the stories told about war—create support for large-scale military engagements at the social and cultural level?

There are several ways in which war stories become significant factors in a citizenry's willingness to engage in war. In the most simple and direct manner, the representations of World War II as a morally just war in which individual soldiers achieved heroism through their participation promoted a public sense that warfare is, or at least can be, both individually and socially meaningful. The fact that World War II was portrayed during the postwar period, almost without exception, as an unqualified "victory" contributed to audiences' identification with that war and to the sense that a war is defined principally by its outcome. The facts of the Axis surrender, signed treaties, and war tribunals underscore the sense of an Allied victory in World War II, but the political, social, and economic realities are far more complex than could be portrayed in Hollywood films, which celebrated the victory as an individual and a national achievement. It was precisely this impression of war as just and as winnable, an impression left by scores of Hollywood World War II films throughout the 1940s, 1950s, and early 1960s, that made it so difficult to assimilate the Vietnam War into broad cultural definitions about who Americans are and how and why they fight their wars. Conversely, the cultural truism that America "lost" the Vietnam War, a conclusion supported by numerous films and narratives, led to public anxieties about whether foreign wars can be won at all. Hesitations about U.S. involvement in El Salvador, Grenada, Panama, Nicaragua, and the Persian Gulf were articulated largely in terms of fears that those wars would become "another Vietnam." Stories told about the Vietnam War thus have established the framework within which subsequent wars are judged.

But if we look at the dates of some of the best-known war stories in U.S. history—Stephen Crane's *The Red Badge of Courage* (1895), Ernest Hemingway's *A Farewell to Arms,* (1925), Otto Preminger's *In Harm's Way* (1965), Francis Ford Coppola's *Apocalypse Now* (1979)—it becomes clear that they all were written a substantial time *after* the wars they depicted were over. This may mean that war stories have less to do with the particular wars they are "about" than they do with other social and cultural issues that can be discussed *through* war stories. Thus we must now ask a slightly different question than before: not, What do war stories tell us about fighting wars? but, What purpose do war stories serve in American culture? One obvious purpose is, as I have noted, the promulgation of ideas about war, but the popularity of war stories long after a war is over suggests that other kinds of stories are being told as well. In particular, I would like to focus on three themes: gender, race, and the idea of what it means to be American.

Because war in the United States has historically been fought almost exclusively by men, war stories offer an ideal place to examine portrayals of masculinity. The ideals of heroism, strength, decisiveness, and the capacity to fight for what is right and good characterize male heroes of twentieth-century popular war stories. They are also the features of many male heroes in westerns, detective stories, and most recently, action-adventure films, suggesting that war stories are parts of larger cultural stories being told about men and women. In addition, these other genres are used to respond to social shifts that have taken place as a result of war. For example, the dark and suspenseful film noir genre that achieved such popularity in the post–World War II period with its negative portrayals of independent and aggressive femmes fatale—typified by films such as The Maltese Falcon (John Huston, 1941) and Sunset Boulevard (Billy Wilder, 1950)—is widely understood to be a response to the increasing numbers of women who entered the paid labor force during World War II and were consequently challenging traditional roles of masculine and feminine behavior.

Because of its clear gender lines—men fight war and women do not—war stories and war veteran heroes are often ideal mechanisms for working through broader cultural and social tensions related to shifting gender roles. For example, the story lines and characterizations of some of the most popular 1980s films—Sylvester Stallone as Rambo in the Rambo trilogy, Chuck Norris as Colonel Braddock in the Missing in Action trilogy, Mel Gibson as police sergeant Riggs in the Lethal Weapon trilogy, or even Bruce Willis as police sergeant John McClane in the Die Hard series—involve the portrayal of Vietnam veterans as heroic figures. In a period when feminism had successfully challenged many of the traditional role models and expectations for men, it is important that a revised and reasserted aggressive masculinity should be depicted through the character of a war veteran, thereby linking heroic masculinities with American patriotism and military service. Feminist critiques of gender constructions in the labor force and in the home were answered with stories about the single remaining arena within which men could distinguish their social identities from those of women: military combat. Representations of female action-adventure heroes, including female soldiers in futuristic warfare scenarios (Alien/s, Terminator 2, Demolition Man, and others) suggest that it is possible for women to mimic but not alter these roles.

War stories told apart from the time periods in which the wars take place are, again, ideal locations for working through contemporary tensions about racial and ethnic differences in the United States. Since the western wars of expansion, American wars have been fought against populations of people who have been marked as racially and/or ethnically different from white

Americans: American Indian, Mexican, Spanish, Japanese, Vietnamese, and, most recently, Iraqi peoples. World War II films meticulously presented a "melting pot" cast of "white" characters, including soldiers from Italian, Jewish, Irish, and other backgrounds. At a time when postwar industrialization was changing the economic terrain of the United States, when urbanization and postwar resettlement caused many people to move from one region to another, and when economic expansion and suburbanization were taking place, interactions between people of different ethnicities was increasing, creating social, economic, and cultural tensions. In such a context, working together was a shared theme, and films that reinforced "melting pot" images were addressing just such tensions. Most films made in the 1980s about the Vietnam War reflected the racial composition of many combat units with their disproportionately large percentages of African American, Native American, and Latino populations.[9] These films portrayed tensions but also showed how the bonding between men that took place in combat units superseded racial differences. These idealized, cross-racial friendships overlooked the quite real economic and social barriers that continued to exist in the 1980s and equally misrepresented the quite real racial tensions that existed among soldiers stationed in Vietnam.[10] It is significant that all the heroes of the Hollywood Vietnam War or action-adventure films in the 1980s were white men; although white and black men might dance to the same music in a bunker in *Platoon*, there were still clear racial categorizations for Hollywood's war stories.[11]

Because they necessarily involve national military engagements, war stories in the United States in the twentieth century have also provided vehicles for the constructions of American national identities. Who we fight and what we fight for, these stories say, tell us about who we are. From the Spanish-American War's affirmation of America's "strength" in a revised Euro-American balance of power to the Persian Gulf War's insistence on the U.S. role in a "New World Order," stories told about wars have been used to construct U.S. global relations and to describe the roles American citizens should play in them. From the story of a Hearst newspaper reporter who "rescued" Evangelina deCisneros from the evil Spaniards who held her captive during the Spanish-American War, to the stories of American soldiers halting German atrocities against women and children in World War II, to the story of John Wayne's character avenging Japanese atrocities in *Back to Bataan* in World War II, to the story of Rambo returning to Vietnam to rescue U.S. POWs held captive by the Vietnamese, to the story of Pete Mitchell (Tom

Cruise) halting a Soviet invasion of U.S. air space in *Top Gun*, war stories depict American characters as protective defenders of oppressed peoples and of just and democratic causes. War stories, then, help Americans construct national and international self-images that speak not only to U.S. military interests but to economic and geopolitical and moral ones as well. It is not accidental that, for example, while Rambo was fighting Soviet soldiers in Afghanistan, Martin Riggs (*Lethal Weapon*) and John McClane (*Die Hard*) were fighting international drug cartels, German terrorists, and Japanese takeovers. At a time when U.S. international economic power is waning, a display of heroic, militarized power can provide compensatory national identities for American viewers.

• • •

Looking at the Vietnam War shows that there is no single "war story" and that war stories can be used at different times for vastly different purposes. These include creating support for a war (*The Green Berets*), protesting against war (*M*A*S*H**), criticizing the national thinking that the war symbolizes (*Apocalypse Now*), celebrating as heroes the men who fought (*Rambo 2*), and using the war story as preparation for the next war (*Under Siege*). These are not simply different viewpoints on the same war but different kinds of war stories, told at different times to achieve differing ends. The "same" war can, therefore, be portrayed in numerous ways and be used to convey widely divergent messages. For this reason, it is important to understand not just the history of a war, but how history is itself one of many stories told about a war in the service of national, social, economic, cultural, and even individual interests.

It was, for example, important for George Bush to construct a history of the Vietnam War in which the United States had to fight "with one hand tied behind our backs," so that he could persuade the American people to believe the Persian Gulf War was winnable, if the United States fought with "both hands." It was equally important that the popular films of the 1980s reconstruct the American soldier, replacing the image of "baby killer" with that of life saver through the story of the rescue of American POWs. Without this regeneration of the U.S. soldier, it would have been difficult to convince the American public that its soldiers were worth supporting in another war. Conveniently, these films also found someone other than the soldier to blame for the loss of the war. It was a Congress that cared more about its international image than about its soldiers or the cause they had been enlisted to fight. This scenario made it possible for George Bush to challenge U.S. senators and congressional representatives with being "un-American" if they failed to support the war in the Persian Gulf. Without the revised Vietnam War stories of the 1980s and the revisionist thinking about the military and the government that characterized the Reagan presidency, the Persian Gulf War could never have been fought.

Conclusion

War stories are always looking back and looking ahead. They are telling the story of a war that has already occurred at the same time they are preparing for a war that has yet to come. Stories are often told by interested parties, parties who have particular points of view about specific wars or wars in general or both. Stories are told to individuals and to nations, and they play a significant role in determining whether individuals and nations are willing to go to war. The stories are important because they tell audiences not simply about wars but about moralities, about men and women, and about one's place in the social order. They describe what is worth fighting and dying for. They ask viewers and listeners to experience, if only for the time of the story, what fighting would be like. And they ask those same audiences to imagine who they would be willing to fight against, at the same time providing images of what enemies would or should look like. If we can visualize the face of an enemy and imagine ourselves in the place of the soldier fighting that enemy—if, in other words, we can tell a story about a people and a place and insert ourselves into it—then we are halfway to the next war.

NOTES

1. James Michener published *Tales of the South Pacific* in 1947, winning the Pulitzer Prize; Rodgers and Hammerstein turned it into a Broadway musical in 1949, winning the Pulitzer Prize for drama and earning more than $5 billion; and the film was released in 1958 by Twentieth Century Fox, winning an Academy Award for best soundtrack.

2. The Department of Defense supplied the following equipment for the filming of *The Green Berets*: rifles and carbines, machine guns, trench mortars, field and heavy guns, airplanes, ammunition wagons, field kitchens, field bakeries, and captured enemy weapons, as well as hundreds of soldiers as "extras" in the film. Wayne's production company paid $18,623.64 for the use of equipment that Congressman Benjamin Rosenthal (D-N.Y.) estimated cost the Pentagon more than a million dollars (Cauley 1990, 74).

3. In a final parental gesture, one of the last flights out of Vietnam after the North Vietnamese Army moved into Saigon in 1975 was a U.S. evacuation of Vietnamese orphans. The plane crashed, and it was later revealed that many of the children were not orphans at all, but children whose Vietnamese parents had placed them for short periods in the orphanage so that they could be cared for during the closing months of the war.

4. Though, as Gustav Hasford depicts it in his Vietnam War novel The Short Times, (1980) after attitudes about the war began to change, soldiers found the film to be more funny than inspiring: "The audience of Marines roars with laughter. This is the funniest movie we have seen in a long time. . . . At the end of the movie, John Wayne walks off into the sunset with a spunky little orphan. The grunts laugh and threaten to pee all over themselves. The sun is setting in the China Sea—in the East—which makes the end of the movie as accurate as the rest of it" (p. 38).

5. Broadcast 27 February 1968 over the CBS television network; quoted Cohan 1983, 214.

6. Although the power of the film's antiwar message outweighed its many flaws at the time, its overt sexism is now difficult to overlook.

7. Taxi Driver (1976; Martin Scorsese) certainly was a popular film that focused on a Vietnam veteran, but its acclaim had less to do with its commentary on the war than with its portrayals of sexuality and violence against women.

8. In addition to public support, Weinberger listed the following criteria for going to war: (1) the combat should be vital to national interest; (2) combat commitments should be wholehearted; (3) combat commitments should have clearly defined goals and objectives; (4) relationships between size of combat forces and objectives should be continually reevaluated; (5) the commitment of combat forces should be a last resort (Weinberger 1990, 442).

9. Blacks constituted a disproportionate percentage of draftees in the Vietnam War. Scholars attribute this less to race per se than to class differences that are affiliated with race in the United States. See Binkin and Eitelberg 1982.

10. For example, blacks and whites who fought together in combat often engaged in separate leisure activities when they returned to their bases. See Terry 1984.

11. The only 1980s Vietnam War film in which an African American man plays the lead was 84 Charlie Mopic (Patrick Duncan, 1989), a harshly critical and realistic depiction of one platoon's long-range reconnaissance patrol mission. It was not until 1994, with Wesley Snipes's leading role in Passenger 57, that a black actor was cast in a mainstream action-adventure film (I distinguish this film from the Shaft films of the 1970s, precisely because these films, though crossover successes, were largely targeting black audiences).

REFERENCES

Baker, Mark. 1981. Nam. New York: Berkeley Books.
Binkin, Martin, and Mark J. Eitelberg. 1982. Blacks in the Military. Washington, D.C.: Brookings Institution.
Caputo, Philip. 1977. A Rumor of War. New York: Ballantine.

Cauley, Leo. 1990. "The War about the War: Vietnam Films and American Myth." In Linda Dittmar and Gene Michaud, eds., *From Hanoi to Hollywood: The Vietnam War in American Film*. New Brunswick, N.J.: Rutgers University Press.

Cohan, Steve, ed. 1983. *Vietnam: Anthology and Guide to a Television History*. New York: Alfred A. Knopf.

Crane, Stephen. [1985] 1944. *Red Badge of Courage*. New York: Scribner's.

Greene, Graham. 1956. *The Quiet American*. New York: Viking Press.

Hasford, Gustav. 1980. *The Short Timers*. New York: Bantam Books.

Hemingway, Ernest. 1929. *A Farewell to Arms*. New York: Scribner's.

————. 1940. *For Whom the Bell Tolls*. New York: Viking Press.

Kovic, Ron. 1977. *Born on the Fourth of July*. New York: Pocket Books.

Michener, James. 1947. *Tales of the South Pacific*. New York: Macmillan.

Terry, Wallace. 1984. *Bloods: An Oral History of the Vietnam War*. New York: Ballantine.

Weinberger, Caspar W. 1990. *Fighting for Peace: Seven Critical Years in the Pentagon*. New York: Warner Books.

Miriam Cooke

12

Subverting the Gender and Military Paradigms

War has become a constant presence in our lives, whether through telecasting of "ethnic cleansings" in Cambodia or Bosnia or Rwanda or through experiencing militarization here at home. We may seem further away from nuclear night than we were as recently as 1989, but smaller-scale, widespread explosions of violence force us to ask why people who were living together in "peace" suddenly begin killing one another. The causes of war must be explored; surely, war is not inevitable; it is only made to seem that way.

Two Paradigms

A bumper sticker on the car in front of me reads, "Subvert the Dominant Paradigm." My mind wanders from the "Morning Edition" story about Serbian aggressions in Gorazda to the two dominant paradigms I study: war and gender.

War is conventionally defined as organized, armed conflict among states, that is, political entities having or aspiring to have a monopoly on armed force within their territory. The goal of war is definitive resolution—victory. Even when such a resolution is not reached, and it rarely is, it is often *said* to have been reached. Victory is declared; fighting ceases. The war is "over." Therefore, the new state must be one of "peace." During peace, society need no longer be divided between spaces where certain tasks are performed by men and others where tasks are performed by women.

Previously, sex segregation was so accepted that few questioned what the philosopher J. Glenn Gray called the "artificial separation of the sexes or, at best, a maldistribution" 1970, 62). Unlike convents and monasteries or boys' and girls' schools, the front and homefront have not usually been analyzed as gendered spaces. Maybe this is because these emergency, gender-specific spaces are not, in fact, so different from peacetime, patriarchal arrangements.

Like war and peace, gender is thought of in binary terms that are said to be "natural." But gender, far from being natural, is a cultural code that describes, prescribes, and thus shapes social expectations for sexed bodies: men and women grow up differently, and most act in ways consonant with their culture's prevalent images and values. Gender is constructed in a discourse that the psychologist Carol Cohn describes as being "not only about words or language but about a system of meanings, of ways of thinking, images and words that first shape how we experience, understand and represent ourselves as men and women, but that also do more than that; they shape many other aspects of our lives and culture. In this symbolic system, human characteristics are dichotomized" (1993, 228–29). Thus, both war and gender are thought of as polarized. If war and gender so powerfully organize the world dyadically, then their reconception and rearticulation may become the instrument for recreating the world.

I am interested in the blurring of binaries in contemporary wars. I am also concerned with how people who have lived through wars tell their stories, because stories profoundly influence how the next wars will be fought— and then told. Until quite recently, most wars were recounted within a narrative frame that the British military historian John Keegan argues has remained essentially unchanged since Thucydides. This frame I call the War Story.

The War Story gives order to wars that are generally experienced as confusion. Nevertheless, military historians force a grid on the anarchy; they arrange experience and actors into neat pairs: beginning and ending, foe and friend, aggression and defense, war and peace, front and home, combatant and civilian. Women are important to emphasizing that such splits occur; in particular, it is said that women's need for protection is the reason men must fight. Thus, the War Story reinforces mythic wartime roles. Outworn essentialist clichés of men's aggressivity and women's pacifism are revived. The world is described as divided between the *politikon*, where men play "political" roles, and the *oikon*, where women are lovers or mothers, including the *mater dolorosa* (weeping madonna) and the patriotic mothers who proudly sacrifice their wombs and their sons for their country. The War Story proclaims that this sex segregation is justified for biological reasons: the men are strong; therefore, they must protect the women, who are weak.[1] It is written in their genes that men shall be active and women passive.

Telling the War Story

War is messy, but until recently it has rarely been told that way. Men have always turned their messy war experiences into coherent stories, poems, memoirs, and even official records.[2] The dichotomies of the War Story organize the confusion so that aggression is not confused with defense, civilian and combatant, home with front, women's work with men's work.

Lebanon's ordeal between 1975 and 1992 offers a telling example of this ordering and dichotomization. I went to Lebanon in 1980 to interview women who had written fiction on the civil war that had been raging in the eastern Mediterranean for five years. I was surprised to find that literary activity was intense, that the war had inspired many to represent their experiences creatively. Women and men were churning out novels, short stories, and poetry. Whereas the women's descriptions of the war seemed to preclude the possibility of arranging the chaos into a coherent narrative, however, most men's war stories lined up oppositions. It was my comparative analysis of women's and men's differing senses of responsibility during the war that gave me a clue as to how the War Story grid could be forced onto even the most intractable chaos.

In general, the women presented the situation as out of control and urged each individual to assume responsibility for ending the war. Responsibility in the women's writings entailed *duties* toward others that had to be fulfilled so that the war might stop. In the men's writings, responsibility was connected to a notion of *rights*: protagonists protected what was theirs against others. In the women's writing, chaos could be acknowledged, because it was only by drawing attention to it that individuals might be induced to become active in ending it. In the men's system, chaos was first disavowed and then transformed into the clarity of friend and foe (Cooke 1988).

It was only years after the writing of *War's Other Voices*, my analysis of the war writings, that I realized that the most enlightening example of how the Lebanese War Story might be told was through photographs. In 1980 and again in 1982, I had noticed war albums with full-page pictures of blood and guts in Beirut living rooms. I assumed that this phenomenon was peculiar to Lebanon, and beyond a cursory glance at the mostly gruesome contents, I paid them little attention.

When I traveled to Croatia in the late summer of 1993, I began to suspect that this expensive packaging and marketing of war images might be more pervasive than I had thought. While in Zagreb, I bought Zoran Jovicic's *War Crimes Committed by the Yugoslav Army, 1991–1992*. This oversized photo-illustrated book with its text in Croatian, English, and German was published in 1993 by the Croatian Information Centre. Although more sober than its Lebanese counterparts, this book also was a handsome production with many stunning photographs. Further, Jovicic or his publishers had added a titillating detail: the last four pages were sealed with a piece of red tape. Like Madonna's presentation of the autobiography, this book was not accessible to the casual browser but had to be bought to be seen in whole.[3] I went straight to the section whose cover page carried the following message in three languages: "WARNING. The sealed pages contain some of many available photos depicting brutal murders and massacres committed by the YU-Army and Serbian irregular units against the civilian population in Croatia during the years of 1991 and 1992." To my relief, but also I must confess somewhat to my disappointment, the pictures were not as grim as I had expected; I had seen worse in the uncensored Lebanese versions.[4] Why had the publisher used the red-tape trick? Clearly, it had made people buy the book and not just skim the pages in the store. Beyond the mercenary motive, however, was a stated moral purpose: "This book has been outlined to identify the crimes committed by the YU-Army" (p. 95). Jovicic and his team of twenty-two photographers were playing the role of detectives and lawyers for the prosecution. Jovicic sent me back to the Lebanese war albums. Maybe they, too, were not just examples of macaber commercialism.

The most popular of the Lebanese albums was *Harb Lubnan* (The Lebanese War) which had first come out in 1977 and was reprinted in 1980. Other than a two-page introduction and a war chronology, it had no written text— there were one hundred sixty pages of photographs with as many as four per page. For the first time, I read the introduction. It was signed by "The Publisher," but it was not clear whether this person was Layla Badi' 'Itani, who prepared this volume, or the photographer, 'Abd'al-Razzaq al-Sayyid, or the editor, Sami Dhabyan, or someone else in the Dar al-Masira publishing house. Unlike the Croatian volume, *Harb Lubnan* did not set itself the task of identifying the enemy, although the format and nature of the subjects photographed suggested sympathies. Its avowed intent was to chronicle the war truthfully.

> "This is exactly what happened. Here it is between the two covers of a book. . . . Photo after photo out of which pour blood, stream rockets, burst shrapnel. A torn-out eye, a cut-off hand, a burnt cadaver, a skinned body may slap you in the face. . . . Here is the nation, Lebanon, which they [indicating the enemy, whoever that might be] crucified for two years. We present it in pictures, events, and documents. . . . We wanted to touch its wounds and then to bring them together in ink on paper because we do not want the tragedy to happen again. . . . We are less interested in whether this war was a victory or a defeat than we are in bringing it into your house, your office, into every corner of your house. . . . May it be a war on war itself and on you if you were one of its instigators, one of those who lit its fire or poured oil on it or failed to put it out. . . . This war might have been noble had the many revolutionaries and fighters not been joined by thieves and criminals, killers, drunks and ignoramuses. . . .
> The war had ended.

The writer urges the reader to look to the present and the future, which must guarantee four aims: that Lebanon remain independent and united; that it be part of a pan-Arab ethos; that it no longer remain indifferent to Israel but confront its territorial ambitions in Lebanon; that it function in terms of its newly awakened consciousness.

What are we to make of such an introduction? It establishes the project as moral: this photojournal is supposed to make us experience the war and its horrors so as to assume responsibility for ending the war. But then, oddly, it announces that the war is over. Now it is time to build the future, and this book aims to play a role in constructing this future. The very last sentence declares: "Our ambition is that you should read with us the brilliant future in the pictures, documents, and events." Although from the perspective of 1994, we know the seventeen-year war was only in its second year,[5] everything about the book says it is time to rebuild. But what this album does is not rebuild but build tout court. The author has used fragments of the Lebanese civil war to build the Lebanese War Story. The volume is a concrete example of how the confusion of war can be streamlined into the black-and-white certainties of a binary narrative.

Let us begin with war and peace. How does this volume frame the action? The covers are a good place to start. The front photo represents the warfront: burnt-out buildings and bullet-pocked walls, sandbags, young men in khaki—two in helmets—alert with their kalashnikovs at the ready, and no women, in fact no civilian in sight. The back photograph is quite different. It suggests that the war is over. We surmise this because young men are sprawled over a tank, they are smiling and chatting, some are even wearing civvies. These masculine soldiers will protect us; they are in charge. We know this because although they are at ease, their tank's phallic gun thrusts out aggressively from the epicenter of the image; it fills the vision; it is pointed at us, between the eyes, so much so that it blocks out part of the image, including the head of one of the "soldiers." He is seated deep into the shaft of the gun and appears to be faced in the direction of a very relaxed man. The homoerotics of the scene are unmistakable. In this space of men and victory, men can love one another both emotionally and physically with impunity. On the right edge of the frame, we can make out the unharmed residential buildings with hints of cheerful orange awnings and a cedarlike tree. This tree serves two functions: it represents the return of life, but above all, the cedar is the tree of Lebanon. Its presence in this photograph suggests that the good guys have won. These cover images are the most important in the entire book, because they are there on the coffee table, next to the afternoon teacup and the preprandial snacks. Family members and their guests can linger over two moments: the middle and the end of the war.

But what about the photographs inside? The images with their captions inside fill out the message of the covers: this is about the move from being at war to beginning peace. This book traces the progression of the war from its onset on 13 April 1975, when members of a fascist militia, the Phalangists, shot up a bus of Palestinians in 'Ayn al-Rummana, a neighborhood in Beirut, to its "end" on 1 May 1977. This ending is anticipated by some boilerplate images and captions. First, "The al-Hoss government has dealt [note the past tense] with many problems that were a legacy of the war"— so the war is dead and the inheritance is being distributed. Next, one sees a tank with helmeted figures silhouetted against the rising sun; it is the beginning of a new day: "They [this "they" is never specified, but at this late stage of the volume "they" are always confident, relaxed young men in some military context] came with the dawn to make fast the peace of Rada'

حرب لبنان

صُـور · وثـائـق · أحـداث

دار المسيرة

The Lebanese War: Pictures, Documents, Events.
Courtesy Publisher Dar al-Masirah.

حرب لبنان

The Lebanese War.

ورشة: جرافة تزيل متراساً من «الاوتوبيسات»! الردع... سلام القوة.

Top: Work detail: tractor removing the barrier of buses.
Bottom: Al-Rada': peace by force.

قبل البدء بعمليات الحكم. أجرى الرئيس الياس سركيس بعض المشاورات والاتصالات.. هنا مع المقدم احمد الحاج قائد قوات الأمن الداخلي. العقيد محمد الخولي. الأمين العام المساعد للجامعة العربية حسن صبري الخولي. ياسر عرفات رئيس منظمة التحرير الفلسطينية. اللواء ناجي جميل قائد سلاح الطيران السوري. هنري لحود محافظ البقاع.

لقاء عند مستديرة المتحف ...

Top: President Elias Sarkis, before taking office, consulting with Major Ahmad al-Haj, commander of Internal Security Forces; Colonel Muhammad al-Khali, assistant general of the Arab League; Hasan Sabri al-Khuli; Yasser Arafat, head of the Palestine Liberation Organization; Brigadier General Nuji Jamil, commander of the Syrian Air Force; and Henri Lahhud, administrator of Al-Bika'. *Bottom*: Meeting at the Museum traffic circle.

وبقيت الطفولة .. تحمل المستقبل

Arab youths: bearers of the future.

ضاع... اين زوجي.. هكذا دخلت الحرب كل بيت!

"I'm lost. . . . Where is my husband?": how the war entered every house.

في باب إدريس، شوارع الأناقة
والجمال.. هل تمشي وسط الموت؟

Bab Idris, streets of elegance and beauty: Will she walk through death?

احد عناصر الارتباط في الشياح اصيب برصاص قناص بتاريخ ٧٥/٦/٣ ..

An Irtibat armed element in Shiyah hit by a sniper's bullet,
3 June 1975.

[Prevention Forces]—peace by force." "They" proceed to enter the city—I say "enter," because, presumably, we are in the city and they are approaching us; they are friendly and relaxed. Next, we recognize another take of the scene on the back cover. This image, however, is much less aggressive: the gun is smaller and off to the right; it is still pointed toward us but not at our eyes; there are more civilians hanging around; a man with a camera and some Roman ruins balance the residence on the right; and in this case there is a caption: "They arrived and the cannons were silent. A smile. A cannon" (p. 141). In other words, we are friendly, but don't mess with us! Then we see two cleanup operations in the devastated city.

The absolute end is conclusively established with four photographs on unnumbered pages, as though they were outside the war that the book had been presenting. The first shows a leader—Kamal Jumblat—lying in state; the captain does not say who he is or that he was assassinated, only that "he is lying on the deathbed between his two companions in life and death." It looks like "Le roi est mort, vive le roi!" The next shows the fortieth-day remembrance of Jumblat's death, being observed, we are told, by 150,000 citizens and, as we can see, by "soldiers" lined up in organized rows; this picture seems to hark back to much earlier pictures of marching soldiers (p. 15) and victorious soldiers (p. 105), but these men look more disciplined. The third photo, a meeting of politicians in earnest and friendly conversation, assures us that things are moving in the right direction: the caption announces, "Before beginning to govern, President Sarkis conducted some consultations and made some contacts," followed by names that include PLO leader Yasser Arafat and the leader of the Syrian Air Force. Thus, we get the impression that all the warring parties are represented here and that they are in agreement. Fourth, a group of civilians—marked by the fact that there are young women among them—meet at the Museum (Mathaf) traffic circle. This Mathaf was one of the most dangerous crossing points from East to West Beirut. This last picture is the most reassuring: if it is safe enough for women to be at the Mathaf, the city will not continue to be divided for long. More than any other image, this one convinces us that peace is at hand.

The photographs create a sense that this was a war like many before it; it could even turn out to have been a good war. As we were told in the introduction, "This war might have been noble had the many revolutionaries and fighters not been joined by thieves and criminals, killers, drunks and ignoramuses." We leaf through commonplace images of war: people running, demonstrating, buying bread, setting up temporary shops in the streets, dragging the wounded out of sniper fire, refugees leaving town, bad guys gleefully celebrating with champagne. We see gutted buildings, exploded cars, streets littered with military debris ("The Game of Death," p. 35), and the charred, bloated, or crushed remains of "collateral damage." We see armored cars carrying troops that are never referred to as the militiamen or thugs they actually were (p. 19); we watch children playing on piles of sandbags. Interspersed among these images of violence are the calm takes of politicians huddled around conference tables. The captions are laconic, such as "A meeting to find a solution," followed by a list of those in attendance (p. 65). Clearly, these men are the ones who are waging war and deploying troops. They know what is going on. Others know that they know and that is why they still trust them (whoever they might be), even if "they" are not always willing to help. In a series of four photographs, a father of five is pictured on his way to parliament to register a complaint about his children's hunger, but "the policeman's and the deputies' hearts are hard." Had they not been hard, the image and the caption seem to say, they could have done something (pp. 74–75).

The images tell the story of a war that separated the men from the women and by extension the combatants from the civilians. Although early on we are allowed to see women soldiers (p. 15), soon women disappear from photographs depicting anything that might be construed to be the front. There is, however, the women who lost her husband and whose desperate search announces that "the war entered every house" (p. 24). At rare intervals, we see women weeping, in one case in the cramped space of a simple home (note the coffeepot, p. 39). Children, representing the quintessential noncombatant, are pictured lost in the ruined streets-become-front. Their jarring presence reminds us of the inevitable transgression of segregation, which they thereby serve to reinforce. The ironic caption reads "Youth continues to be the bearer of the future" (p. 38). There are also occasional images of women defending and preserving, which endanger the home/front binary. In two juxtaposed images (p. 81), a very young father and a mother are holding an infant. The first image suggests domesticity: the "father" is standing quietly by a wall, looking toward what we assume to be his home. He seems contented as he holds the baby, its bottle, and its pillow; the caption reads: "War births. They are trying to escape to peace. He carried him in the first stage." When a father can hold his baby at home, all must be well abroad. The second image suggests present danger: the "mother" is rushing along a street, the baby tightly clasped to her bosom: "And his mother carried him in the difficult stage." The caption announces that she is the one who really protects the weak. But another interpretation of this second image is that when there is danger in the streets, the men are protecting the women who are protecting the children. Thus, the subtext reinforces the binaries of the War Story.

The cause of the war becomes pretty clear: identity. With a cause to defend, combatants line up on opposing sides. Several images of corpses carry captions that explain the cause of their death as being related to their identity: "Streets of corpses. Massacring identity"; "Tragedy. They kidnapped them and killed them. Because of their identity." The captions, and not the photos alone, confirm that the war was about identity politics. The book aims to persuade us that this chronicle of the war is true, total, and unbiased; again, the introduction claims: "This is exactly what happened. Here it is between the two covers of a book." Above all, we—unlike those who merely lived through the war but were not privileged to share this broader vision—are allowed the photographer's special access: we are made privy to the most inaccessible meetings; we get the impression that we have seen all parties to the conflict. We have even been up on the roof and in hideaways with the snipers. We even see those who are supposed to be managing the violence—journalists, through camera control, and politicians, who have otherwise been shown in consultation that promises resolution—out of control, running, ducking, and "jumping" in fear of their lives. Our photographer, Mr. al-Sayyid, is in greater control of the violence than are the politicians: he was able to get a steady shot of the jumping deputies! He is braver than the other photographers who are cowering, feminized by their fear. The caption reads: "The photographers and the journalists were there. . . . But!" The heavy sarcasm seems unwarranted when we think a bit about the angle of his camera; is he not lower than the woman whose frightened face he shoots? So maybe he was a little scared, but that is less important than the fact that our photographer is always there at the right moment: a man is kidnapped on his return from shopping, and al-Sayyid catches the moment of shock, which we can later revisit (p. 65). Two photos of planes: in one, it has just landed with its cargo of flour; in the next, the charred remains are still smoking.

We are not restricted to painful emotions; we can also appreciate the moments of irony that wars produce. Sometimes we shake our heads in disbelief, as when a bulldozer is pictured trying to conquer a mountain of rubble (p. 69). At other times we are moved, as by the photograph of a corpse lying behind the wheels of an abandoned UN car; the caption reads, "A witness to the massacre in Burj Square" (p. 88). And then we smile in relief, as with the militiaman amusing himself by putting together the scattered limbs of a mannequin: "In Bab Idris. Streets of elegance and beauty. Will she walk through death?" (p. 117).

The sense of having had the experience that one is viewing in stills is enhanced by the inclusion of an unmarked section of fifteen full-page color glossies without captions. This section, entitled "Crime. In Color," is introduced by a few lines explaining why color was used. It is "not a luxury, but rather another way of describing. Colors say what black and white cannot. . . . "They have ceased to serve as decoration and have become a *witness for the prosecution of a crime* and of those who committed the crime thinking that they were living a film on a wide screen . . . and in color." This language is much closer to that used in the Croatian volume, which emphasized the ethical aspect of the project.

We are so much there with al-Sayyid that we witness a shooting and the ensuing suffering. "One of the Irtibat armed elements in Shiyah was hit by a sniper's bullet. 3 June 1975." This series compels us to share al-Sayyid's choices: to intervene or to record? To save a life or capture a death? Sometimes the choice is dragged out over several images, as in three shots of a man asking for help (p. 30). If al-Sayyid found three photos good enough for inclusion in this book, how many were there on the contact sheet from which he chose? Did it ever occur to al-Sayyid that he might choose between intervening and recording? Was he, and we with him, inured to the victim's pain and terrible need so that he/we can overlook, literally, the fact that in the last two images this man is looking straight at him/us, screaming at him/us to do something for God's sake? Neither we nor al-Sayyid are going to do anything, however, unless it be to get closer for the perfect shot. As Susan Sontag has written: "Photographing is essentially an act of non-intervention. . . . To take a picture is to . . . be in complicity with whatever makes a subject interesting, worth photographing—including, when the interest is another person's pain or misfortune" (1977, 10, 11). The fact that the man was directly engaging the photographer and begging for help meant that he was peculiarly photogenic.

For al-Sayyid, what mattered was documentation. This was just another event he was representing. But what of the other event, the one that involved him, the wounded man addressing him and us? More than most of the images in this book, this series alerts us to the role of the photographer in war.

He is not a disinterested agent mediating realty; he is using fragments of his individual experience to construct another reality that he projects as objective.[6] These three frozen moments tell us that this book is the sum of an individual's choices. His camera has indeed proven to be what Sontag calls "a sublimation of the gun." He has gained double control over this man's life: the mere act of taking the image is "a sublimated murder—a soft murder" (Sontag 1977, 13); additionally, he has chosen to let him suffer, die if necessary. He has made other choices: of subject matter, of angle, of juxtaposition, and of captioning. Above all, he has chosen to assemble these images in a book that must be read in the order he adopted. As Walter Benjamin has noted, such organization of photographs is comparable to what happens in film, "where the meaning of each single picture appears to be prescribed by the sequence of all the preceding ones" (1968, 226). Once the sequence is broken, the meaning assigned by the context is lost or at least deferred until the advent of another organizer, and so on. That is the power and weakness of photographic technology that allows anyone to subvert a dominant paradigm and then to pastiche together a convincing reality, at least until someone else comes along with a new idea/ideology. Each montage and collage authenticates itself by reference to these transparencies onto the real, which, in fact relay a fragment of someone else's experience. To paraphrase Sontag, 'Abd al-Razzaq al-Sayyid has explored the war, duplicated aspects of it, fragmented its continuities, and fed "the pieces into an interminable dossier, thereby providing possibilities of control that could not even be dreamed of under the earlier system of recording information: writing" (1977, 95, 138). This control has created an immensely powerful visual version of the Lebanese War Story.

Why question the photographer's story? Without the war photographer we would not have the same compelling evidence to prosecute criminals and also to remind ourselves and the world of what the war had been like. It does not give the viewer the filmic sense of having been there. It is the profusion and its arrangement that allow al-Sayyid's fabrication to work so well that we accept this is the way things happened in Lebanon even though this is not the story most people told while the war was raging. Photographs are particularly suitable building blocks in the construction of the War Story. Photography and later film allowed noncombatants to observe and witness war in a way that had never before been possible. The evidence provided by still and moving images of death and destruction from what was said to be the front gave the impression of having been there. This witness, you, may not have actually been there, but you feel that you know what it must have been like because you know what it *looked like*. Those of you who feel guilty about surviving unharmed physically and psychologically can feel partially vindicated. You can appropriate this war as your own, talk about it with the authority of experience, even though what you experienced was a perception of a fragment of what the photographer framed. "War and photography now seem inseparable," writes Sontag. "The feeling of being exempt from calamity stimulates interest in looking at painful pictures, and looking at them suggests and strengthens the feeling that one is exempt. . . . In the real world, something *is* happening and no one knows what is *going* to happen. In the image world, it *has* happened, and it *will* forever happen in that way. . . . The powers of photography have in effect de-Platonized our understanding of reality, making it less and less plausible to reflect upon our experience according to the distinction between images and things, between copies and originals" (1977, 147–48, 158). We have the illusion of having been present at the crucial moments and in the turning-point places.[7] Since we were there, we have a stake in confirming that this war was not fought for nothing. The war may not have deprived us of a loved one, but it robbed us of our innocence. We have an interest in its being told as a good war.

Photography throws into relief what happens when war experiences are codified into the War Story. The connection between what actually happened and its documenting is never transparent. John Keegan graphically illustrates this point when he writes that the General Staff historian's "mind is made up for him by *prevailing staff doctrine about the proper conduct of war* and he will accordingly *select* whatever facts endorse that view, while *manhandling* those which offer resistance" (1978, 34; my emphasis). In other words, the accounts of war that have come down to us are the products of careful screening by politicians, military historians, even creative writers, all of whom have at least some sense of what it is they are doing. Although he understands how and why the War Story has remained unchanged for millennia, Keegan is not so much critical as he is impressed by the inspirational value of such stories (1978, 20). The War Story shapes reality as we would like it to have been or as the government says it was. That is why the War Story is usually written *after* a war at a time when, as Elaine Showalter writes, "canon formation has been particularly aggressive. . . . When nationalist feeling runs high there is a strong wish to define a tradition" (1985, 11).

The resort to a familiar war narrative and attitude is not restricted to governments and militaries who demand that the war they have just fought be told in a particular way; it is almost a reflex. During the Spanish Civil War there was much side-swapping and much confusion, and yet it is now narrated as the romance of right against wrong. As F. R. Benson writes, many idealized the war and explained their participation as "a humanitarian desire for a world in which poverty, injustice and misery might be eliminated." Benson quotes Malraux as having believed that the war could restore to the intellectual "his fertility, his fundamental sense of *belonging* to a definite time, a definite place, and a specific milieu, without which a meaningful life and true understanding of the self cannot be achieved" (1967, 7). In *Homage of Catalonia*, George Orwell notes that he was less frightened by the violence of the Spanish Civil War than he was by the "immediate reappearance in left-wing circles of the mental atmosphere of the Great War" (Dyson 1984, 129). In made little difference that these two wars were utterly different, the one total and the other civil. To be at war entailed a remembering of what other wars had been so as to understand what was happening and to know how to proceed.

Contemporary wars, however, lend themselves ill to the streamlining of the War Story. The film director Francis Coppola is only one example, if one of the best, of the need for a new narrative frame. As he struggled to make sense of the experience of Vietnam, he lit on Conrad and followed him—with his camera crew and a reluctant Marlon Brando—into the heart of darkness. It was there that he shot *Apocalypse Now*. Coppola did not know how otherwise to express the unspeakable that war always is. Wars today increasingly involve combatants and targets rarely officially acknowledged. The stories that today's warriors, many of them women, tell of the wars they have known stray further and further from the binarized structure of the War Story. Since women are no longer everywhere systematically excluded from the military and war, the War Story will eventually have to take account of them.

Derailing the Paradigms: Women in the Military

In the wake of the Cold War and the triumph in the Gulf, an antimilitarist became president of the United States and commander in chief of a military comprising 11 percent women. Congress voted to eliminate the clause excluding women from combat ships and planes. Dearly held beliefs about the appropriateness and feasibility of women fighting to defend the country began to crumble. The arguments of proponents of equal access to all areas of national service, including the military, as constituting a central tenet of citizenship in a democracy began to be heard.

What do advocates for equal opportunity in the military, many of whom are women and feminists, really want? Historian Joyce Berkman argues that feminists' assessment of the "'justness' of their nation's military action would pretty much shape the position they would take on the war. . . . Short of countenancing a global war, most European and American women, with countless feminists among them, support a strong national military establishment" (1990, 150, 157). A less jingoistic perspective is articulated by political scientist Kathleen Jones. She encourages women to "demand access to the military only as a means to acquire the power base from which to redefine the range of responsibilities included in the concept of citizenship . . . and to enrich the meaning of citizenship" (1990, 133). Sheila Tobias is the most instrumental in her argument that women should be allowed to enlist without restriction. War experience, she writes, has been "a convenient stepping-stone for politics" (Elshtain and Tobias 1990, 183). Judith Stiehm criticizes antimilitarists in America whose "interest too often stops when they are no longer threatened, and U.S. women feel threatened only by nuclear war. A serious and consistent critic [of the military] should analyze the wars fought by surrogates, the consequences of profiting from arms sales, the effects of 'winning' miniature wars" (1988, 105).

Some fear that increasing the number of women in the armed forces may strengthen the military and perhaps make the country readier to go to war. They advocate boycotting military service, arguing that war might become less likely if fewer people predicated their lives on its possibility and if citizenship was not linked to war service. Others believe, however, that unilateral demilitarization is not an answer at a time when new nations are expanding their militaries with easily procured arsenals of lethal arms. Also, feminist advocates of equal opportunity in the military want citizenship for all in a strong country whose military is rational and democratic and has a humanitarian commitment to the promotion of freedom and the maintenance of a just peace.[8]

Objection in the United States as elsewhere to women combat soldiers has been vehement. Opponents claim that opening up combat positions for women jeopardizes military effectiveness by disrupting men's cohesiveness. Yet combat duty is clearly not for everyone. Some, including men, are just not qualified, and more may not want to participate. Further, a few women have long been "frontline combatants" without being publicly acknowledged as such. In short, the War Story's dichotomy has never been real.

Wars today challenge more than ever the conventional binaries and their consequent exclusions that have organized war stories throughout history. In the Geneva Convention era, international military lawyers have been entrusted with the task of establishing a war taxonomy, of determining who is a civilian, where a particular event happened, under what circumstances, and so on in order to be able to judge the legality of behavior in a war situation. Yet some are beginning to acknowledge that they are not quite sure how to differentiate the space, activities, and actors of war.[9] We have at our disposal sophisticated surveillance technology, yet not even those who have been trained to observe and judge the conduct of wars can in the final analysis separate the combatant from the noncombatant, distinguish where exactly the fighting is taking place from where it is not, and differentiate who is pulling the trigger from who is stoking the gun from who is receiving the shock of the explosion. Nevertheless, the War Story survives.

Cross-culturally and historically, combat has been reserved for male defenders as that arena in which they could test, prove, and be rewarded for their virility. Keegan writes of men who regret and even repudiate machismo, yet when the fight is on, they deem it necessary. The inclusion in combat of women and of men who are ambivalent about their sexuality may complicate a mobilization and a cohesion made attractive because of its promise to turn boys into men. Just how important is male bonding? Is the military's rhetoric about success of a cause, "cohesion, sense of mission, mood of self-sacrifice, local as well as national patriotism . . . self-confidence and credulity," (Keegan 1978, 277), as well as the hope for immortality as the individual's death is subsumed to the group's survival (Gray 1970, 40–47), sufficient to motivate large numbers of women and gay men to kill and to die?

Women's presence in the quintessentially male domain has made several important differences. Stiehm writes that "it alters the military if service is no longer a way to demonstrate manhood. It alters the assumptions of military incentive systems to have mother-soldiers." It challenges basic beliefs or myths that are "fundamental to the military enterprise: (1) War is manly; (2) Warriors protect; (3) Soldiers are substitutable." She suggests that women who do not understand their own role as protectee will not realize that they are "essential to legitimate violence. The protectee is its justification" (1989, 7, 224, 230). Moreover, women's physical presence has undermined the unmarked aspects of soldiers' lives. They are no longer "our boys," whom we are reluctantly but proudly prepared to sacrifice. Rather, they are women and men who are parents and spouses and who saw in the military a change for employment and even for social mobility. Several myths and realities of the military are having to give, although, as Stiehm notes, they give less easily in connection with women than they do with men; thus, "accommodations are regularly made for fathers that are not compatible with the myth that every service person is always available for worldwide assignment" (1989, 119). Our "neomercenary military" has brought a new focus to the costs of patriotism. As coverage of the Gulf War demonstrated, the new questions raised by the changing face of the military may be responsible for the brevity of the war. Just how long would we be willing to expose mother-soldiers to danger when their babies were waiting at home with their perplexed fathers? And as we focus on mother-soldiers, father-soldiers are calling attention to their needs, too. At the "Just War—Gulf War"—conference at Vanderbilt University in January 1992, an officer in the audience challenged a panelist who had argued for the elimination of women from combat positions. After praising women's achievements in the Gulf War and describing his own and fellow father-soldiers' pain at parting from their families, he urged us to remember that the U.S. military is no longer an institution attracting only single young men; it is now made up of families. Thus, these are simultaneously the families the military is supposed to protect *and* the families who are supposed to do the protecting. The military is no longer so different from civilian society.

When military analysts Mady Segal and David Segal were writing in 1983, they noted that public opinion tolerated women in military roles that had civilian counterparts, but that it had "not gone the next step and defined as acceptable women serving in the traditionally male ground combat specialties that do not have counterparts in the civilian labor force. . . . If the military continues to expand women's participation, or even maintains it at present levels, it will in the process be serving as a critical agent for future social change" (1983, 255–56). But we must not forget the experiences of women after they leave the military or a war zone. They often share the experience of women fighters in revolutionary situations, such as in Algeria and Eritrea. For example, Amair Adhana, a guerrilla fighter in the successful thirty-year struggle of the Eritrean People's Liberation Front (EPLF) against the Soviet-backed dictatorship, told an *Economist* reporter: "In the field, the men respected us—our brains, our strength. . . . They now respect make-up, nice hair, being a proper housewife." Whereas before 1991 the women fighters had been "treated with awe" and their attire and demeanor emulated, by 1994 many of the demobbed women were back in their kitchens.[10] Enlisted women are different from both conscripted women and those in revolutions, however, because they are not doing men's work in an emergency. They have chosen and have been chosen to do as a career what has been considered a man's job.

The thesis thus far rests on a paradox: feminists advocate the opening up of opportunities for serving, but also of course of killing, to women in the hope that they will choose to exercise their right to kill only when they have no other choice. Such a discourse elides the chasm that divides those who speak about national security from those who speak about citizenship rights. It invests hope in the nightmare of the military-effectiveness mavens that a government that sends women and families to war will be more reluctant to fight. It elaborates the link between military and civilian society so that when the military eliminates discrimination, civilian society will follow suit; that when civilian society criminalizes the killing of civilians, the military will do the same.

Feminist pacifists, such as Mary Wollstonecroft, Sara Ruddick, and Klaus Theweleit, remain skeptical about such a paradoxical discourse, questioning the acceptability of any collaboration with a militarized system. Although they affirm the political importance of sexual equality, they doubt the value of swelling military ranks with "natural"[11] advocates of nonviolent resolutions to conflict. If aggressivity is learned and women are as prone to violence as men, the ungendering of the makeup of the military may mean that aggressive behavior will spread throughout society. Such fears seem to be justified by blockbuster movies such as *Alien* whose androgynous female grunts are braver, brawnier, and more brutal than male peers in countering xenomorphs. In his Vietnam novel-memoir *The Things They Carried*, Tim O'Brien describes how the jungle transformed the proper, middle-class Mary Anne into "part of the land. She was wearing her culottes, her pink sweater, and a necklace of human tongues. She was dangerous. She was ready for the kill" (1990, 125). This might be a portrayal of women in Peru's Sendero Luminoso. Israeli women settlers are among the fiercest advocates of the Jews' right to oust Palestinians from their homes in the occupied territories. Throughout the period of the rule of the Imam Khomeini, Americans were regaled with media images of chador-swathed women toting kalashnikovs. The war in Bosnia has shown us Serb women blocking humanitarian aid to Muslims and Croats. These women do not accord well with the traditional images of women as representatives of a culture and of a land to be protected. Their transformation dramatizes their group's determination to destroy whatever stands in its way. Stiehm believes that the "pictures of women with guns appear when a country is under siege. Their purpose is to mobilize civilians. Their purpose is to demonstrate unified commitment. It is to tell an enemy that it will have to occupy the country and pacify every citizen before it can claim victory. But, perhaps most importantly, it is a way of mobilizing young men . . . few men are able to resist the call to service when women are serving" (1988, 96). These women are flat embodiments of the desire of their nation. Feminist pacifists do not take such images lightly, however; they do not dismiss their threat as part of rhetorical hype. They fear that women in combat do not portend a kinder, gentler military but rather prefigure the worst that is yet to come.

In response to such a list of fearsome Amazons I propose another: mother warriors who risk all for their children, real or adopted.[12] Such women fighters have become popular idols of the American screen. This is true of *Terminator 2* and the *Star Wars* trilogy but even of *Alien*, in which the reluctant Sigourney Weaver has to play the part of the ultimate marine, fearlessly diving deep into the bowels of the space colony to save the little girl she had "adopted" from the monsters. The Madres for years successfully opposed the military regimes of Chile and Argentina with nothing more than patience and placards. The Palestinian mothers on the West Bank and in Gaza, Zapatista mothers in Mexico, and the mothers of Soweto have evolved with their children a form of resistance with sticks, stones, and machetes that renders life for the resident oppressor as arduous as possible. In the summer of 1993, Serb and Croat mothers marched on an area where their sons were fighting each other. Iraqi women write about mothers who deliberately refuse to produce cannon fodder.

These activist mothers are committed to a cause, but above all they have adopted responsibility for one another on whose behalf they improvise new forms of resistance and opposition that pay attention to the survival and preservation of the largest number of people possible. Writing of Edna St. Vincent Millay, Susan Schweik notes that the "maternal metaphor allowed her to represent women in active political engagement, and to represent active political engagement as womanly" (1991, 78). These mother warriors have forced themselves onto public awareness. They draw attention to themselves and to the roles they have played and in the playing have transformed. Their activism on the "battlefield" contrasts with expectations that they should be passive or, best of all, absent. They and their counterparts in the military sensitize the world to what happens to women in war. This is especially the case when governments sanction rape as a weapon. News from Bosnia of the Serb rape camps raised a furor. International demonstrations reminded a forgetful world that this is not the first time women's bodies have been officially and systematically targeted. The list of mass rapes of just the last sixty years includes Japanese rapes of Chinese women in the 1930s; Nazi rapes of Russian and Jewish women, Soviet rapes of German women, and Japanese rapes of Korean women during World War II (Brownmiller 1976); American rapes of Vietnamese women in the 1960s and 1970s;[13] Pakistani rapes of Bengali women in the early 1970s; Iraqi rapes of Kurdish women in the late 1980s;[14] and Hindu rapes of thirteen Muslim women in an open, lighted square after the destruction of the mosque at Ayodhya in 1992. These are only the better-known cases; others will surely emerge as consciousness is globally raised about the crime against humanity that was once considered an acceptable means of "softening up" the enemy (Stiglmayer 1994).

The ungendering of combat further undermines the "normality" of rape in war. Women in combat prisons will not rape and may report those who do. If the International Tribunal tries and condemns the Serb rapists and their leaders, officially organized and sanctioned rape will be recognized as a crime against humanity on a par with Nazi genocide and Japanese war crimes.

Many Little War Stories

Never before has the fictionality of the War Story been so obvious. In nuclear-age wars, the women and the children—whom the War Story had described at home and safe because they were defended by their men at the front—are acknowledged to be increasingly attractive as military targets. They are not being protected. Their men cannot protect them. This fact has never before been so openly and widely recognized, because war is no longer the province of military historians, just-war philosophers, and national security analysts and advisers, all of them men. It has become a magnet for humanists, many of whom are women and feminists.

Less rigidly bound by conventions that confine the understanding of war to battle, these cultural analysts of war are revealing connections that may allow for new ways of thinking. For example, the threat of war is in itself a kind of war. It is only with hindsight that we can look back on the Soviet–United States standoff and say, "Yes. I survived the Forty-Year Cold War!" Soon, geologically speaking, the numbers of those who have had that experience, and who know that this war was lived as an uneasy peace, will dwindle. When added to the list of the world's long wars, it will be remembered as devastating. I am not trying to minimize the very real fear we all felt as we imagined and campaigned against the nuclear holocaust for which Hiroshima and Nagasaki seemed to be curtain-raisers, but I want to record a fact that is as true for the Cold War as it is for the hot little wars exploding all over the globe, particularly in Asia and Africa: war behind the front lines, when such lines can be defined, often becomes another normality, a kind of charged "peace." Except in an idealized Kantian formulation of Perpetual Peace, peace is not the opposite of war but rather a provisional tolerance of differences, of the conflicts they engender, and of the knowledge that absolute resolution may not be possible.[15] Peace thus construed is linked with war on a continuum of conflict negotiation spanning absolute nonviolence through mayhem. War is not always unspeakable horror. It can be, but it is more commonly an intensity, a heightened awareness, a massive human displacement, or a preparedness to move from being at peace to being at war.

Can affairs of state function within such ambiguity? When split-second decisions have to be made, can notions of continuity, uncertainty, and instability be tolerated? In general, governance and control have required clearcut categories. Freeman Dyson writes that the *"public voice* of the military establishment cannot be critical of its own purposes. The military machine is designed to carry out the missions which it has established for itself, irrespective of the thoughts and feelings of individual commanders" (1984, 8; my emphasis). Clarity is also essential for the public image of the military. Voters demand attention to their welfare and safety. The wise ruler must create the illusion of peace so that war is always utterly different.

Women's prominence as guerrilla fighters, as military targets of bombs and rapes, and as subjects of debate about the gendering of the military and of combat has complicated the telling of the War Story. These women are telling their counternarratives, which reveal that what we had thought to be self-evidently true, is true only for some. This truth is, of course, that the War Story is not just a story but a paradigm that lies at the heart of our inability to understand war. Women's stories talk openly about how war compels men and women to take over each other's roles. For the duration, men and women fill in for each other, for example, military men work as medics and secretaries, and women work in munitions factories. A few male writers such as Glenn Gray and Erich Maria Remarque even described men who nurtured and loved each other, whereas women such as Helen Zenna Smith, in her 1930 *Not So Quiet . . .* demonstrated that the women who had volunteered, such as the ambulance drivers, became hard and fearless. Performance of new tasks and roles allowed for temporary transgressions of gender-prescribed behavior: women could act like men without losing their femininity, men could act like women without risking the knee-jerk label of "wimp."

It was equally clear, however, that this wavering, this gender instability and ambiguity, had to be sanitized in war's aftermath, and particularly in the War Story. How can we retrieve the detritus? This is the task of the responsible intellectual: to make sure the binary frame narrative does not predetermine the uncovering of the experience. Instead of fixing roles and experiences so that each war is said to repeat the experience of its predecessors, war stories should allow for the narration of war's dynamism and incomprehensibility, but also of other aspects usually excluded from the War Story. A vivid example can be found in the Vietnam stories of Tim O'Brien, in which he describes boredom as "dripping inside you like a leaky faucet, except it wasn't water, it was a sort of acid, and with each little droplet you'd feel the stuff eating away at important organs." For this man to write the story of his experience in Southeast Asia was not to replicate some outworn formula but rather to interrogate memory, to question what had seemed to be so self-evidently true: "Stories are for joining the past to the future. Stories are for those late hours in the night when you can't remember how you got from where you were to where you are. Stories are for eternity, when memory is erased, when there is nothing to remember except the story. . . . If a story seems moral, do not believe it. If at the end of a war story you fell uplifted, or if you feel that some small bit of rectitude has been salvaged from the larger waste, then you have been made the victim of a very old and terrible lie. . . . By telling stories, you objectify your own experience. You separate it from yourself. You pin down certain truths. You make up others" (1990, 37, 40, 76, 179). These stories are not for others only but mostly for oneself, and yet in the process they leave open areas of access for those others who have not had the experience that entitles them to tell the War Story. These stories do not silence, because, as O'Brien suggest provocatively, "a true war story is never about war" (1990, 91).

Such are the stories that Lebanese, Bosnian, Iraqi, Algerian, and Palestinian women are telling today. These stories offer some understanding and an alternative. They describe an experience of war that all can understand because it does not take place in a special, privileged elsewhere but is rather the heightened awareness and management of lethal conflict that is different from ordinary life only in terms of its intensity. What women experience in war repeats in stereo the daily experience of violence that has become ordinary. This telling of the ordinariness of war bypasses the age-old prohibition on women writing about war. In these accounts, women are not trespassing on men's space, threatening to deprive them of the glory of having been where only heroes and martyrs tread. Women's stories reveal that war—at least, war today—entails not glory but massive death and the destruction of innocents. Their experience of war allows them to assign their own meanings to what they have felt and done. What used to be labeled civilian experience—being bombed, raped, and expropriated, salvaging threads of living in a refugee camp—they name combat experience. Everyone can have this experience, and it is this acknowledgment of universality that is critical in re-imagining a world where conflict is a constant fact of life and survival depends on the ability to confront conflict without automatically resorting to violence.

We begin to understand women writers who have represented women in Lebanon, Bosnia, and Eritrea not as passive victims but as active survivors and even resisters. We can recognize the parallels between military women in combat and literary women authorizing themselves to name and inscribe women's experiences in war as "war experiences." If women with their different experiences of war write at the time that war is happening, and if they recognize that the collapsing of feeling and language undergirds the silencing and excluding discourse that finds its authentication in the "authority of experience," they may be able to intervene in how the War Story is finally told and how future wars will be fought and then told. Their iconoclastic stories may make it hard indeed to continue to believe that it is a sweet and appropriate thing to die for one's country.

Women's counternarratives of war and changes in the gender arrangements of the military allow us to frame new questions that reject either/or explanations: When does a war begin? Does the first shot to be fired launch a war, or does one have to take into account the buildup? When does it end? What are we to make of the negotiations of outcome: Saddam as "victor" and Bush as "triumphalist"? If war is not declared, if it is in fact Pure War, how can we "stop something that wasn't a war" (Virilio 1983, 26)? When does a civilian become a warrior? Does being targeted, as in total war, entail transformation? Of is there less at stake in defining who is a civilian when men and women can both be combatants?

I am increasingly persuaded that a binary epistemology facilitates the declaration of war and the consequent semiotic transformations; it sanctions what are otherwise considered crimes. To be militarily effective, people must be convinced that what they do in war bears no relation to actions and their meanings elsewhere. They can be good soldiers only if they believe and do not question the fact that war transforms the meaning of actions. For the duration, violence is normalized, even glorified as the experience of the sublime. Throughout his work Frantz Fanon referred to the violence the Algerians used in their struggle against the French colonizers as "sacred," and Gray has written of the pleasure and glory in heroic killing, while conceding that there is a growing problem: "The warrior who slays an impersonal enemy has traditionally not been regarded as a criminal, a murderer. Yet in the era of total war the distinction becomes ever more blurred. And the dissociation in our lives between soldiering and civilian pursuits grows at the very period when distinguishing between combatants and non-combatants threatens to disappear altogether." Later he writes that this differentiation is essential lest killing be confused with murder. Murderers are criminals, but "killers [i.e., soldiers] come to feel like high priests" (1970, 33–36, xvi, 131–32, 154). Even a pacifist can say that killing may acquire the aura of sanctity if it happens in the right place.

In 1984, the U.S. State Department announced that "it will no longer use the word 'killing,' much less 'murder,' in official reports on the status of human rights in allied countries. The new term is 'unlawful or arbitrary deprivation of life' " (Cohn 1990, 51). Language matters. In women's writings, there is no right place for killing or theft or rape, because the violence of war is not so different from the violence of peace. They reject black-and-white certainties and thus cast doubt on the validity of transformations in the meanings of actions occasioned because of the space with which they are attached.

Once we judge what happens in war by the same standards we invoke to assess equivalent actions and events outside war, we may begin to understand how violence is so often not only justified but actively pursued. We can begin to think in these new ways because all around us the old structures are cracking. Women are in contemporary wars, whether by fiat of a governing body or because they find themselves in a place that has burst into violence. Women who have experienced this explosion of the normal and who have decided to talk and write about it draw attention to the reality of what women and those like them actually do and endure during war. It is by putting women into the war stories that we can begin to recognize the strangeness of the unchanging metanarrative the War Story has always had. If we render transparent the process whereby the War Story not only legitimizes but also necessitates what in peacetime is considered criminal behavior, we may make it a little harder for governments and gangs to sally off to war.[16]

Feminist praxis gave one the courage to be an active witness whose words may serve to subvert the dominant paradigm. These witnesses are elaborating survival strategies that include the forging of alternative visions and stories. They are voicing dissension from the status quo, making visible the linguistic tactics and ideologies of patriotism, nationalism, and patriarchy, and they are examining the role of consciousness and constructing a memory responsible to the future.

NOTES

1. For an excellent discussion of the military's attitude and policies concerning men and women's comparative strength, see Stiehm 1989, 198–205.

2. The U.S. Army History Department has considerable funding (conversation with Judith Stiehm, 15 December 1994).

3. Thanks to Jody McAuliffe for this insight.

4. Susan Sontag notes, "photographic seeing has to be constantly renewed with new shocks, whether of subject matter or technique, so as to produce the impression of violating ordinary vision" (1977, 89). Gray writes of the "lust of the eye," which "requires the novel, the unusual, the spectacular. It cannot satiate itself on the familiar, the routine, the everyday." His description of the burning bombed villages on the French Riviera as "magnificent" is obscene, despite the explanation that the aesthetic appeal of war is not beauty but awe in the face of power that produces a "feeling of the sublime." Part of the satisfaction is survival; as "spectators we are superior to that which we survey . . . the self is no longer important to the observer; it is absorbed into the objects with which it is concerned" (1970, 29, 33, 34, 36).

5. This fact is acknowledged by the preface to the second edition, published in 1980. It affirms that after the Two-Year War was over, it was followed by other wars. The half-page preface is less euphoric, but it continues to urge the importance of living the war through its images, concluding: "Whoever suffers, learns."

6. Sontag writes: "Instead of just recording reality, photographs have become the norm for the way things appear to us, thereby changing the very idea of reality, and of realism. . . . Cameras miniaturize experience, transform history into spectacle. As much as they create sympathy, photographs cut sympathy, distance the emotions. Photography's realism creates a confusion about the real" (1977, 79, 99).

7. "The Real is a complex of dominant and dominated discourses which given texts exclude, separate or do not signify. If the text or picture is going to represent a re-

ality which is different from, and perhaps determinant of, the picture itself, then this representation will be possible through an act of negation, through a demonstration of the incoherence of the system of dominant images. . . . We must not allow ourselves to be expedient of imagining something existing 'before' representation by which we may explain the representation away. . . . We must begin to analyze the real representational practices that go on in a society. . . . We must describe the function of 'specific' individuals within them. . . . Only in this way will we come to understand how ideologies are produced in real representational practices" (Tagg, 1988, 101–2, 211).

8. "Peace will never occur as a consequence of weakness, exhaustion or fear," writes Gray as he comments on Nietzsche's assessments of military power (1970, 226).

9. Conversation with Christine Chinkin, 15 April 1994.

10. "Eritrea: The Kitchen Calls," *Economist*, 25 June 1994.

11. See Fuss 1989 for an illuminating discussion of the tension between constructivist and essentialist language and the political expediency of essentialism on occasion. Biologists are divided about the role of gender in aggressivity, as they are also about whether aggressive behavior is innate or learned.

12. Amy Swerdlow describes the 1960s Women Strike for Peace (WSP) as "a disorganized band of middle-class housewives pleading for the children in the domestic terms they had been taught since childhood. . . . In their concern for the fate of their children, the WSPers were no different from millions of other American women. However, they did differ in their broader perception of motherhood as a social and communal function. . . . The WSPers were not concerned with transforming sex role ideology but rather with using it to enhance women's political power" (1990, 23, 24).

13. Susan Griffin, writing on 7 October 1992 for *USA Today*, underscores the indissoluble link between rape and violence, between sexuality and war: "During combat in Vietnam, rape and murder had become frequent enough to enter the slang of our armed forces. A 'double veteran' referred to a man who had sex with a woman and then killed her. The fact of this deeply ingrained link between war and sexual violence must be confronted and deemed unacceptable by those who prepare men for war."

14. See Makiya 1993, 287, where the author reproduces an Iraqi soldier's identification card, on which his occupation was marked "violation of women's honor."

15. Jean Bethke Elshtain suggests that the dichotomized constructions of war and peace are reinforced by Kant's absolute segregation of public and private. It is in the former that Perpetual Peace can reign, for "genuine peace must nullify *all* existing causes of war" (1990, 264).

16. As Stiehm writes, the existence of enlisted women challenges "basic beliefs about the military. This makes it more likely that both the military and civilians will think carefully about the nature of this institution that has a potential not only to guard but also to threaten the nation" (1989, 7).

REFERENCES

Benjamin, Walter. [1955] 1968. *Illuminations: Essays and Reflections.* New York: Schocken.
Benson, F. R. 1067. *Literary Impact of the Spanish Writers in Arms: Civil War.* New York: New York University Press.

Berkman, Joyce. 1990. "Feminism, War, and Peace Politics: The Case of the World War I." In Jean Bethke Elshtain and Sheila Tobias, eds., *Women, Militarism, and War: Essays in History, Politics, and Social History*. Savage, Md.: Rowman and Littlefield.

Brownmiller, Susan. 1976. *Against Our Will: Men, Women, and Rape*. New York: Bantam Books.

Campbell, D'Ann. 1990. "The Regimented Women of World War II." In Elshtain and Tobias, *Women, Militarism, and War*.

Cohn, Carol. 1990. "'Clean Bombs' and Clean Language." In Elshtain and Tobias, *Women, Militarism, and War*.

————. 1993. "Wars, Wimps, and Women: Talking Gender and Thinking War." In Miriam Cooke and Angela Woollacott, eds. *Gendering War Talk*. Princeton: Princeton University Press.

Cooke, Miriam. 1988. *War's Other Voices: Women Writers on the Lebanese Civil War*. Cambridge: Cambridge University Press.

Cooke, Miriam, and Angela Woollacott, eds. *Gendering War Talk*. Princeton: Princeton University Press.

Dyson, Freeman. 1984. *Weapons and Hope*. New York: Harper and Row.

Elshtain, Jean Bethke. 1987. *Women and War*. New York: Basic Books.

————. 1990. The Problem with Peace." In Elshtain and Tobias, *Women, Militarism, and War*.

Elshtain, Jean Bethke, and Sheila Tobias, eds. 1990. *Women, Militarism, and War: Essays in History, Politics, and Social Theory*. Savage, Md.: Rowman and Littlefield.

Fuss, Diana. 1989. *Essentially Speaking: Feminism, Nature, and Difference*. New York: Routledge.

Gray, J. Glenn. [1959] 1970. *The Warriors: Reflections on Men in Battle*. New York: Harper.

Isaksson, Eva, ed., 1988. *Women and the Military System*. New York: St. Martin's Press.

Jeffords, Susan. [1986] 1989. *The Remasculinization of America: Gender and the Vietnam War*. Bloomington: Indiana University Press.

Jones, Kathleen. 1990. "Dividing the Ranks: Women and the Draft." In Elshtain and Tobias, *Women, Militarism, and War*.

Keegan, John. 1978. *The Face of Battle: A Study of Agincourt, Waterloo, and the Somme*. London: Penguin Books.

Makiya, Kanan. 1993. *Cruelty and Silence: Wars, Tyranny, and the Arab World*. London: Jonathan Cape.

O'Brien, Tim. 1990. *The Things They Carried*. New York: Penguin Books.

al-Sayyid, 'Abd al-Razzaq. [1977] 1980. *Harb Lubnan: Suwar Watha'iq Ahdath*. (The Lebanese war: Photographs, documents, events). Beirut: Dar al-Masira.

Schweik, Susan. 1991. *A Gulf So Deeply Cut: American Women Poets and the Second World War*. Madison: University of Wisconsin Press.

Seager, Joni. 1993. "Blueprints for Inequality." *Women's Review of Books*. 10, 4:1–3.

Sedgwick, Eve. 1990. *Epistemology of the Closet*. Berkeley: University of California Press.

————. 1992. "Nationalisms and Sexualities in the Age of Wilde." In Andrew Parker et al., eds., *Nationalisms and Sexualities*. New York: Routledge.

Segal, Mady Wechsler, and David R. Segal. 1983. "Social Change and the Participation of Women in the American Military. *Research in Social Movements, Conflicts, and Change*. 5:235–58.

Smith, Helen Zenna. 1930. *Not So Quiet . . .* London: Albert E. Marriott.

Sontag, Susan. [1973] 1977. *On Photography*. New York: Farrar, Straus and Giroux.

Stanley, Sandra C., and Mady W. Segal. 1988. "Military Women in NATO: An Update." *Armed Forces and Society*. 14, 4:559–85.

Stiehm, Judith. 1988. "The Effect of Myths about Military Women on the Waging of War." In Isaksson, *Women and the Military System*, pp. 94–105.

————. 1989. *Arms and the Enlisted Woman*. Philadelphia: Temple University Press.

Stiglmayer, Alexandra, ed. 1994. *Mass Rape: The War against Women in Bosnia-Herzegovina*. Lincoln: University of Nebraska Press.

Tagg, John. 1988. *The Burden of Representation*. Amherst: University of Massachusetts Press.

Virilio, Paul. 1983. *Pure War*. Translated by Mark Polizotti. New York: Semiotext.

Judith Hicks Stiehm

13

The Civilian Mind

In 1994–95, we (U.S. citizens) spent close to $270 billion on defense. In 1990, we were 5 percent of the world's population, occupied 7 percent of the Earth's land surface, created 27 percent of the world's GNP, but made 41 percent of the world's military expenditures (Sivard 1993, 37). Since 1990, many nations (particularly the former Union of Soviet Socialist Republics) have reduced military expenditures, but we have not. The result is that we now spend almost as much as the rest of the world *combined*.

The military budget has been treated as untouchable even as federal (and state and local) budgets have been slashed by officials focusing on the debt, the deficit, and lower taxes. The irony is that military expenditures have held steady even though their primary justification, the "Evil Empire," the USSR, has dematerialized. There has been discussion about other missions for the military and some conjuring of new threats, such as North Korea, Iraq (alternatively, Iran), Libya, and Syria—countries branded "outlaws" for seeking to join the nuclear club or for sponsoring terrorism or both. It has also been suggested that the new threat may not be a country but a culture, the prime candidate being Islam. But even though some have claimed that the United States brilliantly won the Cold War by tricking the USSR into spending itself into bankruptcy, and even though we envy the economies of Germany and Japan, which allocate 3 and 1 percent of their GNP to military spending, respectively (we allocate about 4 percent), we have not asked ourselves the hard questions about the relationship between our well-being, our economy, and our military spending (Sivard 1993, 43–44).

Our taxes may have built a strong military, but its very strength also creates an unease. After all, didn't our Founding Fathers warn against a "standing army"?[1] Apart from the cost of such an institution, there is always a concern that if an army exists, it will be used, perhaps even against a country's citizens, not just its foes. Two president-generals, George Washington and Dwight David Eisenhower, used the occasion of their farewell addresses to admonish us against an excessively strong military. Eisenhower did so even though we were then very much engaged in the Cold War. That war has now been concluded. We have reduced the number of people in uniform, but there has been nothing approaching a budgetary demobilization. Spending goes on and on and on.

Our standing army is not only expensive and large; it is self-selected and selective. It is not representative. In the past, whenever we have had a large military(the Civil War, World War I, World War II, and until 1972), it has been a conscripted military. It has depended on citizens (male) fulfilling (often reluctantly) required service. Today, however, almost one-third of our young men are considered ineligible for any form of military service (mostly because of low educational achievement). Also, for almost a quarter of a century, all those who have served have volunteered. Some describe these volunteers as "economically drafted," and it seems certain that for many racial minorities and for women, military pay is better pay than they could hope to receive as civilians (see Moore, Chapter 6 in this volume). Others describe our nonconscripted military as a mercenary military—that is, one that soldiers join for money—and one that we, as a nation, hire out for money. (The example cited is the Gulf War, which incurred incremental costs of $52 billion, covered by some $54 billion raised by Allied nations, including $16 billion from Saudi Arabia, $16 billion from Kuwait, $10 billion from Japan, and $5 billion from Germany [O'Loughlin, Mayer, and Greenberg 1994, 165].) Another description of our military is that it has become professional. Instead of being made up of a large number of young people who expect to serve only briefly, our military is seen as a career choice. Thus, those in uniform are older and are more likely to be parents than in the past. Both trends make our military more expensive. They may also inhibit its use, since we have always preferred to deploy young and single rather than older and married men to combat. (This may be balanced by a belief that since they volunteered, military personnel agreed to accept risks that we would not ask of draftees.)

When one has a professional rather than a conscripted army, one runs the risk of having a military that believes "it knows better." Until recently, our commanders in chief (presidents) had served in World War II or had graduated from a military academy. In 1992, a commander in chief was elected who not only did not serve in the military, but who took care to avoid doing so. When Bill Clinton indicated his plan to change a policy of excluding homosexuals from military service, he faced a minimutiny (abetted by some congressional leaders). What does the future hold if we continue to maintain a powerful, professional military that is commanded by a person (a president) without military experience and, perhaps, without the military's respect? The Supreme Court has long taken a stand of "deference" with regard to military matters (a doctrine developed by Chief Justice William Rehnquist over several decades). If neither the Court nor the presidency is likely to challenge the military, Congress, and more fundamentally, voters (most of whom are civilians) need to think about and make decisions about the military as an institution they authorize and pay for. They need to think about it as one of a number of governmental institutions, not as one that should be unexamined and sacrosanct.

Civilians pay for and are supposed to be served by their militaries. But civilians seem to be profoundly irrelevant to the military and, in turn, to be profoundly disinterested in discussing or debating military expenditures, strategy, or weaponry. Civilians just don't think about force structure, readiness, modernization, and sustainability. Conversely, in examining the major works on warfare, one can scan index after index without finding any entry related to civilians except in some treatises on guerrilla warfare or "low-intensity conflict." But civilians are enormously affected by war. One study (which defines a war as causing one thousand or more deaths, thus defining away, for example, the U.S. invasions of Grenada and Panama) lists 149 wars in the "peaceful" era between 1945 and 1992. During this period more than 23 million persons were killed. Many more millions were injured. More than 60 percent, or 14.5 million of the 23 million dead, were civilians (Sivard 1993, 21).

Current official doctrine concerning the use of our military arises directly from the Vietnam experience. It has three basic provisions. The first is that U.S. troops will not be used without strong public support. The second is that the goal of a mission will be clearly defined and possible to accomplish. The third is that military professionals will be provided with the resources needed to accomplish their mission, and to accomplish it with a minimal loss of U.S. lives.

Few are prepared to argue against popularity, victory, and a casualty-free war. Also, one appreciates the military's need for clarity and its desire to be prepared and then to act effectively. It is ironic, however, that successful military action is portrayed as dependent on public support, for public opinion is also widely perceived as volatile and unreliable. The military needs and wants to know what civilians want and think, but the "civilian mind" frustrates and mystifies. That is why the civilian mind is the topic of this essay. First, I distinguish it from the views of the pacifist and from the more discussed "military mind." Then I explore three characteristics of the civilian mind. Finally, I offer a charge to the reader, who is sure to share with me some of the characteristics of the civilian mind.

The Pacifist, the Militarist, the Civilian

Pacifist and militarist modes of thought require discussion because they offer a crucial contrast to civilian thinking. They thus serve as a probe for an unfamiliar concept—the civilian mind. This concept has been nearly invisible, not because it is rare but because it is common. It is a concept that has never been well articulated. Because it is ordinary, diffuse, and not particularly self-conscious, it has proved difficult to give form. One way to approach it is to tease out a residual or default body of thought—that which remains once the views of pacifists and militarists have been removed.

Self-identified subscribers to pacifism and to militarism are few in number. Probably the best-known pacifist works are those by M. K. Gandhi, and the best-known militarist work is Carl von Clausewitz's On War. My discussion is framed by the U.S. experience and therefore does not draw on these well-known works.

In my Nonviolent Power (1973) I describe two quite different philosophies of nonviolence. Each claims to be moral, but each also claims to have the potential for being effective. The two perspectives, though, are quite different from each other.

The first view I call "conscientious nonviolence." Its unit of analysis is the individual. In it each individual is morally enjoined from the use of even the threat of physical violence. (Some adherents would also forbid the use of psychological violence.) The individual is directed always to act in accord with conscience, always to respect the conscience of others, and when involved in apparent conflict, to appeal to the conscience of his of her apparent antagonist. Conscientious nonviolence assumes that there is a natural harmony of interests and that all human beings have a potential for good.

Violence, coercion, and threats are seen as unnecessary as well as wrong. Nonviolent action intended to foster agreement or reconciliation is directed toward increasing and improving communication. It employs persuasion and such tools of persuasion as empathy, surprise, and even self-sacrifice. There is often a religious commitment associated with this form of nonviolence. Its practice is demanding and perfectionistic. Its adherents are prepared to suffer and even to die.

The second kind of nonviolence I call "pragmatic nonviolence." In this formulation, conflict is seen as real (not just apparent) and even as inevitable. A violent action or response is judged not so much "wrong" as uneconomic or ineffective. The argument against the use of violence and the absolute commitment not to use it are rooted not in the belief that people are basically good but in the belief that people have a potential for the truly terrible. Because of their capacity for great inhumanity, the argument goes, people should absolutely forswear the use of violence, because it will inevitably incite counterviolence. In short, violence should be tabooed.

Nonviolent action is seen as appropriate in a conflict situation, but that action need not be limited to efforts to create better communication. Indeed, pragmatic nonviolent action can be designed to function as a ritualized form of conflict, as a trial by ordeal. Even if violence is forbidden, then, coercion is not.

Coercive acts such as boycotts and sit-ins are often employed for the purpose of altering an opponent's options, not just changing the opponent's mind. Further, in pragmatic nonviolence the unit of analysis is not the individual but the group. Also, it is understood that the crucial role in resolving conflict may belong to "uninvolved" third parties. Nonviolent action, then, may be directed less to an antagonist and more to an audience, an official, a moral leader, or a judge. Indeed, it may be more generally directed—toward the ever elusive public opinion.

The two approaches to nonviolent action usually forge an uneasy alliance when they are practiced in an actual conflict. Practice often involves the charismatic leadership of someone such as Martin Luther King, Jr. In practice, then, King's argument that nonviolence "is right and works too" becomes standard.

Again, the two forms of nonviolence make quite different assumptions but share a response to violence that involves (1) a complete renunciation of the use of force, (2) the recognition that violence may well be used against those who have renounced it, and (3) the understanding that by forswearing violence one may actually tempt some antagonists to a violence they would not have used if they had anticipated retaliation. Even though they know third parties may play a crucial role in the resolution of conflict, those committed to nonviolence do not compel, do not employ, do not even ask others to use violence on their behalf. In this very important way they differ from civilians.

The most familiar discussion of "the military mind" may be Samuel P. Huntington's in *The Soldier and the State,* written in 1957. There it is suggested that what I have called a militarist is a "conservative realist" who assumes that conflict and periodic wars are inevitable. She or he also assumes that hierarchy and authority are appropriate and that ambiguity, individuality, and democracy are not necessarily desirable but may have to be tolerated. (Huntington concluded that "today America can learn more from West Point than West Point from America." He urged Americans to place a higher value on "loyalty, duty, restraint, dedication," even if they seemed antithetical to the culture's liberal and democratic values [1957, 466, 465].)

I would add that a militarist believes that violence "works," that it is effective and, therefore, should be institutionalized, that is, considered legitimate, organized, planned for, and invested in. It should command significant intellectual and financial resources. In any particular situation a militarist might or might not advocate the use of violence (often she or he would not), but the assumption remains that one must be prepared to use it. Finally, I would argue that adopting this position implies one's acceptance of moral responsibility for the use of violence, and, possibly, responsibility for actually wielding it. Civilians are likely to shirk the former and by definition do not do the latter.

If willingness personally to apply state violence is part of the definition of a militarist, the perspective is more likely to be held by men than by women, because our culture has given men a near monopoly on the application of legitimate state violence (see Peach, Chapter 8, and Cooke, Chapter 12, in this volume). Old men make military decisions, young men execute them, and women are exempt even from registering for the draft, although such registration is still required of men. Even feminists who strongly advocate women's equality do not place military participation near the top of their agenda.

What, then, is a civilian? In pursuit of a definition, I have offered descriptions of both the pacifist and the militarist; through their characterization, a definition of the civilian has begun to emerge. A second approach to the task of definition is now in order. This involves, first, immersing one-self in the literature about war and in firsthand accounts of its conduct. Then one can contrast the knowledge gained thereby with the assumptions one once made about the military and war, assumptions that are still made, I sus-pect, by many civilians, particularly U.S. women civilians, for we have been especially sheltered from war's realities.

Except for nurses (see Reeves, Chapter 5 in this volume), American women have enjoyed a near exemption from firsthand experience with a war in progress. Admittedly, Washington, D.C., was burned in 1812; fron-tier life was sometimes hazardous for pioneer and for Native American women; the rigidity of the U.S. Constitution made a sustained and bloody civil war necessary in order to end slavery; and Hawaii (not then a state) was bombed in 1941. Still, because U.S. women have traditionally been barred from combat, and because the United States has conducted its wars abroad for a long time now, few U.S. women have killed or been killed in war. Thus, culture, geography, a powerful economy, and military might have combined to permit Americans, but especially American women, to prac-tice an ostrichlike obliviousness when it comes to war.

This obliviousness permits us to describe our military as a defensive or-ganization even though we fight almost exclusively in other people's coun-tries (see Devilbiss, Chapter 9 in this volume). It permits us to believe that civilians who enjoy protected status under international law are, in fact, pro-tected by that law, and also that wars are conducted according to agreed-on rules—or at least that U.S. soldiers follow such rules. It permits us simulta-neously to believe that state violence is a necessary and effective evil, that unilateral disarmament is foolishness, but that we can, with safety, unilat-erally disarm ourselves versus the most powerful military in the world—our own.[2] Again, U.S. civilians assume they can renounce or refuse the right and the responsibility of using official force but still exercise the right of com-mand, that is, the right to direct others to use force, to use it only for spec-ified purposes, and to use it for our benefit even if it is to their cost.

Technology and terrorism have combined to diminish civilian innocence. We know, even if we prefer not to know, that nuclear weapons and their delivery systems make everyone vulnerable. We know that terrorists who are prepared to die cannot be stopped and that their deeds are often nonattrib-utable. Minicams and satellites can provide extraordinary visual access to the battlefield and even behind enemy lines. Xerox, FAX, and Bitnet connect civilians to global information channels that cannot be controlled as governments might like to control them. Nevertheless, civilian thinking continues and demands our attention.

Civilian thinking assumes that the use of force is sometimes necessary and is appropriately planned and prepared for. It believes that one does not have to accept personal responsibility for the use of force. Thus, like the pacifist, the civilian may refuse to use force, but unlike the pacifist, she or he condones and may support, may encourage, may even demand that others use it. Unlike the militarist, though, the civilian believes that rules exempting civilians not just from using violence but from even experiencing it are real and enforced. Overall, then, there are three things that appear so to characterize civilian thinking that they require further exploration. The first I call willful ignorance. The second is innocence about protected innocents. The third concerns disarmed trust.

Willful Ignorance

Let us set aside the fact that militaries and wars involve secrets, that they involve deception, that they involve censorship. Let us set aside the irony that secrets, deception, and censorship are designed to keep the public (as well as the enemy) ignorant, even though public support is said to be essential to successful military action. Let us set aside even the question as to whether public support should be based on information or on disinformation. It should be remembered, however, that ignorance makes us more susceptible to war stories, stories (and movies) that are not assessed for logic or evidence but that have powerful consequences (see Jeffords, chapter 11 in this volume, and the many references made to John Wayne when young men described how they responded the first time they faced combat).[3] For example, atrocity stories, the classic being the rape of nuns, are powerful mobilizers; stories demonizing an enemy and claiming God's support are grand sustainers; and a wide variety of tales justify a victory or explain away a loss.[4]

My concern here is with ignorance that could be overcome. One kind of ignorance derives from double messages. Jonathan Schell and other analysts of the Vietnam conflict have described the efforts of government to send one message to an enemy government and another (conflicting one) to its own citizens. The dialogue of the Vietnam conflict also taught us the difficulties created by diplomatic language, which means one thing to diplomats (who essentially speak to one another in code) but something quite different to newspaper readers. Double messages and those messages whose "real" meaning is accessible only through translation from diplomatese often make citizens feel betrayed. On the other hand, officials, who have unconsciously been decoding the messages for themselves, feel scapegoated because "everyone knows," for instance, that a "surgical strike" is a bombing raid and that bombing raids inevitably claim old folk, women, children, and babies among their victims.[5] Thus, governments sometimes help citizens ignore what they may well prefer to ignore, but citizens, especially civilians, are often willfully ignorant about things military.

One important thing civilians are willfully ignorant about is means. They may enthusiastically support an end, while leaving the means to others to select and implement. Their preference, of course, is that threats should suffice. When they do not, civilians are unlikely to analyze the relative advantages and disadvantages of air war, tanks, infantry, psychological operations, low-intensity conflict, support with training and materiel, sanctions, bribes, manipulating the electoral process, or destabilization.

Although support for entering into a war may be deemed moral according to the Western tradition that provides a definition of a "just war" (jus ad bellum; see below), there are also rules for the conduct of war (just in bello) that require attentiveness to the means as well as to the end. Thus, failing to consider and support the means to a desired end can be immoral.

Endorsing an end without considering and endorsing the means can also be unwise. When those (civilians) who have supported an end finally grasp the means implied by their endorsement, or simply the means being used, they can feel betrayed. But so can the (military) individuals who in good faith are employing the means they believe have been authorized and are required to achieve the end. Our new doctrine regarding the use of troops (discussed above) addresses the need for a well-defined goal, provision of the means to it, and the requirement for public support. The question is how to assure public support for the means as well as the end. Any elected official will testify to the frustration of connecting means to ends, whether the topic is fighting crime, providing health care, creating adequate schools, or guaranteeing a clean water supply. Citizens can be willfully ignorant of implied costs and, therefore, of necessary taxes. Similarly, civilians can be willfully ignorant of implied deaths and suffering.

There are certain things civilians prefer to believe, and so prefer to believe that they have acquired the power of myths, that is, they are widely shared beliefs, emotionally rooted, and hard to dislodge however illogical or at odds with the facts (Edelman 1971).

One myth is that there is a battlefield. This concept permits one to think of war as something that is fought in a location like a football stadium or a great unoccupied desert where trained, declared antagonists fight according to an agreed-on set of rules and in an agreed-on physical space. The fact is that a nuclear battlefield can be everywhere and a terrorist's battlefield can be anywhere. But *every* battlefield is somewhere, and that somewhere is not agreed-on in advance, is not "distant," and is not uninhabited.

Former battlefields may be fields today, but yesterday they were farms or suburbs or even the heart of a city. Guerrilla wars may be perceived as jungle or mountainous wars, but they, too, are fought in villages where people live, where they work, where they cook, where they sleep, where they pray, where they make love, where they care for their children. All these activities continue even in the midst of conflict, in the midst of danger.

Indeed, "low-intensity wars" may be the deadliest of all for civilians. For example, in the early years (1980–88) of Mozambique's recently concluded civil war, the UN estimates that almost 500,000 children under the age of five died from war-related causes. Similarly, Angola lost 330,000 young children from a total population of only 9.7 million (Minter 1994, 3–4). It is not easy to learn these things. For us, after all, war is something men volunteer to go to by plane or by ship. War usually takes place in locations we have never seen and to which we have given little thought of ever seeing.

A second thing civilians like to believe is that things will go as planned. There is a willingness to take military "can do" responses at face value rather than as professional style or as an effort to create a self-fulfilling prophecy. The fact is there are always snafus—major ones. Sand gets in helicopter engines. Drugs and alcohol are used. Race riots occur. Radios jam. Soldiers don't shoot. Officers are fragged. People have accidents. We kill our own troops. (Of the 148 Americans who died in the forty-three-day Gulf War, 35, almost a quarter, were killed by "friendly fire". [*Miami Herald*, 15 April 1994].) Because military personnel can better distinguish between what is real and what is just "being positive," they are often more cautious about what their forces can do than are the elected officials who command them (Betts 1977).

A third thing civilians like to believe (and which is essentially written into current doctrine) is that wars can be won, they can be conclusive, and right can prevail. But the unconditional surrenders extracted in World War II followed by war-crimes trials conducted by the victors, military occupation, and severely limited rearmament are the exception, not the rule. Sometimes wars end because the antagonists are exhausted; sometimes wars are suspended; frequently they are negotiated. Often things don't seem to change much, and often the result of a war is quite different from the goal of any party to the war.

A fourth thing civilians like to believe is that if one has a mighty military, little blood will be shed. This could be true if one's military is perceived as both mighty and eager to fight; then threats alone may win one's way. Once war begins, however, deaths also begin. And once war begins, limits lose their meaning. General William Tecumseh Sherman's "I am tired and sick of war. Its glory is all moonshine. . . . War is Hell" (Keegan 1976, 6) serves as a solid bottom line. Every war narrative provides details. Those details force acknowledgment that the victims are not just soldiers and that U.S. troops, too, throw POWs out of airplanes, mutilate dead enemies and make souvenirs of body parts, rape women and practice necrophilia, loot stores, shoot children—that our soldiers, too, "literally did anything that we wanted to do. . . . There was no rules at all. . . . There is no honor in war" (Terry 1984, 24, 27, 93, 82, 91, 129).

At some point a reversal occurs. What is willfully not known is forced into civilian consciousness. Something, and it is heard to predict what that something will be, becomes emblematic of a means being used (or an end being pursued) that civilians believe they have not authorized. As an example, there is a picture engraved in the memory of the generation of the Vietnam conflict. It is that of a young girl running down the road nude suffering from napalm burns. (Napalm, a U.S. weapon, is a highly combustible jellylike substance that is dropped from the air.) A second visual from that war was accompanied by audio. The visual is of a cigarette lighter in the hand of a U.S. soldier setting a thatched roof afire. The audio is "We had to destroy the village to save it."

Like World War II, the Gulf War has generally been treated as though it was both just and successful. The war involved 400,000 U.S. troops supported by troops from thirty other countries. It began in January 1991 with a month of air raids. At the end of February a ground campaign was launched and successfully concluded in just one hundred hours. Television provided "real-time" coverage, some from Baghdad itself and much of it of missiles in action in what came to be called the "electronic battlefield." Enormous amounts of information were provided to the press by military officials. But one piece of information was and continues to be unavailable. That is the number of people who died. The U.S. public had been prepared for a large number of U.S. deaths. When the number of U.S. battle deaths turned out to be 148, it seemed almost bloodless—particularly in comparison with the 241 Marines who were killed in a single terrorist attack in Lebanon. The number that was and is missing is the number of Iraqi deaths.[6] Iraq isn't telling. The U.S. military isn't telling. And the public isn't asking.

There are two audio clues that may explain the lack of interest. One was a statement made by General Colin Powell as he explained U.S. strategy on television before the ground invasion. After describing the huge Iraqi force lying in wait, he noted, "We are going to cut it off, and then we're going to kill it." Speaking of the actual fighting, one pilot described the strafing of fleeing soldiers as "a turkey shoot." Would the numbers reveal that the war was essentially a massacre? Is that something we do not want to know?

Three months after the war (in May 1991), the Defense Intelligence Agency estimated Iraq's losses as 100,000 killed in action, 300,000 wounded, and 150,000 deserters (with a 50 percent error factor). The House Armed Services Committee estimated 9,000 killed and 17,000 wounded in the air war and 120,000 killed or deserted in the ground war. An estimate published in *Foreign Policy* two years later gives much lower numbers, especially for the ground war: 7,500 dead and 19,500 wounded. A crucial difference is that these numbers were based on the conclusion that there had been large-scale desertions (withdrawals?) from the battle zone (O'Loughlin et al. 1994, 11). There can be little doubt that the ground war was lopsided and that most of the deaths were military. But what about the air war? How were civilians affected? Were innocents protected? Has the lack of data protected our innocence about the protection of innocents?

Innocence about Protected Innocents

St. Augustine (354–440) is usually credited with developing the concept of the "just war" (jus ad bellum). The just war is one waged under constituted authority, with right intention, and for a just cause. Rules about how a war should be fought (jus in bello) are equally old if not so specifically authored and include the concepts of (1) "necessity" (military), (2) "proportionality" (between ends and means), and (3) "discrimination" (between noncombatants and combatants). Both necessity and proportionality have an obvious potential for limiting the principle of discrimination, but equally tricky is the task of determining just who is a combatant and who is a noncombatant, who is innocent and who is not.

Most would argue that members of the military are an appropriate target in war even though their service may be reluctant or even coerced. Some would argue that in a democratic state all adults are "guilty" because they have at least tacitly consented to their government's decision to make war. There is room for discussion when it comes to determining the status of civilians who work in industries that support the war or hold governmental positions. Typically, though, it is argued that civilians who are not directly engaged in hostilities or resistance, who do not immediately threaten an enemy, should be considered noncombatants, innocents, persons who are to be protected by the strength of their own military *and* by the restraint of the opponent's military.[7]

The concept of the protection of the innocent became a part of secular international law when it was laid out by Hugo Grotius (1583–1645) and further developed by Emmerich von Vattel (1714–67). It was codified in the fourth Geneva Convention following World War II and was interpreted in the Second Protocol of that convention in 1977. In the recent past, a great deal of the debate about the immunity of civilians has derived from the application of technologies, such as the airplane and nuclear weapons, that were attractive because they afforded a high level of protection to the user of the weapon, even if they were indiscriminate with regard to their victims. Ethicists have especially directed their attention to the bombings of World War II, worrying such concepts as "the double effect," "intention," "the incidental," "proportionality," and "necessity" (Wasserstrum 1970). Elegant though they were, these discussions seem to have had little effect on the development of military strategy or on the rate of civilian casualties. Indeed, some argue that the rules of war are at best restraints. Others go so far as to claim that these rules have been deliberately formulated not to humanize war but to legitimate it. The argument is that the rules release military strategists and technicians from moral restraints and, moreover, that they justify the military technology of the most advanced countries while forbidding the tools (such as threatening POWs) available to the less powerful (O'Loughlin et al. 1994, 59–60).

The problem is that whereas civilians call for humanitarian laws to protect the innocent (obviously, this is in their interests), diplomats negotiate those laws, military officers implement them, and no one enforces them.

Further, "necessity" provides a loophole large enough for virtually any strategy or tactic.

Let us return to consideration of the Gulf War, particularly to its air war. Like the ground war, it was a lopsided affair. The United States bombed Iraq. It and most of its forces were not bombed. Further, as Toeffler and Toeffler (1993, 76) note, the air war was actually a dual war. One war was the television war, which featured incredibly accurate Tomahawk missiles and laser-guided bombs. These, representing only some 10 percent of the bombs released, sought (and usually found) very specific targets even in downtown Baghdad (O'Loughlin et al. 1994, 37). The other war involved old-fashioned (World War II) bombing, featuring wave after wave, day after day of "stupid bombs" (one-third of which were cluster bombs) delivered by decades-old aircraft. These "prepared the battlefield," that is, bombarded the Iraqi troops who would later be attacked during the ground war.

Both air wars sought to prevent any communication to, reinforcement of, or supplies for Iraqi troops. Thus, much of the bombing was directed toward communications centers, roads and bridges, civilian industry, and electric power. In short, while emphasizing its efforts to minimize "collateral damage" (civilian casualties), the United States targeted and severely damaged Iraq's infrastructure. General Norman Schwarzkopf reported that 25 percent of Iraq's electrical generating facilities were made "inoperative" and 50 percent more were "degraded." Other reports said Iraq's electrical output was reduced to 4 percent of its prewar capacity (O'Loughin et al. 1994, 71). Thus, even if civilians were not directly targeted as they were in World War II (for the purpose of destroying "morale"), the loss of infrastructure in a technology-dependent society, combined with the effects of sanctions and postwar civil uprisings, had severe consequences for civilians, consequences that extended long after the war was over. Indeed, one observer concluded that civilian deaths would ultimately exceed military casualties, the difference between this and other wars being only that civilian deaths had been "postponed" (O'Loughlin et al. 1994, 58).

Strategies designed to protect one's own troops, strategies that avoid ground combat, can, then be terribly costly to enemy civilians (O'Loughlin et al. 1994, and Toeffler and Toeffler 1993). And these strategies are not confined to the use of weapons of mass destruction. Low-intensity conflict and psyops strategies that are designed to unravel the social structure or to destabilize an economy or a regime may save military lives, but they have appalling consequences for civilian lives. Similarly, attempting to deny resources to a military is likely to mean denying food, electricity, transportation, and communications to civilians, for in wartime any society equips its protectors first.

The fact is that the innocent have never been protected. In recent years, they have been starved in Somalia, slain by the thousands in Cambodia, blown up over Lockerbie, "disappeared" in Central America, and "cleansed" in Bosnia. Innocence about the fate of civilians may be the form of willful ignorance civilians most eagerly embrace. When information is forced on them, when they cannot any longer deny the suffering of noncombatants, they often lose their taste for war. Why?

In any conflict there are leaders, combatants, and noncombatants on both (all) sides. For the most part, the leaders, combatants, and noncombatants of each side identify with and share one another's lot. But to some degree they also identify with their counterparts on the enemy's side.

Leaders understand the responsibilities of other leaders, and if the goal is not unconditional surrender and military occupation, they know that enemy leaders must retain sufficient legitimacy to make negotiations and implement a settlement. Leaders generally fear anarchy more than they do the continuance in office of an enemy leader. Soldiers may have a respect for their counterparts which they do not accord leaders of either side, whom they see as ordering slaughter and sacrifice from highly secure headquarters. And they may view civilians, including their own, as profiteers and/or parasites, while regarding their counterparts as being like themselves—just wanting to stay alive and to do so with honor, but entrapped by politicians and endangered by senior officers whose eyes are on acquiring "stars" and making history. Finally, noncombatants may see themselves as having little responsibility for the war. If they are Americans, they may feel unthreatened (except by the possibility of nuclear war), but at some point, if confronted frequently enough with the knowledge of the suffering of enemy civilians, two responses are typical. One is, "There but for the grace of God . . . "; the other is, "My troops are doing that?" Civilian empathy with other civilians should be expected. That empathy can be powerful. It can cause reconsideration. At a minimum it leads to invocations such as, "We're not at war with the German, Japanese, Russian, Iraqi, fill-in-the-blank *people*."

Civilian enthusiasm for war can erode quickly when it is clear that innocents are not being spared. This is one reason current military doctrine calls for a well-defined mission that can succeed in a short period of time. It is also why the military has spent many millions developing the precision weapons that were so dramatically displayed during the Gulf War. (Again, note that these weapons may not directly kill civilians but may cause many civilian deaths indirectly.)

When wars are in progress, we are able to distinguish between the interests of an enemy's "people" and their leaders. We may even be able to distinguish between the interests of an enemy's soldiers and their leaders. We are less likely to distinguish the different interests of leaders, soldiers, and civilians on our own side. When a war is stalemated or being lost, those interests are particularly divergent and visible. Leaders know that leaders who don't win don't usually continue in office. This makes it difficult for them to compromise or lose even if that would be best for everyone else.

Barbara Tuchman (1984) and Robert McNamara (1995) have both contributed to our understanding of why leaders cannot be trusted to pursue a policy that is good for others if it is not good for them. Leaders find it hard to rethink; they find it hard to accept defeat; they may even prefer national ruin to personal defeat. Thus, Nero fiddled and Hitler retreated to his bunker. Leaders may well try to preserve their honor even at the expense of soldiers and civilians. One must expect this, for the shame of a leader cannot be concealed. It is not private. It is recorded in history, song, and saga. "Honor" can have terrible consequences (Wyatt-Brown 1986). It leads husbands to slay wives; it leads young men to serve as kamikaze pilots or self-sacrificing truck bombers. How are we to determine when honor is blind and when it is admirable, when it should be paid tribute and when it is shameful? (See Jeffords, Chapter 11 in this volume, for an account of the war stories that help us "answer" these questions.)

To summarize, innocents are almost never protected in war, and usually more civilians are killed than combatants. (Wouldn't you prefer to shoot at someone who can't shoot back?) The rules say this should not be the case, and civilians, who would benefit if those rules were implemented, may be particularly willful in maintaining their ignorance about the experience civilians actually have in war. If civilian thinking is characterized by the willful belief that respect will be afforded those with civilian status, and if a shift in civilian support of war is typical when denial of the facts of war is no longer possible, what should be done? A patronizing answer offered by professionals could be to have quick wars, ones that would be over before public support could erode. Another answer would be to take that characteristic into account and force-feed the public with predicted consequences. That might make the nation more war-averse, but it might also mean that once support was offered, it would be steady because informed.

Disarmed Trust

Perhaps the most peculiar but least queried characteristic of civilian thinking is what I call "disarmed trust." To review, the civilian is like the militarist in believing (1) that unilateral disarmament is foolhardy—one simply cannot trust others to refrain from using violence or coercion when it is to their advantage, and (2) that violence can be an effective means to advocate one's interests. Like the pacifist, though, the civilian relinquishes all personal use of state force. Thus, while believing in the necessity for state armament, the civilian accepts personal disarmament. What is peculiar is that civilians trust certain others to use violence on their (the civilians's) behalf, even when it is not to the others' advantage. The disarmed civilian, then, trusts (at least some) specialists in violence to use violence, if you will, altruistically. In general, though, the civilian does not trust others to refrain from using violence to promote their interests.

Civilians are disarmed in two ways. They are disarmed vis-à-vis foreign foes and they are disarmed vis-à-vis their government's specialists in violence. Disarmed trusters are both men and women. The specialists in violence, though, are mostly men, and the professions in which they are trained to use violence are the police and the military.

The use of force by police (at least in the United States) is severely hedged. They do not use weapons of mass destruction. The media keeps an eye on them. Certain interest groups also serve as watchdogs. Although they have authority on the streets, an independent judiciary has final disposition of actions they take. They have only local authority, though cooperation exists between police in different jurisdictions. They are not very well paid or seen as members of society's elite. Thus, police work may be a way of entering the middle class, but it is not often a route to the upper class or to political power.

Even so, a significant portion of the population does not trust its police. Some observe and must deal with corrupt police. Others are wary of police violence, which sometimes places more emphasis on the duty to maintain order than on the duty to enforce and obey the law. Still, citizens have a pretty clear idea about what they would like police officers to do and about the means that are required. There is also a healthy realism about the ability of police forces actually to provide protection and a sense that citizens must work at their own security.

The military is different from the police, and the military of the United States is different from the military of other countries. It is different from the police because it commands breathtakingly powerful (and expensive) weapons, such as more than eighty nuclear submarines, including two Sea Wolves, which cost more than $1.5 billion each. Although the media and some interest groups try to provide routine reporting on the military, when there is a war in progress, criticism is stifled, and when there is no war, there is minimal interest. Occasionally, a particularly absurd expenditure or practice surfaces, but it is hard to get much of the public to concentrate on such issues as the amount and kind of training reserve personnel should receive, the costs and benefits of short-term versus long-term enlistments, or the value of allocating the nation's funding for scientific research through the Pentagon versus the National Science Foundation. The courts rarely review decisions taken by the military. And the officer/enlisted tier system (most police forces operate on a single promotion ladder) ensures that starting at the bottom and going to the top is rare in the military. Further, our military is not local and not even national. It is global, perhaps even more so than our economy. It has access to intelligence that even elected officials may not see, and it routinely conducts its work behind barriers of secrecy and classification.

Our military is different from the military of other countries in two important ways. First, though it may serve as a route to the middle class, it is not a route to what C. Wright Mills called the power elite. Few senior officers make fortunes, and few command institutions of the kind whose influence cannot be denied. It is also not a route to political power. Troops have not put their officers into power in this country, although they do so all over Latin America, Asia, and Africa. U.S. voters have put generals who commanded in a winning war into the presidency, but only one in this century (Eisenhower—and his immediately preceding job was that of university president).

The second important way our military differs from any others is that except for the Civil War, it has been used almost exclusively against foreign enemies and, as noted above, abroad. In many countries a primary role of the military is domestic and political. In addition, in many countries the military is guilty of terrible violations of human rights. Even in countries where elections are held and civilians occupy the presidency, the military may, essentially, hold a veto, as in Chile and Pakistan.

We are probably quicker to recognize a military's political power in Third World nations. Still, the French government was openly challenged by its army from 1958 to 1961, and the army of the former USSR is clearly a potential player in the disarray there. Does a stable, electorally based political system imply that the military is "under control" (civilian), or only that the military sees its interests as identical with those of the government? That is, is the military obedient or just satisfied, or, a third possibility, is it bonded to the citizens it serves, bonded more closely than to the government or to its own members?

Let us suppose that most Americans trust our military to follow the direction of its civilian, elected, commander in chief (the president) and that they trust the commander in chief to use troops only against a foreign enemy. Shouldn't we, nevertheless, ask the question, "Should we just trust, or does history suggest that militaries cannot be counted on to protect rather than exploit civilians?"? If they cannot be, the question becomes, "What are the conditions under which disarmed civilian trust is appropriate and realistic?"

One view is that the military is most supportive of "legitimate" governments, ones chosen by agreed-on participatory procedures and backed by a nation's citizens. In a form of symbiosis, governments are often seen as most legitimate when a nation is threatened by an external foe or when the military is engaged in a limited and successful foreign war.

For decades, global politics was structured as a struggle between capitalists and communists, in particular between the United States and its allies and the USSR and its allies. Once the USSR disintegrated, once "the threat" was gone, allied governments suffered a noticeable loss of legitimacy. Much has been made of President Clinton's "low ratings," but the ratings of the heads of state in Canada, Russia, Britain, France, Italy, Germany, and Japan have been equally low. Apparently, when there is no external enemy, citizens focus on their more immediate (and competing) concerns; unanimity is lost, and national leaders' feet of clay become visible.

An example of what has been called "a lovely little war" is that between Argentina and Great Britain over the Falkland Islands. The Argentinian military government was floundering and calculated that a quick and successful military action would mend things. Unfortunately for it, Prime Minister Margaret Thatcher decided the islands were worth fighting for (or, perhaps, that a winning war would be good for her and Britain). Although they were thousands of miles from the site, the British arrived with the kind of technology that made the war almost bloodless for them, and the war was brief. The Argentine military was soon out of office (but not entirely out of influence), and Thatcher's government rode high. This is precisely the kind of engagement current U.S. military doctrine prescribes. It makes the military happy because it offers an opportunity to perform and to perform well, and it makes the winning government happy because citizens are supportive.

If one aspires to a world in which government stability does not depend on a real or conjured "threat," a world that does not reward those who play the role of bully, what should be done? What could civilians do to strengthen the bond between the military and themselves rather than between the military and the government or among members of the military? (See Burke, Chapter 10 in this volume.)

Some suggestions that have been considered are

Reducing the size of the "standing army"

Keeping the services in competition with one another by modifying the Goldwater-Nichols Act, which has so elevated the chairmen and the Joint Chiefs of Staff that civilian secretaries of the services and of defense find it hard to compete with them

Reinstating conscription so that military service is understood as a citizen's duty (women's, too) rather than as a profession

Reducing the size of or eliminating the military academies so that more officers receive civilian college educations

Creating a single rank hierarchy, thus eliminating the enlisted/officer dichotomy

Channeling research monies to civilians through civilian offices such as the National Science Foundation rather than through the Pentagon[8]

Conclusion

The military is important, and civilians do not want to do without it. But militaries are of many kinds, and we civilians would do well to think about our military to be sure it is the kind of military we want.

Unfortunately, civilians are often willfully ignorant about the military; they are particularly oblivious to the fate of "innocents" in war, and U.S. civilians tend to trust "their" specialists in violence without considering what makes a military trustworthy or untrustworthy. (Trust seems to stem from shared risk and responsibility over the long term—hence recommendations like the one to renew conscription.)

Analyses that balance the expense and the morality of new technology versus its effectiveness in killing without being killed, analyses that take into account third parties, surrogate wars, low-intensity conflict, and the long run, analyses that try to assess the difference between what is good for a country's citizens as opposed to its leaders are complex, and their results would almost certainly be controversial. Civilian denial, inattention, and ignorance, therefore, has a certain logic. It lets civilians enjoy having "clean hands" while asking the military, "as professionals," to do things civilians not only do not want to do but do not want to know about. The civilian/military division of labor also provides justification for murderous acts: they are required of professionals, done out of necessity, and sanctioned by civilians.

I have argued that U.S. women especially embody the "civilian mind"; still, this book began with chapters by three active-duty women officers. Each is an exceptionally fine officer but also very different from the other two. Their essays establish the variety of experiences and personalities as well as the high level of competence found among military officers. It should be clear that these officers' minds could no more be confined by the boundaries of any de- or prescribed "military mind" than the minds of the readers of this volume could fit tidily into what has been put forth as the "civilian mind." Nevertheless, gender matters in the military. The rules are different for women and men, the experience is different for them, and the core activity, combat (and especially close combat, where you might see "the whites of their eyes"), is still quite inaccessible to women (see Peach, Chapter 8, and Devilbiss, Chapter 9, in this volume). Imperfect though they may be, the dichotomies of men and women, military and civilian remain powerful (see Cooke, Chapter 12, and Mitchell, Chapter 3, in this volume).

This fact has been true over space and over time. In all cultures men and women are distinguished from each other, and the ways they are distinguished are myriad—except that almost everywhere men wield the weapons of war and women nurture young children. But there is an asymmetry to this division, for men cannot (at least yet) bear and nurse children. Therefore, women's specialized role is secure. There is no poaching. Women don't have to protect their turf or prove their womanhood. In contrast, men's special role is one that women *can* do. Indeed, some women can do it better than a significant number of men. Further, when they are needed, women do carry out men's reserved role. As a result, the boundaries of manhood require defense and there is a continuing danger that they will be breached, because men's special role, unlike women's, is not protected, is not defined by biology.

There is a second asymmetry. Men's special role is dangerous and unpleasant. (Women's special role is sometimes dangerous, too; and diapers and colic remain annoying; still, they hardly measure up to occupying a resisting village or interrogating a prisoner.) Therefore, it sometimes takes a good deal of coercion to get men to fulfill their special role; one form of pressure is the culturally sanctioned desire to "prove" their manhood. But that can be hard to do when people such as Rhonda Cornum and Virginia Solms are there doing the same thing.

There is a third asymmetry that bears on the gender and civil/military dichotomy: "honor." Honor has different requirements in different cultures, but in our culture, Bertram Wyatt-Brown (1986) argues, the willingness to use violence is required of men in certain circumstances. It is not required of women in the same circumstances. The system of honor includes women, but not as users of violence, certainly not as users of violence on behalf of others, and, most certainly, not on behalf of men. (Note that challenge and testing may be required by honor, but the actual doing of violence may not be; fighting may be required but winning may not; saying one would fight may be required but actually doing so may not.) All of this may help explain why it is hard for military men to accept even the most eager and competent women as their peers, why there is so much concern about bonding, and why women's mere presence can produce such anxiety.[9]

Just as women's military service may not have the same meaning as men's service, so women's civilianship may be different from men's. Women may be considered *mere* civilians, whereas it may be understood that civilian men are potential soldiers. For example, the fall of Srebrenica in 1995 taught us that in an invasion, able-bodied, civilian men will not be treated the same as civilian women.

What is the bottom line? Does understanding the "civilian mind" suffice, or is there a reason to try to change it, and if so, how?

There seem to be two reasons for trying to change civilian thinking. First, it is in the interests of both civilians and the military. Civilians who participate in informed debate about the military may end up saving a lot of money and also getting the kind of military they want. On the other hand, the military is less likely to be asked to do something unwise, or to be sent to accomplish a task but then be denied the means to do it, or even to have its mission changed in midstream. These are very practical reasons. The second reason involves ethical judgments.

Even to introduce the word "moral" into a discussion about the military can be to invite scorn, dismissal, or both. But although there is often not time for such judgments in the midst of war, they are made. They are certainly made after the fact by philosophers, historians, and the tellers of war stories. Assuming discrimination, proportionality, and means are important, wouldn't it be better to consider them before rather than after action? And, even better, in the arming and preparation of our violence specialists? Even if Thucydides' comment—"Justice is a matter for equals. The strong do what they can; the weak suffer what they must"—is not a satisfactory answer, and even if Camus's injunction to be "neither victim nor executioner" is somewhat imprecise, people do care about ethical judgments, and the military, which implements the choices made about the use of state violence, may care even more than civilians. Is it moral, for instance, for one side in a dispute to take advantage of its technology so that it suffers *no* casualties while it inflicts however many casualties it finds necessary on an enemy? If something is important enough to take life, is the proof of its importance how many lives one will take or the number of lives one will offer in sacrifice? How does one distinguish between an arrogant bully and a strong protector?

I hope civilian thinking will change to being informed—not only to making the military salient but to using the tools of logic and evidence when thinking about war. I hope, too, that civilians will weigh their responsibilities attending the conduct of war—their responsibilities to their own military but also their responsibilities to their counterparts, those on the other side, particularly civilians. I hope, finally, that the conditions for mutual trust between civilians and their military will soon be understood and put in place. Now is the time, for in one sense now is the "real" war. That is because it is now, during peace, that we prepare the weapons, the people, and the justifications for the next war.

To have might without right is monstrous. To have right without might is ridiculous. Our goal must be to make might and right congruent. That will require civilians and the military to work together, without minds constricted by the narrowness of either "military" or "civilian" thinking.

NOTES

1. Mary Wollstonecraft, contemporary with but not a Founding Father, described military officers as womanish because they were ornamental and parasitical.

2. This, of course, is not the view held by the private, volunteer, armed groups that surfaced in the mid-1990s. These groups, which have appropriated the name "militia," are deeply distrustful and suspicious of the government and of its capacity for force; they believe they must be prepared to resist the government with counterforce. Those who participate in these militias are civilians but, I would argue, are also militarists, because they believe they must be ready to use violence. They do not, therefore, have "civilian minds."

3. Military personnel also are told and believe war stories. They give meaning and justification to the performance of grisly deeds and the making of great sacrifices. If the stories are later deemed untrue, what was briefly functional can have long-term negative consequences.

4. Different people tell different after-war stories to make sense of chaotic and hideous events. The first ones tend to be rooted in principle, to refer to things higher, larger, or more enduring than human life. Later more attention is paid to the movers and shakers, the heroes and antiheroes, and to the actions and words of public persons, the supposed agents of war, the history makers. Still later, historians usually render a judgment based on impersonal economic forces, suggesting a lack of both autonomous agentry and high principle.

5. Two of the most telling events of the early 1970s were the publication of the Pentagon Papers and the trial of Daniel Ellsberg for releasing those papers. Apparently, it took both events, the publication of "secrets" in the "paper of record" (the New York Times) and the trial of a former official, to make visible things that could have been known long before—if individuals had wished to know them. No new information appeared in The Pentagon Papers, but the manner in which previously obscured information was finally projected—with authority and accompanied by near martyrdom—made old information compelling.

6. During the Vietnam conflict the nightly news regularly reported North Vietnamese, South Vietnamese, and U.S. deaths. The ratio was invariably something like ten to three to one. Much doubt has been shed on both the reliability and the validity of those numbers.

7. Civilians are probably safest in short wars fought at state borders. They are likely to be relatively safe if their country is overwhelmingly stronger than the enemy. They are most endangered when a war is being fought where they live. When war is being fought all around them but is between two states, some definition is given to their status. Most dangerous of all are civil wars and wars of liberation. In those circumstances it is hard to argue that anyone is by definition not a participant and not a threat—including children. Still, even if one cannot tell precisely where to draw the line between combatants and noncombatants, one must not conclude that one should act as if no line existed.

8. Civilians sometimes take advantage of the Pentagon's sacred-cow status for their own purposes; for example, recently the military received substantial unrequested funds to study breast cancer.

9. In the summer of 1995, a board of Naval captains recommended the discharge of a lieutenant commander who had led a helicopter detachment but declared that his religious views (Episcopalian) prevented him from leading women into combat. After resigning, the commander later withdrew his resignation and fought the discharge (Los Angeles Times, 21 May 1995). Note that arguments about women's lack of physical strength have all but disappeared as a justification for excluding women from the military, but the struggle to include them can involve protracted bureaucratic and technical wrangling. See Richman-Loo and Weber, Chapter 7 in this volume.

REFERENCES

Betts, Richard. 1977. Soldiers, Statesmen, and Cold War Crises. Cambridge: Harvard University Press.
Edelman, Murray J. 1971. Politics as Symbolic Action. New York: Academic Press.
Huntington, Samuel P. 1957. The Soldier and the State. Cambridge: Harvard University Press.

Keegan, John. 1976. *The Face of Battle: A Study of Agincourt, Waterloo, and the Somme*. New York: Viking Press.

McNamara, Robert. 1995. *In Retrospect: The Tragedy and Lessons of Vietnam*. New York: Times Books.

Minter, William. 1994. *Apartheid's Contras*. Johannesburg: Witwatersrand University Press.

O'Loughlin, John, Tom Mayer, and Edward S. Greenberg, eds. 1994. *War and Its Consequences*. New York: Harper Collins.

Schell, Jonathan. 1976. *Time of Illusion*. New York: Knopf.

Sivard, Ruth Leger. 1993. *World Military and Social Expenditures, 1993*. Washington, D.C.: World Priorities, Inc.

Stiehm, Judith. 1973. *Nonviolent Power*. Lexington, Mass.: D.C. Heath.

Terry, Wallace. 1984. *Bloods*. New York: Ballantine Books.

Toeffler, Alvin, and Heidi Toeffler. 1993. *War and Anti-War*. New York: Warner Books.

Tuchman, Barbara. 1984. *The March of Folly*. London: Joseph.

Wasserstrum, Richard, ed. 1970. *War and Morality*. Belmont, Calif.: Wadsworth.

Wyatt-Brown, Bertram. 1986. *Honor and Violence in the Old South*. New York: Oxford University Press.

About the Contributors and Index

About the Contributors

Carol Burke is associate professor in the Writing Seminars Department and associate dean for academic affairs at Johns Hopkins University. She is the author of *Vision Narratives of Women in Prison*, *Back in Those Days*, *Plain Talk*, and *Close Quarters* and coauthor of *The Creative Process*.

Miriam Cooke is professor of Arabic literature at Duke University. She is author of *The Anatomy of an Egyptian Intellectual: Yahya Haqqi* and *War's Other Voices: Women Writers on the Lebanese Civil War*. She edited *Opening the Gates: A Century of Arab Feminist Writing* with Margot Badran, *Gendering War Talk* with Angela Woollacott, and *Blood into Ink: South Asian and Middle Eastern Women Write War* with Roshni Rustomji-Kerns.

Rhonda Cornum, whose story is told in detail, is an Army lieutenant colonel currently doing a residency in urology at Brooke Army Medical Center in San Antonio, Texas.

M. C. Devilbiss holds an M.A. in religion from the Lutheran Theological Seminary in Gettysburg and an M.S. and Ph.D. in sociology. She was a platoon officer in an Army basic training company during the Vietnam War and served in the enlisted ranks in the Air National Guard. She is the author of *Women and Military Service*.

Susan Jeffords is divisional dean of the social sciences and professor of English and women's studies at the University of Washington. She is author of *The Remasculinization of America: Gender and the Vietnam War*, and *Hard Bodies: Hollywood Masculinity in the Reagan Era* and coeditor of *Seeing Through the Media: The Persian Gulf War*.

Billie Mitchell is a military officer, college professor, and parent. The pseudonym she has used is a tribute to the Army general and pilot who literally exploded the myth of Naval invulnerability to air power; in 1925, over Navy protests, Billy Mitchell bombed and sank several over-age battleships. For this and outspoken criticism of the military, he was court-martialed and found guilty. History vindicated him.

Brenda L. Moore is assistant professor of sociology at the State University of New York at Buffalo. She is the author of *To Serve My Country, to Serve My Race: The Story of the Only African American Wacs Stationed Overseas during World War II.*

Lucinda Joy Peach has a J.D. from New York University and a Ph.D. in religious studies from Indiana University. She is assistant professor in the Legal and Ethical Studies Program at the University of Baltimore.

Connie L. Reeves is a retired Army officer who served as an aviator, a military intelligence officer, and a foreign area officer. She is currently a graduate student at George Washington University working on women's military history.

Nina Richman-Loo is a program analyst in the Office of the Under Secretary of Defense for Personnel and Readiness. She chairs the Department of Defense Cockpit Accommodation Working Group.

Virginia Solms (a pseudonym) is an active-duty officer who made good at a military academy and has enjoyed a highly successful career as a pilot and commander during a period when she (and others) marked a number of "firsts" for women in the U.S. military.

Judith Hicks Stiehm is professor of political science at Florida International University and author of *Nonviolent Power, Bring Me Men and Women: Mandated Change at the U.S. Air Force Academy,* and *Arms and the Enlisted Woman.*

Rachel Weber is a doctoral candidate in the Department of City and Regional Planning at Cornell University. Her interests lie in the area of deindustrialization of the military industrial complex.

Index

References to photographs are in boldface.

Academies, 187n. 43, 206, 213, 217, 218.
See also Air Force Academy; Naval Academy; West Point
Accountability ethic, 157, 163–74, 179–81, 184n. 18
Adams, Maj. Charity E. (Charity Adams Earley), 117, 119
Adhana, Amair, 258
AEF, 91, 92
AFQT, 65
African Americans: in the military, 123, 127, 132, 164, 167, 216, 271; and unemployment, 127, 127 Table 6–1, 128
African American women, 115–16, 129; in the military, 116, 117, 123–24, 127, 129, 132, 133n. 3, 182n. 3; and military drawdown, 131, 133; occupations of, in the military, 130–31, 132; percentage of, in the military, 182n. 3; and unemployment, 128, 128 Table 6–2; in WAAC, 117, 118–21, **125**, **126**; in WAC, 117, 112–21; during World War II, 115, 117, 133n. 6
Aikens, Pvt. Ann, 119–20
Ainsworth, 2d Lt. Ellen, 104
Air Force, 6, 60, 150, 227; African American women in, 129, 129 Table 6–3, 130, 182n. 3; anthropometrics used by, 141, 142, 143; gays in, 33, 34; gender of personnel in, 61 Table 4–1; gender, rank, and ethnicity of personnel in, 66 Table 4–2; pilot training standards in, 142–43, 144, 145 Table 7–3; white women in, 129, 129 Table 6–3, 130; women and combat in, 173, 182n. 4, 182–83n. 8; women in, 61 Table 4–1, 66 Table 4–2, 68, 69, 132, 182n. 3 (see also Military women). See also Military

Air Force Academy, 61, 65
Air Force Nurse Corps, 106, 107, 108, 110
Alcott, Louisa May, 83
Alexander, Capt. Eleanor Grace, 110
Alien, 229, 259, 260
All-Volunteer Force, 127, 164
Ambulance corps, 85–86
American Expeditionary Force (AEF), 91, 92
American Nurses' Association, 88, 91
Andrews, Capt. Bill, **17**, 18, 20
Angels from Hell, 222
Annapolis. See Naval Academy
Anthropometrics, 138, 139 Figure 7–2, 139, 141, 142, 143
Apocalypse Now, 224, 225, 228, 231, 255
Arafat, Yasser, **244**, 249
Armed Forces Qualifications Test (AFQT), 65
Army, 3–4, 60, 150, 164, 266n. 2, African Americans in, 133n. 3; African American women in, 129, 129 Table 6–3, 130, 182n. 3; and childbearing, 186n. 40; gays in, 30–31, 33; and gender equality, 36, 174; gender integration in, studied, 166–67; gender of personnel in, 61 Table 4–1; gender, rank, and ethnicity of personnel in, 66 Table 4–2; pilot training standards in, 144, 145 Table 7–3; publication by soldiers in, 35–36; reasons for women joining, 38–41, 42; white women in, 129, 129 Table 6–3, 130; women and combat in, 65, 146, 159–60, 166–67, 168, 170, 182n. 4, 182–83n. 8, 183n. 9, 10, 184n. 18; women in, 3, 30–31, 39, 61 Table 4–1, 66 Table 4–2, 67, 69, 116, 132 (see also Military women). See also Military
Army Air Aeromedical Research Laboratory, 8

Army Medical Department, 76, 88, 90, 103
Army Medical Service Corps, 4
Army-Navy Nurse Act, 105
Army Nurse Corps, 89, 90, 106, 111; rank
    and promotion for, 98, 107; during the
    Vietnam War, 108, 109–10; during
    World War I, 91, 97, 116; during World
    War II, 99–103, 104, 105–6
Army Reorganization Act of 1818, 79
Army Reorganization Bill of 1901, 90
Army School of Nursing, 92
Army Student Nurse Program, 107
Aspin, Les, 136, 146, 158, 159
A Team, The, 226
Athletics, 56n. 10
Augustine, St., 281
Aviation Medicine Clinic, 8

Back to Bataan, 230
Baker, Kristin, 57n. 15
Baker, Mark, 227
"Balkan Nurses," 105
Ball, Mary Ann (Mother Bickerdyke), 84, 86
Barbour, Margaret, 122
Barkalow, Carol, 54, 57nn. 14, 15, 182n. 1,
    183n. 12; and woman as man at West
    Point, 51–53, 57n. 16, 57–58n. 17
Barrows, Comdt. Gen. Robert, 161, 183n. 16,
    184n. 23
Barton, Clara, 84
Battle Cry, 227
Bat 21, 225
Becker, Maj. Jane, 108
Beguines, 76
Bell, Bessie S., 91
Benson, F. R., 255
Berger, Joseph, 56n. 8
Berkman, Joyce, 256
Berry Plan, 4–5
Bettelheim, Bruno, 214
Bickerdyke, Mother (Ball, Mary Ann), 84,
    86
Blackwell, Dr. Elizabeth, 81
Born Losers, The, 222
Born on the Fourth of July, 225, 226
Born on the Fourth of July (Kovic), 226–27
Bosnia, 235, 259, 261
Boys in Company C, The, 223
Britain, nursing in, 75, 79–80, 82

Bryan, Col., 9
Bush, George, 159, 225, 231, 232

Cadet Nurse Corps, 103. *See also* Army Nurse
    Corps; Navy Nurse Corps
Cambodia, 235
Camus, Albert, 292
Canada, 69, 88
Caputo, Philip, 227
Care ethic, 157, 177–81, 187–88n. 50,
    188n. 51
Carter, Gladys, 121
Carter, Jimmy, 186n. 36
Cellar, Senator Emanuel, 162
Cheney, Richard, 19, 159
Childbearing: and an ethic of care, 178, 179;
    and women in combat, 170–72, 176,
    181, 185nn. 31, 32, 186nn. 33, 34, 35,
    36, 37, 38, 39, 40; and women in the
    military, 55, 69, 182n. 2
China Beach, 225
Chrome and Hot Leather, 222
Citadel, 38, 41, 56n. 4
Citizenship, 133n. 1, 177; and combat
    restrictions, 116, 175–76, 187n. 47,
    256
Civilians: defined, 275–76; and militarism,
    273, 275, 277, 286; and the military, ix,
    272–73, 289, 291–92, 293n. 8; myths
    believed by, 278–80; and pacifism, 273,
    275, 277, 286; and protected innocents,
    281–85, 289; and warfare, 272–73,
    276–77, 282, 293n. 7; and willful igno-
    rance, 277–81, 289–90
Civil War, 271, 287; African American
    women in the military during, 115; med-
    ical advances during, 86–87, 88; mortal-
    ity rates during, 86; nursing during, 74,
    78, 80–87, 89, **93**, 111, 112; war stories
    of, 220
Clark, William D., 164
Clausewitz, Carl von, 273
Clinton, President Bill, 136, 142, 272,
    288
Coast Guard, 60, 61 Table 4–1, 66 Table
    4–2, 201. *See also* Military
Coast Guard Academy, 25
Cohen, Moshe, 8
Cohesion, 216, 217, 218

Cohn, Carol, 236
Cold War, 39, 222, 255, 262, 270, 271
Color Parade, 207, **211**
Combat; and aircraft design, 136, 150; and
    the care ethic, 179; definition of,
    158–59, 163, 182nn. 5, 6; women in. *See*
    Women in combat
Coming Home, 223, 226
Compensation, 70, 70 Table 4–3
Confederate Army, 81, 85
Conference Report of the 1994 Authoriza-
    tion Act, 152
Conquest Mentality, 196–98, 200
Conscientious nonviolence, 273–74
Continental Army, 76, 77
Coppola, Francis Ford, 224, 228, 255
Cornum, Rhonda, 3–14, **16**, **17**, 18–23,
    159, 169, 291
Coughlin, Paula, 38
Crane, Stephen, 220, 228
Crawford v. Cushman, 186n. 40
Crimean War, 74, 79, 82, 111
Croatia, 238
Cronkite, Walter, 222
Crying Game, The, 51

DAB, 136, 151
Dalton, Navy Secretary, 185n. 32
D.A.R., 88, 90
Daughters of the American Revolution
    (D.A.R.), 88, 90
Davis, Jefferson, 85
Deer Hunter, The, 223–24
Defense Acquisition Board (DAB), 136, 151
Defense Advisory Committee on Women in
    the Service, 151–52
Defense Intelligence Agency, 281
Defense Manpower Data Center, 70
Defensive Model, 196, 198, 199, 199 Table
    9–1, 200, 201
Delano, Jane A., 91
Demolition Man, 229
Department of Defense (DOD). *See* Military
Department of Transportation, 60
De Pauw, Linda, 70
Desegregation. *See* Integration
Desert Shield. *See* Gulf War
Desert Storm. *See* Gulf War
Deutch, John, 146

Dhabyan, Sami, 238
Dickens, Charles, 78, 79, 111
Die Hard, 229, 231
Disease, 74, 77, 78, 86, 92, 100, 109; dur-
    ing the Spanish-American War, 88, 89,
    90, 115
Dix, Dorothea Lynde, 82, 84
DOD. *See* Military
Donovan, 2d Lt. Pamela Dorothy, 110
"Don't ask, don't tell, don't pursue" policy,
    33–34, 40, 182n. 3
Dorn, Edwin, 151
Draft, 61, 271; of nurses, 104; and race,
    123–24, 233n. 9; and women, 69, 177,
    183n. 14, 186n. 36, 275
Drag, 53
Drawdown, and African American women,
    131, 133
Drazba, 2d Lt. Carol Ann Elizabeth, 110
Dunant, J. Henri, 80
Dunlap, Sgt., 22
Durkheim, Emile, 214
Dyson, Freeman, 262

Earley, Charity Adams (Maj. Charity E.
    Adams), 117, 119
Economy of the male gaze, 52, 57n. 16
Education: and African Americans, 117–18;
    and enlisted personnel, 69; and officers,
    61, 65, 69
Edwards, Sarah, 83–84
Eglin Air Force Base, Florida, 7
84 Charlie Mopic, 233n. 11
Eisenhower, Dwight David, 271
Eliade, Mircea, 214
Ellsberg, Daniel, 293n. 5
El Salvador, 228
Elshtain, Jean Bethke, 161, 267n. 15
Enlisted personnel, 60, 65, 69; and African
    American women, 129, 129 Table 6–3,
    130; compensation for, 70 Table 4–3;
    and ethnicity, 66 Table 4–2, 67; and
    white women, 129, 129 Table 6–3
Equal Rights Amendment, 124
Ergonomics, 138
Ethnicity: and officer rank, 66 Table 4–1, 66
    Table 4–2, 67; and war stories, 229–30,
    233n. 11
Expert Field Medical Badge Course, 5

Falkland Islands, 288
Fanon, Frantz, 265
Farewell to Arms, A (Hemingway), 228
Faulkner, Shannon, 38, 49
Femininity, 21, 161–62, 183n. 13, 200
Feminism and feminists, 74, 229; and the
    ethic of care, 178, 187–88n. 50; and the
    military, 37, 38, 54, 151–52, 256, 275;
    and military nurses, 74; war criticized by,
    36, 37; and women in combat, 259–60,
    267n. 11
Field Artillery, 39
First Blood, 224–25
Flexible Power Mentality, 196
Folklore, in military academies, 206, 218
For Whom the Bell Tolls (Hemingway), 220
Frankenstein, 52, 57n. 14
French and Indian Wars, 76
Full Metal Jacket, 225

Gandhi, Mohandas Karamchand, 273
Garber, Marjorie, 42, 43, 57n. 13
Gardens of Stone, 225
Gardiner, 2d Lt. Ruth M., 104
Gavin, Denise, 42, 53, 57–58n. 17
Gays: and military policy, 33–34, 40; and
    military service, ix, 33–34, 39, 42, 164,
    182n. 3, 216, 257, 272. *See also* Lesbians
Gender, 236; and aggressivity, 259, 267n.
    11; and military service, 20, 32, 40–41,
    290–91; and officer rank 66 Table 4–2,
    67; and professional success, 20–21, 22,
    23; and war stories, 228–29, 237; and
    weapons design, 136–38, 140, 146, 149,
    150, 151, 153–54. *See also* Gender discrim-
    ination; Gender ideology
Gender discrimination, 7, 36
Gender ideology; defined, 161; and the ethic
    of accountability, 174, 179–80; and the
    ethic of care, 179, 180; and the masculin-
    ity of war myth, 161–62, 165–66,
    183nn. 11, 12, 14, 15, 16, 184n. 17;
    and the protection of women myth,
    169–70; and women in combat, 157,
    160–61, 162, 174, 179, 180, 183nn. 15,
    16, 184n. 17; women linked with peace
    in, 161–62, 183nn. 11, 12, 14, 184n. 17
Geneva Convention, 92, 282
Germany, 270, 271

G.I. Bill, 105, 122
Gibson, Mel, 226, 229
Gilligan, Carol, 48, 178
Glenn, Senator John, 175
Go Tell the Spartans, 223
Graham, Lt. Col. Annie Ruth, 110
Grant, Dan, 19
Gray, J. Glenn, 236, 262, 265, 266n. 4,
    267n. 8
Green Berets, The, 222, 226, 231, 232–33n. 2,
    233n. 4
Greene, Graham, 221
Grenada, 69, 225, 228, 272
Griffin, Susan, 267n. 13
Grotius, Hugo, 282
Gubar, Susan, 36
Gulf War, 10–11, 230, 255, 271; civilians
    affected in, 283, 285; deaths in, 279,
    281; precision weapons of, 283, 284–85;
    public interpretation of, 234; and Viet-
    nam War stories, 224, 225, 228,
    231–32; women captured in (*see* Prison-
    ers of war); women in, 3, 8–14, 18–19,
    69, 156, 157, 159, 167, 169, 173, 185n.
    26, 186n. 37, 258

al-Haj, Maj. Ahmad, **244**
Hammond, Ruth, 122
Hancock, Cornelia, 84
Harb Lubnan, 238–40, **241–48**, 249–53
Hasford, Gustav, 233n. 4
Hasson, Esther Voorhees, 90
Heaven and Earth, 225
Hemingway, Ernest, 220, 228
Herbert, Sir Sidney, 79
Herndon Monument, 205, 206, 207, **212**
Higbee, Lenah S., 97
Hill, Admiral Virgil, 210
Hill Street Blues, 226
Hobby, Col. Oveta, 119
Holm, Maj. Gen. Jeanne, 186n. 35
Homage of Catalonia (Orwell), 255
Homosexuals. *See* Gays; Lesbians
Honor, 285, 291
Horton, Mildred McAfee, 117
Hospitals: during the Civil War, 81, 82, 84,
    85–86, 87; in colonial America, 75, 76;
    in the nineteenth century, 78–80, 88;
    during the Revolutionary War, 76, 77;

during the Vietnam War, 109; during World War I, 92, 97; during World War II, 101
House Armed Services Committee, 281
Howard, J. Daniel, 218
HSI, 150–51
Hultgreen, Lt. Kara, 160
"Human Engineering Design Criteria for Military Systems, Equipment, and Facilities," 139
Human Systems Integration (HSI), 150–51
Huntington, Samuel P., 275

In Harm's Way, 228
Insignia, 53, 54
Integration, 10, 65, 124, 167
Integration Act. *See* Women's Armed Forces Integration Act
Iraq, 3, 8, 11, 13, 270, 281
Israel, and women in combat, 185n. 30

Jamil, Brig. Gen. Nuji, **244**
Janis, I. L., 216
Japan, 270, 271
Jepsen, Senator Roger, 184n. 19
Johnny Got His Gun, 223
Joint Primary Aircraft Training Systems (JPATS), 136, 137, 151; accommodation of eligible women for, 142–43, **147,** 149–50, 152, 153; acquisition strategy for, 141–42; and anthropometric data, 143, 144, 144 Tables 7–1 and 7–2, 145–46, **147, 148,** 149; sitting height specifications of, 140, 141, 141 Figure 7–3, 142, 149; and training, 137, 137 Figure 7–1
Jones, Kathleen, 256
Jones, 2d Lt. Elizabeth Ann, 110
Jovicic, Zoran, 238
Jumblat, Kamal, 249
Justice ethic, and women in combat, 157, 174–77, 179, 180, 181, 187nn. 43, 45, 46, 47, 48
Just war, 280–82

Kant, Immanuel, 262, 267nn. 15
Keegan, John, 236, 254, 257
al-Khali, Col. Muhammad, **244**

Khomeini, Ruholla, 259
al-Khuli, Hasan Sabri, **244**
King, Martin Luther, Jr., 274
Kinney, Dita H., 90
Klinker, Capt. Mary Therese, 110
Korb, Lawrence, 184n. 19
Korean War, 123, 172, 223; nursing during, 106–7, 111
Kovic, Ron, 227
Kuwait, 8, 13, 271

Lacan, Jacques, 43
Lahhud, Henri, **244**
Lane, 1st Lt. Sharon Ann, 110–11
Lebanon War, 251; stories of, 237–52, 266n. 5; women in, 250–51
Lesbianism, as an accusation, 33, 38, 39
Lesbians: coming out as, 26–27, 30; and military service, ix, 30–31, 34, 164, 182n. 3; at West Point, 26–27, 30. *See also* Lesbianism
Lethal Weapon, 226, 229, 231
Letterman Research Institute, 3, 4–5
Libya, 69, 270
Lincoln, Abraham, 81, 83
Lombardi, 1st Lt. Jane A., 110
Lykins, Maxine, **95**

MAAG, 108
Maass, Clara Louise, 89
MacArthur, Gen. Douglas, 99
MacCoun, Robert, 216
Magnum, P. I., 226
Male bonding, 42, 166–67, 257, 291
Malraux, André, 255
Maltese Falcon, The, 229
Marines: African Americans in, 133n. 3; African American women in, 129, 129 Table 6–3, 130; gender of personnel in, 61 Table 4–1; gender, rank, and ethnicity of personnel in, 66 Table 4–2; and the Navy, 60, 67; white women in, 129, 129 Table 6–3, 130; women and combat in, 146, 160, 182n. 4, 182–83n. 8, 183n. 16; women in, 61 Table 4–1, 66 Table 4–2, 117, 182n. 3, 186n. 34 (*see also* Military women). *See also* Military
MASH, 106, 109
M*A*S*H*, 223, 231, 233n. 6

Massachusetts Bay Colony, 75
McConnell, Capt. Viola B., 106
McGee, Dr. Anita Newcomb, 88–89, 90
McNamara, Robert 285
McPeak, Air Force Chief of Staff Gen. Merrill, 161
Media, 34, 227, 283, 286, 287; Vietnam War viewed by, 222–23; and women at West Point, 26, 50; and women in combat, 111; and women in the Gulf War, 157, 170, 186n. 37; and women in the military, 20, 23, 41–42
Medical Civil Action Program, 109
Medical Unit, Self-contained, Transportable (MUST), 109
Mexican War, 79
Miami Vice, 226
Michener, James, 232n. 1
Midwives, 75
Militarism, 273, 275, 277, 286, 292n. 2
Military, ix, 31, 42, 69, 195; benefits offered by, 175, 187n. 44; budget and expenditures of, 270; careers in, 271; and the care ethic, 178, 180, 181; changing mission of, 195, 196–97, 199 Table 9–1, 201–2; combat defined by, 158–59, 182nn. 5, 6; commanders in chief of, 255, 271–72; compared to that of other countries, 286–87; discharges in, 33, 185n. 32; downsizing of, 173–74; and gender equality, 37, 116, 256; gender of personnel in, 61 Table 4–1; gender, rank, and ethnicity of personnel in, 65, 66 Table 4–1, 66; male rites of passage in, 214–16; and political power, 287–89; and racial equality, 116, 118–21, 124; as self-selected and selective, 65, 271; training in, 195, 214; unease caused by strength of, 270–71; weapons of, 138, 287; women in, ix, 3, 4, 11, 12–13, 20, 33, 38, 69, 116, 157, 182n. 3, 216, 256 (*see also* Military women); and women in combat, 172–73; women's feelings about, 4, 11, 12–13, 20. *See also* Air Force; Army; Coast Guard; Marines; Navy
Military academies. *See* Academies
Military Assistance Advisory Group (MAAG), 108
Military Personnel and Compensation Subcommittee, 124

Military women, 41–42, 54; African American (*see* African American women); benefits for, 175, 187nn. 44, 45; and career advancement, 68, 175, 187nn. 45, 46; career opportunities for, 124, 151–52, 160, 175; challenges posed by, 257–58, 267n. 16; circumstances affecting increase in, 69–70, 123–24; combat viewed by, 173, 187n. 42; as fake men, 40, 42–43; military nurses viewed by, 111–12; motivations of, 38–41, 42, 271; and nursing (*see* Nursing); occupations of, 69, 130, 131–32; percentage of, 61 Table 4–1, 66 Table 4–2, 67, 123, 124, 127; professionalism of, 57nn. 14, 15; public opinion of, 258–59; roles of, 195, 196, 200–202; sources of information about, 70; views of, 36, 41, 44, 47, 48–50, 52, 55, 162, 176, 184n. 22, 187n. 43
Militia, 292n. 2
Millay, Edna St. Vincent, 260
Mills, C. Wright, 287
Minerva: Quarterly Report on Women and the Military, 70
Minorities, 271
Misogyny, 37
Missing in Action, 225, 229
Mobile Army Surgical Hospital (MASH), 106, 109
Moore, Robin, 222
Morrell, David, 224
Moskos, Charles, 174, 187n. 48
Motherhood. *See* Childbearing
Murphy, Audie, 226, 227
MUST, 109

Nam (Baker), 227
National Association for the Advancement of Colored People, 121
National Council of Negro Women, 121
National Defense Act, 98, 116
National Guard, 69
National Institutes of Health, 143
Nationalism, 56n. 10
National Organization for Women, 124
National Women's Political Caucus, 124
Naval Academy, 61, 65; civilian faculty of, 210, 213; Color Parade at, 207, **211**; folklore at, 206, 209; male rites of passage at,

205, **211**, 213, 215; marching chants at, 208–9; women at, 205, 206–7, 208, 209–10, 213; women viewed at, 205, 207, 208, 209–10
Naval Reserve Midshipmen's School, 117
Navy, 137, 140, 150, 227; African Americans in, 133n. 3; African American women in, 129, 129 Table 6–3, 130, 182n. 3; anthropometrics used by, 141, 142, 143; career advancement of women in, 187n. 46; gender of personnel in, 61 Table 4–1; gender, rank, and ethnicity of personnel in, 66 Table 4–2; and the Marines, 60, 67; nurses in, 86, 90 (see also Navy Nurse Corps); occupations of women in, 132; pilot training standards in, 142–43, 144, 145 Table 7–3; policy on gays in, 33, 34; pregnancy policy of, 186n. 34; uniforms worn by, 40–41; white women in, 129, 129 Table 6–3, 130; women and combat in, 159, 160, 163, 170, 182nn. 4, 7, 182–83n. 8, 184n. 17; women in, 61 Table 4–1, 66 Table 4–2, 67, 117, 182n. 3, 213 (see also Military women). See also Military
Navy Nurse Corps, 90–91, 97, 98, 111, 116; during the Vietnam War, 108, 110; during World War II, 99–100, 102, 103, 104, 105–6. See also Navy, nurses in
Neumann, Erich, 214
Nicaragua, 225, 228
Nietzsche, Friedrich Wilhelm, 267n. 8
Nightingale, Florence, 79–80, 82, 85
"1988 Anthropometric Survey of U.S. Army Personnel," 143
Noddings, Nel, 178
Nonviolence, 273–75
Nonviolent Power (Stiehm), 273
Norris, Chuck, 225–26, 229
Norton, Anne, 57n. 16
Notes on Hospitals (Nightingale), 80
Notes on Nursing (Nightingale), 80
Not So Quiet (Smith), 263
Nunn, Sam, 152
Nuns, 76, 79
Nurse Corps. See Army Nurse Corps; Navy Nurse Corps
Nurse Draft Bill, 104
Nurses, 111, 200; contract, 89–90, **94**; decorations and citations awarded to, 83, 84,

85, 89, 97, 101, 104, 105, 110; military training for, 100, 102; models for, 79, 82, 97; rank and promotion for, 98, 104, 106, 107. See also Nursing
Nurses' Associated Alumnae, 88
Nursing, 73–74, 75; during the Civil War, 80–87, 89, **93**, 111, 112; in colonial America, 74–76; during the Korean War, 106–7, 111; in the nineteenth century, 78–80, 87–88; professionalization of, 73–74, 78–80, 111; during the Revolutionary War, 76–78; during the Spanish-American War, 88–90, **94**, 111; training of, 74, 76, 87; in the twentieth century, 98–99, 107; during the Vietnam War, **96**, 108–11, 112; during World War I, 91–92, **93**, 97–98, 111; during World War II, **95**, **96**, 99–106, 111, 112. See also Nurses
Nursing schools: in the nineteenth century, 80, 81, 87, 111; in the twentieth century, 91, 92, 97, 103

O'Brien, Tim, 220, 259, 262
Occupations: and African Americans, 118; of African American women in the military, 130–31, 132; and combat, 175; of women in the military, 69, 130, 131–32
OCS, 4, 65, 217
Offensive Model, 196–98, 199, 199 Table 9–1, 200, 201
Office of the Secretary of Defense (OSD), 136, 141, 150
Officer Candidate School (OCS), 4, 65, 217
Officer Candidate Training, 117
Officer culture, 218
Officers, 60, 66; African American women as, 129, 129 Table 6–3, 130–31; compensation for, 70 Table 4–3; education of, 61, 65, 69; and gender and ethnicity, 66 Table 4–2, 67; white women as, 129, 129 Table 6–3
On War (Clausewitz), 273
Ordeal, 56n. 10
Orlowski, 1st Lt. Hedwig Diane, 110
Orwell, George, 255
OSD, 136, 141, 150
Owens v. Brown, 184n. 17

Pacifism, 273, 275, 277, 286. *See also* Peace
Palestine Liberation Organization, 244, 249
Panama invasion (1989), 69, 225, 228, 272
Parachute school, 6
Paris Is Burning, 51
Passenger 57, 233n. 11
Peace: defined, 262, 267n. 15; and an ethic
  of care, 178–80, 188n. 51; and gender
  roles, 235–36; maintenance of, 256,
  267n. 8; women linked with, 178–80,
  188n. 51, 236–37. *See also* Pacifism
Peacemaking. *See* Peace
Peay, Gen. J. H. Binford, 159
Penis-envy, 39–40
Pentagon Papers, 220, 293n. 5
Perpetual Peace, 262, 267n. 15
Pershing, Gen. John J., 91
Persian Gulf War. *See* Gulf War
Phallocracy, 41–42, 55
Photography, 252, 266nn. 4, 6, 266–67n. 7
Platoon, 225, 226, 230
Plebe indoctrination, 213, 215, 217–18
Police, 286–87
Powell, Gen. Colin, 19, 281
POWs. *See* Prisoners of war
Pragmatic nonviolence, 274
Predator, 226
Pregnancy. *See* Childbearing
Pricely, Mary, 78
Prisoners of war, 280; nurses as, 99, 100,
  105, 111; and plebe indoctrination,
  217–18; in war stories, 230, 231;
  women as, 18–20, 22–23, 69, 169, 170
Pro-fensive Model, 196, 198–99, 199 Table
  9–1, 200, 201–2

Quiet American, The (Greene), 221

Race. *See* Ethnicity
Racism, 118–21
Rambo, 225, 226, 229, 230, 231
Rank, 60, **63, 64**
Rape, 33, 170, 261, 267n. 13
Ray, Aldo, 227
Reagan, Ronald, 224, 225, 227, 232
Red Badge of Courage, The (Crane), 220, 228
Red Cross, 74, 80; American, 84, 89, 90,
  91, 103, 104–5; International, 80
Registered Nurse Student Program, 107

Rehnquist, Chief Justice William, 272
Religiosity, 56n. 10
Religious orders, 79; nursing during Civil
  War by, 81, 84, 85, 86, 87
Remarque, Erich Maria, 263
Reminiscences (Taylor), 115
Reppy, Judith, 153
Reserve Officer Training Program (ROTC),
  4, 6, 61, 65, 69, 217
Retirement, 69
Reverby, Susan, 88
Revolutionary War, 75, 76–78, 115,
  157
Richards, Linda, 87
Roberts, 1st Lt. Mary, 104
Roe, 2d Lt. Elaine, 104
Roosevelt, Franklin Delano, 103, 104, 117,
  121
Rosenthal, Congressman Benjamin, 232n. 2
Rostker v. Goldberg, 177, 187n. 47
ROTC. *See* Reserve Officer Training Program
Roulstone, Capt. Doug, 166
Rourke, 2d Lt. Virginia, 104
Rowlandson, Mary, 220
Royal Military Academy (Duntroon, Aus-
  tralia), 214, 215–16, 217
Royal Military College (Kingston, Canada),
  214
Ruddick, Sarah, 178, 259
Rumor of War, A (Caputo), 227
Rwanda, 235

Sands of Iwo Jima, 227
Sanitary Commission, 81–82, 84, 86
Sarkis, Elias, **244**, 249
Saudi Arabia, 9, 19, 271
al-Sayyid, 'Abd al-Razzaq, 238, 251, 252
Schell, Jonathan, 277
Schroeder, Patricia, 124, 159
Schwarzkopf, Gen. Norman, 19, 159, 283
Schweik, Susan, 260
Segal, David, 258
Segal, Mady, 258
Segregation, 10, 118–21, 164, 236
Selective Service Training Act, 116–17
Senate Armed Services Committee, 152
Senate Armed Services Manpower Subcom-
  mittee, 164
Servicemembers Legal Defense Network
  (SLDN), 33–34

Sexual harassment, 33, 37, 176, 213
Sexuality: in the military, 27, 32–33; and war, 267n. 13; at West Point, 27; of women soldiers, 39, 40
Seymour Johnson, North Carolina, 7
Shaft, 233n. 11
Shalikashvili, Gen. John, 41, 183n. 10
Sherman, Gen. William Tecumseh, 280
Short Times, The (Hasford), 233n. 4
Showalter, Elaine, 254
Siege Mentality, 196, 198
Sisters of Charity, 76, 81, 87, 89
Sisters of Mercy, 86, 89
Sisters of St. Joseph, 81
Sisters of the Holy Cross, 81, 89
Slaughterhouse Five, 223
SLDN, 33–34
Smith, Helen Zenna, 263
Smith, Maj. Frances K., 108
Smith, Maj. Genevieve, 106
Smith, Maj. Helen D., 108
Soldier and the State, The (Huntington), 275
Solms, Virginia, 24–27, **28**, **29**, 30–34, 291
Sontag, Susan, 253, 254, 266nn. 4, 6
South Pacific, 221–22, 232n. 1
Spanish-American War, 74, 115, 230; nursing during, 88–90, **94**, 111
Spanish Civil War, 255
Stamaris, Sgt. Daniel, 18
Standing army, 271
Star Wars, 260
Sternberg, Surgeon General George M., 88–89, 90
Stiehm, Judith, 30, 151; on women at West Point, 56nn. 7, 9, 12; and women in combat, 179, 185n. 25, 260; and women in the military, 256, 257–58, 267n. 16
Stone, Oliver, 225, 227
Sullivan, Army Chief of Staff Gordon, 159–60
Sullivan, Betsy, 85
Sullivan, 1st Lt. Mary Ann, 101
Sunset Boulevard, 229
Swerdlow, Amy, 267n. 12
Swisshelm, Jane, 84
Syria, 270

Tailhook scandal, 38, 152, 176, 213, 218
Tales of the South Pacific (Michener), 232n. 1

Taxi Driver, 233n. 7
Taylor, Susie King, 115
Terminator 2, 229, 260
Thatcher, Margaret, 288
Theweleit, Klaus, 259
Things They Carried, The (O'Brien), 259
Thucydides, 292
Thurmond, Strom, 152
Tobias, Sheila, 256
Toeffler, Alvin, 283
Toeffler, Heidi, 283
To Hell and Back, 227
Tokenism, 175
Tompkins, Sally Louisa, 85
Top Gun, 227, 231
Tour of Duty, 225
Triage, 109
Truman, Harry S, 133n. 8
Truth, Sojourner, 83
Tubman, Harriet, 83, 115
Tuchman, Barbara, 285
Two-Year War, 239, 266n. 5
Typhoid fever, 115

Uncommon Valor, 225
Under Siege, 226, 231
Unemployment, 127, 127 Table 6–1, 128, 128 Table 6–2
Uniforms, 60–61, **62**
Union Army: African Americans in, 115; nursing in, 81–84, 85, 86, 87
United States Military Academy, 24–26
United States Supreme Court, ix, 272
United States v. St. Clair, 183n. 14
United States v. Schwimmer, 187n. 47
Universal Soldier, 226

Vattel, Emmerich von, 282
Vietnam War, 74, 272; deaths in, 293n. 6; double messages from the government about, 277–78, 293n. 5; nursing during, **96**, 108–11, 112; and parentalism, 222, 233n. 3; racial tension during, 230, 233nn. 9, 10; rape of Vietnamese women by Americans during, 261, 267n. 13; war stories of, 220–27, 228, 231–32, 255; women in, 123, 156, 158, 185n. 29
Vietnam War Memorial, 221
Violence, 56n. 10

WAAC. *See* Women's Army Auxiliary Corps

WAC. *See* Women's Army Corps

WAC Band No. 2, 120–21

Walker, Dr. Mary Edwards, 83

Walter Reed Army Hospital, 6, 13, 91, 92

Walter Reed Army Institute of Nursing
(WRAIN), 108

War: ambiguities of, 264–65; as a charged
peace, 262, 267n. 15; and civilians,
272–73, 276–77, 282, 293n. 7; defined,
235; goals of, 278, 280; as just, 281–82;
as masculine, 161–62, 165–66, 169,
173, 180, 183nn. 11, 14, 15, 236–37;
myths of, 279–80; and nursing, 73–74,
75; and photography, 252–54, 266–67n.
7; and the protected innocents, 282–85;
and public support, 272–73, 277, 278;
and sexuality, 267n. 13; stories of (*see*
War stories); women in, 36–37, 263–64,
265–66, 276

War Crimes Committed by the Yugoslav Army (Jovicic), 238

War Department, 117, 118–20

War of 1812, 78

War of Independence. *See* Revolutionary War

War's Other Voices (Cooke), 237

War stories, 257, 285; confusion organized
in, 237, 266n. 2; cultural analysis of,
261–62; and cultural attitudes, 227–28,
233n. 8; defined, 220; and gender, 237,
262–63; and history, 231, 254; of
Lebanon, 237–52, 266n. 5; and the legit-
imization of criminal behavior, 264, 265,
266; and military personnel, 277, 292n.
3; and national identity, 230–31; and
photographs, 237–38, 266n. 4; purposes
of, 228–31, 232; and race, 229–30,
233n. 11; and sex segregation, 236–37;
types of, 277, 293n. 4; of Vietnam,
221–27, 255; and women, 255, 259–61,
262–64, 267n. 12

Washington, George, 76, 271

Waters, Mary, 78

WAVES, 117

Wayne, John, 227, 277; World War II films
of, 220, 222, 226, 230, 232n. 2, 233n. 4

WCS, 43

Weapons design: and anthropometrics, 138,
139, 139 Figure 7–2; and enhanced ac-

commodation, 150–51; and gender,
136–38, 140, 146, 149, 150, 153–54
(*see also* Joint Primary Aircraft Training
Systems [JPATS]); and milspecs, 139–40

Webb, James, 209–10, 217

Webbites, 209

Webster, Chaplain Alexander, 185n. 31,
186n. 37

Weinberger, Caspar, 227, 233n. 8

Welcome Home, Johnny Bristol, 223

West, Army Secretary Togo, 159, 160, 164

West, Maj. Harriet, 119

West Point, 61, 65, 275; application to,
24–26; changes women brought to, 46,
48–49, 56n. 11; and gender discrimination, 36; male-centeredness of, 48, 56n.
7; military women viewed at, 36, 44, 47,
48–50, 52; official purpose of, 44, 49;
program at, 44–47; sex-role attitudes of
male cadets at, 48–50, 56n. 8; sexual
maturation at, 27; social success of
women at, 47–50, 51, 53–54, 56n. 12;
women as fake men at, 43, 51–52, 53,
57nn. 13, 14, 16, 57–58n. 17, 58n. 18;
women at, 38, 39, 41, 42, 43–44,
50–54, 55, 56n. 9, 57n. 16; women's
performance at, 44–47, 48

West Point Skydiving Team, 56n. 6

Whiting, Willie, 122

Whittle, Reba Zitella, 105

Whole candidate score (WCS), 43

Who'll Stop the Rain? 223

"Who, What, When, Where, Why"
(Cronkite), 222–23

Wollstonecroft, Mary, 259, 292n. 1

Women, ix, 22, 39, 54, 206; in combat (*see*
Women in combat); in the military (*see*
Military, women in; Military women);
protection of, 162–63, 169–72, 173,
179, 184n. 17, 185nn. 30, 31, 32,
186nn. 33, 35, 36, 37, 38, 39, 40, 236,
250–51, 261

Women Accepted for Volunteer Emergency
Service (WAVES), 117

Women in combat, 37, 65, 69, 154,
255–56, 290; assumptions and beliefs
challenged by, 156–57; challenges posed
by, 257–58; and citizenship, 116,
175–76, 187n. 47, 256; and combat air-

craft, 31, 136, 147, 150, 153, 159 (*see also* Joint Primary Aircraft Training Systems [JPATS]); and combat support positions, 156, 182n. 1; and the ethic of accountability, 157, 163–74, 180–81, 184n. 18; and the ethic of care, 157, 177–81, 187–88n. 50; and the ethic of justice, 157, 174–77, 179, 180, 181, 187nn. 43, 45, 46, 47, 48; feminist view of, 259–60, 267n. 11; and gender ideology, 157, 160–61, 162, 174, 179, 180, 183nn. 15, 16, 17; as guerrilla fighters, 185n. 29, 262; historically, 157, 158; and inefficiency, 164–65, 166–69, 173, 180, 181, 184nn. 18, 19, 20, 21; and the masculinity of war myth, 169, 173, 180, 185n. 27; and the need for personnel, 173–74; and nurses, 111–12; opposition to, 159–60, 256; and paradigms of the military, 200; personal stories of, 3, 7, 12, 20, 22, 31–32; and physical strength and stamina, 39, 153, 167–69, 170, 181, 184n. 23, 184–85n. 24, 185nn. 25, 26, 293n. 9; and the protection of women myth, 162–63, 169–72, 173, 179, 184n. 17, 185nn. 30, 31, 32, 186nn. 33, 35, 36, 37, 38, 39, 40; and psychological considerations, 169, 170, 181, 185nn. 27, 28, 29; public and military opinions on, 172–73, 186–87n. 41, 187nn. 42, 43; race and class dimensions of, 177, 187n. 49; and religious views, 293n. 9; studies on, 166–67, 184n. 21; and war stories, 259–61, 262–63; and women's advancement, 67. *See also under individual wars*
Women in the Military, 70
Women's Armed Services Integration Act, 123, 157, 158, 182nn. 2, 4, 184n. 17
Women's Army Auxiliary Corps (WAAC),

116; African American women in, 117, 118–21, **125**, **126**; background of women in, 117–18; and overseas service, 117, 133n. 6; racism in, 117, 118–21; recalled by women in, 121–23; treatment of, in Europe, 122–23
Women's Army Corps (WAC), 116, 133n. 4; African American women in, 117, 112–21; background of women in, 117–18; and overseas service, 117, 133n. 6; racism in, 117, 118–21, 133n. 8; recalled by women in, 121–23; treatment of, in Europe, 122–23
Women's Central Association of Relief, 81
Women's Equity Action League, 124
Women's Research and Education Institute, 70
Women Strike for Peace (WSP), 267n. 12
Working Uniform Blue Alpha (WUBA), 207–8, 218n. 1
World War I, 116, 271; African American women in, 115–16; nursing in, 91–92, **93**, 94, 97–98, 111; war stories of, 220
World War II, 108, 138, 271, 279–80; African American women in, 115, 117, 133n. 6; African Americans in, 116, 133n. 3; Hollywood representations of, 220, 226–27, 228, 230; nursing during, **95**, **96**, 99–106, 111, 112; and protected innocents, 282, 283; war stories of, 220; women in, 158, 169
WRAIN, 108
WSP, 267n. 12
WUBA, 207–8, 218n. 1
WUBA Klux Klan, 210
Wyatt-Brown, Bertram, 291

Young Women's Christian Association, 121